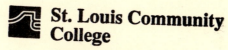

A REFERENCE COMPANION
TO DYLAN THOMAS

"My saying shall be my undoing." Dylan Thomas, by Hugh Olaf de Wet. *Courtesy of the Art Collection, Harry Ransom Humanities Research Center, The University of Texas at Austin.*

A REFERENCE COMPANION TO DYLAN THOMAS

James A. Davies

Greenwood Press
Westport, Connecticut • London

Library of Congress Cataloging-in-Publication Data

Davies, James A.
    A reference companion to Dylan Thomas / James A. Davies.
      p. cm.
    Includes bibliographical references and index.
    ISBN 0–313–28774–0 (alk. paper)
    1. Thomas, Dylan, 1914–1953—Criticism and interpretation—
Handbooks, manuals, etc. 2. Wales—In literature—Handbooks,
manuals, etc. I. Title.
PR6039.H52Z6225   1998
821'.912—dc21   97–24572

British Library Cataloguing in Publication Data is available.

Library of Congress Catalog Card Number: 97–24572
ISBN: 0–313–28774–0

First published in 1998

Greenwood Press, 88 Post Road West, Westport, CT 06881
An imprint of Greenwood Publishing Group, Inc.

Printed in the United States of America

The paper used in this book complies with the
Permanent Paper Standard issued by the National
Information Standards Organization (Z39.48–1984).

10 9 8 7 6 5 4 3 2

Copyright Acknowledgments

To JEN—again.

Contents

Acknowledgments

For invaluable help of various kinds I wish to thank Dannie Abse, Walford Davies, Paul Ferris, David Howell, John Pikoulis, Glyn Pursglove, M. Wynn Thomas, and the library staff of University of Wales Swansea, Swansea Central Reference Library, and the National Library of Wales, Aberystwyth. Needless to say, I remain responsible for all errors and opinions in this volume.

During 1993 I was Andrew W. Mellon Foundation Fellow at the Harry Ransom Humanities Research Center, University of Texas at Austin: I am grateful to its Director, Professor Thomas F. Staley, and his staff (especially the reading room staff and Leslie Wearb, Photoduplication Coordinator, Art Collection) for making my stay so pleasant and profitable and for subsequent assistance. I am also grateful for permission to draw on the HRHRC's extensive Dylan Thomas Collection and associated material (including the frontispiece photograph). Thanks are due for the friendship and hospitality shown to me in Austin, in particular by Janice and Bill Rossen, Beverly Bardsley, and other members of the late Gareth Morgan's Shakespeare reading group.

Sections of this book were read as papers, as follows: ESSE Conference, Bordeaux (1992); Sixth Annual Conference of the Association for Welsh Writing in English, Gregynog, Powys (1993); British Studies Faculty, University of Texas at Austin (1993); Fifth and Sixth International Conferences on the Literature of Region and Nation, Budmerice, Slovakia (1994), and the University of New Brunswick at St. John, New Brunswick, Canada (1996). In each case I am grateful to those who contributed to discussion, and to the conference organizers.

I thank George F. Butler, Maureen Melino, Jason Azze, and Charles Eberline of Greenwood Press for their care and attention during the publishing process.

Without my wife's encouragement and support this book would not exist. The dedication is yet another hopelessly inadequate response.

Introduction

Dylan Thomas died in 1953. Almost a half century later his life and work can still generate reactions of extraordinary intensity. All too often, even in these sophisticated literary-theoretical times, achieving a balanced assessment of his work can be subverted by its problematic relationship with his life. Critical discussions have too frequently degenerated into ad hominem attacks.

This reference companion offers a candid account of Thomas's life that does not seek to minimize his faults of character, his reprehensible behavior, and the extent to which he wasted his talent. It willingly accepts what it knows to be true, that serious readers of Thomas are increasingly fascinated by the paradox that, as Yeats put it, the man who writes the poems is, in a sense, "never the bundle of accidents and incoherence that sits down to breakfast." [1] As Thomas himself wrote, "I, in my intricate image, stride on two levels." He may not have been the kind of man we would hope for as a son-in-law, and we are all relieved that he will never come to live next door, but he wrote poetry, in particular, and prose that can still touch the heart, and he has made a disturbing, substantial, and, I would argue, important contribution to twentieth-century literature.

Second, perhaps seemingly paradoxically, given the preceding, this companion discusses Thomas's work as being constantly alive to its own time. Of course he was a "process" poet—and attention is paid to that—but his work emerged from specific personal, social, and historical circumstances that it reflects and explores. That is, this reference book takes a critical view of Yeats's and Thomas's distinction between man and poet, recognizing both its wisdom and its limitations. Though it is often hard to accept that such a flawed character wrote such superb poetry, of course there is a relationship, albeit often complex, between the "accidents and incoherence" and Thomas's pages. Certainly this reference book, especially the critical study, is written out of a conviction that Thomas is an important social poet of a special kind, one whose strengths are linked to his bourgeois, suburban, middle-class upbringing in the 1920s and 1930s.

Third and finally, this reference companion offers a selective critical history. From the thousands of responses to Thomas as man and as poet, the most important are grouped into what the present writer considers to be that history's four major elements.[2] This approach seeks to expose the controversies that have dogged Thomas in death as they did in life: the variable response of the London literary establishment, Welsh arguments about his ''Welshness,'' let alone about his worth, English attempts to dismiss him, often, it seems, *because* he was Welsh, and many American attempts to pin down his achievement and assess his worth. From a matrix that has often been petrifying, Thomas is now escaping.

This reference companion appears at a crucial moment in his continuing literary existence. The popularity of poems such as ''Fern Hill'' and ''Do not go gentle into that good night'' is indisputable. His historical importance has never been in question; it is possible to understand the period from, say, 1936 to 1953 in terms of Thomas's literary career: the reaction against Auden, 1940s romanticism, the Movement-led reaction. But we now know much more about Thomas's life, and at a time when the zeitgeist is no longer congenial to simple moralistic dismissal, especially when knowing more increases understanding. Much of his work has become available in scholarly editions, so that many of the basic requirements for informed criticism now exist. Further, the questioning of the monolith that was English literature, in particular the increasing concern with British literatures in English (Scottish, Irish, Anglo-Welsh) and thus with the ''interstitial perspectives'' this reference book begins to explore in the section on ''Fern Hill,'' is creating conditions conducive to fostering new interest in and modern perspectives on this most famous of Welsh writers. Informed reconsideration is a constant literary necessity that, as far as Dylan Thomas is concerned, this reference companion seeks to further.

NOTES

1. W. B. Yeats, ''A General Introduction to My Work,'' in *Modern Poets on Modern Poetry*, ed. James Scully (London: Collins, 1966), 15.

2. Necessarily, this is a personal judgment surrounded by apologies. In addition, a critical history of the substantial work on Dylan Thomas done in non-English-speaking countries—particularly in France, Italy, and Japan—is much needed.

Abbreviations

The following abbreviations are used for frequently cited editions of the works of Dylan Thomas and for the site of an important collection of his manuscripts:

CL   Thomas, Dylan. *The Collected Letters*. Ed. Paul Ferris. London: Dent, 1985.

CP   Thomas, Dylan. *Collected Poems, 1934–1953*. Ed. Walford Davies and Ralph Maud. London: Dent, 1988.

CS   Thomas, Dylan. *Collected Stories*. Ed. Walford Davies. London: Dent, 1995.

HRHRC   Harry Ransom Humanities Research Center, University of Texas, Austin.

PM   Thomas, Dylan. *Poet in the Making: The Notebooks of Dylan Thomas*. Ed. Ralph Maud. London: Dent, 1968.

Chronological Summary

1834   William Thomas born at Llanybydder, Carmarthenshire, Wales. Educated at the University of Glasgow, he became a Unitarian minister and a Radical leader, ending his life as a schoolmaster. As Gwilym Marles, he wrote poetry and fiction in the Welsh language. Gwilym Marles was the uncle of Dylan Thomas's father and the source of the middle name of both Dylan Thomas and his sister.

1876   The poet's father, David John Thomas, born at The Poplars, Johnstown, Carmarthenshire (now part of Carmarthen), one of at least four children. His father, Evan Thomas, was a railway guard.

1879   Gwilym Marles died, aged forty-five.

1882   The poet's mother, Florence Williams, born at 29 Delhi Street, St. Thomas, Swansea, Wales, the youngest of seven surviving children. Both parents were from the Llansteffan peninsular in Carmarthenshire. Her father was a railway porter, then a railway inspector. Her aunt, Annie Jones, farmed Fernhill.

1895   David John Thomas entered the University College of Wales, Aberystwyth.

1899   Graduated with First Class Honours in English. Became English master at Swansea Grammar School.

1900   Left for Pontypridd County School.

1901   Returned to Swansea Grammar School, where he remained until his retirement in 1936.

1903   30 December, David John Thomas married Florence Williams. Their first home was in Sketty Avenue, Swansea.

1906   Birth of Nancy Marles Thomas, the poet's sister. The Thomases then lived at 31 Montpellier Street in central Swansea.

1914   Summer, David John and Florence Thomas, then of 51 Cromwell Street, Swansea, purchased 5 Cwmdonkin Drive, Uplands, Swansea.

           27 October, Dylan Marlais Thomas born at 5 Cwmdonkin Drive, Uplands, Swansea.

1925   September, entered Swansea Grammar School, where his father was now senior English master. He had previously attended Mrs. Hole's private school at 22 Mirador Crescent, Uplands.

December, published his first poem, "The Song of the Mischievous Dog," in the *Swansea Grammar School Magazine*, which he was to dominate and edit.

1926   June, won the under-fifteens handicap mile at the school sports.

1927   14 January, "His Requiem" (signed "D. M. Thomas") published in Cardiff's *Western Mail*. In 1971 it was discovered that this poem by Lilian Gard had been taken from *Boy's Own Paper* of November 1923.

1928   Probably began his friendship with Daniel Jones.

1929   Until 1931, a leading member of the school Dramatic Society. Prominent in the Debating Society.

1930   27 April, the date of the earliest surviving notebook poem ("Osiris, Come to Isis").

1931   Amateur acting with Swansea Y.M.C.A. Players.

Summer, left school to train as a reporter on the local paper, the *South Wales Daily* (later *Evening*) *Post*.

1932   Began meeting his friends at the local Kardomah Café.

Until 1934, amateur acting with Swansea Little Theatre.

December, ceased being a journalist.

1933   18 May, *New English Weekly* published "And death shall have no dominion."

28 June, Thomas's poem, "The Romantic Isle" broadcast. He had entered it in the BBC Poetry Competition. The poem has not survived.

Summer, first visit to London.

27 August. His father's cancer diagnosed.

3 September, first poem ("That sanity be kept") published in the *Sunday Referee*, leading to correspondence with Pamela Hansford Johnson.

1934   23 February, first meeting, in London, with Pamela Hansford Johnson.

25 March, awarded the *Sunday Referee*'s second "Poets' Corner" prize, guaranteeing the publication of a book of his poems.

May, first recorded visit to Laugharne, with Glyn Jones.

13 November, moved from Swansea to 5 Redcliffe Street, Fulham Road, London SW10.

December, *18 Poems* published.

1935   c. January, left Redcliffe Street for Colehearne Road, before returning to 5 Cwmdonkin Drive, his base until 1937.

c. March, began friendship with Vernon Watkins.

May, stayed in Derbyshire with A. J. P. Taylor and his wife Margaret.

Published poems and reviews in London magazines.

July–August, stayed in County Donegal with Geoffrey Grigson.

1936   April, met Caitlin Macnamara in the Wheatsheaf pub, Rathbone Place, W1.

            April/May, in Cornwall with Wyn Henderson.

            July, called at Richard Hughes's home in Laugharne; quarrelled with Augustus John over Caitlin.

            10 September, *Twenty-five Poems* published by Dent. David Higham, then with Curtis Brown, later part of Pearn, Pollinger & Higham, arranged the Dent contract and became Thomas's lifelong literary agent.

            December, Thomas father retired from Swansea Grammar School.

1937   April, Thomas's parents moved from 5 Cwmdonkin Drive to Marston, Bishopston (near Swansea). They remained there until spring 1941.

            21 April, first radio broadcast, reading poetry (including his own).

            11 July, married Caitlin Macnamara at Penzance Registry Office.

            late summer (to spring 1938), Dylan and Caitlin stayed with Mrs. Macnamara (Caitlin's mother) at New Inn House, Ringwood, Hampshire.

1938   May (until July), moved into 2 Gosport Street, Laugharne.

            July (to July 1940), moved to Sea View, Laugharne.

1939   30 January, Llewelyn Edouard Thomas born in Cornelia Hospital, Poole, Dorset (the Thomases were staying at Ringwood).

            24 August, *The Map of Love* published.

            3 September, World War II began.

            20 December, *The World I Breathe* published in the United States by New Directions.

1940   c. April, found unfit for military service.

            April, *Portrait of the Artist as a Young Dog* published. U.S. edition published by New Directions.

            July (until November), Dylan and Caitlin Thomas stayed with John Davenport at the Malting House, Marshfield, near Chippenham.

            21 August, began contributing to BBC Radio on an occasional basis (scriptwriting, acting, reading).

1940–41   With John Davenport, wrote *The Death of the King's Canary*.

1941   Began writing *Adventures in the Skin Trade*.

            April, sold his notebooks.

            c. summer (until 1945), worked for the Strand Film Company, Golden Square, Soho, scripting propaganda films. Strand was succeeded by Gryphon Films, for whom Thomas also worked. Became well known in London's wartime club and pub scene, centered in Soho.

            Autumn, the first chapter of *Adventures in the Skin Trade* published in John Lehmann's *Folios of New Writing*.

            Late autumn, lived at 13 Hammersmith Terrace, W6.

1942   Summer, Caitlin and Llewelyn stayed at Gelli, Talsarn, Dyfed. Thomas visited.

Thomas's friendship with Ruth Wynne Owen.

Autumn (for periods until early 1943), the Thomas family lived at 3 Wentworth Studios, Manresa Road, Chelsea, SW3.

1943   February, *New Poems* published in the United States by New Directions.

15 February, broadcast "Reminiscences of Childhood."

3 March, Aeronwy Bryn Thomas born in Chelsea.

1944   Summer, staying with parents at Blaen Cwm cottage.

September (to summer 1945), the Thomases lived in Majoda, New Quay, Dyfed.

2 October, failed to turn up as best man at Vernon Watkins's wedding.

14 December, recorded "Quite Early One Morning" for the BBC (the talk was broadcast on 31 August 1945).

1945   March, Majoda and its inhabitants machine-gunned by a drunken army captain jealous of his wife's friendship with the Thomases.

Summer, staying with parents at Blaen Cwm, where he wrote "Fern Hill."

Autumn, living in the basement flat of 6 Markham Square, Chelsea, SW3 (the home of Caitlin's sister Nicolette Devas).

September (until his death), made frequent BBC broadcasts.

December, awarded the Levinson Prize by *Poetry*.

6 December, recorded "Memories of Christmas" for the BBC (the talk was broadcast on 16 December).

1946   7 February, *Deaths and Entrances* published.

March (until April 1947), the Thomases lived in a one-room summerhouse in the garden of A. J. P. and Margaret Taylor's Magdalen College home at Holywell Ford, Oxford.

8 November, *Selected Writings* published by New Directions.

1947   January, member of the National Liberal Club.

April (until August), in Italy, first at Rapallo, then near Florence, finally on Elba.

15 June, "Return Journey" broadcast.

August/September (until April/May 1949), the Thomases' home was at the Manor House, a small cottage in South Leigh, Oxfordshire, owned by Margaret Taylor.

1948   March, working on what became *Under Milk Wood*. Scriptwriting for Gainsborough Films.

1949   March, visited Prague for a writers' conference, as the guest of the Czech government.

March, became member of the Savage Club.

April/May, moved to the Boat House, Laugharne.

May, John Malcolm Brinnin invited Thomas to read at the Poetry Center, New York City, and offered to arrange a reading tour.

24 July, Colm Garan Hart Thomas was born.

In great financial difficulties and failing to honor BBC commissions.

1950   20 February, flew to New York for first U.S. tour: Poetry Center and colleges and universities across the United States and in Canada. Heavy drinking; scandalous behavior.

1 June, sailed back to Britain. Despite substantial U.S. earnings, further problems with money.

November, continuing work on *Under Milk Wood*.

1951   January, visited Iran to write a filmscript for the Anglo-Iranian Oil Company.

October (until 20 January 1952), left the Boat House temporarily to live at 54 Delancey Street, Camden Town, NW1, owned by Margaret Taylor.

1952   20 January, sailed to New York, with Caitlin, for second U.S. tour. Further scandalous behavior and squandering of earnings.

22 February, first recordings in New York for Caedmon Records.

28 February, *In Country Sleep and Other Poems* published in New York by New Directions.

16 May, Dylan and Caitlin sailed home from New York.

Pursued by the Inland Revenue over unpaid income tax. Money trouble; marriage increasingly turbulent.

10 November, *Collected Poems, 1934–1952* published.

16 December, D. J. Thomas, the poet's father, died.

1953   31 March, American edition of *Collected Poems* published.

16 April, death of Thomas's sister Nancy.

21 April, arrived in New York for third U.S. tour. Began affair with Elizabeth Reitell. Heavy drinking.

14 May, in New York, first performance with actors of *Under Milk Wood*.

14 May, *The Doctor and the Devils*.

May, met Stravinsky in Boston. Thomas agreed to write the libretto for a new Stravinsky opera.

Dr. Milton Feltenstein treated Thomas for a broken arm.

2 June, flew back to London from New York. Unhappy; struggling to write.

19 October, flew to New York for his fourth U.S. tour. Continued affair with Elizabeth Reitell. Attended New York rehearsals and performances of *Under Milk Wood*. Heavy drinking; seemed mentally disturbed. Generally unwell suffering from gastritis and gout. Possibly also suffering from delirium tremens.

4 November, Dr. Feltenstein injected Thomas with morphine, which exacerbated his condition.

5 November, Thomas, in a coma, admitted to St. Vincent's Hospital.

9 November, Dylan Thomas died without regaining consciousness.

I

LIFE

1

1914–1934

He was very small and light. Under a raincoat with bulging pockets, one of which contained a quarter-bottle of brandy, another a crumpled mass of poems and stories, he wore a grey, polo-necked sweater, and a pair of very small trousers that still looked much too big on him. He had the body of a boy of fourteen. . . . [He had] hair the dull gold of threepenny bits springing in deep waves and curls . . . eyes, the colour and opacity of caramels when he was solemn, the colour and transparency of sherry when he was lively. . . . He looked like a brilliant, audacious child, and at once my family loved and fussed over him as if he were one.

When Pamela Hansford Johnson published this description, Dylan Thomas had been dead for seven years; more than a quarter of a century had passed since they had first met and, for a comparatively brief period, been strongly attracted towards each other. It was how she remembered him when they first met, on the doorstep of 53 Battersea Rise, SW 11, the home that she shared with her widowed mother, and where she made her own first successful literary beginnings, on the "dull grey" evening of Friday, 23 February 1934.[1] She wrote in her diary: "Charming, very young looking with the most enchanting voice."[2] At this moment we glimpse Thomas at his most appealing: nineteen years old, mad about literature, redolent with high promise, his pockets stuffed with his writings and a provocative bottle. He was beginning to conquer literary London; his poems, including the precociously brilliant "And death shall have no dominion," "The force that through the green fuse drives the flower," and "A process in the weather of the heart," were already being published in metropolitan places.

Thomas stayed with the Johnsons for ten days, charmed Pamela's mother, and behaved impeccably. The two young writers walked and talked, met Pamela's friends, went to the theatre, and sat decorously in pubs. If his life had ended on Pamela's doorstep or when he left Battersea Rise to return to Swansea, we would now, of course, think less of him as a poet but would regard him, with fond bitterness, as another marvellous boy, as a younger Keats or as a civilian Wilfred Owen or John Cornford: attractively heroic, with infinite potential, struck down in youth's full flower. We would have a believable context for Augustus John's famous portrait in the National Museum of Wales in Cardiff.

There is no doubting the underlying affection of Pamela's recollection, though with hindsight we detect the novelist's hand at work. The details are shrewdly chosen not only to re-create the attractions of the young man who became her de facto fiancé but also to suggest aspects of character and behavior that had tragic implications: the ominous bottle, the literary chaos implicit in the crumpled papers, the suggestions of poverty in "threepenny bits," the persistent sweet eating, possibly diabetic in origin, in "caramels," the further alcoholic associations of "sherry," his childlike dependence, and, overall, his strange, unorthodox attraction for women.

The young writer who stood so appealingly on the Johnsons' doorstep was the product of a complex matrix of influences and experiences.[3] His father's family was from rural Carmarthenshire, mainly working-class but with one local luminary, the minister and poet Gwilym Marles. He was the family's high flier in the social as well as the intellectual sense and was thus commemorated eponymously by the next Thomas (Dylan's father) to have intellectual and social ambitions. The poet's paternal grandfather, Evan, moved from the heart of rural Wales to make his home in Johnstown, then a village close to the county town of Carmarthen, and took a further crucial step away from country life and limited horizons by becoming a guard on the Great Western Railway. Railway workers had steady, reasonably paid jobs and, comparatively speaking, some social standing. They had escaped the hovel down the muddy lane and the economic depression that swept through Welsh rural areas in the second half of the nineteenth century. They had become a small part of the industrial revolution that transformed Wales up to World War I.[4]

Dylan Thomas's father, David John Thomas, grew up in a Welsh-speaking community dominated by work and by the chapel; his parents were active members of Heol Awst Congregational Church in Carmarthen.[5] He grew up as " 'Jack' Thomas, a poor boy with brains, he used to say later."[6] Yet those brains did not take him to Carmarthen's old and famous Queen Elizabeth Grammar School, but to the far inferior National Model and Practising School and then the Carmarthen Boys' Board School. He spent a year at the National Model and Practising School as a pupil-teacher and then, exceptionally for one in his position, won, by examination, a Queen's Scholarship to the University College of Wales at Aberystwyth. The scholarship gave him free tuition, a maintenance grant, and an opportunity that he seized. He had great ability, worked hard—apart from an interest in singing, he appears to have had no extracurricular interests—and took an ordinary degree in 1898. One year later he was the only graduate of the three University of Wales colleges to gain First Class Honours in English. His professor was C. H. Herford, who left Aberystwyth in 1901 for the English chair at Manchester. In 1899 the external examiner was an even more famous figure, Professor W. A. (later Sir Walter) Raleigh, then at Liverpool, who became the first professor of English literature at Oxford.[7] D. J. Thomas's widow recalled, without evidence, that the young man was then offered a fellowship, "the first fellowship in Aberystwyth."[8] If this was so, which is doubtful, he did not take it up.

These brief encounters with famous professors help us to understand why D. J. Thomas felt such a bitter sense of failure at having become no more than a provincial schoolmaster, particularly when he saw contemporaries who, in his opinion, were less able and certainly had poorer degrees advance further. But that bitterness came later. Initially, he had a passion for literature and a good post at a good school, Swansea Grammar School. Mrs. Thomas recalled that he was first employed as a temporary teacher to cover illness. He then moved to Pontypridd County School, where his stay was very short. Trevor Owen, Pontypridd's headmaster, was promoted to take charge of Swansea and took D. J. Thomas with him into a permanent post.[9]

The town, as it then was, in which D. J. Thomas was to spend the rest of his working life has been described by the poet Edward Thomas, who had family in the area and knew it well.[10] For him, Swansea before the Great War was a place of abrupt contrasts: the ugly and the squalid in a magnificent setting. In general, Edwardian Swansea was a prosperous sprawling place of docks and works and smoke and smells, of slums and bustling streets, of dominating hills and of the sea. It still had odd reminders of its past, former country cottages or farmhouses trapped by the advance of industry. Edward Thomas was excited by it, at once hostile and fascinated. His survey noticed new building and new streets on the hillsides, the beginnings of Swansea's expansion that led to the development of the Uplands suburb and, in 1914, the building of Cwmdonkin Drive. Though, as has been said, D. J. Thomas came to feel that he deserved more, he had done well, given his background: when he moved into the new house at 5 Cwmdonkin Drive, later described by his son in a mixture of fact and pretentious inaccuracy as "a mortgaged villa in an upper-class professional row,"[11] he established himself as a middle-class, home-owning, professional man. His contemporaries back in working-class Johnstown would have found the odor of drying plaster in the rooms of 5 Cwmdonkin Drive to have been the sweet smell of comparative success.

In transforming himself socially, in changing from the "Jack" known to his relations, his wife, and himself to the "D. J." known to colleagues, pupils, and Swansea acquaintances, he played a small part in the fundamental change overwhelming Welsh society in the first decades of this century: the rise of its middle class. In smaller Welsh places this new middle class did not always detach itself physically from the community it served: as late as the 1950s professional men often lived in the same valley streets as miners and steelworkers. But like began to cling to like, particularly after 1914 and in the larger places, such as the Radyr, Rhiwbina, and Roath Park areas of Cardiff, possibly in Newport, and, of course, in the Mumbles, Sketty, and Uplands areas of Swansea. That said, in between-wars Wales, a country still mainly rural or socially mixed, the middle-class suburb into which D. J. Thomas moved and in which Dylan Thomas grew up was a new and unusual phenomenon.

It was almost wholly English-speaking. A few could speak Welsh, but even fewer did so. Welsh belonged to the old, poor, rural world from which many had escaped. English was the passport not only to social and material advancement but also, for D. J. Thomas and others like him, to a vibrant language, a greater literature, and a wider world. Certainly he did not hark back nostalgically and guiltily to some muddy linguistic womb; his attitude was typical of most other first-generation migrants to the brave new world of urban gentility. He was not absolutely hostile to Welsh; at one point in his career he taught it in evening classes. He simply had little need of it.

In social terms, Jack Thomas had come a long way. The times were propitious. In those golden Edwardian years before World War I the Welsh middle class became increasingly prosperous and, for the first time, a significant social presence. Edwardian, middle-class west Swansea was anglicized, prosperous, pious—chapel membership boomed during this time—and comfortable. Even schoolmasters, particularly those in the academic grammar school, taught boys sifted socially through entrance examinations and fee paying, had almost absolute power in the classroom, and enjoyed short working hours. It was, in its way and up to a point, a gentlemanly existence.

These new suburbs were dominated by what one social historian has described as the "work ethic," "social ethic" and "domestic ethic."[12] In home as in suburb, gentility dominated, often expressed, as might be expected, in terms of keeping up standards, possessions, and status symbols, conservative cultural interests, accent, and a stress on regularity, order, and ritual; social historians have noted that in such areas the young were made to acquire "habits of cleanliness, punctuality, politeness."[13]

The Uplands, which included Cwmdonkin Drive, became a "sophisticated middle-class suburb, in which bards, ministers and academics were thick on the ground."[14] Within it were private junior schools, churches and chapels, a cinema, a respectable pub, and a busy shopping center. Swansea Grammar School and the new University College were within walking distance. It was an affluent area, though D. J. Thomas, on his schoolmaster's pay, bought too many books and drank too much beer to make ends meet easily or at all; he taught Welsh evening classes and occasionally borrowed from relatives, while his wife—who hardly ran a tight domestic ship—paid tradesmen in rotation. But his job was secure, the mortgage always paid; they employed a "live-in" maid.

Even though it was an unusual Welsh place, it was not an alien wedge, a "Little England" beyond financial exigencies and the language of heaven. It was Welsh enough; from southeast Wales it would have looked very Welsh indeed. It was probably less sure of itself than a comparable English area and, certainly, less generally affluent. Its social parameters were more Welsh than

English in being less harsh. The occupation range was wider—Thomas's close friend, the painter Alfred Janes, for example, was the son of a greengrocer—and a grammar-school teacher had more status than in, say, Surrey. Yet as a middle-class enclave it probably felt itself to have more in common with, say, parts of Bristol than, say, parts of Tonypandy.

The "three ethics," plus cleanliness, punctuality, and politeness, are not qualities that come readily to mind when we think of Dylan Thomas or of life at 5 Cwmdonkin Drive. Though there is much evidence to confirm the malicious truth of Caitlin Thomas's comment that "no blue-blooded gentleman was a quarter as gentlemanly as Dylan's father,"[15] and though we know how desperately Jack Thomas aspired to be the cultivated gentleman, yet important aspects of his suburban lifestyle were at odds with these aspirations, despite the fact that his social position, intelligence, and intellectual interests might seem to have been well suited to middle-class suburban life in Swansea's Uplands. Despite his fierce yearning for the genteel, Jack Thomas seems to have derived little pleasure or satisfaction from living where he did.

Considered in terms of conventional middle-class habits, his home life was, to say the least, unusual. He could not stand gossiping women and could be very rude to those rash enough to drop in for a chat with Florence. After a few drinks his temper could flash and he would swear—at times at his wife and her acquaintances—with alarming proficiency. He was intensely vain: when he began to go bald, he took to wearing his hat in the house in defiance of etiquette. He was always formally dressed in jacket, collar, and tie. More often than not, he simply withdrew from domesticity. Evening after evening he sat in his study, alone and immaculately dressed, surrounded by his books, to mark essays or read his life away. There he nursed disappointments that included failure as a poet as well as his schoolmastering fate. There he dreamed, perhaps, of being a gentleman scholar, a man of letters in his leisured library.

Later each evening he would go out for a drink: to the Uplands Hotel or to the Bush in Sketty. Sometimes he drank alone, sometimes with socially and intellectually inferior pub acquaintances who called him "professor." He drank a lot, despite the effect on his temper, part of the rage against life for which he is remembered, his fierce response to the mainly trivial circumstances of his existence. Such drinking was, as has been suggested, probably one reason why he was sometimes short of money and, gallingly, had to be helped out by his wife's relations. Outside the home the best that could be said for him was that, predictably, he was a fastidious and slightly dandiacal dresser, though even that was unusual in a sartorially conformist age. In school he despised most of his colleagues, and all were wary of his temper and sharp tongue. His wife recalled that he never worked a full term,[16] an index both of his hypochondria and of his attitude to teaching. She put it down to ill health. He had little contact with neighbors, no close friends, and no faith (his agnosticism would have removed him from the cultural possibilities of chapel life); he dissociated himself from the Welsh-speaking world (which closed further cultural doors), did not serve in the Great War, which caused some problems for him, and belonged, so far as we know, to no clubs or organizations.

Why all this was so is now almost impossible to explain fully. What is clear is that we discern the clash of two different ways of living. One was suburban life, essentially middle-class, restrained, cultured, and genteel, into which D. J. Thomas had worked his way. The other had elements of typical working-class life of the period, the world that, as it turned out, Jack Thomas had never wholly left: the husband as income earner and so all-powerful, self-indulgent, slightly feckless, prone to roughness, not much interested in domestic and family life, drinking regularly outside the home. In such tensions between the bourgeois and the proletarian, between D. J. and Jack, we might detect a fundamental insecurity or disappointment with the new life. Certainly the latter was present, not simply in a general bitterness about the extent of his rise through the social ranks, but in a more specific grievance. He felt that his academic achievements, his Aberystwyth "First," deserved much more. It was said that he applied for the first chair of English at the new University College of Swansea and that he remained convinced that W. D. Thomas, who was appointed in 1921 from a junior post at the University of Saskatchewan and had a generally undistinguished career, had inferior qualifications.

D. J. Thomas's social problems were not helped by his marriage in 1903. Florence Williams was six years younger than her husband and a product of Swansea's east side. Like her husband's parents, hers had also fled from agricultural Dyfed. Both were born around 1840 on small Dyfed farms, and their flight was a longer and perhaps braver one than that of Evan Thomas. It took them to working-class St. Thomas, on the edge of Swansea's dockland, where George Williams, also a railwayman, had eight children by his wife Anna. Seven survived, Florence being the youngest. George Williams was a chapel deacon at St. Thomas's Canaan Congregational Church; the family was grimly respectable. Some of the children began to move up through the social ranks: the eldest, Thomas, became a clergyman and married money; daughter Theodosia married David Rees, the minister at Canaan, who, as a fine preacher and scholarly man, later moved to Paraclete Chapel in middle-class Mumbles, to which the young Dylan was taken by his mother. Brother John worked in the docks but built up a cargo-handling business that made him comparatively prosperous. He owned houses in St. Thomas, and it was he who helped out—much to D. J.'s chagrin—when sister Florence went short.

Florence Williams became a seamstress in a local draper's. Many years later she told Ethel Ross that she met D. J. at a fair in Johnstown. After their marriage on 30 December 1903 at the Congregational Church in Swansea's Castle Street, they settled in Sketty Avenue, where, during 1904, a first child was born but did not survive. In this there is perhaps an explanation for what, on the face of it, was an unlikely liaison. The birth so soon after the marriage suggests—at this distance in time it can never be more than a suggestion—that D. J., to use the phrase of the time, "had to marry her." Florence Williams may have been a pretty, lively young woman, but, as the youngest of a large family, she had been much spoiled and was certainly no intellectual. Nor did she appear to have much social ambition. Though she married a highly intelligent schoolmaster with much social self-consciousness, she remained, it seems, resolutely working-class. As Florence Thomas, she became a kind, loving, thoughtless, slightly feckless wife and mother with, so far as we can tell, no intellectual interests whatsoever, who increasingly got on her husband's nerves and who retained strong links with St. Thomas and with the peasant world from which her family had come. George Tremlett noted shrewdly that she ''brought to the family home in the Swansea Uplands the habits and customs of an ancient past. She baked her own bread, bottled preserves, made cakes and jams, barely mixing with her suburban neighbours.''[17] In that second sentence, if we substitute ''reading serious literature'' for those culinary activities, we have D. J. It seems that he came to despise her, but sexually, at least, the relationship survived: Pamela Hansford Johnson recalled Florence excusing herself after lunch because ''Jack likes me to go up on the bed with him.''[18]

Thus both parents lived uneasily, to say the least, in their new social world. Both came from families that demonstrated social change and mobility with all its resultant tensions and insecurities. Further, Dylan Thomas's mother was unable, through character or conduct, to offer her son—or daughter—any admirable alternative to her husband's bourgeois intellectual desires. ''My mother came from the agricultural depths of Carmarthenshire,'' he told Pamela Hansford Johnson, ''a pettier woman I have never known.''[19] In being what she was, she fostered contempt for urban and rural working-class life. The son turned to the father, who at least offered something to admire—intelligence, knowledge of literature, perhaps social achievement—even though, as matters turned out, D. J.'s biggest influence on his son's work was exerted through his constant implicit demonstration of the clash between ''Jack'' and ''D. J.'' that too often made 5 Cwmdonkin Drive crackle with social tension.

Dylan Thomas recalled hearing of ''a country called 'The Front' from which many of our neighbours never came back,''[20] but the first windows properly open on his life during the years immediately following the Great War, that ''massive watershed in Welsh social history.''[21] The war itself brought prosperity to Wales: docks, mines, and steelworks boomed with the war effort, and agriculture benefitted from increased demands for food production. But from the early 1920s until World War II much of Wales was devastated by economic depression, mass unemployment, and despair as the demands of war ended, overseas markets, particularly for coal, were lost, and the internal-combustion engine began to dominate. Swansea—and, in particular, the western suburbs that included Uplands, with a significant continuing high level of domestic employment—survived this period better than many Welsh places: the anthracite coal field of West Wales, plus tinplate, enabled the area to survive and even, to some extent, to remain buoyant until well into the 1930s. Indeed, during the 1920s Swansea's docks were expanded and continued to boom. Thomas grew up on a island, as it were, of comparative affluence surrounded by seas of unemployment. Though he once insisted that outside Swansea was only "a *strange* world, coal-pitted, mountained, river-run, full, so far as I knew, of choirs and sheep and story-book tall hats, [moving] about its business which was none of mine,"[22] that he was increasingly aware of that world and its dreadful deprivations is evident from early letters and from *Portrait of the Artist as a Young Dog*. Whereas D. J. Thomas came to a boomtown and may well initially have caught something of its material excitement, the sense that things would happen and that ambitious ability would have its due reward, his son grew up as that ambition faded and the town's development faltered. The father may well have communicated to the son a deepening sense of limited horizons.

The house at 5 Cwmdonkin Drive is deceptive: it is semidetached, with a narrow frontage but much depth. The main door is at the side, leading into a hallway into which the three main ground-floor rooms open. The front room, overlooking the Drive, was the parlor, "kept for best"; the middle room was D. J.'s study, lined with books; at the rear is the kitchen with scullery, with a small garden and washhouse behind. Upstairs are four bedrooms and a bathroom. Dylan Thomas's bedroom was next to the bathroom. He described it as "*very* tiny. I really have to go out to turn round. . . . Hot water pipes very near. Gurgle all the time. Nearly go mad. Nice view of wall through window."[23] It was his sanctuary, and in so frequently withdrawing to it, he followed his father's example.

Daughter Nancy was already eight when her brother was born, and the midwife recalled that Dylan's birth aroused "tremendous excitement because of the years between. Mr Thomas celebrated so well I had to take his boots off and put him to bed."[24] The birth was registered seven weeks later; the names were unusual. Dylan is from the medieval Welsh collection of prose romances now known as the *Mabinogion*; he makes a brief appearance as the child of Aranrhod who, at birth, makes for the sea. In 1914 the name was virtually unused. Marlais is a pious nod towards Gwilym Marles. D. J.'s initial euphoria did not last. The baby's crying exasperated him: he would shout, "Put the little bugger through the window," and Addie, the maid during Dylan's first two years, would take him off to her own bed in the tiny boxroom.[25] Such complaints apart, D. J. left all to the doting mother. The young Dylan had an angelic appearance; he became and expected to be the pampered center of attention. Mrs. Thomas could never see her son in other than a favorable light and certainly indulged him absolutely.

The flavor of the childhood years is caught, in part, by Dylan Thomas's story "Patricia, Edith, and Arnold." Patricia is the live-in maid who takes the young Dylan to Cwmdonkin Park. The boy is physically provocative, curious, and observant. Patricia, in using the excursion to meet her boyfriend, has moved beyond the permissible. She is uneasy that, as she complains to her friend Edith, "He notices everything."[26] The boy is very much the young master, the story heavily suggestive of the beginnings of bourgeois authority, redolent with between-wars class difference. Equally significant is a photograph from about 1920

of Dylan, aged five or six, with his sister Nancy, then a teenager, taken somewhere on the west side of Swansea Bay.[27] Nancy accepts being photographed;
the boy, dressed typically for the time in jacket, short trousers, and shirt and
tie, seems unwilling. His head is lowered, hair slightly tousled, expression re-
sentful. It could perhaps be entitled "Study of a Later Rebel." Together, the
story and the photograph dramatize complementary characteristics: conventional
middle-class assumptions and inevitable reaction. Despite Thomas's later lifestyle, both remained important.

Certainly both were fostered by the Uplands of Thomas's upbringing. It had
become an attractive place. Cwmdonkin Drive itself had houses only on one
side; on the other was a private school, Clevedon College, with its small playing
field. Beyond the college was Cwmdonkin Park, complete with drinking fountain, bowling green and pavilion, tennis courts, and many trees. It was, and
remains, one of the most attractive parks in a city of many such. There Thomas
played with his friends. At first war games dominated; later they ranged "armed
and desperate, from end to end, from the robbers' den to the pirates' cabin, the
highwayman's inn to the cattle ranch, or the hidden room in the undergrowth
where we held beetle races and lit the wood fires and roasted potatoes and talked
about Africa and the makes of motor-cars."[28]

On Sundays his mother took him to chapel, defying the frowning agnosticism
of D. J. They went either to Walter Road Congregational Church, on the main
road into central Swansea, or to Paraclete, her brother-in-law's chapel at Newton. When Dylan Thomas was born, his father was a distant thirty-eight; as has
been noted, he remained distant. But though he played little or no part in his
children's upbringing, most evenings during their respective childhoods he
would sit them on his knee in his study and read to them before bedtime. What
he read to Nancy is not known; being eight years older than her brother tended
to blur her presence in the latter's upbringing. To young Dylan he often read
Shakespeare in the belief, presumably, that something would be gradually absorbed even by one too young to understand. Or perhaps D. J. simply found
children's stories too irksome to contemplate. Though home life was stable, it
was not happy; Jack Thomas's brooding presence saw to that. But for young
children not yet sensitive to parental irksomeness or hostility, it was probably
happy enough. Thomas never suggested otherwise.

Little more is known of Thomas's preschool years, though the most detailed
attempt to sum him up psychologically attaches great importance to this period.
It has been argued that it produced an orally fixated, breast-obsessed human
being who became frightened of the wider world and so sought extreme forms
of escape. Whether or not we would wish to describe him in this way, certainly
we know that his mother indulged him, spoiled him, and so contributed to his
"hedonistic and hypochondriacal trends."[29] The "Notebook" poem "The first
ten years in school and park" suggests further complications: an early inner life
of high and fearsome imagination, of "bogies scared from landing and from
corner," and a sense, beginning early, of being "caught between, / The field

and the machine.''[30] For hypersensitive, indulged, and self-indulgent Thomas, the trap opened early.

His mother believed that there was good reason to indulge him. She believed him to be "delicate," like his sister, possibly asthmatic or, at least, with a weak chest. Florence Thomas dreaded tuberculosis, which she believed—there is no factual evidence—had killed her father. All Dylan Thomas's life, particularly in childhood, his bones broke easily.

Maternal concern kept him from school until he was seven, by which time he had become unruly, the terror of baby-sitters, the boy who took what he wanted, usually without asking. When his mother eventually let him go, it was to a private, fee-paying infants' school at 22 Mirador Crescent, near Cwmdonkin Drive, kept by the elderly Mrs. Hole. Thomas recalled it with great affection:

Never was there such a dame-school as ours: so firm and kind and smelling of galoshes, with the sweet and fumbled music of the piano-lessons drifting down from upstairs to the lonely schoolroom, where only the sometimes tearful wicked sat over undone sums or to repent a little crime, the pulling of a girl's hair during geography, the sly shin-kick under the table during prayers. Behind the school was a narrow lane where the oldest and boldest threw pebbles at windows, scuffled and boasted, lied about their relations . . . and smoked the butt-ends of cigarettes, turned green, went home, and had little appetite for tea.[31]

The lonely schoolroom reappears in "Return Journey" when Mirador School is recalled as a place of practical jokes, of storytelling, and of mild discipline: "When they were bad, they sat alone in the empty classroom, hearing, from above them, the distant, terrible, sad music of the late piano lesson."[32] The affection was genuine, but we have always to be wary of Thomas's re-created memories, here, perhaps, remembering Thomas's abiding enthusiasm for Dickens and the extent to which the nostalgic image of the lonely boy in the deserted schoolroom depends upon the similar scene in A Christmas Carol.

The painter Mervyn Levy was a contemporary of Thomas's. There is no reason to doubt his opinion that, educationally, Mirador School was useless. The school was in part of Mrs. Hole's home; it catered for girls up to sixteen and for boys from seven to eleven. She charged ten pounds per year and had twenty or so pupils from homes that regarded the local state school as socially undesirable. Her drunken middle-aged son made periodic appearances that thrilled and frightened the children. Thomas claimed that he learned to read and count, but little was taught. They said a prayer, sang a hymn, and were kept amused mainly through playing games and listening to stories.

For Thomas, it was the worst kind of educational beginning.[33] The school failed to give him the solid grounding in the three Rs that would have supported his grammar-school career. Worse, it did not counter his undisciplined ways. Of angelic appearance, cherubically curled, effectively he did what he liked, and all indulged him. If he was caught making mischief, he blamed others; if he wished to avoid any task, he complained of stomach pains; if he was treated at all harshly, he complained to his mother, who would visit the school in a rage. He was the worst kind of teacher's pet, constantly demanding attention. Given a part in the school play, he simply played the fool. In the lane behind the house he led the boys in competitions to establish who could urinate highest up a wall. The most positive recollection of that period of his life was that he learned to recite great chunks of Shakespeare; he owed that to D. J.

The boy who entered Swansea Grammar School shortly before his eleventh birthday was, if not yet "roaring," certainly on the wrong side of "wild." He was the product of a poor school and a vibrant imaginative life, the latter sustained against the authoritarian pressures of suburban circumstances that later were to press relentlessly upon him. "Patricia, Edith, and Arnold" describes the solitary child at play. "Reminiscences of Childhood" recalls gregarious activities and the attractions of the park. In the later "Return Journey" he added throwing stones at swans on the small reservoir that then filled a corner of the park and damaging flowers and trees, as well as fighting with his friends. Such anarchic violence was even more at odds with the prim suburb.

Two other factors furthered his imaginative development. One was visits to the Uplands Cinema, only a short walk from his home. There, in the age before talkies, Thomas began a lifelong interest in film that fed important imagery into his poems and eventually led to substantial lucrative work as a scriptwriter. In one of his most vivid early poems Thomas's fellow Swansea writer, Vernon Watkins, described the excited and dishevelled boys gripped by horror films in that local fleapit.[34]

Second, of particular importance, given that the Thomases never had family holidays, nor, seemingly, family outings to new places, there were visits to his mother's relations in Newton, part of the Mumbles area of Swansea, and at Fernhill farm on the Llansteffan peninsular in south Carmarthenshire, and to his father's family in Johnstown. In Newton he stayed with his uncle, the Reverend David Rees of Paraclete Chapel, who drew him into the world of chapel religion despised and ignored by D. J. There was much mutual hostility. David Rees thought Thomas mad. Thomas hated him with gusto: in a notebook poem of 1933 he is "The Reverend Crap, a pious fraud . . . The Reverend Crap, a holy pimp" (*PM* 222). Tremlett plausibly suggested that there may also have been visits to Florence Thomas's other brother, Thomas Williams, who became minister of Nicholaston Hall Chapel, on Gower.[35] Such visits were important in that they exposed Thomas to active Nonconformity, to Bible reading, and to the cadenced tradition of Welsh chapel preaching. He acknowledged as much when he recalled that "the great rhythms had rolled over me from the Welsh pulpits; and I had read, for myself, from Job and Ecclesiastes; and the story of the New Testament is part of my life."[36]

Even more important were young Dylan's regular holidays with Aunt Annie and Uncle Jim at Fernhill farm.[37] This was no peasant's hovel. It had been built in the 1720s and had been, at various times, a manor house and the home of the district's assistant hangman. Substantial, suggesting height and hinting at elegance, the main building forms three sides of a small courtyard with gates opening onto the road to Llangain. The young Dylan stayed amid faded grandeur: a Regency staircase, panelled doors, plaster cornices. Outside were gardens, farm buildings, an apple orchard, and fields. In "The Peaches," seemingly set in the years following the Great War, the house is delapidated, the farm in ruins: "The house smelt of rotten wood and damp and animals. . . . The ramshackle outhouses had tumbling, rotten roofs . . . There was nowhere like that farm-yard in all the slapdash county, nowhere so poor and grand and dirty" (*CS* 131–32).

Thomas's visits to Fernhill comprised one of his life's great formative experiences, explored and re-created not only in "The Peaches" but also in "After the funeral" and, much later, in "Fern Hill." The history of the house, intensified by its isolation and its darkening trees, appealed to his sense of the macabre. The association of his childhood and beautiful rurality, his consciousness of the power of nature in all its color, fecundity, and teeming life—rather than its detail; he was no Gilbert White—and of the nature of childhood, and his awareness of the unremitting toil and narrowness of his aunt's life and the extent to which his drunken uncle ruined both farm and substance penetrate and shape much of his finest work. It fostered his strong sense of the declining, the fading, the wasted, the lost that became, in his writing, a ramifying theme: "The Peaches," for example, not only is about individuals but also suggests a way of life, a whole society, in irreversible decline.

Encounters with Uncle Jim also remind us that irresponsible, at times reckless, drinking, perhaps alcoholism, is an unavoidable theme in Thomas's family history: as well as Uncle Jim, there was D. J., who, in his earlier days, was said to have a severe drinking problem that he later struggled to control. To judge from "The Peaches," the impressionable Dylan regarded the farmer's drinking as a fascinating eccentricity; and alcohol and pubs seemed acceptable parts of the life of a father he always respected. The conventionalizing of heavy drinking and of visiting dingy pubs was the childhood impression most fraught with later tragic implications.

Of his visits to Johnstown we know less. "A Visit to Grandpa's" perhaps captures something of a young boy's sense of a strange world, registering Jack Thomas's relations as a further set of eccentrics. Certainly the Johnstown Thomases were another chapel-dominated family. They were also, for a sophisticated "Swansea Jack," another family out in the sticks. In both "The Peaches" and "A Visit to Grandpa's"—those explorations of maternal and paternal relations—is the boy's sense of his own superiority as he views his relations from his urban-suburban, middle-class pedestal.

Park, cinema, visits to relations, indulgent dame-school, doting mother, distant, bitter father, and equally distant older sister combined to create a ten-year-old unused to discipline, prone to wildness, intensely imaginative, growing up in a bourgeois suburb that, in seeking to order and contain, developed a creative tension on which his finest writing, perhaps all his writing, came to depend. In the summer of 1925, when school uniform was bought for him and childhood came to an end, quite a few observing adults must have hoped that the grammar school, in the popular phrase, would sort him out. They were to be disappointed.

Dylan Thomas entered Swansea Grammar School in September 1925. He may have sat for the entrance examination; more probably he paid fees, which would not have been more than five pounds per term. The same Trevor Owen who in 1901 had brought D. J. Thomas with him from Pontypridd was still headmaster of a school of four hundred or so boys. He was to retire in 1929. Paul Ferris, who entered the school fifteen years later, commented that in Thomas's time the school "was permissive for those days, even lax."[38] Trevor Owen was genial and generally ineffective. He rarely used the cane; there were no compulsory games. Boys were left to discover their own academic strengths, which was fine for some but obviously open to abuse. D. J. was senior English master, still contemptuous of most of his colleagues, still regarding them as his intellectual inferiors. They continued to fear his temper and sharp tongue and tried to avoid him. Though the school generally may have been lax, in his classroom D. J. was a martinet. If any boy stepped out of line or failed to appreciate the great literature set before him, he was subject to verbal abuse and/or physical violence. But D. J. could also be a fine teacher whose reading to the class, particularly from Shakespeare, was often remembered as inspiring long after boys had left the school. He was good at preparing boys for Oxbridge.

Dylan Thomas took full advantage of the lax regime and of having such a father as a power in the school. As a product of Mirador School, he was one of the worst-educated entrants and was allowed to become intellectually lazy, a trait that was to blight his life. He absented himself from as many lessons as possible, played truant frequently, and often avoided examinations through feigned illness that always deceived his mother. For such nefarious acts he was rarely punished, probably because of D. J.'s volatile presence. Neither—and probably for the same reason—did he suffer any academic penalty: when he entered the school he was placed in the "A" stream, and though he did very badly academically—hardly bothering with any subject save English, at which he was very good—he was never demoted. As he moved through the school, he became insolent and contemptuous of his subjects. D. J. seemed never to intervene.

Thomas's contempt for all school subjects except English is difficult to understand. P. E. Smart, close to him at school, suggested that "Dylan was already instinctively excluding from his life everything that might distract him from his fixed path."[39] Daniel Jones made a similar point in stating that the "early stand against the academic was very valuable to Dylan; he would have needed twice the time to accomplish all that he did accomplish if he had not discerned clearly and from the beginning the things that were of no use to him, or if he had not steadily ignored them."[40] In both these reactions is the whiff of special pleading. More to the point is John Davenport's belief, reported by FitzGibbon, that "Dylan was very clever but intellectually almost incredibly lazy.''[41] FitzGibbon qualified this by insisting that Thomas, as the writer of complicated, demanding poems—and, we might add, some of the letters and thoughtful replies to questionnaires—could hardly have been intellectually lazy. He simply found the academic approach "distasteful in the extreme." Davenport seems closer to the truth. The consequence of attending Mirador School and Swansea Grammar School under Trevor Owen and of having a doting mother who connived naïvely at the evasion of any academic challenge was that during his formative years he was rarely put under any intellectual pressure.

Even more puzzling is why his father, the classroom martinet, did not make him work. To this there is no apparent answer, though we can surmise that he simply failed to counter the boy's wildness, or that perhaps his own disappointments raised subconscious questions about the worth of academic study that prevented intervention or made it half-hearted. The son careered through the school to failure—in all subjects except English—in the public examinations of 1930; the father, it seems, stood or fumed by.

Yet outside the classroom Dylan Thomas's attitude was very different. His extracurricular interests were at the opposite extreme to his academic indifference. He was a talented athlete who, during his first summer term, in 1926, won the handicap mile for under-fifteens at the school sports. Because of his age and small size he was given a hundred yards start. He is said to have kept the newspaper cutting recording this success in his wallet all his life. Other highlights of his school sporting career include victory in the quarter mile and mile, both for under-fifteens, in July 1929. In 1930 he finished second in the senior cross-country. Thereafter, presumably, precocious smoking and drinking ruined his form.

He became a pillar of the Dramatic Society, doubtless helped by the elocution lessons to which his father sent him to counter the Welshness of his speech, and that gave him the slightly haughty accent but generally superb voice production so apparent in his recordings. He acted in John Galsworthy's *Strife* and in John Drinkwater's *Abraham Lincoln* and *Oliver Cromwell*. In the last-named he played the title role—''he looked as young and as fresh and clean as if he had just come off the cover of a chocolate box''[42]—as he had done in Galsworthy's *Strife*. During his last two years at school he helped found a reading circle linked to the Dramatic Society. Galsworthy's *Escape* was their first choice. Thomas's acting was generally admired, and he made out-of-school appearances with the local Y.M.C.A. Players, who performed mainly thrillers and farces. He became a member of the Y.M.C.A.'s Junior Department, which gave him further acting opportunities.

During 1931, his last year at school, he also helped found a Debating Society, serving as its first secretary. At the first meeting, he spoke for the proposition ''That modern youth is decadent'' and was, as he told his schoolfriend Percy Smart, gleefully provocative in attacking a whole range of sensitive subjects, from religion to sex.[43]

His main extracurricular activity was writing for the school magazine, which had been founded by D. J. in 1901. When Dylan was in the middle school, he became a subeditor and then editor of three issues before leaving school.[44] The magazine's contents were always vetted by D. J.; here, at least, the father must have been pleased with the son. Thomas's first contribution was "The Song of the Mischievous Dog," submitted in his first term, when he was eleven and had been writing poetry for at least two years. It was the first of many; some, we have since learned, were written in collaboration with his friend Daniel Jones.[45] All are technically assured and skilfully rhymed. He shows a gift for parody: "Little Miss Muffet," for instance, was in the style of early Yeats. As Victor Golightly has stressed, the school magazine was where Thomas could experiment with different styles and respond to numerous influences to produce what Thomas himself described as "endless imitations."[46] The most important influence was that of the poets of the Great War. He was born during the first Battle of Ypres and certainly into the late 1930s, as will be seen, was haunted by the historical context of his birth and by the recent dreadful carnage. The decade of the 1920s was dominated by memories of the war and by books about it. Literary-minded boys like Dylan Thomas, growing up after the war, were avid readers of the poetry. This is evident in Thomas's essay on "Modern Poetry" and in a series of war poems. The first, published in 1927, when Thomas was twelve, was "The Watchers"; the second, published the following year, the tenth anniversary of the Armistice, was "Missing"; the third, in 1930, was "Armistice." Wilfred Owen's work, in particular, became very important to Thomas, but these poems are more in the manner of a Laurence Binyon. That is, they are consoling poems in which the dead are glamorized or inspire fine sentiments in the living. They are gestures towards a readership made up of grammar-school boys and their suburban, middle-class, perhaps petit bourgeois parents, some, inevitably, bereaved by the war.

"Modern Poetry" is one of two impressive essays, the other being on silent films. Both demonstrate an impressively wide range of reading and viewing and the ability to marshal material and develop arguments that make Thomas's disastrous classroom showing all the more puzzling. For D. J., who once hoped that his son would go to Oxford, reading these essays must have been a galling experience.

Thomas's final contributions were made after he had left school, during the period from 1931 to 1934. They consisted of three short stories, "Brember," "Jarley's," and "In the Garden." All three are dark and assured, with supernatural elements. We should remember that by 1934 he had already made his mark on the London literary world.

At school he was bullied, like all newcomers, though, at first, probably more often than most, given his small size and cherubic appearance. He was thrown into the playground bushes and jammed into the wastepaper bin when classes began. When he responded aggressively—he never lost that aggressive streak—and with the swearing that became a hallmark and that he derived from D. J., the bullying ceased. But, to judge from his autobiographical fiction, most of his leisure activities were of the usual kind. He played cricket with his friends or watched it at the county ground, went to the beach and to the fairground, camped on Gower, and responded to the multifarious activities of adolescence.

Such normality must not be overstressed. In three important respects Thomas was very different from his fellows. The first, already noted, was that puzzling contempt for all school subjects except English, a contempt carried to indifferent extremes far beyond simply disliking school. The second—perhaps one way of expressing a general contempt for all authority—was his wild behavior. He would lie his way out of trouble. He was known to be a thief: sister Nancy complained that when her friends visited, he stole money from their handbags. Sweets on unattended shop counters and the contents of charity boxes were fair game. Sometimes he would use the money to buy cigarettes, or even cigars, to smoke in the cinema. In company he could say outrageous things: Ferris reported an occasion at a friend's home when Thomas was offered a fresh fig. He bit into it and commented, ''God it's like chewing a girl's cunt.''[47]

Even more serious and puzzling were two clear instances of plagiarism. On 14 January 1927 the *Western Mail* published a poem by ''D. M. Thomas'' entitled ''His Requiem.'' He was then twelve years old. For this he received a check for ten shillings, which his proud parents kept as a memento. He pinned the cutting to his dressing table. In 1971 it was discovered that the poem was by Lilian Gard; Thomas had lifted it from *Boy's Own Paper* of November 1923. Two years later, in 1929, he offered the editor of the *Swansea Grammar School Magazine* a poem entitled ''Sometimes.'' To the editor it seemed familiar; it was traced back to Arthur Mee's *Children's Encyclopaedia*. When D. J. was informed, he was furious. Oddly, both poems were trifles; Thomas's own light verse of the time is more vigorous and interesting.

The third difference was in the nature of his secret life. This last had two main elements. The first emerged from his friendship with Daniel Jones, which began, according to Jones, during Thomas's first week at the grammar school, but which probably began in 1928.[48] Jones, two years older than the young Dylan, was the brilliant boy of whom much was expected. As a mutual friend put it, ''Dr Jones seemed to be (and indeed in my opinion was) a giant, intellectually, whereas Dylan seemed to be a somewhat feckless but very likeable person.''[49] In school Jones specialized in English, which he read at the University College of Swansea, obtaining a First before writing an M.A. thesis on Elizabethan poetry. A distinguished career in music followed: he wrote nine symphonies, two operas, and much else. After army service in World War II he lived in Swansea for the rest of his life.

When the friendship began, Daniel Jenkyn Jones lived at Warmley in Sketty's Eversley Road, a road of larger and even more solidly bourgeois houses than Cwmdonkin Drive, which was a mile away. His father was a prominent local musician of pantheistic tendencies, a friendly man who read widely and enthusiastically and was an amusing raconteur. His mother, who was also musical, wove tapestries and had exhibited her work in London. His elder brother also composed and played. His cultured aunt, who lived with the family, tutored Daniel before he entered the grammar school. Warmley was a spacious, casual, cultured home.

The home at 5 Cwmdonkin Drive was very different: "D's father a heavy drinker, a morose dark household," Bill Read noted during an interview with Mervyn Levy.[50] Though at first Daniel Jones called on his friend, D. J.'s brooding presence weighed heavily on the boys, with the result that Warmley became Thomas's second home. It was a place of much boyish activity—fights, cushion throwing, garden cricket—that surrounded a solid intellectual core. The boys tried their hand at painting and at carving stone and played fantastic games, inventing, as Jones wrote, a "whole mythology of composers, instrumentalists and singers,"[51] as well as a radio station. This last was WBC (Warmley Broadcasting Company), on which they read poems and performed short plays, often listened to and criticized by members of the family, early training for Thomas's important broadcasting career. Most important, for Thomas, they tried out on each other their various compositions—poems and musical pieces—and collaborated in the writing of poetry, calling the author Walter Bram.[52]

The extant worksheets demonstrate how Jones dominated the partnership. Even his handwriting, compared to Thomas's rather childish lettering, is confident and adult. In their collaborations he always wrote the odd lines, Thomas the even ones. This meant, of course, that Jones always took the lead and, because he had read more widely, knew more about music, and had more varied diction than his friend, set an agenda that widened Thomas's range of response. Such writing exercises developed Thomas's cultural awareness and subjected him to the kind of intellectual pressure he was able to avoid at school. Together they began to map out their future, to dream of "a future spread out beyond the window" and, in Thomas's case, of conquering "smoky London paved with poems" (CS, 164).

Through Thomas's unnamed fictional persona in "One Warm Saturday" he refers to the obsession that was the second strand of his secret life: "I must go home and sit in my bedroom by the boiler" (CS, 226). There, certainly from April 1930, in his bedroom's cramped privacy, he began filling his notebooks with poems and stories that were often fair copies of earlier drafts. They were not an absolute secret: Daniel Jones knew of them and heard Thomas read some of the poems during their sessions at Warmley. Thomas's friend Percy Smart, coeditor of the school magazine, also knew of them and wrote later that, as well as the conventional poems published in the magazine,

he was of course already producing verse of the kind which many people can't understand, and I remember asking him why he did it: what was the point of writing "privately" in this way. But he couldn't really understand the question: he wrote, he said, what was in him, and it was really quite irrelevant whether anyone else even read it.[53]

The biographical significance of the notebooks lies in the evidence they provide of the intense, erotic, obscure, strange, imaginative world at the center of Thomas's teenage existence. The powerful originality of that world was soon to be recognized: the first two extant notebooks, covering the period 1930 to 1932, contain early versions of six important Thomas poems, including two of his finest: "How shall my animal," "Today, this insect," "The spire cranes," "Why east wind chills," "The hunchback in the park," and "Out of the sighs." They were all written before he was eighteen.

The simple contrast—the bright, seemingly normal teenager with the secret, intense, imaginative life—will not do. It is complicated by Thomas's anarchic public activities: bad language, thieving, plagiarism, and contempt for school. These can, of course, be seen as reactions against bourgeois norms and suburban pressures. Filling the notebooks, the main element of that secret life, was the result of regular, disciplined activity, of intellectual struggle, at once a contrast to suburban life and an extension of it. Outer and inner worlds cannot be separated. Thomas needed the suburban, middle-class framework; as will be seen, it found its way into a poetry otherwise reactive via the strict forms and tight structures he imposed upon it.

In December 1930, during his last year at the grammar school, Thomas wrote a further letter to Percy Smart, who had left school to work in a bank. Its main purpose was to accept a contribution from Smart for the school magazine. But the letter also contained a disturbing outpouring of despair as he imagined a future of utterly conventional failure. Thomas told his friend that nothing, not even writing, seemed worthwhile.[54] Though to some extent this is typical teenage angst, it is not only this. The mood is echoed in the notebooks in such lines as "For, if I could, I'd fly away" and "Christ, let me write from the heart," written in June 1931 (*PM* 119, 120). Such despair—and perhaps some fear— at being trapped in the way of life imposed on most provincial grammar-school boys reminds us that Thomas's anarchic behavior should not simply be condemned as the actions of a spoilt young man. It expressed deeper needs that could only be properly satisfied within an ordered world. Seemingly, Thomas never understood this; certainly his eagerness to heed the siren call of disorganized bohemia was the beginning of his tragedy.

Three weeks after the notebook entries he was no longer a schoolboy. FitzGibbon suggested that the three years between leaving school and going to London in 1934 comprised "the most important period of his life as a poet."[55] This is arguable, given that by the time he left school, the main traits in his character—too often seen simply as the expense of single-mindedness in a waste of moral faults—had been established. But it is certainly true that in the first eighteen months after leaving school it was his further misfortune to choose a short-lived career that served only to develop those faults. He became a journalist on the local paper, the *South Wales Daily Post*, which soon became the *South Wales Evening Post*.

Though Swansea escaped the worst of the 1930s economic depression, it was difficult to find employment. Given Thomas's abysmal school record, we should accept his mother's statement that he got the job because of D. J.'s influence. Dylan Thomas began in the reading room, then, after a few weeks, became a junior reporter. Most of his work was appalling: he failed to learn shorthand and was usually neither accurate nor conscientious. The exception is a series of careful, detailed, and often shrewdly critical articles on "The Poets of Swansea" written for the *Post*'s companion paper, the *Herald of Wales*, articles pointing to an intellectual potential destroyed by indulgence and bad schools. It must be added that his iconoclastic approach even to the work of E. Howard Harris, a notoriously egotistic local poet, gave his editor much concern.

His time as a local journalist increased his knowledge of Swansea and particularly of its crisis areas and low life: the hospital, the police station, the mortuary and its sad cargo, and the docks area with its sleazy pubs and loose women. He cultivated a "reporter's image" influenced by American films: a pulled-down porkpie hat, dangling cigarette, and check overcoat. His role model was Freddie Farr, a hard-bitten man in his forties who was one of the senior reporters and became the central character in "Old Garbo," and whose hard drinking Thomas began to emulate:

I liked the taste of beer, its live, white lather, its brass-bright depths, the sudden world through the wet brown walls of the glass, the tilted rush to the lips and the slow swallowing down to the lapping belly, the salt on the tongue, the foam at the corners. (*CS*, 217)

Implicit in such a marvellous description are significant suggestions of escape into a world of immediate physical sensation, slightly repulsive yet eagerly sought animality, and a slackening of control. Because he was small and had a low capacity for alcohol, because getting drunk struck a small blow against provincial conformity, and perhaps because he was afraid of literary failure and the small-town trap, he got drunk with increasing frequency: "at least four nights of the week," he told Trevor Hughes.[56] Out of such regular pub crawling emerges Thomas the life and soul, the convivial raconteur, roles that hastened his downfall. All such activity doubtless had an effect on his efficiency as a reporter.

A further important element in this essentially urban social life was the circle that met regularly at the Kardomah Café in central Swansea. The building, utterly destroyed during World War II bombing, was at 14 Castle Street, opposite the *Evening Post* offices. The all-male group met for morning coffee, perhaps for lunch. It included Charles Fisher, who also worked for the *Post* and who became a published poet, the painter Alfred Janes, already in art school but often in Swansea, Daniel Jones, Mervyn Levy, first met in Mirador School and, like Janes, studying to be a painter, and Tom Warner, a musician who became a schoolteacher. Wynford Vaughan Thomas, later famous as a war correspondent, broadcaster, and travel writer, came and went. Vernon Watkins was a later addition. Doubtless others, grammar-school acquaintances with jobs in the town center, also made appearances. The flavor of these occasions is caught in "Old Garbo," in which the Kardomah is the Café Royal:

Most of the boys were there already. Some wore the outlines of moustaches, others had sideboards and crimped hair, some smoked curved pipes and talked with them gripped between their teeth, there were pin-striped trousers and hard collars, one daring bowler.
    "Sit by here," said Leslie Bird. He was in the boots at Dan Lewis's. (*CS*, 213)

It is also recalled in the broadcast "Return Journey" when the Passer-By recalls:

I haven't seen him since the old Kardomah days. . . . Him and Charlie Fisher—Charlie's got whiskers now—and Tom Warner and Fred Janes, drinking coffee-dashes and arguing the toss . . . [about] music and poetry and politics. Einstein and Epstein, Stravinsky and Greta Garbo, death and religion, Picasso and girls.[57]

Thomas had many faults, a number veering more to the mortal than the venial; he sorely tried the patience of all who knew him. Yet he kept his friends; those he made during his Swansea upbringing stayed loyal to the end. He was hardly a good friend in the fullest, most selfless sense. Rather, he was marvellous company, fun to know, and brought out, in so many of those who knew him more than superficially, an affection that was often protective. A further aspect of his tragedy is that the attractive side of Thomas became more and more difficult to find.

For two years or so after leaving school Thomas also continued his interest in acting. He joined Swansea Little Theatre, then based in the Mumbles area of Swansea close to congenial pubs. The Little Theatre had broken away from the Swansea Amateur Dramatic Society in order to develop a more serious repertoire that would include plays by Shakespeare, Chekhov, and Ibsen. By the time Thomas joined, such idealism had faded: though he took leading parts in George Farquhar's *The Beaux' Stratagem* and William Congreve's *The Way of the World*, he also appeared in Noel Coward's *Hay Fever*, H. F. Rubinstein's *Peter and Paul*, and Rodney Ackland's *Strange Orchestra*.[58] He toyed briefly with a career in the theatre but was probably always a limited actor: his voice, compellingly magnificent though it could be, was never the most flexible of instruments. His brief association with the Little Theatre was important in developing public presence and a sense of the dramatic, qualities that were to help him when he worked for the BBC and when he gave readings. It was also important in being one of the few occasions when he made common cause with his sister Nancy, otherwise a strangely peripheral figure in his life; she and her future husband, Haydn Taylor, were members when Thomas joined. Further, in Swansea in the 1930s the theatre was still regarded as slightly daring, so that joining a drama group was cocking a small snook at provincial respectability. Ultimately, however, the Little Theatre was too disciplined for Thomas. He liked to nip out for a quick one during rehearsals; one producer objected, and an altercation followed. Thomas walked out, leaving the cast at the dress-rehearsal stage. Thereafter his interest faded away.

It was, in any case, always subservient to his literary ambitions. In 1931 he tried to further these ambitions through what proved to be an abortive attempt to start a magazine entitled *Prose and Verse*. An advertisement in the *Evening Post* brought in a short story by Trevor Hughes, who became a friend and the original of Raymond Price in "Who Do You Wish Was With Us?" Other friends rallied round. As so often with such proposed publications, it was intended mainly as a showcase for the founder, whose own poetry, short fiction, and nonfictional prose would have dominated the first issue.[59] But publication required subscriptions in advance. They were not forthcoming, either then or in 1933 when the project was revived.

By the close of 1932 Thomas had left the *Evening Post*, probably by mutual and amicable acceptance of the inevitable. In a letter to Trevor Hughes he invented the offer and refusal of a five-year contract, some indication of bourgeois shame at having failed to hold down his first job. In what followed he struck a more genuine note:

What I feared was the slow but sure stamping out of individuality, the gradual contentment with life as it was, so much per week, so much for this, for that, so much left over for drink & cigarettes. That be no loife for such as Oi![60]

But what to do? The subtext here is uncertainty, Thomas poised between regular work in a provincial town and some kind of literary career.

At 5 Cwmdonkin Drive life had become unbearable. This is vividly evident in Nancy's letters to Haydn Taylor:

Mother grumbled at me & I asked her to shut up. Daddy heard & threw a book at me, hit me & behaved in a back street way. Finally after using language I couldn't repeat—it was filthy—said, "Who are you? Nobody cares what happens to you, it's a pity you're alive. All you and your beautiful brother do is to take my money from me." . . . I honestly do wish I was dead. . . . Last night Dylan said one day he'd strangle me.

Thomas, now unemployed, stole money from his family and from Nancy's visiting friends and disappeared to the pub. If he had no money, he spent his time at Warmley. "What will become of him Heaven knows," Nancy wrote with unexpected concern.[61] Early in 1933 she escaped into marriage to Haydn Taylor and a move to London. She left a household dominated by a Jack Thomas raging against his lot in life, that rage intensified, we now know, by the painful beginnings of cancer of the tongue.

It is always tempting to write off Thomas as an unscrupulous rogue. The reality is always more complicated, as is evident from two descriptions of him at this crucial point in his life. The first is by A. E. Trick, who befriended

Thomas during 1932. Bert Trick was a former engineer who lost his job in the depression and then became a clerk before giving that up to run a grocer's shop in Glanbrydan Avenue, at the point where middle-class Uplands met working-class Brynmill. He was sixteen years older than Thomas and had strong Marxist sympathies. Thomas became part of Trick's circle, which fluctuated in numbers between three and twelve and which met as a discussion group either at Glanbrydan Avenue or, unexpectedly, on Wednesdays at 5 Cwmdonkin Drive after D. J. had gone out, "usually in Dylan's father's book-lined den with the Grecian statuettes."[62] The group included Tom Warner and Alfred Janes from the Kardomah group. Subjects included literature, art, music, religion, and, particularly, politics. Trick gave Thomas some sense of the political currents of the 1930s; to the end of his life Thomas held left-wing views even if they were never clearly defined. Trick's recollection of Thomas is unusual:

Dylan as I knew him was not the drunken, roistering figure that legend has tended to weave round him. He was deeply religious—in the broadest sense of the word. He had a wonderful compassion, and the only time I ever saw him enraged was when he saw an act of cruelty or violence against man or beast.

He loved people and loved Swansea. Even the eccentrics and odd characters were his kinsfolk be they Swansea people. At heart he was a shy person and loathed being on show or made the Lion of the Evening. His rudeness and seeming uncouth behaviour on such occasions was his defensive mechanism.[63]

There is much here that points to Thomas's ambivalence about his birthplace and which helps explain later behavior.

Trick's stress on Thomas's shyness and consequent defensiveness, and on his sensitivity, is a link with the second account. This is by Thomas Taig, then a lecturer in the Department of English at the University College of Swansea. Taig produced Little Theatre plays in which Thomas appeared. He wrote: "I think of him as infinitely vulnerable, living from moment to moment in a heightened awareness of sense-impressions and emotional tensions, the victim rather than the master of his environment." He acted parts, Taig believed, as a desperate defence mechanism because he felt the trials of the world so intensely.[64] One example is his letter about the death of Ann Jones, his aunt at Fernhill:

The odour of death stinks through a thousand books & in a thousand homes. I have rarely encountered it (apart from journalistic enquiries), & find it rather pleasant. It lends a little welcome melodrama to the drawing-room tragi-comedy of my most eventful life.[65]

There is much more in the same vein. The affectedly cynical and callous pose is evident both here and, perhaps less successfully, in the notebook poem that, in the event, was the first draft of "After the funeral." Neither in letter nor draft does Thomas wholly succeed in hiding the deep regard for his aunt expressed more openly in the finished poem.

In both accounts this sense of an inner life so different from the outward persona, and of Thomas as sensitive victim, is one way to understand the predicament already expressed in terms of the tension between and interpenetration of the ordering bourgeois world, Thomas's wild behavior, and his intense and dynamic inner life. Certainly he showed different sides of himself to different people, but in the end, all can be seen in terms of discrepancies between appearance and inner reality and of a bourgeois provincial's fear of stepping out of the common way.

The year 1933 was a key year in Thomas's literary career. He was eighteen. In his room's privacy he wrote fluently and furiously, filling his notebooks, creating a strange world of neosurrealistic shifts, intense sexuality, and disturbing physical introspection. Haunted by social and familial tension and by imaginings triggered by violence much of which stemmed from the still-looming presence of the Great War, it was a world away from a suburban upbringing. He was sending his work to editors and in 1933 had his first success. Thomas's fascination with the Great War, apparent in the school-magazine sequence and throughout the notebooks, was especially evident in 1933 when he and Bert Trick had a competition for the best poem about "Immortality." Trick was also obsessed with the war, as his poem, with its reference to "Lungs chewed by poison gas / Attempt to sing," demonstrates. Thomas's poem was the notebook version of "And death shall have no dominion," which, together with the famous final version, has for too long been regarded as a straightforward poem of simple affirmation. As will be seen, both versions should now also be understood as war poems, in part because of Bert Trick's influence.

The notebook version, unchanged, was accepted by A. R. Orage and published in the *New English Weekly* in May, becoming Thomas's first poem to appear in a London magazine. Thomas was doubtless delighted; he was also furious when he discovered that there was no payment. Only a month later "The Romantic Isle," Thomas's entry for a BBC poetry competition, was broadcast. During the summer he paid his first visit to London, staying for at least part of the visit with his sister and her husband Haydn Taylor, who lived in a houseboat on the Thames at Chertsey. It is said that he called on Orage and Sir Richard Rees, who edited the influential *Adelphi*. A month later Rees published "No man believes." In September 1933 "That sanity be kept" was published in the *Sunday Referee*'s new feature, "The Poets' Corner," which was edited by Victor Neuburg, the strange, bisexual literary journalist who had been a friend of Aleister Crowley. The *Sunday Referee* was a newspaper with serious pretensions trying to tap a more literary market. It awarded prizes for the best poems, the major award being the sponsorship of a volume of poetry by the major prizewinner. In October 1933 Neuburg published "The force that through the green fuse drives the flower." Years later William Empson recalled that this poem made Thomas famous.[66]

For all its Neuburg-inspired razzmatazz, the *Sunday Referee* was outside the mainstream of London's serious literary world. That Thomas should have turned so eagerly to the newspaper and that he should have maintained his connection for so long—the last poem it published, "Incarnate devil," appeared on 11 August 1935—are indications of his struggles for general recognition. Even after the early acceptances Geoffrey Grigson, editor of the highly regarded *New Verse*, rejected a number of Thomas's poems. Sir Richard Rees, while publishing work by Thomas, was uneasily puzzled by the nature of the material; Thomas reported to Pamela Hansford Johnson that his poems reminded Rees of "automatic or trance-writing," the kind of poetry that he (Thomas) regarded as "worthless as literature. . . . The note has depressed me more than the usual adverse criticism."[67] In Rees's response Thomas sensed general incomprehension and exclusion.

To break through, as Thomas then proceeded to do, to a dominant position in metropolitan literary life was a great and courageous achievement. He was, after all, an unknown and very young provincial writer of startlingly original and often very difficult poems. In his letter accompanying the poems Grigson was to reject he referred to having "developed, intellectually at least, in the smug darkness of a provincial town. . . . Grinding out poetry, whether good or bad, in such an atmosphere as surrounds me, is depressing and disheartening."[68] He sought a world in which he could feel at ease; in 1933 it was not Wales. Thomas belonged to an English-speaking, Welsh middle-class world that separated itself from nationalist, Welsh-speaking Wales. He thought his world to be philistine, though at its most ambitious it looked—as it has always done—to the wider world for which education, travel, and even accent had prepared it. In Thomas's case his parents paid for elocution lessons to eliminate the singsong cadences of a Swansea Jack. In Wales there was virtually nothing for Welsh writers in English; automatically and eagerly they looked to London.

Thomas once stated that on his first visit to London he was too frightened to leave Paddington railway station. That seems an exaggeration, though London, for the 1930s Welshman or other provincial, could seem a fearsome world. For the young aspiring writer, this was not simply because of the city's bewildering size and bustle—it remained affluent when so much of Britain was economically depressed—but also because of the incestuous nature of the metropolitan literary world during the 1930s.[69] At a time when only four in a thousand went on to higher education and only one in a thousand went to Oxford or Cambridge, most writers of standing were from comfortable professional families, educated at public schools and Oxbridge. During the 1930s that world was beginning to narrow even further, for an increasing number of writers—including William Empson and Charles Madge—were part of the first generations to have read English literature at the ancient universities. They were often disciples of I. A. Richards and his advocacy of close reading, or of F. R. Leavis, whose *New Bearings in English Poetry* (1932) championed Hopkins, Hardy, T. S. Eliot, close reading, and moralistic judgment and became increasingly influential.

In addition, many writers came from literary families and had fathers or relations in influential posts. Stephen Spender's father edited the *Westminster Re-*

view, John Lehmann's *Punch*; Evelyn Waugh's father was managing director of Chapman and Hall. Though, as Cunningham pointed out, such fathers, and others, "produced the wrong kind of writing,"[70] meaning writing inimical to the younger generation, nonetheless, they could hardly help but be influential; Evelyn Waugh, after all, was published by his father's firm. Other writers were related to each other: Cunningham offered another list that includes John Lehmann and Christopher Isherwood, who were Graham Greene's cousins, and Julian Bell, who was Virginia Woolf's nephew.[71] Numerous writers were linked through homosexual proclivities: Auden, Isherwood, Spender, Plomer, Lehmann, Forster—the list is long. The London literary world before World War II was a huge in-group, or a cluster of small in-groups, whose members puffed each other's works and gave each other literary jobs. Though powerful critics, such as the Leavises, attacked such damaging inclusiveness, they themselves had their own Cambridge-dominated following.

Metropolitan literati affected left-wing views, yet were almost wholly isolated from a working class they really feared. A corollary of their socialism—in some cases, their communism—was that they derided the suburban middle classes, particularly those in the provinces, let alone in far-off Wales. A further corollary was that social realism and direct political awareness, in poetry as well as the novel, were much in vogue in order to demonstrate, respectively, general social concern and a response to troubling times. Paradoxically, given so much socialist sentiment, their literary world was intensely elitist and had, at its center, T. S. Eliot, who was hardly either socialist or social realist or the purveyor of directly political work.

The period's vogue for travelling, with expenditure often recouped through volumes of impressions brought out by the best publishers, from the early 1930s onwards brought writers face-to-face with the ominous zeitgeist and so furthered the politicizing of their texts. In 1932 the Nazis became the largest single party in the Reichstag; on 30 January 1933 Hitler became chancellor; persecuted Jews were beginning to leave Germany. For a sensitive, insecure Welsh writer of seemingly apolitical poems, 1933 was not a propitious time to march on London.

Following Thomas's return to 5 Cwmdonkin Drive and further filling of notebooks, his father, then fifty-seven, was diagnosed in late August as suffering from cancer of the tongue; in September he underwent a course of radium-needles treatment at University College Hospital in London. He was there for a week and then, for the rest of 1933, travelled between Swansea and London for further treatment. Though he returned to school in January 1934, he was, his son told Trevor Hughes, "weak and uncured."[72] He recovered to live another twenty years, but he was, comparatively speaking, chastened by his narrow escape and perhaps by the fact that not a single colleague visited him during his four months away from school. D. J. began to keep his temper, to mellow. Or, we might say, the illness knocked some of the spirit out of him.

His son was deeply upset by the illness. Suddenly he faced the possibility of his father's death. As a result, his writing began to mature. In the months immediately following the diagnosing of cancer we see the emergence of Thomas's "process" poems, his fierce sense of life in his body and his body as microcosm of the wider, natural world, a metaphor for cosmic actions. "The force that through the green fuse" is the most famous example. Further, during that same period we find in his notebooks a series of fatherly poems that sometimes are also process poems and that include "Before I knocked," "Jack my father, let the knaves," "The eye of sleep turned on me like a moon," and "All that I owe the fellows of the grave," this last with its strangely compelling lines about familial tensions:

> O all I owe is all the flesh inherits,
> My fathers' loves that pull upon my nerves,
> My sisters' tears that sing upon my head,
> My brothers' blood that salts my open wounds. (*PM*, 254)

It seems no accident that in the notebook poems of this period, September through November 1933, Thomas often turns to the persisting presence of the Great War. As will be seen, Armistice Day 1933 inspired a furious outburst against the war to Pamela Hansford Johnson and the first draft of "When once the twilight locks no longer," above all else a poem about the conflict into which he had been born. Death and violence always haunted him; from this moment on, relations with his father—and his father's own social predicament—became a second central dynamic.

Despite his father's illness, Thomas must have been cheered when, as has been noted, on 3 September 1933, the *Sunday Referee* published "That sanity be kept." A few days later he received an admiring letter from a young woman named Pamela Hansford Johnson, and they began to correspond. The letters are remarkable for their length. Thomas did not preserve her letters to him. Of the hundred or so Johnson estimated Thomas wrote to her, only twenty-five survive. They amount to fifty thousand words.

During October 1933 Johnson won the first *Sunday Referee* major poetry prize, the coveted sponsorship of her first volume. Parts of Thomas's letters to her consist of detailed criticism of her work: enthusiastic praise but also objections that were invariably vehement and could be savage. She was a very different kind of poet, as is obvious from Thomas's satirical reversal of roles:

She, too, wrote vul-gar poems, and it was nothing for her to use the horrible word "Cancer" twice in one stan-za. And the little poet went all flower-faced, and wrote a lot of verses about the sun coming up and the moon going down.[73]

Thomas's letters show off magnificently. He sounds off at poets past and present. He hates Wordsworth, "a human nannygoat with a pantheistic obsession," Matthew Arnold, and David Gascoyne—"if he is so young there *is* a hope that the poetry will drop away from him and that the sore it leaves will soon heal." He attacks, ungratefully, the *Sunday Referee*: with the exception of their own work, it printed mostly "schoolgirl posies plucked from a virgin garden."[74]

But there is also a despairing note beyond posturing. The Armistice Day letter shows us one form of haunting. Another is his personal predicament. Sometimes the letters are from Blaen Cwm, cottages near Fernhill owned and occupied by his mother's family, visited occasionally for short holidays. When he travelled there, each industrial town on the journey was

a festering sore on the body of a dead country. . . .

It's impossible for me to tell you how much I want to get out of it all, out of narrowness and dirtiness, out of the eternal ugliness of the Welsh people, and all that belongs to them, out of the pettinesses of a mother I don't care for and the giggling batch of relatives. . . . And I *will* get out. In some months I will be living in London. . . . I'm sick, and this bloody country's killing me.

Having reached Blaen Cwm, he stayed in "a rat-infested cottage in the heart of Wales. . . . It is raining as I write, a thin, purposeless rain hiding the long miles of desolate fields."[75] When he writes of Swansea, he continues the note sounded in the letter to Grigson: "Swansea is a dingy hell, and my mother is a vulgar humbug; but I'm not so bad, and Gower is as beautiful as anywhere."[76]

At times he exaggerates for effect, as when he writes, from his leafy, Uplands suburb, of being brought up "amid the terrors of the Welsh accent and the smoke of the tinplate stacks,"[77] but there is no doubting his depression. Equally, as in the Gower reference, there is no doubting the developing ambivalence of his response to the environment of his upbringing. In this respect his reference to having grown up in a "provincial villa" is revealing in combining the hostility implicit in the adjective with the class-conscious desire to impress that governs his choice of noun, a reminder that class fuels Thomas's writing as much as it does that of any other 1930s writer.

To his distant correspondent he was free with his views. They included his support of socialism and, interestingly, enthusiastic advocacy of sexual relations for the young. This last reminds us of Thomas the shocker, ever concerned to disturb what he doubtless sensed to be Johnson's conventional suburbanism. He wrote of his own ill health, including the ever-mysterious—and seemingly untrue—comment that a doctor had given him only four years to live. He described his daily routine: waking at 9:30 when his mother brought him the paper and breakfast; reading in the morning; pub at lunchtime; reading or writing or walking in the afternoon; evenings filled by drama rehearsals or the pub; returning home, he sometimes wrote in bed. Johnson, who at this time had a full-time job as well as furthering her writing career, must surely have been struck by the leisurely pace of Thomas's life.

He offered information on his books, contrasting his father's library—"all the accepted stuff, from Chaucer to Henry James"—with his own: "nearly all poetry, and mostly modern at that.'' Of course, he wrote about his own work: ''Through my small, bonebound island I have learnt all I know, experienced all, and sensed all. . . . I employ the scenery of the island to describe the scenery of my thoughts.''[78] He told her that he always read his poetry aloud.

At Christmas 1933 they exchanged presents: he sent her a copy of Robert Graves's poems, she gave him cigarettes. In January 1934 he wrote to tell her that he was about to come to London, for two reasons: ''One is to see you, & the other is to look for a job.''[79] The insertion of this gesture at conventional respectability was significant; he sensed what would appeal, even though what appealed was not, in the end, able to be offered by the young man who stood on Pamela Hansford Johnson's doorstep on 23 February 1934.

NOTES

1. Pamela Hansford Johnson, ''The Man,'' in *Dylan Thomas: The Legend and the Poet*, ed. E. W. Tedlock (London: William Heinemann, 1960), 23–24.

2. Pamela Hansford Johnson, extracts from Diary, photocopies of manuscript, Dylan Thomas Collection, Harry Ransom Humanities Research Center, University of Texas, Austin. In subsequent references this location is abbreviated as HRHRC.

3. Constantine FitzGibbon, *The Life of Dylan Thomas* (London: Dent, 1965), is the official biography. Paul Ferris, *Dylan Thomas* (1977; Harmondsworth: Penguin Books, 1978), is the standard life. John Malcolm Brinnin, *Dylan Thomas in America* (London: Dent, 1956), is valuable for that aspect of Thomas's life. Basic biographical information has been drawn from these works. Specific usage is referenced.

4. For detailed historical background, see Kenneth O. Morgan, *Rebirth of a Nation: Wales, 1880–1980* (New York and Cardiff: Oxford University Press & University of Wales Press, 1981); John Davies, *A History of Wales* (Harmondsworth: Penguin Books, 1994), chap. 8.

5. George Tremlett, *Dylan Thomas: In the Mercy of His Means* (London: Constable, 1991), 14.

6. Ferris, *Dylan Thomas*, 10.

7. For information in this paragraph I have consulted Ferris, *Dylan Thomas*, 10–11; *The Calendar of the University of Wales, 1896–97, 1897–98, 1898–99, 1899–1900* (Newport, Monmouthshire: Mullock & Sons, 1897–1900); E. L. Ellis, *The University College of Wales Aberystwyth, 1872–1972* (Cardiff: University of Wales Press, 1972); C. H. Herford, ''Impressions of Aberystwyth, 1887–1901,'' in *University College of Wales Aberystwyth: The College by the Sea*, ed. Iwan Morgan (Aberystwyth: Cambrian News 1928), 96–100; and Bill Read, *The Days of Dylan Thomas* (London: Weidenfeld and Nicolson, 1964).

8. Ethel Ross, undated notes of an interview with Florence Thomas, manuscript, Dylan Thomas Collection, HRHRC.

9. Ibid.

10. Edward Thomas, ''Swansea Village,'' *The English Review* 17 (June 1914): 316–24. The essay was collected in Edward Thomas, *The Last Sheaf* (London: Cape, 1928), 151–166.

11. Dylan Thomas, *The Collected Letters*, ed. Paul Ferris (London: Dent, 1985), 216. Letter to Wyn Henderson, 9 March 1936. This edition is abbreviated as *CL*.

12. David C. Thorns, *Suburbia* (London: MacKibbon & Kee, 1972), 93.

13. Roy Lewis and Angus Maude, *The English Middle Classes* (London: Phoenix House, 1949), 239.

14. Peter Stead, "The Swansea of Dylan Thomas," in *Dylan Thomas Remembered* (Swansea: Dylan Thomas Society, Wales Branch, 1978), 22.

15. Caitlin Thomas, *Leftover Life to Kill* (London: Putnam, 1957), 57.

16. J. E. Ross, " 'We Had Evidence and No Doubt,' " *Gower* 16 (1964): 50.

17. Tremlett, *Dylan Thomas*, 14.

18. Pamela Hansford Johnson, *Important to Me: Personalia* (London: Macmillan, 1974), 147.

19. *CL* 43. Letter to Pamela Hansford Johnson, dated [early November 1933].

20. Dylan Thomas, "Reminiscences of Childhood (First Version)," in *The Broadcasts*, ed. Ralph Maud (London: Dent, 1991), 3. The talk was recorded and broadcast during 1943.

21. Morgan, *Rebirth of a Nation*, 169.

22. Thomas, "Reminiscences of Childhood (First Version)," 3.

23. *CL*, 146. Letter to Pamela Hansford Johnson, [c. 3 July 1934].

24. Ross, " 'We Had Evidence and No Doubt,' " 49. This was recalled by Mrs. Gillian Williams, the midwife attending Dylan Thomas's birth.

25. Ferris, *Dylan Thomas*, 26.

26. Dylan Thomas, *Collected Stories*, ed. Walford Davies (1983; London: Dent Everyman, 1995), 152. Subsequent references to this edition, abbreviated as *CS*, are included in the text.

27. The photograph is now owned by Jeff Towns, the Swansea bookseller who specializes in Dylan Thomas material.

28. Dylan Thomas, "Reminiscences of Childhood," *Broadcasts*, 17.

29. B. W. Murphy, "Creation and Destruction: Notes on Dylan Thomas," *British Journal of Medical Psychology* 41 (1968): 150.

30. Ralph Maud (ed.), *Poet in the Making: The Notebooks of Dylan Thomas* (London: Dent, 1968), 193–94. Subsequent references to this edition, abbreviated as *PM*, are included in the text

31. Dylan Thomas, "Reminiscences of Childhood (First Version)," 7.

32. Dylan Thomas "Return Journey," *Broadcasts*, 188.

33. See FitzGibbon, *Life of Dylan Thomas*, 37–39, for a scathing and entertaining account.

34. Vernon Watkins, "Elegy on the Heroine of Childhood," in *The Collected Poems* (Ipswich: Golgonooza Press, 1986), 5.

35. Tremlett, *Dylan Thomas*, 18.

36. See Dylan Thomas, "Poetic Manifesto," *Texas Quarterly* 4, no. 4 (Winter 1961): 45–53. This is most conveniently found in Dylan Thomas, *Early Prose Writings*, ed. Walford Davies (London: Dent, 1971), 154–60. The passage quoted is on 157–58.

37. The farm's name is Fernhill (one word). The title of Thomas's most famous poem is "Fern Hill" (two words).

38. Ferris, *Dylan Thomas*, 43.

39. P. E. S[mart], " 'Under Milk Wood'—and Reminiscence of School Days," *Spread Eagle*, April 1954: 134.

40. See Daniel Jones, "The Man," *Dylan Thomas: The Legend and the Poet*, ed. E. W. Tedlock (London: Heinemann, 1960), 18.

41. FitzGibbon, *Life of Dylan Thomas*, 49.

42. *Swansea Grammar School Magazine* 27, no. 1 (April 1930): 10.

43. Dylan Thomas, letter to Percy Smart, 7 March [1931], MS 23068E, National Library of Wales.

44. The most detailed discussion of Thomas and the *Swansea Grammar School Magazine* is Victor Golightly, " 'Eggs Laid by Tigers,' " *New Welsh Review* 28 (Spring 1995): 35–38. See also Ferris, *Dylan Thomas*, 53–55.

45. Dylan Thomas, *The Poems*, ed. Daniel Jones, rev. ed. (1974; London: Dent, 1982), xv.

46. Thomas, "Poetic Manifesto," *Early Prose Writings*, 156.

47. Ferris *Dylan Thomas*, 49.

48. See Thomas's short story "The Fight" in *Portrait of the Artist as a Young Dog*, which, Daniel Jones stated in *My Friend Dylan Thomas* (London: Dent, 1977), 95–6, is an "accurate" account of their first meeting and the early days of the friendship. The story's opening indicates that the young Thomas had been at the Grammar school for some time; his age is given as fourteen.

49. Ferris, *Dylan Thomas*, 49.

50. Bill Read, notes of an interview with Mervyn Levy, manuscript, Dylan Thomas Collection, HRHRC.

51. Jones, *My Friend Dylan Thomas*, 23.

52. Jones, *My Friend Dylan Thomas*, 26, suggested primly that the name came from Bram Stoker, the author of *Dracula*. Ferris, *Dylan Thomas*, 358, reminded us that "bram" is Welsh for "fart."

53. P. E. S[mart], *Spread Eagle*, 134.

54. Dylan Thomas, letter to Percy Smart, [c. 6 December 1930], MS 23068E, National Library of Wales.

55. FitzGibbon, *Life of Dylan Thomas*, 68.

56. *CL*, 7. Letter to Trevor Hughes, dated [February 1932].

57. Thomas, *Broadcasts*, 183.

58. See Ethel Ross, *Dylan Thomas and the Amateur Theatre* (Swansea: Swansea Little Theatre, n.d.).

59. Dylan Thomas, letter to Percy Smart, [early 1931], MS 23068E, National Library of Wales.

60. *CL*, 10. Letter to Trevor Hughes, dated [late 1932/early 1933].

61. Quoted in Ferris, *Dylan Thomas*, 73–74. Letters from Nancy Thomas to Haydn Taylor, c. 23 October 1932 and 13 January 1933.

62. HRHRC manuscripts, Thomas, D. Misc., draft of Bert Trick, "The Young Dylan Thomas," *Texas Quarterly* 9, no. 2 (Summer 1966): 36–49.

63. Ibid.

64. Thomas Taig, "Swansea between the Wars," *Anglo-Welsh Review* 17 (1968): 23–32.

65. *CL*, 13. Letter to Trevor Hughes, [February 1933].

66. William Empson, "Books in General," *New Statesman*, 15 May 1954: 636.

67. *CL*, 51. Letter to Pamela Hansford Johnson, dated [week of 11 November 1933].

68. *CL*, 19–20. Letter to Geoffrey Grigson, dated [summer 1933].

69. Good accounts of the literary 1930s include Samuel Hynes, *The Auden Generation: Literature and Politics in England in the 1930s* (London: Bodley Head, 1976); Bernard Bergonzi, *Reading the Thirties: Texts and Contexts* (London: Macmillan, 1978);

Valentine Cunningham, *British Writers of the Thirties*; and Adrian Caesar, *Dividing Lines: Poetry, Class, and Ideology in the 1930s* (Manchester and New York: Manchester University Press, 1991).

70. Cunningham, *British Writers of the Thirties*, 115.

71. Ibid 134. The links are numerous and amazingly complex.

72. *CL*, 89. Letter to Trevor Hughes, dated [early January 1934].

73. *CL*, 46. Letter to Pamela Hansford Johnson, dated [5 November 1933].

74. *CL*, 26, 27, 28. Letter to Pamela Hansford Johnson, dated [15 October 1933].

75. *CL*, 29–30. Letter to Pamela Hansford Johnson, dated [late October 1933].

76. *CL*, 63. Letter to Pamela Hansford Johnson, dated [?early December 1933].

77. *CL*, 43. Letter to Pamela Hansford Johnson, dated [early November 1933].

78. *CL*, 76, 39. Letters to Pamela Hansford Johnson, dated [25 December 1933] and [early November 1933], respectively.

79. *CL*, 95. Letter to Pamela Hansford Johnson, dated [January 1934].

2

1934–1944

Pamela Hansford Johnson (1912–81) was two years older than Thomas. At first she believed that they were both twenty-one, Thomas having lied about his age. When, much later, she learned the truth, it was the beginning of the end. We can see Thomas's lie as part of the posturing that marks the torrential letter writing that began the relationship. Though much of what he wrote to her is undoubtedly sincere, there is also much of Thomas the literary fat boy: showing off, trying her out, being provocative, but with his wildness and ruthless dishonesty carefully eliminated. For Pamela, the relationship was to be the gradual and fatal discovery of the extent to which the real Thomas differed from the epistolary one.

Pamela's father, who died when she was eleven, had been a colonial civil servant on the Gold Coast; she lived with her mother, who was from a theatrical family, in slightly struggling circumstances, at 53 Battersea Rise, Wandsworth. She had been educated in Clapham, had left school at seventeen, and was working as a secretary in a bank in central London, writing poetry and fiction in her spare time. In 1950 she was to make a second marriage to the scientist and novelist C. P. Snow, becoming Lady Snow when he was ennobled. Derek Patmore, who knew her after her marriage to Snow, wrote nastily that "they were made for each other—for she had always been as ambitious as he. . . . the Snows were a mutual admiration society."[1] That may have been so; certainly she was always ambitious. But her diaries when she met Dylan Thomas—and her later autobiographical writings—reveal a charming young woman, yet with an inner steel and determination.[2] She was, like Thomas (and, indeed, like C. P. Snow), a person from a lower-middle-class background who eventually, through great efforts and talent, achieved metropolitan literary fame. In September 1933, when she wrote to Thomas praising "That sanity be kept," she had recently broken off a two-year-long engagement. As has been noted, the *Sunday Referee* was publishing her poetry and was about to sponsor her first—and last—volume of poetry, for she quickly realized her limitations as a poet and was already working on her first novel, to be published by Chapman and Hall as *This Bed Thy Centre*.

Her life was hardly eventful: work in the bank, boyfriends, small visits, some parties. It was the suburban round. Her health was variable: she suffered from migraines invariably brought on by emotional stress. What the diaries convey, above all, is the work ethic: despite her full-time job, she probably produced more prose during her friendship with Thomas than, letters apart, he produced during his lifetime. She valued order, keeping appointments, respectability, and religious faith (she occasionally attended church). This is not to say that she was prissy: she was an attractive, passionate young woman seeking to break out of suburban restraints into a productive literary life.

Thomas entered her life at a propitious moment. Following the broken engagement, she was eager to fall in love again, particularly with someone whose ambitions matched her own. He was obviously flattered by her praise of his work and equally willing to be smitten. Almost certainly she was his first serious girlfriend. When she sent her photograph, he liked the look of her well-defined, slightly oriental features but shrewdly caught from it the essence of her personality: "I did not expect you to be so full and bright and strong, with such a British chin. What a dominant personality."[3] He returned to these qualities in subsequent letters; they made him uneasy. When Thomas met her in February 1934, he had gone almost fourteen months without regularly paid employment. Life at home was not good: he and Nancy were at daggers drawn, not least because he continued to steal small amounts of cash from her and her visiting friends. Matters were not improved by his mother always taking his part. Meanwhile, his father's moods were increasingly black. Though by the end of 1933 Thomas had made a few small beginnings, he was racked with worry about his work. In September 1933 Richard Rees had published "No man believes" in his prestigious *Adelphi* and had asked to see more, yet, as has been noted, when more poems were sent, Rees rejected them because they were too suggestive of automatic writing, much to Thomas's dismay. He took the bold and unusual step of sending the poems and Rees's letter to T. S. Eliot, then editor of The *Criterion*, asking him for an opinion. Eliot was later to publish poetry and prose by Thomas; on this occasion, prompted by a second letter, he praised Thomas's beginnings and returned his work. This did little to assuage Thomas's concern.

Following his arrival at the Johnsons' house on Friday, 23 February 1934, he stayed for ten days; they immersed themselves in each other's cultural and literary lives. They walked and talked, went to the theatre, wrote a few collaborative poems, criticized each other's work, went to the local pub, and occasionally sat in the garden of the Six Bells in Chelsea, "which seemed to us a cultural Mecca."[4] When he returned home, he wrote quickly declaring his love. "I don't know how I feel or what to do," Pamela confided to her diary.[5]

Her reply made him apologize for his hasty declaration. His letter mentioned subsequent illness. Whatever the truth of that—it may have been an attempt to foster sympathy—on the personal front this was, for Thomas, an uncertain time: no London job had materialized, and with Pamela he was having to tread carefully. But his literary career began to flourish: poems and the occasional story were accepted by London magazines. "Light breaks where no sun shines," published in the *Listener* during March 1934, drew letters from Geoffrey Grigson, Stephen Spender, and T. S. Eliot. In the same month he won the *Sunday Referee*'s second book prize and began to prepare *18 Poems* for publication.

Despite such metropolitan success, he was still living at 5 Cwmdonkin Drive and wondering how to proceed. Ferris commented shrewdly:

Now that he thought himself in love with Pamela . . . he found himself thinking about practical bourgeois matters like getting a job. All his life part of him hankered for stability and an "ordinary life." . . . [Caitlin] used to laugh at him for being bourgeois at heart.[6]

This moment was his last close encounter with such permanent respectability. The vital move was never made, and the rest of his relationship with Pamela can be dealt with speedily and predictably. At Easter 1934 he returned to Battersea Rise. D. J., in London for cancer treatment, was introduced. "Father nice," reported Pamela's diary. That summer, when she and her mother visited Swansea, she found the father "adorable as usual." In the summer of 1935, even though the affair with Thomas was effectively over, she stayed on her own at Cwmdonkin Drive and sat up late talking and drinking beer with "Pop": "V. jolly evening & we all got rather beery," she reported.[7] A different note is struck by her later reminiscence, which refers to D. J.'s heavy drinking. He would return from the pub well lubricated and with more bottles of beer,

to which he would sit me down. He had had cancer of the tongue: and would relate to me night after night, the horrible sufferings his radium treatments had caused him. Florrie used to blame me for "encouraging him"; God knows I did not, for he was unstoppable. All I could do was drink up and listen.[8]

He even began teaching her Welsh.

This is an unexpected side to D. J., who probably saw in Pamela not only an attractive young woman but also what he had hoped his son would have been: a writer of consequence—her first novel had then been published—whose work emerged from an ordered, hardworking life. Further, she was a great contrast with Florence: here was an intelligent woman who must surely have made D. J. feel, despairingly, the limitations of his marriage. Like father, like son, as will be seen.

Through the spring and summer of 1934 Thomas made a number of visits to London, meeting Spender and T. S. Eliot and trying to foster literary contacts. He also began a friendship with the Welsh writer Glyn Jones, significant if only because links with Welsh writers, despite Thomas's own reservations about many of them and a general indifference to the idea of "Anglo-Welsh" writing, became a significant element in his literary career. Jones's family, like Thomas's, was from the Llansteffan peninsular. From there, in May, Glyn Jones took Thomas to Laugharne, which he described to Pamela as "the strangest town in Wales."[9] He wrote to her at length of its drab quiet.

There followed—so he told Pamela—a brief fling, luridly described, with a girl in a Gower bungalow, the truth of which is now impossible to verify. Doubts occur because at this point in his relationship with Pamela, Thomas's willingness to confess all suggests that he was hoping she might break it off. In the event, she forgave him. However, the relationship, to judge from the diaries, declined from rapture into rows over his disorganized life, rows that intensified when he moved to London.

This occurred in November 1934, when he moved from Swansea to his first London address, a large bedsitter in "the quarter of the pseudo-artists" that he shared with his Kardomah friend, the artist Alfred Janes. Elsewhere in the house was Mervyn Levy, once his classmate at Mirador School: "Hark, hark, the parish pump," Thomas wrote to Bert Trick.[10] During his few months at Redcliffe Street, living independently for the first time, he went wild; he dressed flamboyantly, was frequently drunk—particularly at Art College dances, where he often pretended to have DTs—usually dirty, and sometimes incontinent, and wrote little or nothing. In Ferris's scathing phrase, he was "the naughty boy from the provinces."[11] Stupidly self-indulgent is nearer the mark. Pamela, whose first novel, published in April 1935, was a great success, reaching a fifth impression during May, now knew his real age. In Thomas's roaring world she felt a stranger. She wrote:

Then I did go to see them. They had reached a peak of artistic romanticism. . . . They greeted me uproariously; and at once I knew that I was not wanted. I was no longer of their kind. That I had written a successful book made it, for Dylan, worse: like Scott Fitzgerald, I don't think he wanted another writer in the family.

I went away stunned with misery.[12]

Thomas's own first volume, *18 Poems*, was published during December 1934, the *Sunday Referee* combining with David Archer's Parton Press. It emerged from the most prolific period of Thomas's writing career: all eighteen had been written since August 1933.[13] Publication was supported by an interview in the *Sunday Referee* in which Thomas, out of the wildness he made no attempt to control, spoke of a writer's insecurity and confided that "there are times when I'd give much to be a bank clerk in a safe job."[14] Fear of chaos and a deep desire for order were sustained creative hauntings as Thomas prepared to rush to destruction.

Not until well into 1935 did *18 Poems* begin to make its way. Desmond Hawkins, in *Time and Tide*, offered a rave review, but one that tended to limit Thomas's achievement: his poetry, Hawkins wrote, "is personal or universal, but not social."[15] This set the tone for other leading London magazines that, in general, gave the book a good reception. It was a crucial moment in Thomas's life, one for which he had worked and about which he had thought since he was very young. Through sheer talent, a marvellously original way with words, and the ability to project onto paper the intense, compelling emotional life of a young man at once unified with and estranged from the natural and suburban world, he had forced an incestuous literary world to take notice of him. His reaction, strangely, was not to work at consolidation but to continue the wild life. He, Janes, and Levy had already left Redcliffe Street for nearby Coleherne Road, but he was not always there. He began to sleep where he could and with whomever, following drunken evenings. The relationship with Pamela fell apart. "Still says he loves me but can't resist Comrade Bottle. Am just watching & praying. What else can I do?" she wrote in her diary on 5 January 1935.[16] After a while, for "watching and praying" she substituted an Australian named Gordon Stewart, who was soon "darling Neil" who sent her flowers and became her first husband. She saw much less of Dylan and was relieved.

From 1935 to 1937 Thomas was back at 5 Cwmdonkin Drive, from which he made frequent visits to London, staying wherever he could. In March 1935 he met the poet Vernon Watkins in Swansea and began another close friendship. Watkins was eight years older than Thomas and had spent four years of his childhood in the Uplands. His father was a prosperous bank manager with Lloyds Bank who had sent his son to Repton and Cambridge. But Watkins left Cambridge after only one year and became a bank clerk in Cardiff. A nervous breakdown followed, his father pulled strings, and he was transferred to the St. Helen's Road, Swansea, branch of Lloyds Bank. There he stayed until his retirement in 1966, living at first with his parents at Redcliffe, on Caswell Bay, and then at Heatherslade, on Pennard Cliffs. When he married, he and his wife settled and brought up a family further along the cliffs, in a small bungalow called the Garth. His own work was yet to come; his first volume, which made him that prestigious literary animal, a "Faber Poet," did not appear until 1941. He was dedicated to poetry; after reading *18 Poems* he sought a meeting with the author and was encouraged in this by the Reverend David Rees, Florence Thomas's brother-in-law at Paraclete Chapel. As has been noted, Rees hated Thomas and almost certainly believed that Watkins might help Thomas move in more respectable circles.[17]

The friendship lasted until Thomas's death; indeed, Watkins wrote his friend's obituary. But it was very one-sided. Watkins idolized Thomas and his work; Thomas valued Watkins's literary judgment and often sent poems for Watkins's criticism. But it is doubtful whether he thought much of most of Watkins's poetry or greatly valued the friendship. Thomas was too self-centered and too often disorganized by alcohol to be a true friend. He even failed, disgracefully, to turn up as best man at Watkins's wedding. Watkins became an occasional member of the Kardomah circle in its final months, but his ordered life would never merge with Thomas's chaos. David Rees's hopes came to nothing. In that sense, for Thomas, Watkins was another unheeded possibility.

On Thomas's frequent visits to London he wrote nothing of consequence. Through Grigson's influence he began to review thrillers for the *Morning Post*, a task he carried out on almost a weekly basis from April 1935 until September 1936. This was the first of many time-consuming ventures into hackwork. For the most part London meant drinking and drunken behavior. "I'm coming to town for three days in the first week of November," he wrote to his sister and brother-in-law, "and am already preparing my small jar of red paint."[18] At about this time he is believed to have caught and recovered from gonorrhea. His behavior was such as to worry even like-minded friends. They arranged "retreats" for him. One was to a cottage in Derbyshire with the A. J. P. Taylors, whose first wife, Margaret, was to become Thomas's lifelong patron and would-be, possibly actual, lover. He stayed with Geoffrey Grigson in an isolated studio in Donegal. Grigson had to return early; Thomas stayed on to write, then left without paying the owner for food and lodging. Through this he lost Grigson's friendship. It was replaced by that with Edith Sitwell, who, after initial hostility to Thomas's work, became one of his most fervent and influential champions. Even the "retreats" were not free from excessive drinking, but they were periods when some work got done, though probably not a lot and, of that, too much of the wrong kind. Of course, most writers, particularly poets, take on hackwork to keep the wolf from the door and to buy time for serious concerns. Thomas's hackwork too often only bought hours in the pub and left him no time at all.

During 1935 and for the last time, he published a poem in a local Swansea newspaper, the *Herald of Wales*. "Poet: 1935" was revised from the notebook draft of March 1933 (part was used much later, in 1943, in Thomas's "Reminiscences of Childhood" broadcast, when he described it as unpublished). It is a poem about the loneliness and insecurity of his life as a poet, in which "he's a stranger, outside the season's humour," and "Even among his own kin is he lost." He ends with the lines quoted in the broadcast:

> See, on gravel paths under the harpstrung trees,
> Feeling the summer wind, hearing the swans,
> Leaning from windows over a length of lawns,
> On tumbling hills admiring the sea,
> I am alone, alone complain to the stars.
> Who are his friends? The wind is his friend,
> The glow-worm lights his darkness, and
> The snail tells of coming rain.[19]

Such lines, though discursive, are lyrically persuasive in offering familiar ambivalence: the young man is both attracted towards his ordered suburban world and alienated from it. For Thomas, the word "alone" is his tolling bell; loneliness could be seen as one of his writings' central concerns. He struggled to write, to make his way, to find a comfortable place in a world that in 1935 was darkening. We begin to understand why he turned so desperately to quick comforts. Enter Caitlin Macnamara, with superb timing.

Thomas met her in April 1936, probably at the Wheatsheaf pub in "Fitzrovia's'' Rathbone Place. She was with the painter Augustus John, whose model and mistress she then was. Her parents were faded and straitened Anglo-Irish gentry. They had separated; her mother lived in Blashford, Hampshire. Caitlin was a year older than Thomas, had striking good looks, and had once tried to be a dancer. The attraction was immediate and mutual. Caitlin recalled that they immediately stayed together at the nearby Eiffel Tower Hotel, charging the bill to Augustus John's account. As a friend of Thomas once put it: "Caitlin didn't care a bugger what anyone thought. She was an aristocrat, and that was that."[20] She had none of Thomas's petit bourgeois scruples or desires for order. She was wild and disorganized. They fell in love. For Thomas, the equally wild product of an indulgent home and lax schools, Caitlin Macnamara was exactly what he did not need.

In the spring of 1936 Thomas went to Cornwall to stay with Wyn Henderson, the mother of his friend Nigel. While there, he was hardly the pining suitor: he had a brief affair with Wyn and another, even briefer, with Wyn's acquaintance, Veronica Sibthorp. During the summer he and Fred Janes invited themselves to Richard Hughes's home in Laugharne, where Augustus John and Caitlin were then staying. That furthered the affair, though at the expense of John's jealousy. In the autumn he and Caitlin were corresponding, then living together intermittently in the homes of acquaintances.

Thomas's volume *18 Poems* was reissued in February 1936. There was now pressure on him to prepare a second volume. This he did: *Twenty-five Poems* was published by Dent in September 1936. Two volumes in two years; all seemed well with Thomas's literary career. Yet already there were warning signs. Eighteen of the poems were revisions of notebook poems, though some of these—notably "Why east wind chills" and "And death shall have no dominion"—were extensively revised. Counting the sonnet sequence "Altarwise by owl-light" as a single poem, Thomas is known to have written seven new poems since publishing *18 Poems*. He used them all, including "Now" and "How soon the servant sun," which Vernon Watkins begged him to exclude on grounds of obscurity. Few would consider any of the new poems to be Thomas's finest achievements, though the "Altarwise" sequence has famously fascinated distinguished commentators. The new poems are more difficult, at times certainly more obscure, than the revisions. Possibly this indicates greater problems with his material. Possibly he did not apply himself with his earlier dedication because of Caitlin and general self-indulgence. In the twenty-two months between the two volumes, as well as the seven new poems, Thomas wrote three new short stories, thirty-one mainly potboiling reviews, and a number of letters. He revised much earlier material, including some stories. In September 1936, when *Twenty-five Poems* was published, his career seemed to lack impetus. For a professional writer, he was not really writing much.

Because Thomas was returning so often to earlier drafts, it is difficult to discuss chronological development. What can be done, of course, is to study development in terms of what he chose to publish. *Twenty-five Poems* is different from *18 Poems*. For a start, it is more variable in quality, if only because, as has been noted, it contains new poems difficult or impossible to understand. Other poems—revised from notebook drafts—are among Thomas's finest; they include "Why east wind chills," "Ears in the turrets hear," and "I have longed to move away." Such poems are among his most approachable, though, in Thomas's work, this is not a sure indication of quality. These poems return us to "Poet: 1935": they wrestle with the relationship between his personal desires, his uniqueness as a writer, and the hostile world of the respectable bourgeoisie. It is surely no accident that the opening poem, the new "I, in my intricate image," is about the divided self and struggles to explore that predicament. Part of such wrestling and struggling is a sense of a lost Eden as Thomas's Swansea links were severed.

This last point should remind us that Thomas's work reflects and explores the real world, not only personal circumstances but also the wider context that impinged upon them. Central to the former are his relations with his father and his engagement with what his father represented in terms of the period's social shiftings. The recurrence in his work of the "Hamlet" theme is an important manifestation of this. As for the wider context, its main features are all too familiar: by 1936 Hitler controlled Germany; the Austrian chancellor, Dolfuss, had been assassinated; anti-Jewish decrees had been passed in Germany; Italy had invaded Abyssinia. During 1936 Germany reoccupied the Rhineland; the Spanish civil war began; Edward VIII abdicated; general economic depression led to the Jarrow hunger marches and, in South Wales, general despair and emigration. One of the contentions of this volume's critical section is that such events helped shape Thomas's work. Suffice it here to note that such poems as "The seed-at-zero," "Out of the sighs," "The hand that signed the paper," and "And death shall have no dominion" and the prevalence of violent imagery are at the text/context interface. Thomas was haunted by violence, conscious of an increasingly violent world closing in on him.

Equally revealing of self, world, and wider world are his short stories of the mid-1930s. These are strange narratives full of horror and violence in bourgeois settings. "The Orchards" makes what is surely a personal statement: the narrator, significantly named Marlais, walks away from what seems to be Cwmdonkin to a picnic in a far-off field only to discover that he is still in the ordered, attractive, but unfulfilling middle-class world he thought he had left behind. The fiction reflects Thomas's letter to Vernon Watkins written from Cornwall during April 1936:

Here the out-of-doors is very beautiful, but it's a strange country to me . . . and I'd rather the bound slope of a suburban hill, the Elms, the Acacias, Rookery Nook, Curlew Avenue, to all these miles of green fields and flowery cliffs and dull sea. . . . I'm not a country man; I stand for, if anything, the aspidistra, the provincial drive, the morning café, the evening pub . . . that's the trouble with the country: there's too much public world between private ones. And living in your own private, four-walled world as exclusively as possible isn't escapism, I'm sure; it isn't the Ivory Tower, and, even if it were, you secluded in your Tower know and learn more of the world outside than the outside-man who is mixed up so personally and inextricably with the mud and the unlovely people.[21]

Once again we are reminded of "Poet: 1935" and, more strongly, of the "WARMDANDYLANLEY-WORLD" letter he wrote to Daniel Jones from Donegal during August 1935. This describes the attractions of growing up in Swansea with his friend, their fantastic games and dreams of fame. There is much sentimentality and wishing for the moon:

We must, when our affairs are settled, when music and poetry are arranged so that we can still live, love, and drink beer, go back to Uplands or Sketty and found there, for good and for all, a permanent colony; living there until we are old gentlemen, with occasional visits to London and Paris.

Such escapism is recognized as such, as is reality: "But now of course all the things are different; we must peck on and snoot away in an unlovely city until we can manage our own fates to a Walesward advantage."[22] Jones later commented shrewdly that in this letter is a realization that Thomas would never be at ease with his world and so was condemned to be "an onlooker."[23] His tragedy, Jones believed, lay in the fact that this was not what he wanted.

Twenty-five Poems was published by Dent after negotiations conducted by David Higham. Higham was to remain Thomas's agent for the rest of the latter's life, after which he became a trustee of Thomas's estate. At Dent, Richard Church was Thomas's editor. He was a poet of a Georgian disposition, and Thomas's poetry was not to his taste. He enraged Thomas by calling it surrealistic. "I have very little idea what surrealism is", Thomas told Church, "until quite recently I had never heard of it. . . . I read regrettably little modern poetry. . . . I am not a communist."[24] He told Edith Sitwell that had he not signed a contract with Dent, he would have gone elsewhere. By May 1936, as Church put it to Thomas, he decided "to let you and the public face each other."[25]

Thomas's denial was probably strategic. Surrealism was hard to avoid, and some saw him as part of the movement. His work appeared in Roger Roughton's surrealist magazine *Contemporary Poetry and Prose* and in *transition*. He read some of his poems at the International Surrealist Exhibition held in London during June and July 1936 and contributed to the general chaos by handing around cups of string. But Thomas believed in the craft of poetry and in its intellectual element. He had little sympathy with the movement's principles.

Twenty-five Poems received a more varied reception than had Thomas's first volume, some responses confirming—though in the belief that all were later poems—what has already been noticed, that Thomas's work was not developing. Concern was expressed about his obscurity, concern that Thomas himself shared. "I feel, more than ever," he wrote, "to be tightly packing away everything I have and know into a mad-doctor's bag, and then locking it up: all you can see is the bag.''[26] Yet in one way *Twenty-five Poems* furthered his reputation: Edith Sitwell provided a rave review in the wide-circulation *Sunday Times* in which she insisted that she "could not name one poet of this, the youngest generation, who shows so great a promise, and even so great an achievement."[27] This helped the book to sell out and to be reprinted.

Thomas was finding a readership and becoming well known. Yet once again, as if crushed into self-indulgence by expectations, he allowed his career to founder. In the twelve months following the publication of *Twenty-five Poems* he wrote very little. There were mitigating circumstances. On that wider stage events were grim. The Nazis continued their relentless progress; writers fought and died in Spain; outside London—and particularly in South Wales—unemployment undermined communities. In April 1937, the month of Guernica, his father having retired from teaching, Thomas's parents moved to Bishopston, a small village on the Gower side of Swansea. The house at 5 Cwmdonkin Drive was rented out; it was not sold until some years later.[28] Also in April Thomas made his first radio broadcast, reading his own poetry and that of Auden and John Crowe Ransom. Thus began an activity that was to become almost a career in itself. Much was bread-and-butter work; all was a distraction from his poetry. But most of his writing for radio is far superior to hackwork, and some—including "Reminiscences of Childhood," "Memories of Christmas," "Return Journey," and, eventually, *Under Milk Wood*—is of high quality.

A major distraction was women. During 1937 Thomas continued his involvement with Veronica Sibthorp—from whose address he wrote to Caitlin during the spring—and had an affair with the American writer Emily Holmes Coleman, fifteen years older than Thomas, previously married with a child, and with a history of mental instability. According to David Gascoyne, Thomas lived with her until he decided to marry Caitlin. On 10 June 1937 he wrote to his parents from the Sibthorp home in Cornwall, telling them that he would be marrying in Penzance Registry Office in a week's time. D. J. was appalled—his son was penniless—but though he persuaded Haydn Taylor, his son-in-law, to see what could be done to stop the wedding, he had to admit helplessness. The wedding was delayed when the would-be happy pair drank the money saved to buy the special licence. Eventually it took place on 11 July 1937 "with no money, no prospect of money, no attendant friends or relatives, and in complete happiness."[29] Pamela Hansford Johnson wrote in August to offer good wishes, and Thomas told her that he was "full of worries and happiness."[30]

The Thomases honeymooned in Cornwall at the homes of friends and acquaintances. They were absolutely penniless. Thomas's two successful volumes of poetry had made next to nothing. In the case of *Twenty-five Poems*, which was reprinted three times, finally selling out in 1950, Thomas made fifty-eight pounds, or slightly more than four pounds a year.[31] They stayed at Bishopston, then with Caitlin's mother at Blashford, where they remained for some months.

They cadged or borrowed or sponged. They drank a lot, and initially Thomas wrote very little: "My work is shocking," he told a friend.[32]

He was very jealous of all attentions to Caitlin shown by others, with good reason, it seems, given Caitlin's subsequent uncertainty about the father of their firstborn and her relief that he looked like Dylan.[33] From the first the marriage was stormy. But they were in love, and within a year Caitlin was pregnant. Marriage had heightened Thomas's emotional life, and his writing career began again.

In late 1937 he once more began revising poems from the notebooks. They became some of his most famous pieces, such as "After the funeral" and "Once it was the colour of saying." He wrote a series of important new poems, including "I make this in a warring absence," his poem about marital strife, two poems about imminent and actual childbirth—"A saint about to fall" and "If my head hurt a hair's foot"—and "Twenty-four years," his superb birthday poem. He began writing stories in a new, "realistic" style; they became *Portrait of the Artist as a Young Dog*, which he completed in 1939. Reviewing novels for the *New English Weekly* brought in small amounts. So did the anthologizing of his work that was now beginning: Faber's *Welsh Short Stories* and *The Faber Book of Short Stories* both reprinted "The Orchards"; *The Year's Poetry, 1937*, published by the Bodley Head, included "We lying by seasand" and "It is the sinners' dust-tongued bell." There were hints at other possibilities. Early in 1938 the young American publisher James Laughlin contacted Thomas, hoping to publish his work in the United States and promising a small advance. George Reavey, a friend of Thomas linked to the Europa Press in Paris, tried—though unsuccessfully, much to Thomas's annoyance—to arrange publication there of *The Burning Baby*, a selection of Thomas's early stories.

Also in 1938 Henry Treece, then unknown to Thomas, projected a book-length study of his work. His queries drew from Thomas a series of important letters seeking to clarify his aims and procedures. Thomas was not writing with the fluency of his late teens, nor with the thrust and energy of the run-up to *18 Poems*, when he was desperate to make his name. His working methods had become more laborious, involving many worksheets on which he tried out words and phrases and the writing out of whole new drafts if small changes were made. He also had less time.[34] Though, marriage initially stimulated the muse, his new wife was demanding. She required much attention, not only sexually; she did little to impose order on her husband's life. But she did provide a permanent point of reference—replacing, it could be said, 5 Cwmdonkin Drive—and increasingly made possible a more stable environment: for example, the couple's stay at Blashford from summer 1937 until spring 1938. There Thomas reverted to his Cwmdonkin routine: up late, doing little in the mornings, drinking with Caitlin at lunchtime whenever funds permitted, perhaps walking through the fields, writing during the afternoons, and then back to the pub in the evening. The real working day—when it was one, given visits to London, writing letters, and so forth—could hardly have been more than three or four hours, which, together with his writing methods, explains why Thomas wrote so little.

Money, or rather the absence of it, worried him more and more. He made very little, so that when James Laughlin mentioned a small advance and U.S. publication, Thomas gave him the works in a more basic sense:

I *must* have some money, and have it immediately. I live entirely by my writing; it can be printed only in a small number of advanced periodicals, and they pay next to nothing, usually nothing. I was married recently—against all sense, but with all happiness, which is obviously more sensible—and we are completely penniless. I do not mean that we just live poorly; I mean that we go without food, without proper clothes, have shelter on charity, and very very soon will not have even that shelter. I have now less than a shilling; there is no more to come; we have nothing to sell, nothing to fall back upon. If I can be tided over for a little time, I think I will be able to work hard enough to produce poems and stories that will provide some kind of food and shelter. If not, there is no hope at all.[35]

The letter is powerful and no doubt took hours out of one day. Such appeals were to be more frequent time-consumers. Special pleading apart, they reflect desperate worry. Of course, marriage had its positives, but it also harassed his bourgeois conscience. There is no evidence that Caitlin cared much. Such worry made him aggressively and selfishly bitter. He may also have been frightened at his parlous predicament as the world closed in. What is certain is that through the late 1930s he often quarrelled, and not only with Caitlin. Since the Irish visit he was estranged from Geoffrey Grigson; he referred to Richard Church as ''a cliché-riddled humbug and pie-fingering hack.''[36] He vilified George Reavey for failing to place ''The Burning Baby.'' He rarely had a good word for his literary contemporaries. It was as if he felt the London literary world to be against him, oddly, given the great success achieved in less than five years. Yet he could write of himself, ''I have achieved poverty with distinction, but never poverty with dignity; the best I can manage is dignity with poverty, and I would sooner smarm like a fart-licking spaniel than starve in a world of fat bones.''[37] We catch a late glimpse of his mother's spoilt boy.

In April 1938 he wrote from Blashford to Richard Hughes about the possibility of moving to Laugharne. Hughes found them a small cottage, and during May, after a short stay at Bishopston, and with Caitlin pregnant, they moved into the strangely named Eros, 2 Gosport Street, Laugharne. For the first time in their marriage they had their own home. It was described by Thomas, in typically negative jokiness, as ''pokey and ugly, four rooms like stained boxes.''[38] The cottage had no running water; they relied on a pump in Laugharne's main square and on an earth-closet in the garden. They lived there, in a boozy, disorganized way, relying on handouts, until July. Vernon Watkins visited, as did Charles Fisher of the old Swansea Kardomah gang; James Laughlin almost did.

In the popular mind Dylan Thomas is perhaps more associated with Laugharne than with Swansea, even though life at the Boat House, which is invariably part of the association, was still some years away. Pronounced "Larn," it is an ancient town no bigger than a village set on the estuary of the river Tâf on the Carmarthenshire coast. Across the estuary is the Llansteffan peninsular, with Fernhill farm and innumerable members of Thomas's mother's family. Laugharne is barely three miles west of Fernhill, but in ethos and atmosphere it is worlds away. The town, with some fine Georgian houses, usually in a state of disrepair, lies between the ruined Norman castle and the Norman church of St. Martin of Tours. Its mayor is still called the Portreeve, and it has ancient rights and ceremonies. In fiercely nonconformist and Welsh-speaking Carmarthenshire it developed into an English-speaking and Anglican enclave. Laugharne had always attracted writers: Landor had visited, as had Coleridge. Edward Thomas had spent holidays there. Richard Hughes, sustained by his wealthy wife, Frances, and by royalties from *A High Wind in Jamaica*, lived in style at Castle House, in whose garden the castle lay. The industrial revolution had passed Laugharne by. There was no railway station; the only industry was a small factory that boiled the cockles gathered in the estuary. In the 1930s it was a beautiful, crumbling, isolated, incestuous, and eccentric place with "three good pubs . . . the best bottled mild in England,"[39] hedonistic drinking, and an undercurrent of fights and feuds. Its isolation bred lawlessness and fecklessness.

Much was controlled by the Williams family, led by Ivy and her husband Ebie, who owned and ran Brown's Hotel. George Tremlett, an authority on Laugharne, believed that it "was and is a mainly working-class town, although its eighteenth-century houses in the main street give it delusions of grandeur."[40] Richard Hughes and his like comprised the squirearchy. Thomas, who described himself as " 'lower middle class' in attitude and reaction,"[41] in such a place would have had his middle-classness more clearly defined, and this despite—or perhaps because—he was penniless and an intellectual poet with a naturally aristocratic wife who had credit in all the shops. Such placing was emphasized by their links with the Hugheses: Thomas and Caitlin attended the parties at Castle House for writers and artists down from London. Lance Sieveking of the BBC met Thomas at one such function. He recalled him as dirty and dishevelled; when suddenly he smiled and spoke, his whole personality lit up entertainingly: "It was obvious that they were all very fond of him, and I could understand why."[42] This was a world in which Thomas was comfortable. Laugharne was just right for an unconventional Swansea man with little or no Welsh, literary inclinations, and intermittent rural leanings.

It had always been a place for cheap living: when Coleridge visited, it was the resort of half-pay officers in the aftermath of Trafalgar. In the late 1930s meagre domestic budgets were augmented by poached game, or salmon, or cockles, or a few free vegetables. It was a bolt-hole where the Thomases could eke out small means, with the occasional helping hand from Richard Hughes and, more frequently, from Ivy and Ebie Williams, who became friends, and through the tradesmen's credit that often went beyond the call of duty. It was also a long way from London, the distracting nature of which Thomas understood all too well. London was a version of Sodom and Gomorrah, the "bum city" in which, as a latter-day version of Lot's weak-willed wife, he was "struck on the hot and rocking street."[43] But though this withdrawal, seemingly, to the margins of society, let alone of literary life, came at a time when the world was bursting into flames, it is wrong to describe him, as Glyn Jones did, as "quite unconcerned with social, political and industrial problems."[44] As Thomas wrote, indignantly and more accurately, in 1938:

Surely it is evasive to say that my poetry has no social awareness . . . that you actually consider me unaware of my surroundings, out-of-contact with the society from which I am necessarily outlaw. You are right when you suggest that I think a squirrel stumbling at least of equal importance as Hitler's invasions, murder in Spain [there follows a long list of 1930s phenomena] . . . but I *am* aware of these things as well.[45]

As early as 1933, under Bert Trick's influence, he had written his one overtly political poem, "The hand that signed the paper." But, as will be seen, much of his work reflects and responds to social and political events in more subtle and less dated ways.

In 1938 the Spanish civil war entered its third year. Elsewhere the only-too-well-known dark sequence proceeded with seeming inevitability. The Nazis occupied Austria; *Kristallnacht* took place on 9 November 1938, by which time a stream of refugees was arriving in Britain. The policy of Appeasement began in 1936 and reached its nadir in September 1938 when Chamberlain and Daladier, at their infamous "peace in our time" meeting with Hitler in Munich, without consulting the Czechs, ceded the Sudetenland area of Czechoslovakia to Germany. Czechoslovakia was invaded in March 1939, Poland in September 1939. Britain declared war on Germany on 3 September 1939.

In Britain the decade saw the advance of Sir Oswald Mosley and his fascists; in 1934 Thomas and Bert Trick had been part of a hostile crowd when Mosley spoke in Swansea. The pacifist Peace Pledge Union, with which Thomas's friend Glyn Jones was associated, began its futile progress in 1936.

At the same time, particularly in Wales, there was terrible economic depression: the male unemployment rate in Wales in 1932 was 38 percent, rising in places through the decade, to 70 percent. By 1937 even Swansea, which, as has been noted, had been cushioned by big-town buoyancy and the comparative prosperity of the West Wales anthracite coal industry, registered an unemployment rate of 20 percent. Agricultural areas, such as Carmarthenshire, were equally depressed. The result was large-scale emigration from Wales, particularly to places in south-east England, such as Dagenham, Cowley, and Slough, that remained prosperous.

Against such a background too rapidly foregrounding itself in the lives of many, Caitlin and Dylan settled down in Laugharne. After less than three months in waterless Gosport Street they moved across the town to Sea View, a four-story house near the castle, which they rented from the ubiquitous Williamses. A stream of friends came to stay. In nearby Llanybri was the Welsh editor Keidrych Rhys and his wife, the still vastly underrated poet Lynette Roberts. From time to time they also stayed: "I've just come back from a week of flagonned ale & elementary small talk at Laugharne," Rhys reported to Henry Treece, and, a month later, "I was down in Brown's Hotel with the Laugharne playboy this week-end, collaborating? on a radio script!!! Last time I got so drunk & the girl made me sleep alone & downstairs on the couch."[46]

We gather from this that living in Laugharne did not change Thomas. Though excessive drinking of the kind he practiced in London was a rarer occurrence in Laugharne, yet it happened from time to time, and he always drank regularly twice a day. No wonder he wrote so slowly. Further, though living was cheaper, the Thomases continued to lurch from one financial crisis to another. Yet they should have been better off. As has been noted, Thomas was writing and reviewing fairly steadily if not prolifically, was beginning to be anthologized, was beginning to broadcast, and was preparing his third volume, this time of stories as well as poems, which he entitled *The Map of Love*; through 1938 and 1939 it all yielded a small but regular income. In addition, unknown to Caitlin, Thomas was also receiving thirty dollars a month—then about seven pounds—from an admirer in the United States, this having been arranged by James Laughlin. The value of this remittance is best judged against Tremlett's reminder that "the average unskilled working man's wage at that time was only £4 a week, and in Laugharne it would have been less."[47]

All was frittered away, mainly on drink, which invaded most days. Visits to Carmarthen on market day, for example, when the pubs stayed open all hours, meant long sessions. Caitlin was at first a reluctant drinker and quarrelled with her husband about his high consumption. But she was also jealous of his way of life and determined to tear from it what she felt was her due. Her reward, later, was alcoholism. Thomas had expensive tastes. He made frequent visits to London, which meant more boozing; he thought nothing of using taxis, even for long journeys; in an echo of Cwmdonkin life he insisted that Caitlin have a maid. The result was that Thomas devoted more valuable time to often futile attempts to raise money. An orchestrated appeal to the Royal Literary Fund came to nothing, much to Thomas's disgust. A more predictable flop was a scheme for a number of people to contribute small amounts regularly to what he called "Thomas Flotation Limited." He lavished time and skill on begging letters, which rivalled poems and stories as his main literary activity. These produced small amounts from time to time; Vernon Watkins was always good for a touch.

Though shopkeepers in Laugharne gave credit, the Thomases taxed even local tolerance until, with Caitlin's pregnancy well advanced, they placated some tradesmen and fled to Blashford. There they stayed for Llewelyn's birth on 30 January 1939 and for two months after that before returning to Sea View. "Vernon [Watkins] came to stay with us sometimes," Caitlin later recalled, "and he said later that this was the happiest period of our lives together. I think he was right."[48] Gwen Watkins recalled Vernon Watkins seeing Sea View again after the war: "When he saw it again, and remembered how happy they had been there in spite of their poverty, he told me he felt ill with sorrow and desolation."[49] Watkins's moving poem "To a Shell" recalls that time.

In July 1939 Thomas replied to a letter from the Welsh writer W. T. Davies, later well known as Pennar Davies, who, seemingly oblivious to the darkness gathering over Europe, was canvassing support for a Welsh literary society. Thomas was always sceptical about such proposals. He replied diplomatically that so far as younger Welsh writers were concerned (he himself was only twenty-five), "perhaps a new passion and tolerance could be brought to their thinking about and creating of a living literature in this mismanaged, discouraged, middlebrow-beaten, but still vigorously imaginative country." In a second letter he was more frank: "I don't think it does any harm to the artist to be lonely *as* an artist. (Let's all 'get together', if we must, and go to the pictures.)"[50] The exchange is important for two reasons. First, the subtext tells us much of Thomas's uneasy relationship with other Welsh writers. By that time he was not wholly without honor in his own country, but it is true to say that honor did not exactly overflow in his direction for a variety of reasons that included his lifestyle, lack of Welsh, lack of sympathy with nationalist issues, and startling originality as a poet. He did not endear himself to the Welsh-speaking, nonconformist world. Second, we catch one of the last glimpses of that young man on Pamela Hansford Johnson's doorstep: courageous, determined, single-minded, determined to be true to his literary vision. As we shall see, such glimpses became rarer.

The declaration of war on 3 September 1939 was the beginning of the end of life at Sea View. At first the literary world collapsed. Magazines closed; paper shortages began. A BBC broadcast involving Thomas was cancelled. *The Map of Love* had been published on 24 August; its commercial impact was almost wholly nullified by the war. Dent had expected a four-figure sale, but by the end of 1939 only 280 had been sold, fewer than of *Twenty-five Poems*, and sales were never to recoup the long-spent advance of seventy pounds. The volume was reviewed widely, generally respectfully, though Cyril Connolly, in the *New Statesman*, thought that too much of Thomas's work was nonsensical and fake.[51] In December 1939, in the United States, James Laughlin published *The World I Breathe*, forty poems selected from Thomas's first three volumes, plus eleven stories. Thomas's poems had already appeared in *New Directions in Poetry and Prose* and in *Poetry*, the latter magazine having awarded him the Oscar Blumenthal Prize for 1938. *The World I Breathe* was his first American volume and was widely reviewed. Among those who responded favorably were Conrad Aitken and John Berryman.

But America was far away. In Britain Thomas faced a crisis: he was twenty-five and so eligible for military call-up. Friends and acquaintances were leaving for the forces. Even in easygoing Laugharne some of those returning in uniform did not take kindly to Thomas's continuing civilian presence. He wrote at the end of August: "This war, trembling even on the edge of Laugharne, fills me with such horror & terror & lassitude. . . . But everything, including all our happiness—depends on Hitler, Poland, & insanity." The second crisis—the loss of almost all his literary income—combined with the first in a letter to Nancy Pearn of Higham's: "As I don't intend fighting anyone, my position is being made most uncomfortable: and a little money would, at least, ease it." He wrote to his father:

These are awful days & we are very worried. It is terrible to have built, out of nothing, a complete happiness—from no money, no possessions, no material hopes—& a way of living, & then to see the immediate possibility of its being exploded & ruined through no fault of one's own. . . . If I could pray, I'd pray for peace. I'm not a man of action; & the brutal activities of war appal me.[52]

"I don't know what to do," he wrote to Desmond Hawkins on the day England declared war, "declare myself a neutral state, or join as a small tank."[53] Though in all such statements is some sense of personal grievance, some self-pity, as if the war was a deliberate personal inconvenience, there is no doubting that Thomas was greatly disturbed. His early poems are haunted by the Great War; *The Map of Love*, his volume of 1939 and his most important response to the decade's accumulating darkness, is profoundly affected by the historical moment, sometimes overtly, as in "A saint about to fall," everywhere indirectly through form, structure, and a new kind of violent diction. World War II was the new horror. It was almost the last effective catalyst for his poetic imagination.

He made frantic attempts to avoid military service. As early as 1934 he and Bert Trick had associated themselves with pacifist movements. They had offered their services as "active propagandists" to the Swansea branch of the No More War Movement.[54] Now he considered conscientious objection and contacted the Welsh nationalist politician Gwynfor Evans, who was secretary of the Welsh Pacifist Movement, asking him, as Evans later recalled,

to help him find a way of keeping out of the forces without going as a conscientious objector before a tribunal, which may have directed him to unpleasant work. . . . But I do remember that I was impatient, not to say intolerant, of his (it seemed to me) unheroic position. . . . I had no interest in assisting people to easy options. If Dylan was a pacifist, I don't think his letter to me showed it.[55]

Given the earlier letter to Ithell Davies, Evans was not being wholly fair to Thomas, but his attitude was understandable; Thomas's attempts to evade the draft were anything but dignified.

He tried for a reserved occupation, complaining bitterly about those who succeeded in finding one. He railed against the atmosphere and sentiments of war that had already taken over pub life even in Laugharne. To Bert Trick he wrote furiously—and, as it turned out, prophetically—about trying to get some "mild job, in the film-writing racket. . . . I can't raise up any feeling about this War at all and the demon Hitlerism can go up its own bottom: I refuse to help it with a bayonet."[56] The violence of this nonviolent statement seems at odds with the sentiment. Undeterred, Thomas considered collecting writers' "Objections to War" and wrote to a number of his friends soliciting their contributions. His purpose was to associate himself strongly with pacifist sentiment that might perhaps persuade some tribunal to free him from the war effort. All his friends did not reply as he would have wished. He observed a tribunal in action in Carmarthen and noted that all objected to war service on religious grounds. No hope for him there, he felt. Despite everything, Thomas, in Laugharne, was writing fiction; most days he walked to the gazebo on the castle walls, lent him by Richard Hughes, and wrote the last stories of *Portrait of the Artist as a Young Dog*. On 18 December 1939 he and Caitlin took part in a "Laugharne Entertainment" for the Red Cross. Caitlin danced; Thomas took a main part in a short farce. After that, in the kitchen of Castle House, they drank a fair amount, and Thomas told Richard Hughes, "What the people of Laugharne need is a play about themselves, a play in which they can act themselves."[57]

The Thomases spent Christmas with Dylan's parents at Bishopston, then a much longer period at Blashford. They were still there during March 1940, but they had been to London during that time, using Lorna Wilmott's flat. She was the first wife of the painter Rupert Shepherd, whose portrait of Thomas—painted at Sea View during the same year—is now in the National Portrait Gallery. When the Shepherds returned to their flat, they discovered that the Thomases had pawned all their valuables. Police action was threatened, and the Thomases somehow recovered most of what they had stolen. Such despicable action at least indicates how desperate for money they had become. It was difficult to find worthwhile markets for his poems and *Portrait* stories.

The struggle to avoid conscription was resolved in April 1940 when he was required to register for military service. A medical examination followed—possibly more than one—that classified him as "Grade III": unfit for military service but liable for other kinds of war work. The reason, Thomas always stated, was scarred lungs, a legacy of some earlier tuberculosis. The postmortem in New York showed nothing of the sort, and reasons for the classification remain a mystery. One rumored explanation was that matters were arranged in Wales by a friendly doctor. Caitlin always believed that Thomas fooled the medical board through excessive smoking and drinking during the twenty-four hours before the examination.[58]

Though, as has been stated, Thomas had pacifist tendencies throughout the 1930s, his attempt to evade military service was not a creditable episode. His work was attuned to the zeitgeist. After Guernica and the Spanish civil war, after *Kristallnacht* and the advance of the Nazis, he was well aware of the dangers of fascism. It was not as if he was always a peace-loving man: in his cups he was often ready to pick fights, particularly in defence of Caitlin. There seems little doubt that his desire to avoid the draft was motivated by a mixture of a small amount of principle, much psychological horror, and not a little self-indulgence and cowardice. The extent of his self-centeredness is best judged by the glee with which he received the medical board's decision. He immediately went out to celebrate. How that was received by those less fortunate we can only imagine. Thomas's reputation as a "conchie" was to lead to friction and fights and even to the occasional beating by infuriated servicemen home on leave.

April 1940 is one of the moments when we need to separate the often discreditable life from the magical writing. The life, as has been noted, is typified by Thomas's mainly cowardly self-centeredness, the writing by the publication of *Portrait of the Artist as a Young Dog*, his stories of Swansea life during the 1930s that have remained among his most popular and highly regarded works. There were useful reviews but, necessarily, few of them. The war destroyed the volume's immediate prospects in much the same way as the outbreak of war had ruined those of *The Map of Love*.

In April 1940 the family was back at Sea View. Thomas had evaded conscription but now had to struggle to make ends meet. "Since the war," he wrote to James Laughlin, in the hope of securing an advance for the American edition of *Portrait*, "all my little sources of money have dried up, I haven't seen one penny now for over a month and am living on suspicious credit."[59] The atmosphere in Laugharne had changed. Caitlin, who believed Thomas's attitude to military service to be cowardly, recalled that he received "a damned good hiding" one night in Laugharne.[60] Writs were served upon them, even by those tradesmen who, in the best Laugharne manner, had been tolerant of slow payment. The writs threatened distrainment of their meagre possessions. As Thomas put it to Stephen Spender, who was trying to coordinate efforts to help him out, believing that Thomas was about to be called up, "I've had to sneak my family away from our home in Carmarthenshire, because we could no longer obtain any credit and it was too awful to try to live there, among dunning and suspicion, from hand to mouth when I knew the hand would nearly always be empty."[61] As so often with Thomas's requests for money, the sentence is nicely shaped, perhaps too much so, for Thomas worked with increasing effort and time at begging for a living. He was unjustifiably annoyed when he learned that the writer Alec Waugh, Evelyn's brother, had urged John Davenport to "advise Dylan to write more stories and fewer letters."[62] He told Spender he owed seventy pounds, which Spender raised from various artistic friends via an appeal in *Horizon*, Cyril Connolly's new magazine. To these latter, including Sir Edward Marsh, Sir Hugh Walpole, and Francis Brett Young, Thomas wrote beautifully ingratiating expressions of gratitude.

Thomas looked increasingly to a future sustained by charity and so kept all promising options open. His letter to Spender was written in May 1940 from

Bishopston, where the Thomases had fled to escape immediate financial consequences and Laugharne's hostile atmosphere. They encountered the natural resentment of those whose lives the war had turned upside down and who regarded Thomas as a useless, feckless sponger who somehow had deceived the doctors and revelled in the fact. However, with debts paid and hostility lessened, probably because those who had beaten up Thomas had been posted out of range, they returned to Laugharne intent on carrying on at Sea View. He wrote emotionally to Francis Brett Young, "People's kindness to me, a stranger, has altered everything, made me happy, & allowed me to begin my own work again."[63] Yet matters were as desperate as ever: "TA for the great pound. I heard it singing in the envelope," he told ever-obliging Vernon Watkins, who was about to enter the RAF.[64] In July 1940 the Thomases gave up Sea View and left Laugharne. They were not to return permanently until 1949.

The war changed almost everything. Certainly it broke up the literary world of the late 1930s. Thomas was not the only writer to behave discreditably: Auden and Isherwood had scuttled off to America at the first hint of conflict; others followed or went to neutral Eire. There, in 1940, Thomas's friend Roger Roughton, who in 1936, aged nineteen, had been editor of the distinguished if short-lived magazine, *Contemporary Poetry and Prose*, gassed himself in a Dublin hotel. Yet thoughts of discreditable behavior return us to the dichotomy between life and work. Whatever must be said about Thomas's behavior during the war, the war itself gave rise to some of his finest poetry. He completed five poems in 1939 and six more in 1940, excluding "Request to Leda," a parody of a William Empson villanelle. During 1940 and 1941 he also wrote the unfinished novel *Adventures in the Skin Trade*, writing that has not really had its due, mainly, one suspects, because of Thomas's own attitude towards it: "I dislike it," he admitted. "It's the only really dashed-off piece of work I remember doing."[65] By the close of 1941 he had completed four more poems, two of which—"On the Marriage of a Virgin" and "The hunchback in the park"—were revised from the notebooks.

In late April or early May 1941 Thomas sold his poetry notebooks, the fruits of his teens, his prose notebook with drafts of his early stories, worksheets of "Ballad of the Long-legged Bait," and a manuscript of a short story to Bertram Rota, the London book dealer, for an unspecified sum that could not have been much more than £20, given that Rota sold them to the State University of New York at Buffalo for £41.10.0 or $140. Thomas was twenty-six, and it is customary to note that when he sold the notebooks he was the same age as Keats when the latter died. Whether this fact is any more than coincidence is not known. Caitlin argued that Thomas wanted a clean break with his earlier writings: "I've pretty well exhausted all the stuff in there; there's nothing more I want to use," she recalled him saying.[66] This is possible. What is certain is that he needed the money: in late August 1941 they were still penniless, and he was "still looking for a film job, & have been offered several scripts to do 'in the near future', which might mean weeks.''[67] Later, and probably for much the same reason, he sounded Rota about selling his (Thomas's) first editions.

Of the poems written during 1940 and 1941, the last to be published was ''Deaths and Entrances,'' which appeared in *Horizon* in July 1942. Thomas was then silent for two years, until, in April 1944, *Poetry London* published ''Last night I dived my beggar arm'' and ''Your breath was shed,'' neither of which was thought good enough to be collected by Thomas either in *Deaths and Entrances* or *Collected Poems*. From May 1944 and through 1945, the war's last year, Thomas had what turned out to be his final burst of sustained productivity (or at least of publishing), during which ten more poems, including some of his most famous, such as ''Poem in October,'' ''Fern Hill,'' ''A Refusal to Mourn,'' and ''In my craft or sullen art,'' were written or completed and published. Except for the two years of silence, the period from 1939 through 1945 was probably Thomas's finest as a poet. When the family left Laugharne in 1940, they stayed with their friend John Davenport. He was wealthy through scriptwriting in Hollywood, through inheriting money, and through marrying a wealthy American. Much of this money went towards buying a large Georgian house, the Malting House, in the Gloucestershire village of Marshfield, near Chippenham, and filling it with expensive modern paintings. He installed two grand pianos in the music room and kept a superb wine cellar. To the house came a stream of visitors from the music, art, and literary world, all of whom, one way or another, strove to avoid the war. The Thomases, with baby Llewelyn, stayed there until November 1940.

These were dark days. During May 1940 British troops were driven out of the Low Countries; the Dunkirk evacuation took place from 27 May to 4 June. Paris was captured by the Germans on 14 June. On 10 July the Battle of Britain began, ending in British victory on 15 September. In November 1940 the Germans began bombing British towns and cities. Swansea was bombed regularly through the summer of 1940; on 1 and 2 September it suffered its first blitz, incurring extensive damage. Thomas wrote to Vernon Watkins:

I can't imagine Gower bombed. High explosives at Pennard. Flaming onions over Pwlldu. And Union Street ashen. This is all too near. . . . Are you frightened these nights? When I wake up out of burning birdman dreams—they were frying aviators one night in a huge frying pan: it sounds whimsical now, it was appalling then—and hear the sound of bombs & gunfire only a little way away, I'm so relieved I could laugh or cry. . . . I get nightmares like invasions, all successful.[68]

Relieved or not, Thomas awake remained terrified. Caitlin recorded that at Marshfield, when he heard German planes droning overhead on their way to bomb nearby Bristol, he would hide, whimpering, under the bedsheets.

For Swansea the worst came on 19, 20, and 21 February 1941 when a three-night blitz destroyed the whole center of the town. Familiar landmarks of Thomas's upbringing, the Kardomah, the newspaper offices, the Three Lamps pub, and much else, were completely obliterated. He felt the loss very deeply. Bert Trick met Thomas and Caitlin in central Swansea after the third night's bombing. Thomas was very upset. "Our Swansea is dead," he told Trick, and so, for him, it was. Trick never saw him again.[69]

Despite the war, the stay at Marshfield had its idyllic moments. The Thomases had a base and were fed and watered. There was convivial company. They cycled through quiet villages on sunny afternoons. If they felt guilty about the way they lived while, above and elsewhere, men died for them, they did not record it. Thomas and Davenport were close friends. The latter was a pugnacious, volatile man, a failed poet, a highly cultured man of letters. The pair amused themselves—and Thomas, certainly, took his mind off the war—by writing *The Death of the King's Canary*, a satire of contemporary literary life in the form of a "whodunit" about the death of the poet laureate; it contained parodies of contemporary poets. In its day it was regarded as libellous. It was not published until 1976, when both authors and some of the targets were long dead, and the jokes had fallen flat. This was not all Thomas achieved during his summer at Marshfield. Though he told Vernon Watkins that because the war dominated his thinking, "I can't do much work, either,"[70] he did complete four poems, including "Deaths and Entrances," the first of his superb series of war poems. He also wrote three scripts for the BBC Latin American Service. This was a new departure; his earlier broadcasts had been readings mainly of his own work. Now he began what became a substantial career. As Caitlin might have put it, not altogether fairly, he was learning to be a hack. His first script was broadcast without problems, the second had to be rewritten, the third was rejected. Such a downward graph suggests a poor learner, or, more probably, less and less care.

During their stay at the Malting House the Thomases' marriage began to deteriorate. Caitlin had a brief fling with William Glock, later controller of music at the BBC and another of Davenport's guests. The couple spent a night in a Cardiff hotel, Caitlin buying clothes for the occasion by selling some possessions from Sea View. The night was a failure; the affair was unconsummated. It was discovered by Thomas through his mother's suspicions and led to a huge row during which Thomas struck her, threw a knife at her, and refused to sleep with her. This last, Caitlin recalled, lasted for some time.[71] The marriage was close to ending, and though it lasted until Thomas's death, it was never the same again. Trust had been destroyed. Thereafter the marriage was full of wild infidelities on both sides that hastened the final, fatal chaos. They left Marshfield and spent what was doubtless, for Caitlin, an uncomfortable Christmas at Bishopston with her in-laws.

In the spring of 1941 they were briefly in Laugharne staying at Castle House with Frances Hughes. Richard Hughes was away in the navy. The Thomases pilfered and generally misbehaved: "We are apt to be rather too 'at home' in other people's houses," Caitlin later wrote apologetically to Frances Hughes.[72] As usual, they were penniless. Though exempt from military service, Thomas expected noncombatant work. While he waited, he wrote begging letters and fulsome thanks to those, like Vernon Watkins, who came up with money. Whenever funds materialized, they spent them in local pubs or in Swansea pubs where they met old friends home on leave. They visited Thomas's parents, who, to escape the bombing, had left Bishopston for one of the cottages at Blaen Cwm.

In July 1941 they made another abrupt departure from Laugharne, probably, Tremlett has speculated, because of continued hostility towards the gloating draft dodger.[73] They were desperate for money. Caitlin took two-year-old Llewelyn to Blashford, where he was to be left with her mother. Llewelyn was often to be left. Though Caitlin felt guilty, she felt a stronger urge to be, as she put it, "in the in-place where the action was."[74] In some ways, given Thomas's increasingly cavalier attitude to his family's welfare, she could hardly be blamed. Unfortunately, her presence was never a restraint. Thomas went directly to London hoping for writing work, either from the BBC or, using John Davenport's connections, from a film industry responding to the government's demands for propaganda. He needed something: Dent saw the first part of *Adventures in the Skin Trade*, for sight of which it had agreed to pay, and turned it down in no uncertain terms, one reader urging Thomas to "pull himself together for a much more carefully thought out and deliberately written job of work."[75] Dent was exasperated, having advanced Thomas money for various projects—a travel book, an anthology—that came to nothing.

Literary London in wartime was a strange place. Though magazines had closed in 1939, the next twelve months saw a partial revival. The defunct *New Writing* was born again as *Penguin New Writing; Poetry London*, with which Thomas had been originally associated in 1939, reappeared in 1940; Cyril Connolly's *Horizon*, the most distinguished of 1940s literary magazines, began life in January 1940. Fitzrovia was still the artistic center, with the Wheatsheaf pub—where, of course, Thomas had first met Caitlin—the place for literary socializing. The war, which, like all wars, placed many on the verge of sudden death, undermined conventional behavior: life was freer, looser, with more living for the day. Inevitably, with so many away from home and family, frightened into escapism, and in a bombed and blacked-out city that turned transient strangers into sudden friends, drinking and immorality burgeoned, and money was borrowed thoughtlessly. The literary world itself, which had always inclined to the bohemian, became a more intense microcosm of wartime London, full of writers on leave or in reserved occupations where they were often treated warily by the powers that employed them. They made common cause and fostered a flourishing cameraderie. Thomas—this time with Caitlin—had entered yet another laxly hedonistic world. But work did not at first materialize, and Thomas despaired. He wrote bleakly to Vernon Watkins:

We've been having an awful time, and I have felt like killing myself. We arrived with no money, after leaving Llewelyn in Ringwood, and have had none since. In Laugharne that was not so bad. In stinking, friendless London it is unendurable. . . . We are prisoners now in a live melodrama and all the long villains with three halfpence are grinning in at us through the bars.[76]

Help was at hand. A year earlier, through Ivan Moffatt, an American film director who was a friend of John Davenport, Thomas had met Donald Taylor, who ran Strand Films. Strand was booming. It was the largest maker of documentary films, many of which—essentially propaganda films—it was creating for the Ministry of Information as part of the war effort. Taylor was recruiting writers and in the autumn of 1941 hired Thomas as a scriptwriter. Here at last was his reserved occupation. It was also well paid. Thomas started at eight pounds per week, which became ten and eventually twenty plus expenses,[77] first for Strand and then for its successor, Gryphon Films, which Taylor eventually closed down when the war ended.

Apart from his brief career as a journalist, his association with Strand is the only instance of Thomas having a regular job with colleagues, an office, office hours, obligations, and a salary. It was not a constant nine-to-five regimen: on occasion, as long as the writing was done to time, it could be done anywhere. But at other times office hours were necessary, interspersed with work on location. Though Thomas was hardly the model company man—he usually dressed in a check jacket and grey flannels, was rarely punctual, and was often inclined to persuade his colleagues to adjourn to the pub—yet, in general, he worked within an ordering framework and in a professional way. Julian Maclaren-Ross, who worked with Thomas at Strand, has emphasized his serious and responsible approach to his job. He refused to keep alcohol in the office; he drank only moderately at lunchtime, often in the back bar of the Café Royal.[78]

By and large we can accept this, though we should keep in mind that wartime consolidated Thomas's reputation as the great drinker, famous among the bars, the drinking clubs, the Soho pubs: David Tennant's Gargoyle Club, the Horseshoe Club in Wardour Street, the Ladder Club in Bruton Place, Frisco's in Frith Street, and such pubs as the Antelope in Sloane Square, the Helvetia and the Swiss Tavern in Old Compton Street, the French House in Dean Street, the Wheatsheaf, the Café Royal, the Markham in Markham Square, the Anglesea, and the King's Head and Six Bells in Cheyne Walk, where he surely must have recalled that in another life he and Pamela had sat and dreamed of literary fame. In Caitlin's words:

His pubbing became relentless. He would go out in the evening with a chrysanthemum in his lapel, pretending to be a queen. He would dress up in fancy clothes, saying he was "an actor from the BBC", then offer to bite the caps off bottles of beer if he could have the beer. Some of his pub games were incredibly childish, if not embarrassing. One was called "cats and dogs": he would get down on his hands and knees and crawl round a bar, biting people's ankles and howling like a dog. . . . He would pour drinks into other people's pockets; and once I heard that he unbuttoned his trousers and offered a girl his penis. . . . Dylan also had an enormous repertoire of obscene songs, dirty limericks and "blue" stories. . . . Dylan had acquired a reputation as the pub fool and he had to keep it up at all costs.[79]

Ferris commented that a "streak of violence" runs through so many memories of Thomas at this time: slicing off companions' ties with a razor blade, for example,[80] and numerous reports of him picking fights with soldiers.

Though to many on many evenings he seemed the greatest entertainer, the funniest man in the world, yet drinking devoured his time, as it did at every point in his adult life. We might also wonder how long each morning it took Thomas the scriptwriter to get under way. This was certainly the period that saw Thomas at his most professional; it was also the time when heavier drinking began to put his most important talents under severe pressure.

Thomas had always been keen on the cinema; he had, after all, contributed a confident essay on silent films to his school magazine. He liked the work, particularly when he accompanied the film crew on location throughout Britain. He quickly became knowledgeable about film technique and skilled at his craft. All in all, he worked as part of the team on fourteen documentaries, doing his own basic research and writing the scripts for voice-overs either wholly or, occasionally, collaboratively. Through this work he extended his knowledge of current affairs, of Wales, particularly of economically depressed South Wales, of some of the technicalities of mining, and even of antibiotic drugs, dyes, and agriculture. The work was not intellectually demanding, but we can at least admire Thomas's consistent objective professionalism.

As has been noted, Thomas, not altogether successfully, wrote scripts for the BBC in 1940. Occasional work followed during the next three years: small parts in drama productions and poetry reading. In February 1943 he broadcast "Reminiscences of Childhood," his first important contribution to radio. New opportunities that were in a more writerly medium than the film work began to open up.

That film work was to be one source of great marital tension. One reason was the peripatetic nature of the Thomases' wartime life, which came to involve frequent separations. Early in the war they spent a period together in Hammersmith Terrace, in a studio owned by A. P. Herbert. From autumn 1942 until early 1943 the Thomases lived at 3 Wentworth Studios, Manresa Road, in Chelsea. This was a dirty and damp room plus curtained kitchen. The leaking roof was mainly of glass, which made it dangerous during air raids. Even while they rented the studio, the couple were frequently elsewhere, often leaving Llewelyn at Blashford. They stayed at Bosham, in Sussex, in a cottage with squalid facilities belonging to Thomas's drinking pal, the art critic T. W. Earp. Occasionally they stayed in Markham Square with Caitlin's sister, Nicolette Devas, where Thomas, offended by a cold greeting, urinated against their living-room wall. Elsewhere, doubtless for much the same reason, he was known to defecate on the floor. They spent numerous unrecorded nights with friends.

Sometimes they went to Blaen Cwm to see Thomas's parents. That was rarely cheering: D. J. hated the place and its squalid facilities. Most of his books had been sold; intelligent conversation was at a premium. Having worked his cultured way into the urban bourgeoisie in his youth, he doubtless grasped the bitter irony that retirement, in wartime at any rate, had returned him to the world of the peasantry. That there was no alternative must have been hard to bear.

The couple were often apart. Through the summer of 1942 Caitlin took Llewelyn to Laugharne to stay with Frances Hughes and to Talsarn, a small village in Dyfed, to stay with friends. Thomas came occasionally to Talsarn, which is on the river Aeron. They believed that their daughter, Aeronwy, was conceived there, hence her name. She was born in St. Mary Abbot's Hospital in Chelsea on 3 March 1943. Caitlin was then twenty-nine and reluctant to lose more freedom. She recalled, with retrospective guilt, that they often left baby Aeronwy alone under the glass roof in the middle of an air raid while she and Dylan got drunk in the pubs. On one occasion they returned to find her being comforted by a neighbor. Donald Taylor became so concerned about Aeronwy staying in wartime London that he took the family to his home at Beaconsfield for a couple of months.

"You and I have not been together . . . for what seems months & months,"[81] Thomas wrote to Caitlin in 1943. During the following year he is known to have stayed for a time at a vicarage in Chiswick. He took to disappearing for a night or more at a time. He went on location with the film crew from Strand. Other women began to enter his life.

These are difficult to document. "I never thought he was a genuine womaniser at all"[82] was always Caitlin's view. She considered that her husband needed women to boost his self-confidence. Both of them increasingly had affairs and relationships as the marriage slowly fell apart. Strangely, Thomas's most serious relationship was not, it seems, strictly an affair. In 1942 he was in Bradford making a documentary about the theatre in wartime. Almost certainly, as John Ackerman suggested, Strand was filming the London Old Vic's touring production of *The Merry Wives of Windsor* as part of *CEMA*, a film celebrating the Council for the Encouragement of Music and Art.[83] In Bradford, Thomas met the actress Ruth Wynn Owen, who was from Anglesey. More than a year later he was still writing to her:

In London, I mean to write you every day, but the laziness, the horror and selfpity that London drizzles down on me, stop everything but the ghost of a hope that perhaps you will ring. . . . Of you I have only the still picture from the silliest film in the world, which is still the best film for the one reason that it allows me to send you now, with all my heart, my love.[84]

Thomas sounds sincere. She was married, refused to become his mistress, was still pursued, and was apparently in love with him. Nothing came of it. In parallel with his letters to Ruth Wynn Owen were those to Caitlin, effusive letters, often at the edge of the erotic but remaining strangely childish. Such letters protested far too much about the pain of absence, written, as we know, amid a life of scriptwriting, hard drinking, and womanizing. He told her too often that his life in London counted for nothing. When Thomas, of all people, wrote to his wife, "I have to say to you that I love you in life & after death, and that even though I drink I am good. I am not drinking much,"[85] we wonder as much about the sobriety as the sincerity of the writer.

Until early 1943 their base remained the Manresa Road studio. There, sometime during their stay, Bill Brandt took their photograph. It presents Thomas as man of letters, at ease amid solid, even elegant furniture in a book-lined room. Most of the books belonged to Daniel Jones, who had become an officer in the army. The unscrupulous Thomases were selling them to raise cash. No photograph could be more misleading,[86] for a second source of marital tension was Thomas's financial fecklessness. Though Caitlin, when she was present, did her share of spending, in general, while her husband spent his money in London's bohemia, she was left to struggle to bring up the children in dreadful accommodation and persistent poverty. He spent everything. His failure even to allow for future tax demands was to aggravate the financial worries that hastened his final tragic slide. He was always begging: "Could you temporarily (oh cringing word) help me with a little money, however little" is a typical attempt.[87] So far as Caitlin was concerned, he was always penniless and always either begging or apologizing.

What made matters worse for her was that she did not even benefit materially from work—film scriptwriting—that she regarded as the waste of a great talent, the selling out of a great poetic soul. Caitlin had her faults, but she was often shrewd about Thomas's writing. She had reservations about his occasional work for radio. That for films she regarded as essentially hackwork. In general she was probably right. We can be impressed by the professionalism and by the amount Thomas wrote for films—FitzGibbon estimated that "he probably put more words on paper in this professional capacity than in any other"[88]—but we know, with Caitlin, that it was an unfortunate diversion from his proper task. Working for Strand stopped him from writing poetry.

Paradoxically, the order now imposed on his working life—albeit not that of a poet—was accompanied by increasing personal chaos fuelled by an obsessive self-indulgence, Cwmdonkin Drive's spoilt boy writ large. Two instances make the point.

When Llewelyn was born, Caitlin had had a long and difficult labor. In March 1943 Caitlin entered St. Mary Abbot's Hospital in Chelsea for the birth of their daughter, Aeronwy Bryn. The birth was only slightly easier than Llewelyn's, and delivery took place in the middle of a tremendous air raid. Thomas was not at the hospital; he was at home, in the dilapidated studio, in bed with Pamela Glendower, a mutual friend. Caitlin recalled with some bitterness that Thomas was not present and was not seen until some days after the birth, when he appeared wearing an old dressing-gown, which was obviously not his own, and bedroom slippers: he was unshaven and his hair was all over the place; he looked completely shagged out. Dylan had had one hell of a week of dissipation while I was going through my labour. . . . He didn't seem very concerned, either for me or the baby.[89]

Certainly he was not sufficiently concerned to collect her and their new daughter from the hospital. Mother and daughter found their own way to Manresa Road. The studio was unimaginably dirty and squalid; Thomas was out drinking with the FitzGibbons.

Equally reprehensible was his treatment of Vernon Watkins, whose wedding took place in London at two o' clock on 2 October 1944. Thomas was best man but failed to turn up. Not until four weeks later did the Watkinses hear from him. Then he sent an apologetic note enclosing a creased and dirty letter in pencil that, said Thomas, had been written on the wedding day and believed posted only to be found, those four weeks later, in a pocket. It blamed a slow train and his own failure to remember the name of the church. In Gwen Watkins's opinion Thomas's excuses were lies and the letter a fake, written much later and creased to simulate pocket wear. She was probably right, particularly since it is now known that Thomas was in a London publisher's during the early afternoon of the wedding day.

Thereafter Gwen Watkins was always wary of Thomas; he was too often the liar. His behavior was too often reprehensible. Though Vernon Watkins forgave him for not turning up, that friendship was not what it had been, mainly because Thomas could no longer be bothered to respond to the poems Watkins sent him. When Thomas was drunk, his behavior could be maniacal: Gwen Watkins recalled that he "would walk up to the tallest man in uniform in the pub and insult him, his country and the war so grossly that almost inevitably a fight developed."[90] Such conduct was doubtless fuelled by masochistic guilt. Thomas was a greatly troubled man who hated seeing his friends in uniform. Sometimes Gwen Watkins glimpsed a different side of him:

Dylan reading the draft for *August Bank Holiday* and asking nervously at the end, "Do you think it's any good, really?"; Dylan lying on the grass at Pennard and talking about Dickens; Dylan playing Statues with Dan and Vernon in the evening light; Dylan in Swansea looking at the bomb-sites, wet-cheeked with cold and grief, saying "Where we used to go is nowhere at all now". And Dylan saying to me, "You think I'm not a serious person: but I am. I have to be serious to write my kind of poems".[91]

Once again we recall the young man on Pamela's doorstep. As drink began to rot commitment and control in the last decade of his life, there were few such moments.

The war may have marked the beginning of the end for the Thomases' marriage, but that end never quite arrived. In their wild, disorganized lives they were constants for each other, satisfying, it seems, mutual masochistic desire.

Caitlin considered that "after each great crisis in our lives he would go through another period of creativity and calm; it was almost as though I were provoking him."[92] The point is persuasive. Thomas's carefully crafted, ordered, and structured poems were a consequence of his innate bourgeois/suburban upbringing, a reflection of that upbringing's capacity to order emotional and physical experience. We see a similar desire at work in his life with Caitlin: the constant tension, quarrels, violence, and hard drinking, in retrospect, made such poems desperately necessary.

In 1941 Thomas completed "The hunchback in the park." For the next three years he wrote no poetry of note—his only poetry in 1942 was "A Dream of Winter," which consisted of captions to photographs—and hardly any at all. Then, in May 1944, he published "Ceremony after a Fire Raid" in the magazine *Our Time*. Thus began a final sequence—prolific by Thomas's standards—of fine poems culminating in *Deaths and Entrances*, probably his greatest volume. To put this another way: "Ceremony after a Fire Raid" and the poems that follow it show him still able to transform terrible personal and national experiences into literary art. His failure to continue such ordering transformations is yet another reason for the final tragedy.

NOTES

1. Derek Patmore, "A Few of My Contemporaries," unpublished memoirs (1964), typescript, Patmore, D., Works, HRHRC.

2. This description of Pamela Hansford Johnson is based mainly on the following: E. W. Tedlock (ed.), *Dylan Thomas: The Legend and the Poet* (London: William Heinemann, 1960), 23–4; Pamela Hansford Johnson, *Important to Me: Personalia* (London: Macmillan, 1974); HRHRC manuscript, Thomas, D., Misc. FitzGibbon: Photocopies of entries in Johnson's diary, 1933–35.

3. *CL*, 37. Letter to Pamela Hansford Johnson, [early November 1933].

4. Tedlock, *Dylan Thomas*, 24.

5. Pamela Hansford Johnson, diary, entry for 8 March 1934, HRHRC.

6. Paul Ferris, *Dylan Thomas* (1977; Harmondsworth: Penguin Books, 1978), 104.

7. Pamela Hansford Johnson, diary entries for 3 April 1934, 17 September 1934, and 1 September 1935, respectively, HRHRC.

8. Johnson *Important to Me*, 148.

9. *CL*, 135. Letter to Pamela Hansford Johnson, dated [c. 21] May [1934].

10. *CL*, 177. Letter to Bert Trick, dated [December 1934].

11. Ferris, *Dylan Thomas*, 120.

12. Johnson, *Important to Me*, 145.

13. See Ralph Maud, *Entrances to Dylan Thomas' Poetry* (Pittsburgh: University of Pittsburgh Press, 1963), 121–48, and Dylan Thomas, *Collected Poems, 1934–1953*, ed. Walford Davies and Ralph Maud (London: Dent, 1988), 177–95, for full details of chronology and provenance.

14. Interview with Dylan Thomas, *Sunday Referee*, 30 December 1934: 3.

15. Desmond Hawkins, review of *18 Poems*, by Dylan Thomas, *Time and Tide*, 9 February 1935: 204.

16. Pamela Hansfond Johnson, diary entry for 5 January 1935, HRHRC.

17. Gwen Watkins, *Portrait of a Friend* (Llandysul: Gomer Press, 1983), 2.

18. *CL*, 202. Letter to Nancy and Haydn Taylor, 27 October 1935.

19. Dylan Thomas, *The Poems*, ed. Daniel Jones, rev. ed. (1974; London: Dent, 1982), 48.

20. Quoted in Ferris, *Dylan Thomas*, 164.

21. *CL*, 222. Letter to Vernon Watkins, dated [c. 20 April 1936].

22. *CL*, 198–99. Letter, to Daniel Jones, dated 14 August 1935.

23. Daniel Jones, *My Friend Dylan Thomas* (London: Dent, 1977), 44.

24. *CL*, 204–5. Letter to Richard Church, dated 9 December 1935.

25. Richard Church to Dylan Thomas, quoted in *CL*, 227n.

26. *CL*, 223. Letter to Vernon Watkins, postmarked 20 April 1936.

27. Edith Sitwell, review of *Twenty-five Poems*, by Dylan Thomas, *Sunday Times*, 15 November 1936: 9.

28. Documented information provided by Wm. Parry & Co., Solicitors, Swansea, who handled a subsequent sale of 5 Cwmdonkin Drive. Thomas's parents eventually sold the property on 20 April 1943.

29. *CL*, 255. Letter to Vernon Watkins, 15 July [1937].

30. *CL*, 255. Letter to Pamela Hansford Johnson, dated 6 August 1937.

31. Ferris, *Dylan Thomas*, 147–48.

32. *CL*, 260. Letter to Desmond Hawkins, [?September 1937].

33. Paul Ferris, *Caitlin: The Life of Caitlin Thomas* (London: Hutchinson, 1993), 78.

34. Thomas could, though, usually find time to be kind to young writers. The young Welsh poet Meurig Walters sent him poems during early 1938. Thomas wrote back encouragingly, praising "Rhondda Poem," which Walters had published in the *Welsh Review*. He helped place Walters's work in Julian Symons's journal *Twentieth Century Verse*. In 1939 he had hoped to read "Rhondda Poem" as part of a BBC reading. World War II intervened. (See *CL* 274; letter to Meurig Walters; 10 March 1938; Ralph Maud (ed.), *Wales in His Arms: Dylan Thomas's Choice of Welsh Poetry* (Cardiff: University of Wales Press, 1994), 19.)

35. *CL*, 284. Letter to James Laughlin, dated 28 March 1938.

36. *CL*, 273. Letter to Henry Treece, [February or March 1938].

37. *CL*, 280. Letter to Henry Treece, 23 March 1938.

38. *CL*, 304. Letter to Henry Treece, 16 June 1938.

39. *CL*, 304. Letter to Henry Treece, 16 June 1938.

40. George Tremlett, *Dylan Thomas: In the Mercy of His Means* (London: Constable, 1991), 77.

41. *CL*, 304. Letter to Henry Treece, 16 June 1938.

42. Quoted in Tremlett, *Dylan Thomas*, 79.

43. Dylan Thomas *Collected Poems, 1934–1953*, 67. Where required, subsequent references to this edition, abbreviated as *CP*, are included in the text.

44. Glyn Jones, *The Dragon Has Two Tongues* (London: Dent, 1968), 173.

45. *CL*, 310. Letter to Henry Treece, 6 or 7 July [1938].

46. Keidrych Rhys, letters to Henry Treece, 3 May 1939 and 21 June 1939, manuscripts, Dylan Thomas Collection, HRHRC.

47. See Tremlett, *Dylan Thomas*, 81, 189n. The admirer was the poet Emma Swan.

48. Caitlin Thomas with George Tremlett, *Caitlin: A Warring Absence* (London: Secker & Warburg, 1986), 58.

49. Gwen Watkins, *Vernon Watkins: Poet of the Elegiac Muse* (Swansea: University College of Swansea, 1973), 15.

50. *CL*, 388. Letters to W. T. Davies, dated July 1939 and [July 1939].

51. Cyril Connolly, review of *The Map of Love*, by Dylan Thomas, *New Statesman*, 16 September 1939: 404.

52. *CL*, 401, 401, 402. Letters to Vernon Watkins, postmarked 25 August 1939; to Nancy Pearn, [late August 1939]; and to D. J. Thomas, 29 August 1939, respectively.

53. *CL*, 407. Letter to Desmond Hawkins, dated 3 September 1939.

54. Quoted in *Sotheby's Sale Catalogue: English Literature and History*, 24 July 1995. Letter from Dylan Thomas and A. E. Trick to Ithell Davies, [c. 8 August 1934].

55. Gwynfor Evans, letter to Bill Read, 24 October 1963, manuscript, Dylan Thomas Collection, HRHRC.

56. *CL*, 417. Letter to A. E. Trick, 9 September 1939.

57. Quoted in Constantine FitzGibbon, *The Life of Dylan Thomas* (London: Dent, 1965), 248. The idea for the play that eventually became *Under Milk Wood* was in Thomas's mind throughout the 1930s. Bert Trick recalled a day in 1932 that Thomas spent at the Tricks' at their holiday bungalow near Swansea when he talked of writing "a sort of Welsh *Ulysses*," all the action to take place within twenty-four hours. (See Kent Thompson, "Dylan Thomas in Swansea," unpublished Ph.D. diss., University of Wales, Swansea, 1965, 299.

58. Caitlin Thomas with Tremlett, *Caitlin: A Warring Absence*, 72.

59. *CL*, 449. Letter to James Laughlin, dated 15 April 1940.

60. Tremlett, *Dylan Thomas*, 88.

61. *CL*, 451–52. Letter to Stephen Spender, dated 13 May 1940.

62. *CL*, 476. Letter to John Davenport, 27 January 1941. Davenport had told Thomas of Alec Waugh's note.

63. *CL*, 459. Letter to Francis Brett Young, dated 4 July 1940.

64. *CL*, 454. Letter to Vernon Watkins, dated [?Summer 1940].

65. *CL*, 485. Letter to Vernon Watkins, 22 May 1941.

66. Caitlin Thomas with Tremlett, *Caitlin: A Warring Absence*, 83.

67. *CL*, 493. Letter to Vernon Watkins, 28 August 1941.

68. *CL*, 463. Letter to Vernon Watkins, dated [Summer 1940].

69. Ferris, *Dylan Thomas*, 184.

70. *CL*, 464. Letter to Vernon Watkins, dated [Summer 1940].

71. Caitlin Thomas with Tremlett, *Caitlin: A Warring Absence*, 74–75.

72. Quoted in Ferris, *Caitlin*, 90.

73. Tremlett, *Dylan Thomas*, 91.

74. Ferris, *Caitlin*, 89.

75. Quoted in Ferris, *Dylan Thomas*, 187.

76. *CL*, 493–94. Letter to Vernon Watkins, dated 28 August 1941.

77. Dylan Thomas, *The Filmscripts*, ed. John Ackerman (London: Dent, 1995), xi.

78. Julian Maclaren-Ross, *Memoirs of the Forties* (London: Alan Ross, 1965) 118–134.

79. Caitlin Thomas with Tremlett, *Caitlin: A Warring Absence*, 82.

80. Ferris, *Dylan Thomas*, 196.

81. *CL*, 509. Letter to Caitlin Thomas, dated [?1943].

82. Caitlin Thomas with Tremlett, *Caitlin: A Warring Absence*, 88.

83. Dylan Thomas, *Filmscripts*, 19.

84. *CL*, 507–8. Letter to Ruth Wynn Owen, dated 19 September 1943.

85. *CL*, 506. Letter to Caitlin Thomas, dated [?1943].

86. The photograph can be found in Caitlin Thomas with George Tremlett, *Caitlin: A Warring Absence* (London: Secker & Warburg, 1986), 80–81.

87. *CL*, 507. Letter to Wynford Vaughan-Thomas, [?September 1943].

88. FitzGibbon, *Life of Dylan Thomas*, 63.

89. Caitlin Thomas with Tremlett, *Caitlin: A Warring Absence*, 84.

90. Gwen Watkins, *Portrait of a Friend*, 104.

91. Ibid., 115.

92. Caitlin Thomas with Tremlett, *Caitlin: A Warring Absence*, 178.

3

1944–1949

During the summer of 1944, as flying bombs fell on London, three of the Thomases—Caitlin, Dylan, and Aeronwy—were at Blaen Cwm. They stayed for five or six weeks, Donald Taylor having willingly agreed that Thomas could leave dangerous and distracting London to work on his filmscripts in Wales. Such scripts included the lyrical and patriotic *Our Country*, one of his best pieces of film writing. Prior to the return to Wales the family had stayed at Taylor's home in Beaconsfield. There Thomas and Taylor had worked on *The Doctor and the Devils*, a screenplay for a feature film based on the body-snatching exploits of Burke and Hare. Taylor's new company, Gryphon Films, the successor to Strand, had begun to look beyond the propaganda documentary to entertainment for a postwar world.

At Blaen Cwm, where Thomas was living cheaply on a regular income, far away from cronies, drinking clubs, and associated immoralities, in the heart of beautiful Dyfed, with time for more than filmscripts, it was as if his lyrical energy, held back for years, suddenly poured forth. Vernon Watkins wrote of his friend, "The chief part of his creative writing was done in the landscape and among the people to whom he was most deeply attached."[1] So it was in that summer at Blaen Cwm. He completed "Ceremony after a Fire Raid," then "Poem in October"—his "Laugharne poem: the first place poem I've written,"[2] begun some years earlier but never finished—and the intricately shaped "Vision and Prayer."

This was a different kind of poetry, more direct, more approachable, seemingly simpler (a relative term in Thomas's case). In this change can be detected the influence of Thomas's film work: the simplifying of complex experience into propaganda, the need to appeal to a popular audience. A lesser influence, as yet, was his radio work, which required a similar directness. Such shaping forces, distorted by later circumstances, were not always good influences on the poetry of his final years. Now they helped uncover the lyrical seam, combining, almost certainly, with a feeling of relief at having escaped the continuing, escalating threat of London in wartime and at having survived drink, debauchery, and marital strife, though he was still haunted by the war. The Thomases were back in Wales. Though the war had not yet ended, the poems, at least in part, assert implicitly, "Look, we have come through!"

Llewelyn was still at Blashford, where he had spent most of the last three years being looked after by Caitlin's mother. In September 1944 his parents and sister moved to a small bungalow called Majoda, near New Quay, a small fishing village on Cardigan Bay. Majoda was built of wood and asbestos; it had magnificent sea views but no main services. Water came from a rain tank or from a tap on the main road, lighting from bottled gas, and heating from paraffin; the squalid lavatory was outside. Rent was only one pound per week, but though Thomas continued to receive his salary from Gryphon, they were still hard up and sometimes hid from the landlord. Accommodation was cramped, life stable but chaotic. Thomas was adapting *Twenty Years A-Growing*, Maurice O'Sullivan's study of life in the Blasket Islands off the coast of Eire, as a feature film. When Donald Taylor wrote anxiously asking after progress, Thomas replied:

Reason for the badness & slowness is that this little bungalow is no place to work in when there's a bawling child there, too: the rooms are tiny, the walls bumpaper-thin, & a friend arrived with another baby with a voice like Caruso's. Now, however, I have just taken a room in a nearby house: a very quiet room where I know I can work till I bleed.[3]

For once he bled fairly profusely. Apart from adapting *Twenty Years A-Growing*, he was continuing to write poems. Oscar Williams, the American anthologist and poet, wrote asking for some. He had tried in 1942 only to be told by Thomas that he had no poems to send. Now matters were different, and Williams placed a number of poems in American magazines and journals. He asked Thomas for a piece on war and poetry, but without success. Perhaps that was just as well: he contracted to supply the publisher Peter Lunn with a prose work entitled, as the synopsis has it, *A Book of Streets, Words and Pictures about Streets, Streets in London*. A fifty-pound advance was paid that Thomas spent, but he never wrote a word, the publisher finally resorting to legal action to get his money back.

James Laughlin wrote proposing a volume of selected writing and asking for Thomas's suggestions regarding contents. "You ask me to tell you what I consider are my best 20 odd poems, my best 4 stories, and the 2 best chapters of the autobiographical *Portrait*," Thomas replied. "These I have written down on a separate sheet, enclosed."[4] The list includes such recent poems as "Vision and Prayer" and "Poem in October," but out of the early work he chose some of his most difficult lyrics, including "I see the boys of summer," "When, like a running grave," "I, in my intricate image," two sonnets from the "Altarwise" sequence, "I make this in a warring absence," and "Ballad of the Long-legged Bait." He left out a number of his more direct poems, such as "Especially when the October wind," "This bread I break," "The hand that signed the paper," and "Twenty-four years." These last, along with others, Laughlin added to the volume. Possibly Thomas's choice reflects some subconscious concern at the way his writing had changed. The strange, compelling imagination of his work in the 1930s seems far away when we read "Poem in October" or "Fern Hill"; the latter are beautiful, disconcerting, but less intense, perhaps less original.

During his time at Majoda, interrupted by a few visits to London, mainly in connection with his scriptwriting, Thomas completed at least ten poems, including some of his most famous such as, "A Refusal to Mourn," "This side of the truth," and "In my craft or sullen art." It was his final creative flourish; he was to write fewer than ten poems during the rest of his life. He also wrote "Quite Early One Morning" for the BBC. This affectionate portrait of New Quay, exploring the thoughts and dreams of its inhabitants, is an important precursor of *Under Milk Wood*, as were his verse letters to T. W. Earp, full of everyday incidents humorously described, and his unpublished poem about Oxford,[5] and as the *Book of Streets*—which, the synopsis suggested, would have moved through time from noon to midnight—would have been.

This burst of creativity emerged, as always, from a settled routine: pottering, reading, or writing letters in the morning, the pub—invariably the Black Lion, with its "gently swilling retired sea-captains in the snug-as-a-bug back bar"[6]— at lunchtime, writing in the afternoon, then back to the pub in the evening. It is an indication of Thomas's propensity to chaos that this routine can be regarded with some satisfaction. In practice it meant very few hours of actual work for a man with a low tolerance of alcohol, often sleepy with lunchtime beer on warm autumn days. But this was a great improvement on a wartime routine that, so far as serious work was concerned, appeared to allow no time at all.

The Thomases' nearest neighbor was Vera Killick, an acquaintance of Thomas's from Swansea days and now a friend of Caitlin's, who had stayed with her at Talsarn. Vera and her baby lived nearby; William Killick, her husband, was a commando officer, usually away. In February 1945 Donald Taylor had become increasingly concerned at Thomas's slow progress with his filmscripts. A confused telephone conversation led him to believe that Thomas wanted to stop scripting documentaries. Despite fence-mending letters, in March Taylor dispatched his colleague John Eldridge, with a Jewish woman assistant, to New Quay. Killick was home on leave, felt excluded from his wife's friendship with the Thomases, and suspected the relationship. At the Black Lion the woman assistant accused Killick of anti-Semitic comments. A brawl followed, during which Thomas scuffled with Killick. The Thomases returned with friends to Majoda to carry on drinking. They were disturbed by the drunken captain firing submachine-gun bullets through the bungalow's asbestos walls before bursting in, emptying the gun's magazine into the living-room ceiling, and threatening the group with a hand grenade. Thomas behaved coolly. A calmer captain eventually left. The police were called. Charges of attempted murder were brought against Killick, only to be thrown out by the jury at Lampeter Assizes for lack of evidence.

It is difficult to estimate the importance of this incident for Thomas's life and work. His cool behavior, which could be seen as bravery, could also suggest that he had lost self-concern. That loss may well have been linked to the shattering of such belief as he might have had that New Quay was the long-sought sanctuary. The realities of debt—which had destroyed life in prewar Laugharne—had not been avoided; now even the realities of war had penetrated that quiet place. Certainly a darker, more despairing note enters his letters during the rest of 1945. Other worries pressed: his father, he told Vernon Watkins, was "awfully ill these days, with heart disease and uncharted pains."[7] Though he was writing poetry again, he worried about his loss of creative fluency. He wrote unhappily to Watkins of his inability to impose order on his life: despite his continuing regular income from Gryphon Films, his financial affairs were sliding into chaos.

In June 1945 he was in "worse-than-Belsen London,"[8] staying with the FitzGibbons and writing a letter to Caitlin that is so chillingly ingratiating that we sense immediately that the marriage was in difficulty. Despite that description of London and his financial problems, he, with his family, was looking to return. He was restless and depressed, as he had been for some time. At the close of 1944 he had ended a letter to Oscar Williams, "It is the last evening of the bad year and I am going out to celebrate myself sick and dirty. Make what you can of 1945."[9] He had also lamented the impossibility of making a living in Britain out of poetry. Thomas had entertained vain hopes of James Laughlin finding him something in America. Those hopes recur through the letters of this period. The shooting intensified this desire to get out, in some way to escape his troubles. Thus when Oscar Williams, only a few weeks after the shooting, raised the possibility of an American visit, Thomas responded with alacrity, "I'd love a little ladleful from the gravy pots over there—a lick of the ladle, the immersion of a single hair in the rich shitbrown cauldron—though naturally I expect nothing."[10] Nothing was what came his way.

The war in Europe ended on 8 May 1945. A few weeks later the owner of Majoda reclaimed the bungalow, and the Thomases had to leave. They went back to Blaen Cwm, described disparagingly as "a breeding-box in a cabbage valley,"[11] and stayed until the autumn. During August the atomic bombs were dropped on Hiroshima and Nagasaki; their effect, the possibility of absolute catastrophe, was to haunt Thomas for the rest of his life. He was preparing *Deaths and Entrances* but was irresponsibly slow with the proofs. In September he wrote the disturbing and nostalgic "Fern Hill," the most famous of his poems, which, as will be seen, can only be fully understood in its historical context. He returned the proofs to Dent and added "Fern Hill," "which I very much *want* included as it is an *essential* part of the feeling & meaning of the book as a whole."[12] By the end of September the Thomases were back in London, living in the basement flat of Caitlin's sister's Markham Square home.

Postwar Britain was a grim place. The country was bankrupt; it recovered only slowly from the devastation of the war. Rationing was not to end completely until well into 1953. A Labour government struggled with great problems. The weather was terrible. It was the period of the Cold War. There were paper shortages; the Third Programme closed down temporarily. Perhaps paradoxically, there was a mood of suppressed hedonism that made the general populace inimical to serious concerns.

After "Fern Hill" Thomas did not complete another poem until July 1947. He was once again distracted into easier work. The war's end saw Gryphon Films wound up and so the end of his salary. Through Donald Taylor he became a scriptwriter for J. Arthur Rank's Gainsborough Films and worked on a number of feature films. These included *The Three Weird Sisters*, a melodrama set in a Welsh mining valley, which attacks nonconformity and demonstrates Thomas's leftist sympathies, and *No Room at the Inn*, which starred Freda Jackson, Hermione Baddeley, and the young Dora Bryan. In 1948 he contracted to write three scripts for Sidney Box: *The Beach of Falesá, Me and My Bike*, and *Rebecca's Daughters*. None reached the screen during Thomas's lifetime. In 1949 he began scripting *Vanity Fair*, but this came to nothing. When, in 1944, Thomas scripted *The Doctor and the Devils* for Gryphon, he was paid £365. For the three abortive scripts of 1948 he earned £2,000. Such figures provide a sharp perspective on his continuing and constant appeals for money, though there is little doubt that he never seemed to have any and that his family was invariably penniless. This was so despite the fact that he still allowed nothing for future tax demands. The subtext of Thomas's life is fecklessness.

He loved working in films, both the work itself, at which he could be very good, and the sociability that went with it. There is no doubt that Thomas found working in film a fascinating activity. As has been noted,[13] he wrote more for films than for any other literary medium. If to his filmscripts is added his writing for radio, his output of poetry and creative prose is dwarfed. In the postwar period it is more accurate to describe Thomas as a scriptwriter and public performer who occasionally wrote other things.

In December 1945 *Poetry* awarded him its Levinson Poetry Prize. It was worth $100 and came as Thomas continued to try for an American visit. This last, for the penniless poet, required some kind of sponsorship. Despite his efforts, nothing turned up.

Meanwhile, there was the radio. The decade of the 1940s was its great age in which the written script and spoken voice dominated. This was to be the case until 1953, when the televising of the queen's coronation began radio's steep decline. From 1945 onwards Thomas's career as a broadcaster flourished, particularly so when the "highbrow" Third Programme began in 1946. Thomas gave readings, took part in discussions, wrote scripts, occasionally chaired programs, and acted in dramas and documentaries. From 1946 until his death, Thomas made an average of twenty broadcasts a year. His peak was fifty-three in 1946, falling to twenty-eight in 1947 when he was in Italy for four months, twenty-eight in 1948, nine in 1949, seven in 1950, when he spent three months in the United States, ten in 1951, only four in 1952 (four months in the United

States), and then seventeen in 1953, despite two and a half months in the United States and his death in November. In his best year Thomas earned almost £600, once again a sizable sum for its time.

"As a broadcast verse speaker, he was outstanding," wrote John Arlott, who produced many programs to which Thomas contributed. Arlott linked Thomas's success as a reader to the nature of his poetry, which he regarded as being in the oral tradition. He left an attractive and affectionate picture of Thomas in the BBC studio:

He would sit through rehearsals smoking endlessly: he took production like a professional actor and, when he stepped up to the microphone to read, made a happily extravagant figure. Round, with the roundness of a Tintoretto urchin-cherub, and in a large, loose tweed jacket, he would stand, feet apart and head thrown back, a dead cigarette frequently adhering wispily to his lower lip, curls a little tousled and eyes half-closed, barely reading the poetry by eye, but rather understanding his way through it.[14]

On 7 February Dent published *Deaths and Entrances*. Apart from two poems, the volume collected work from the period following *The Map of Love* (1939). The exceptions were "On the Marriage of a Virgin" and "The hunchback in the park," revised versions of poems in the notebooks of 1932 and 1933. Thus Thomas, now thirty-two and well into the last decade of his life, continued to make use of teenage inspiration. The quality of the revised poems is not an issue, but their presence in this volume is a telling comment on the decline of his lyric gift. *Deaths and Entrances* is notable for the group of poems about the London blitz that is Thomas's unique contribution to the literature of war, poems inspired by his disturbed marriage and Llewelyn's birth, and "Lie still, sleep becalmed," the moving poem that, in part, may well be addressed to his father. The volume also includes his two famous rhapsodies about childhood, "Poem in October" and "Fern Hill."

The whole volume is powerful, troubled, uneasy, and probably Thomas's finest achievement. Certainly it is his least solipsistic volume, dominated as it is by the war. Dent printed 3,000 copies, then reprinted another 3,000 a month later. Its success revived interest in his earlier books. Apart from Geoffrey Grigson, who made fierce attacks on Thomas's coherence and surprising ones on his "formal awkwardness,"[15] *Deaths and Entrances* was acclaimed. Reviewers stressed Thomas's greatness, maturity, and outstanding achievement as a poet. His early champion, Edith Sitwell, praised the volume in *Our Time*.[16] Thomas wrote a letter of thanks that does not quite escape ingratiation and that ended with flattery and the perhaps inevitable reference to being "miserably poor."[17] She still regarded him as one of the greatest of poets and, once again, began to take an interest in his career. Thomas visited her, sometimes with Caitlin, and attended her celebrity luncheons. With Edith Sitwell he was always perfectly behaved, probably because he valued her patronage and believed—again in vain—that she could further his American ambitions.

George Tremlett is one who has written perceptively and convincingly of the changes to Thomas's life during the postwar period, the combination of high status as a poet, following *Deaths and Entrances*, and fame as a voice on the radio. He was regarded differently: he received new and great respect, accompanied by new and greater expectations. Tremlett suggested that this new status can be best understood by regarding Thomas as a precursor of the modern pop star, the prisoner of his public reputation. To an extent the comparison is persuasive. Certainly, Thomas had become famous, and, like many a pop star, he did not handle fame very well.[18]

He continued to drink heavily. In late 1945 he complained to Oscar Williams of being "at war with the lining of my stomach."[19] Three months later he was in St. Stephen's Hospital in London, apparently suffering from alcoholic gastritis. Thomas was undeterred, for this was the time when he had become even more "famous among the bars,"[20] holding court in a variety of London pubs, at once brilliant raconteur, mimic, parodist, and drunk. Here was the lovable Dylan, for whose egotistic yet marvellously entertaining company his friends would forgive him much. But here also was egocentricity as self-centered callousness, as two anecdotes reveal. The poet Dannie Abse, then the young admirer, tried to approach Thomas in a pub only to be brushed off in some confusion by Thomas falsely denying knowledge of a mutual Swansea acquaintance. The second, also in a bar, was much nastier and involved

telling an anecdote about a visit to the barber, and being interrupted by one of his audience who had just been called to the telephone. Lamentably, said the man, his wife had just had a stillborn child, the third they had lost. Thomas said, "Well, lamentably, you're a stillborn little couple, aren't you?" and went on with his monologue.[21]

Having left New Quay, Thomas and his family stumbled along in debt, existing almost wholly on the charitable kindness of friends. His earnings were more than adequate, but he kept knowledge of this from Caitlin and spent almost all of what he earned on himself. At this point Margaret Taylor reentered Thomas's life. Her patronage was to sustain the family until Thomas's death. A. J. P. Taylor was now a fellow of Magdalen College, Oxford, and living at Holywell Ford in a house in the college grounds. The Thomases were there for Christmas 1945 and part of January. In March 1946 they moved into a one-room summerhouse in the Taylors' garden close to the river Cherwell. It was very small: "It is, I think, a converted telephone kiosk,"[22] Thomas wrote. It was damp, draughty, and squalid, with no mains services. There, in the midst of utter chaos, they lived on Caitlin's interminable stews. Aeronwy was only three; she was bathed and slept in the Taylors' house. Thomas, it seems, had the use of a room in Magdalen in which to work; Margaret Taylor later provided a caravan.

Margaret Taylor regarded Thomas as a genius. She found him sexually attractive and had her own private means and the urge to patronize. She also wrote poetry with dreadful prolificity. Thomas encouraged her, wrote long critiques, and asked to see more. Privately, he thought little of her work and showed even less gratitude for her substantial material help. Once, when desperately hard up, he was heard to say, "I'll have to see if I can squeeze Maggie's left breast and get some money."[23] He was thirty-one, she was forty; her closeness to Thomas plus her tendency to organize their lives frequently enraged Caitlin. A. J. P. Taylor could not stand Thomas. His wife's friendship was one reason why Taylor's marriage foundered.

Neither the room in elegant Magdalen nor the caravan enabled Thomas to write more poems. This worried him: "I want very very much to write again," he told Edith Sitwell.[24] He complained to Vernon Watkins, among others, about working conditions. On a visit to Thomas's parents at Blaen Cwm he wrote revealingly:

I'm here for a week or so, and, in this tremendous quietness, feel lost, worried about the future, uncertain even of now. In London, it doesn't seem to matter, one lives from day to day. But here, the future's endless and my position in it unpleasant and precarious. Do write and tell me if there are any hopes of our ever selling our pictures old or new? I've reached a dead spell in my hack freelancing, am broke, and depressed.[25]

A desire to write poetry may be in the subtext; a concern for lucrative hackwork dominates. His work for radio continued, and after *Deaths and Entrances* his fame increased. He read at the Wigmore Hall. In August 1946 *Picture Post*, then at the height of its fame, commissioned him to write a piece on "Puck Fair" in County Kerry, but it made the mistake of advancing Thomas money for the visit. This trip was made with Caitlin and their friends Bill and Helen McAlpine. Freed from Cherwell squalor, they cut loose. "We ate ourselves daft", Thomas told Watkins.[26] They also drank themselves stupid. Caitlin recalled that Thomas and Bill McAlpine tried to spend the entire four days of the fair standing at a bar drinking Guinness. They lasted two days and nights before collapsing and spent longer in bed recovering. *Picture Post* never received the article.

By late summer the Thomases were back in their Oxford summerhouse, where they were to stay, much to A. J. P. Taylor's chagrin, until April 1947. In November 1946 James Laughlin's New Directions published *Selected Writings of Dylan Thomas*, which included the poems and stories on Thomas's list plus many others. The volume included a reproduction of Augustus John's idealized portrait and an introduction by the American academic John L. Sweeney. This was the most substantial collection of Thomas's work yet published and a major consolidation of his American reputation.

In January 1947 Thomas wrote a long letter to his parents as a rather belated New Year's greeting. He inquired solicitously about them and other members of the family, described a festive Christmas larded with references to dining out with Oxford dons that, one guesses, were included to please D. J., referred to future plans and possibilities, and enclosed a review of *Selected Writings*. It had

had a good reception. There were hopes of moving to a proper home either in a cottage belonging to Magdalen or in a house in Richmond owned by Helen McAlpine. There was news of the children: Llewelyn was delicate but Margaret Taylor had promised to help. The letter—all of which was no doubt specially written for anxious and aging parents—describes a bustling, busy, fascinating, and successful life. Yet the darker element is not wholly hidden: he was not managing any serious writing. The letter imposes on Thomas's life the conventional, middle-class framework—family, work, plans, visits, success—that here, even allowing for what his parents wanted to hear, he seemed desperately to want.[27] But this was the bass note; elsewhere there were stranger tunes.

He made frequent visits to London, usually with expenses paid, to work for the BBC and to further his scriptwriting career with Gainsborough Films. He complained constantly about money; in Oxford the family lived in damp squalor sustained by Margaret Taylor's handouts. Yet, as has been noted, his earnings were substantial. He dressed well to go to London, became a member of the National Liberal Club early in 1947, made long journeys by taxi, ate out at Wheeler's and the Café Royal, and drank much with cronies in noisy pubs. Even in Oxford, with Alan Taylor at home minding the children, the Thomases, often with Margaret Taylor paying for the drinks, pub-crawled and drank themselves silly. He often ended up, as he put it, as "a piece of cold lamb with vomit sauce."[28] To echo Tremlett's shrewd comment, he was on an ego trip, playing the part of the successful writer and broadcaster.

He complained so much to so many that he was desperately poor that Edith Sitwell, believing that the family needed a period in a cheaper country, and appalled at his desire to go to expensive and corrupting America, exerted influence on the Society of Authors. It awarded Thomas a travelling scholarship of £150 that comprised the whole of its scholarship money for 1947. It recommended Italy, which, during the worst British winter of the century, must have appealed greatly.

During that winter, in February 1947, Thomas returned to snowy Swansea to research "Return Journey." This was broadcast in June 1947, repeated on numerous occasions, and eventually filmed. It has remained one of his finest and most popular pieces. "Return Journey" is a moving exploration of himself when young that discovers a teenager mad about literature and with power over words who closely resembles the likeable young man who stood on Pamela Hansford Johnson's doorstep. It was written—with what Thomas must surely have seen as stabbing irony—by a fat, dishonest, and feckless sponger who could not resist a drink, yet who almost always kept his friends, was still to write a few superb poems, and could still have his moments of impressive kindness. He wrote a warmly appreciative letter to Emlyn Davies, who illustrated Thomas's poems and who, remarkably, had moved into 5 Cwmdonkin Drive when the Thomases left in 1937. To a Harry Klopper who sent poems, he wrote at length, not liking the poems much but in as kind a manner as possible, using, as Ferris pointed out,[29] a few of the same phrases he used when responding to Margaret Taylor's poems.

The Thomases went to Italy in April 1947, taking both children, Caitlin's sister Brigit, and Brigit's small son. They went by train, which took three days and much chasing of lost luggage. At first they stayed at San Michele di Pagana, near Rapallo, on the Italian Riviera, in a small expensive hotel that they could not really afford. Thomas worried about money, for the £150 scholarship had been substantially reduced by his bank overdraft. He hoped in vain to work for the British Council. From San Michele they visited Rome, where, apart from a tour of the Vatican and the Sistine Chapel, they mainly wandered about. They took a bus trip to Florence and stayed near the cathedral. At intervals Thomas wrote reassuring, determinedly humorous letters to his parents and patrons. He told the former, in what is a rare instance of the adult Thomas indulging in demanding reading, that he had been reading *Romola* and so could find his way about the old city. Perhaps familiarity reassured him, for during their visit they rented a small villa in Scandicci, five miles outside the city, up in the hills.

They moved in on 12 May. Thomas told his parents, "Our garden is full of roses. Nightingales sing all night long. Lizards scuttled out of the walls in the sun. It is very lovely."[30] That July he wrote very differently to a friend:

I am awfully sick of it here . . . drinking chianti in our marble shanty, sick of vini and contadini and bambini, and sicker still when I go, bumpy with mosquito bites, to Florence itself, which is a gruelling museum. . . . I can write only early in the morning, when I don't get up, and in the evening, when I go out.[31]

This strangely philistine man, whose only education was early reading and who exerted himself intellectually only when writing, paid dearly for his lack of proper schooling. He came to hate Florence not only because of the summer heat—though he constantly complained about it—and the language (he learned no Italian), but because he had no interest in art or architecture or in the cultural conversation of the Florentine intellectuals who met him in Florence or visited the villa at Scandicci. When they talked, he sometimes fell asleep. Doubtless he missed his cronies and sessions in the pub. Lacking such escape, he preferred to listen to the radio from London, particularly to the cricket commentaries of his friend John Arlott. Thomas's literary achievement depends a great deal on reflecting his provincial and suburban sensibility. There is a strange dichotomy and an equally strange relationship between the narrowness of the man and the intellectual range of his poetry.

While in Italy he wrote one poem, about his daughter, which he entitled "In Country Sleep." Most of it was written in a small farmhouse near the villa, which, on hot afternoons, was the coolest place he could find. The poem marks a return to his earlier, more "difficult" manner, significant in that it may well indicate his struggles to put together a coherent poem. Possibly it is unfinished, or abandoned, given that Thomas made a prose synopsis of a further section that never got written. Some years later he told an American student that the poem was started "in cold blood,"[32] which may have meant that he felt he simply *had* to write something, given the expectations of friends, sponsors, and probably the Society of Authors.

Caitlin loved everything about Italy: the heat, the villa, the cook who came with the building, the frankly appraising attitude of Italian men. She learned enough Italian to get by. Possibly she had affairs while in Florence, and this may have been part of Thomas's unhappiness. Certainly they quarrelled. When they were apart, Thomas wrote abject letters stressing his continuing love.

They spent their last two weeks on Elba, a place recommended by a translator they met in Florence. Thomas liked it much more than Florence, though he continued to complain, humorously and at length, about the heat, longing, he wrote, for "the cyclonic Siberian frigidity of a Turkish bath!"[33] Rio Marino, where they stayed, was a working-class town of iron-ore miners and fishermen, thus freeing Thomas from tourists and intellectuals. Caitlin bathed a lot and took a secret lover.[34] Dylan occasionally sat in the shallows reading the *New States-man*.

They returned to a small cottage, inaptly named the Manor House, that Margaret Taylor had bought and furnished for them. It was in South Leigh, a small "cowpad village"[35] west of Oxford. The caravan was brought from Oxford and set up in the garden for Thomas to work in. The cottage was another squalid dwelling: no electricity, a coal fire the only means of heating water, an outside lavatory. Caitlin struggled with coal and heavy kettles. She cooked more long-lasting stews. Thomas did nothing about the house except expect to be waited on. He was not there much but was usually in London broadcasting or working for Gainsborough Films. In the short term the latter boomed, for, to save foreign currency, the government imposed a quota on foreign films, thus benefitting British studios. When the quota was removed after 1948, the contraction of the British film industry was one reason why Thomas's film career ended.

Until it did, he was well paid. In the tax year 1947–48 he earned over £2,400, or about £41,000 in its modern equivalent. At Higham's suggestion he took on an accountant to try to order his increasing tax liabilities. Back at South Leigh Caitlin and the children, and Thomas when home, continued to live like the muddy poor. Cordelia Locke, who lived in the village and was friendly with Caitlin, thought that she had a terrible time. It was a quiet place, which must sorely have taxed Caitlin's patience. Sometimes she and Thomas rode bicycles; they became local characters. Inevitably they were regulars at the village pub, though they were rarely seen drunk. Thomas sometimes went to Witney market. When he introduced "Country Magazine," a touring radio program featuring local people, he did so from the Fleece Inn in Witney.

Thomas continued his expensive and feckless lifestyle. Even as he frittered away his earnings, he worried about money. Ferris has well observed that "in the very act of spending the money like a bohemian, he was worrying like a family man with a mortgage."[36] But he did nothing to correct his spending; he simply took on further expensive commitments, such as doctors' bills for Llewelyn (the Thomases used private medicine even after the free National Health Service began in July 1948) and the high cost of private education. Llewelyn was sent to Magdalen College School.

The marriage continued to deteriorate: more violence crept in, a harsher edge, less tolerance. To judge from Thomas's letters to Caitlin, he was, as yet, anxious to keep the relationship going. Hardly any letters to him have survived; he may simply have thrown them away or lost them.[37] His side of the correspondence seems frightened and insincere. Philip Larkin described Thomas's letters as "all snivelling and grovelling and adoring and so very impersonal."[38] This is perceptive, for the letters, as will be seen, certainly reflect the fact that Thomas was hardly involved—and little concerned—with day-to-day family life. He rarely showed his feelings for either his children or his wife. When the former became demanding, he kept out of the way. All that was Caitlin's world, where she performed chaotically, wildly, and heroically. Lacking the ballast of mutual familial involvement, the marriage placed unremitting stress on the central personal relationship. Because both Dylan and Caitlin were, respectively, fundamentally amoral and immoral, because Dylan was self-indulgently dishonest and irresponsible, because Caitlin's wild streak meant that she could not provide the controlling center he so desperately needed, and because both of them were so often drunkenly out of control, that unremitting stress generated tension so unbearable at times that it broke out into dreadful violence.

Cordelia Locke corroborated this in recalling how destructive they were: "There was this strange battle going on between them all the time—a battle resolved only at night when at last they were alone & face to face."[39] They destroyed themselves and they often destroyed those around them. Despite this, she valued their company, their zestful liveliness: "Just to be with them was like having a double whisky."[40] Caitlin, she considered, "brought a gayety [*sic*] and perfection to her domestic life that I've never seen before or since." As for Thomas:

To me Dylan was a daft kind of saint, hag-ridden at times by pity and compassion for the grief of human beings. He drank, made love, spewed up words of great beauty and great bitterness in an attempt to come to terms with his desperate feelings.[41]

These are words that echo those of Bert Trick and others who detected and pitied Thomas's open emotional wounds.

In 1948 his mother, then sixty-five, broke her leg at Blaen Cwm and had to be hospitalized in Carmarthen. Nancy, long divorced from Haydn Taylor and living in Devon with her second husband, came back to help out temporarily. She had met that second husband, Gordon Summersby, while she was a Field Army nurse during the war and had married him in India. They were planning to go back. She had to return to Devon, so she was unable to supervise Mrs. Thomas's convalescence. D. J. could not help much: he was now over seventy, aging rapidly and with failing eyesight. Thomas moved them into a rented cottage in South Leigh and then into the Manor House. Nancy sent money, but the huge extra burden—two aged and infirm parents-in-law, two young children, little help from her husband, a poky cottage without decent facilities—was Caitlin's.

She later claimed that she had not been consulted. Matters were not improved either by that or by the fact that Thomas's parents were not passive guests. They were appalled by Manor House life; their remonstrations were not well received. A furious and harassed Caitlin, with the children, went to stay with her mother at Blashford. Margaret Taylor, in a move that finally broke up her marriage, moved in to look after Thomas's aged parents and Thomas himself, when he was there. The man of the house busied himself with broadcasts and scriptwriting and continued to fritter away his substantial earnings. He spent with desperate hedonism and continued to worry, plagued, as he recognized, by "my still only half squashed and forgotten bourgeois petty values."[42] He wrote no poems.

In March 1949 he was invited to Prague as part of a delegation of writers to a conference organized by the Czechoslovakian Writers' Union. It was organized by the newly empowered Communist party, strange company for Thomas, despite his long-held and vaguely defined left-wing sympathies. He drank a lot but was not the gross drunkard. He even seemed to enjoy meeting Czech writers. Prague, he told Caitlin, was very beautiful. He also told her that he was cold and lonely, but his reactions to foreign places and people were so much more favorable than they had been in Italy that they have to be regarded as indicative of his relief at being away from the tensions of South Leigh. Certainly Thomas's provinciality was less in evidence.

Out of his constant worry came explanations of his inability to write poetry: South Leigh was too near London and the distractions that included not only cronies in pubs but also his money-making activities. He hankered after a return to Wales, preferably to Laugharne, where he and Caitlin had been happy and he had been productive. To add to general concerns, Caitlin was pregnant again. Thomas became desperate to move. He persuaded the still-infatuated Margaret Taylor to look for a house for them in South Wales.

Without Margaret Taylor it is hard to see how the Thomases would have survived. But her help was not altruistic. She wanted an affair with Thomas. Caitlin always believed, possibly incorrectly, that she never succeeded. With her marriage over, Margaret Taylor had hopes—quickly dispelled when Caitlin discovered them—of being part of a threesome in Wales. But Caitlin did not oppose the move: one of her most admirable traits, as has been noted, was her constant belief in Thomas's genius as a poet. Her husband's rewarding hackwork was still not helping at home; she continued to believe that it was a corrupting distraction and that returning to Wales would return him to poetry. So they and Margaret hunted for a home. They rejected the Old Rectory at Rhossili as being too far from a pub, then considered Gosport House, on the western edge of

Laugharne, and even leasing Castle House, Richard Hughes's former home. Eventually they found the Boat House, for which Margaret Taylor paid £3,000, plus extra for repairs. She was to charge the Thomases rent, though at Manor House that arrangement had been honored mainly in the breach.

In May 1939 the Thomases moved to the Boat House, Thomas's most famous home. The house is a three-story cottage built in the early nineteenth century. It is tucked under a cliff a little way from central Laugharne and on the very edge of the estuary of the river Tâf, with its sea birds and herons. Across the water are the green slopes of the Llansteffan peninsular; to the west is Sir John's Hill, named after Sir John Perrott, to whom Queen Elizabeth I gave Laugharne Castle. When the tide is in and the sun shines—or even when it doesn't shine—it is a beautiful and tranquil place.

The house had six small rooms and a kitchen; a balcony jutted out over the water. At first they used a well; then Margaret Taylor paid for mains water and electricity. It was not luxury—damp was a constant problem—but it was better than they had had. On the path above the house was what became the equally famous work shed, once a garage, now equipped with a stove, which Thomas used as a study. He installed his parents in part of a Georgian house called the Pelican in Laugharne's main street, and suddenly life took a turn for the better. "I think those few months," wrote Caitlin, "through 1949 and early 1950, were the last period of happiness or near-happiness that we had together."[43] Caitlin was six months pregnant but exerted herself to make the house warm and comfortable. Thomas settled back into a familiar routine: pottering in the morning, which included reading, perhaps the odd letter, and, almost every day, a visit to his parents. He did the crossword with his father. At midday he would drink beer in Brown's, then return to the work shed to write or think or sleep, drowsy with beer on warm summer afternoons. Each late afternoon he returned to the Boat House for a bath, during which he would consume dolly mixtures or pickled onions. Then he would eat a meal and return to the pub, sometimes with Caitlin.

For once he kept his writing for radio more in its place and began, slowly, to write poems again. "Over Sir John's Hill" was the first, the only one he completed during 1949. That and "Do not go gentle into that good night" rank among his finest. There were only four more in four years. This final release of lyrical energy completes a pattern: each release is less prolific than its predecessor. There is no doubt that he was de facto running down as a poet. Whether this was because drink, marital tension, intellectual laziness, and general hedonism had so sapped his creative determination that he could only cope with such less demanding forms of writing as letters, broadcasts, and *Under Milk Wood*, or whether he turned to those forms and to hedonistic drinking because he knew his poetic gift was in decline, is difficult to decide. Charity suggests the latter, realism the former.

Compared to South Leigh, Laugharne was a very long way from London, but Thomas still made regular visits, mainly linked to his BBC work and the last few filmscripting projects. He still made no attempt to curb extravagance. In March 1949, on John Davenport's instigation, he left the National Liberal Club, where, since 1947, he had been a most unlikely member, and joined the Savage Club. He found the latter more congenial; National Liberal members tended to frown when he entertained noisy guests after an evening pub crawling. Following his American visits, the Savage became a convenient address for correspondence, usually from women, that he wished to keep from Caitlin. But with a family to support, London clubs were an expensive self-indulgence.

Early in May Thomas received a letter from John Malcolm Brinnin, then a little-known poet and academic who had been appointed director of the Poetry Center at New York's Young Men's and Young Women's Hebrew Association. Suddenly, after years of Thomas's unsuccessful hinting and angling, America beckoned. Brinnin offered Thomas $500 for a reading at the Poetry Center. He also offered to arrange other readings. Thomas took some weeks to reply, which might suggest nervousness or Caitlin's hostility. His letter is very businesslike, as if Thomas, sensing an approaching jackpot, had considered matters with care. He suggested a visit of about three months early in 1950 and raised the questions of travelling expenses and other possible sources of income.

During 1949 he argued with the BBC over work, refusing a contract to script *Peer Gynt* from a prepared translation. He had asked, not unreasonably, given the size of the task, for more money and time. He began his last filmscripting project for Gainsborough Films in July, a treatment of *Vanity Fair* meant to be a vehicle for the British film star Margaret Lockwood. Nothing came of it, and Gainsborough had no more work to offer. At about the same time his relations with the BBC deteriorated. He failed to adapt *Peer Gynt* and quarrelled further about conditions; he failed to complete an adaptation of William Wycherley's *The Plain Dealer*. His income was now in decline. Though when he was in Laugharne his work-shed sessions continued, there was an increasing sense of general disorganization.

In July Caitlin was rushed into Carmarthen Hospital. Colm Garan Hart Thomas was born on 24 July 1949. He was Thomas's favorite child, mainly, it seems, because he was an undemanding baby. His arrival increased the financial pressure. John Davenport, once wealthy but now struggling, wrote asking for a ten-pound loan. Thomas made excuses but, only a few months later, tried his own begging letter on his friend:

They've stopped sending coal, & will, any moment, stop sending milk: essential things in a baby-packed, freezing house. I'm summonsed for rates. No more meat. I cannot write a cheque, of course, so that we are—for the first time in years—literally without one shilling.[44]

Once again Margaret Taylor helped them out. Further relief came in August when Marguerite Caetani, owner and editor of *Botteghe Oscure*, bought "Over Sir John's Hill." David Higham, who with Thomas's accountant had begun ordering Thomas's finances, began to send him ten pounds per week out of money left after demands for income tax. Higham also drew up a business plan for Thomas. It set deadlines for his uncompleted BBC work and estimated that the American tour would enable him to build up sufficient capital to buy time to complete, at long last, *Adventures in the Skin Trade* and the radio play that became *Under Milk Wood*.

Throughout 1949 Thomas's poetry writing became a painfully slow activity. After "Over Sir John's Hill" he began "In the White Giant's Thigh" and took a year to complete it. "Poem on his Birthday," which he began in October 1949, was not finished until July 1951. "Do not go gentle into that good night," for some his masterpiece, may have had its origins in 1945, when D. J.'s health had given much cause for concern. Thomas was not able to finish it until mid-1951.

Thus at the start of 1950 he was sorely troubled. Three matters would have been much on his mind. The first would have been his marriage. During Dylan's often indeterminate absences in London Caitlin, stranded in Laugharne, took lovers. Quarrels, some violence, and a mutual distrust were the inevitable consequences. The second was his loss of poetic prolificity. The third was his visit to America, which, he probably thought, would solve all his problems.

NOTES

1. Dylan Thomas, *Letters to Vernon Watkins*, ed. Vernon Watkins (London: Dent and Faber & Faber, 1957), 20.

2. *CL*, 518. Letter to Vernon Watkins, 26 August 1944.

3. *CL*, 529–30. Letter to Donald Taylor, dated 28 October 1944.

4. *CL*, 541. Letter to James Laughlin, dated 10 February 1945. For Thomas's list, sent with a later letter, see *CL*, 544.

5. See James A. Davies, "Dylan Thomas in Oxford: An Unpublished Poem," *Notes and Queries* n.s. 44 (1997): 360–61. In the text of the poem in this note, lines 22–23 should read:

> And never dare to smile, to show time's fag-stained mould,
> Comb, over the blitzed bits, my gravely tumbled hair[.]

6. "The Crumbs of One Man's Year," *CS*, 322.

7. *CL*, 548. Letter to Vernon Watkins, dated 28 March 1945.

8. *CL*, 555. Letter to Caitlin Thomas, [24 June 1945].

9. *CL*, 537. Letter to Oscar Williams, dated 31 December 1944.

10. *CL*, 550. Letter to Oscar Williams, dated 28 March 1945.

11. *CL*, 557. Letter to Oscar Williams, 30 July 1945.

12. *CL*, 569. Letter to A. J. Hoppé, 18 September 1945.

13. By Constantine FitzGibbon, *The Life of Dylan Thomas* (London: Dent, 1965), 62.

14. John Arlott, "Dylan Thomas and the Radio," *Adelphi*, First Quarter 1954: 121, 124.

15. Geoffrey Grigson, "How Much Me Now Your Acrobatics Amaze," in *Dylan*

Thomas: The Legend and the Poet, ed. E. W. Tedlock (London: William Heinemann, 1960), 161.

16. Edith Sitwell, review of *Deaths and Entrances*, by Dylan Thomas, *Our Time*, April 1946: 198–99.

17. *CL*, 583. Letter to Edith Sitwell, dated 31 March 1946.

18. George Tremlett, *Dylan Thomas: In the Mercy of His Means* (London: Constable, 1991), chap. 8.

19. *CL*, 576. Letter to Oscar Williams, dated 5 December 1945.

20. Quoted in Paul Ferris, *Dylan Thomas* (1977; Harmondsworth: Penguin Books, 1978), 220n. The phrase was Richard Burton's.

21. Quoted by Ferris, *Dylan Thomas*, 129. The remark was recorded by Richard Burton, who was present as part of Thomas's group.

22. *CL*, 587. Letter to Vernon Watkins, 27 April 1946.

23. Quoted in Paul Ferris, *Caitlin*: The Life of Caitlin Thomas (London: Hutchinson, 1993), 97.

24. *CL*, 583. Letter to Edith Sitwell, dated 31 March 1946.

25. *CL*, 600. Letter to Donald Taylor, 26 August 1946.

26. *CL*, 599. Letter to Vernon Watkins, dated 26 August 1946.

27. *CL*, 614–17. Letter to D. J. and Florence Thomas, 12 January 1947.

28. *CL*, 618. Letter to T. W. Earp, 1 March 1947.

29. *CL*, 592n.

30. *CL*, 629. Card to D. J. and Florence Thomas, postmarked 19 May 1947.

31. *CL*, 649. Letter to T. W. Earp, 11 July 1947.

32. Quoted in Ferris, *Dylan Thomas*, 227.

33. *CL*, 657. Letter to Margaret Taylor, 3 August 1947.

34. Caitlin Thomas with George Tremlett, *Caitlin: A Warring Absence* (London: Secker & Warburg, 1986), 102.

35. *CL*, 692. Letter to John Davenport, 17 November 1948.

36. Ferris, *Dylan Thomas*, 232.

37. See Ferris, *Caitlin*, 101. He reported that Thomas's mother "supposedly burnt" Caitlin's letters after his death.

38. Philip Larkin, *Selected Letters, 1940–1985*, ed. Anthony Thwaite (paperback ed., London: Faber & Faber, 1993), 758.

39. Cordelia Locke, letter to Bill Read, n.d., manuscript, Dylan Thomas Collection, HRHRC.

40. Ferris, *Dylan Thomas*, 229.

41. Cordelia Locke, letters to Bill Read, 31 October [1963], 8 November [1963], manuscript, Dylan Thomas Collection, HRHRC.

42. *CL*, 676. Letter to C. Gordon Glover, 25 May 1948.

43. Caitlin Thomas with Tremlett, *Caitlin: A Warring Absence*, 117.

44. *CL*, 714. Letter to John Davenport, 30 July 1949.

4

1950–1953

All his life Thomas admired Dickens. Caitlin recalled that at home, interminably, he often used to read aloud from the novels. Dickens was a strong influence on his prose. Though there were, of course, great differences, their lives were similar so far as the American experience was concerned: both saw visiting America as the desirable response to uneasy private lives and the lack of financial security, both gave themselves to a demanding public, and both were destroyed by the whole affair. Dickens's reading tour was large-scale, a matter of national interest; he approached it with a fierce commercialism and wise advisors. He ruined his health, and shortened his life, but made much money. Thomas commanded a narrower audience; he read to packed houses mainly on university campuses. In other crucial ways his tours were like his predecessor's, and not only because they precipitated his death. "I'll go to America," says the troubled young man in what is, arguably, Dickens's greatest comic novel. In 1950 Dylan Thomas was Martin Chuzzlewit redivivus.

In early 1950 his life seemed more chaotic than ever. The previous October he had failed to turn up to speak at the annual British Medical Association dinner in Swansea. He had been in London, had been involved in a drinking spree with friends, and then had been in a car accident on the return journey to Swansea; a drunken Thomas had then fallen asleep in a Bristol hotel. Not until January did he send the BMA secretary a long and carefully contrived excuse. Glyn Jones had called on him at Christmas and had been shocked at his ugly, bloated appearance. He seemed to be abandoning himself. Matters were not improved by broken ribs, the legacy of a fall or a fight, the regular exercises of the perpetual drunk.

Arrangements were proceeding for the American tour. Thomas left these to Brinnin and was very dilatory in answering letters. When he did so, he asked for money in advance to pay his airfare. He also wrote to Laughlin asking whether he could help to obtain reading engagements. Always he pleaded crushing poverty. Laughlin, however, wanted new poems. Thomas made excuses.

The trip was to make money, so it was decided that he would go alone, Caitlin remaining at Laugharne with the children. After receiving his air ticket he had to scramble for the visa for which he had neglected applying. He left Wales for London in February. Oddly, given his poverty, but typically, he had expensive dentistry, took part, unexpectedly, in a performance of the Picasso play *Desire Caught by the Tail* at the Rudolf Steiner Institute, and then flew to New York on 20 February. The flight, with landings in Dublin, Gander, and Boston, took seventeen hours. Thomas, hung over from his cronies' send-off, could not sleep or read. He sat in the lounge bar separate from the main cabin and reflected, semidrunkenly, on what lay ahead.

He may well have recalled that at first London had frightened him; he had responded with drunkenness, foolery, and determined anti-intellectualism. Perhaps he had always been frightened. Certainly his response was still much the same. But in London "there was always Paddington station and the train to Wales."[1] America had no such easy escape route. The provincial suburbanite, whose life had been drunk out of control, must have been desperately afraid as he sat in the empty bar of the drumming plane. So how to cope with what lay ahead? As one biographer has suggested, he "had to decide which Dylan of his wide repertoire he would show to the Americans. . . . [He] opted for the poet-performer and pub-clown . . . the talented shocker who could amuse."[2] In that choice, if choice it was, lay the beginning of the end.

He landed at Idlewild Airport before dawn on a freezing winter morning and was met by John Malcolm Brinnin. At first Brinnin seems to have irritated Thomas: the poet Harold Norse recalled that on his first full day in New York, Thomas asked, apropos his host, "How can I get rid of this bastard?"[3] But relations improved; Ferris considered that "Thomas seems genuinely to have liked him."[4] Brinnin was a Northeast U.S. intellectual, a former college lecturer, a poet, and a literary impresario with strong enthusiasms. He also had a puritan streak, and there is no doubt that he was appalled by some of Thomas's behavior. Even nonpuritans were horrified at times. But he stuck by him, helped him, and tried to mitigate the effects of his worst excesses.

Thomas's reputation as a wild man who liked a drink had gone before him. Initially, Brinnin made the mistake of indulging the latter part of it. Thus at Idlewild he immediately took Thomas to the airport bar for what he felt he would like: fortification against the cold by means of a liquid breakfast of scotch and soda. He then drove him into Manhattan. Given Thomas's reputation, all Brinnin's friends had declined to accommodate the visitor, so he took him to the Beekman Tower Hotel. Once in his room on a high floor, Thomas seemed overcome by the overwhelming view of Manhattan's towers, so they had another drink, and then, though it was still early, instead of leaving him to sleep, Brinnin took him off to the Irish bars on Third Avenue, believing that Thomas would find them congenial reminders of London.

So he did and was drawn back to them during his first days in New York, when he, as usual, drank too much, with predictable results. Confused lunches, obscene replies at academic receptions to questions about his work, and crude advances to women were par for the course for Thomas in his cups. At one reception he swung Katherine Anne Porter, then sixty years old, high above his head. His drunken behavior in the hotel included his familiar party piece of pretending to be a dog and then biting a guest. He was soon asked to leave and moved to Midston House on 38th Street. Whether he was unhinged by alcohol— the habitual beer drinker drank more spirits in his first three days in the city than, probably, in his life up to that point—lack of food, jet lag, general fatigue, fear, or anger that he was being received into academic, rather than popular, rumbustious America is difficult to gauge. What is certain is that he behaved dreadfully and seemed not to care. The only remark that seemed to affect him was made by Jane Lye, the wife of a former British acquaintance, who had last met Thomas ten years earlier. She said, "in a sinking voice: 'Oh, Dylan—the last time I saw you you were an *angel*.' . . . Dylan winced."[5]

Drunkenness apart, Brinnin thought Thomas to be in poor health, particularly subject to coughing fits. Yet on the evening of Thursday, 23 February 1950, at the Poetry Center's Kaufmann Auditorium, he coughed and retched offstage, then gave a poetry reading that held a packed hall, a thousand or so people, spellbound. He read poems by Yeats, Hardy, Lawrence, Auden, MacNeice, and Edith Sitwell, and then he read his own. He received a standing ovation. Two days later he repeated the triumph.

Off the platform he roared on. He stayed briefly at Brinnin's Westport home, where he again drank too much and behaved badly, then began the reading tour Brinnin had arranged. He described the travelling in a letter to Caitlin:

I have been driven for what seems like, and probably are, thousands of miles, along neoned, jerrybuilt, motel-ed, turbined, ice-cream-salooned, gigantically hoarded roads of the lower region of the damned, from town to town, college to college, university to university, hotel to hotel.[6]

In most places his behavior continued to be deplorable. Ivan Moffatt, once of Strand Films, met Thomas in Hollywood and thought him greatly changed: he was drinking more, and this, Moffatt felt, had made him rougher, almost wholly insensitive to the feelings of others. Throughout his visit he insulted academics, particularly those who tried to talk to him about his work; he urinated on carpets and in flowerpots; he stole from his hosts; he made crude and drunken advances to numerous women; he was invariably drunk and could be grossly obscene. In Hollywood he may or may not have been offensively suggestive about Shelley Winters's breasts; his drunken behavior certainly offended Charlie Chaplin. The persisting popular image of Thomas owes much to these first three months in America.

Yet evening after evening he read marvellously to packed houses, with an effect best summed up by the reaction from a student at the University of Michigan. Listening to Thomas read, he recalled, "was an experience I'll remember for the rest of my life. . . . Dylan Thomas made poetry come alive. Listening to his beautiful voice, I was touched in my heart by poetry, not in my head."[7] Further, Thomas's behavior off the platform was not always indefensible. In late March, after an exhausting seventeen performances in twenty-nine days, he found himself in Iowa City, with his next engagement thirteen days away. Suddenly freed from the demands of travel and performance, he drank some beer, entertained with stories, complained to his host that, present company and Robert Lowell (then teaching at Iowa State) excepted, he couldn't stand academics, and generally behaved normally. There were occasional problems if he drank spirits: he missed a dinner engagement and insulted a doctor's wife. By Thomas's standards this was almost exemplary behavior.

As always throughout his life, he made some friends. One was Ruth Witt-Diamant, who lectured at San Francisco State College and ran the city's Poetry Center. She insisted that he move from a hotel into her home. They remained friends until his death. The English Faculty at Berkeley took to him and voted that he be appointed to the Speech Department. Typically, Thomas did not help his cause by failing to turn up at a Berkeley party given in his honor, though he was not given the job because the dean, worried about Thomas's reputation, exercised his veto. He enjoyed meeting other writers: Henry Miller at Big Sur; Malcolm Lowry, whom he had known in London, in Vancouver; and Christopher Isherwood in California.

He had two and possibly three serious affairs. One was always denied by the woman. One was with a woman who is now dead. Of her Brinnin wrote that she was

a poet, a small somewhat boyish girl, shy and charming, a writer of high talent well known in *avant garde* circles. But this affair was short-lived, and Dylan seemed regretful when he spoke of it. . . . I had the feeling that he had neglected her not by intention but by default.[8]

The most serious was with "Sarah," now known to have been Pearl Kazin, the sister of Alfred Kazin, the famous literary critic. She was a magazine executive, a high-powered career woman whom Thomas probably met through his efforts to publish in American magazines: he sold a conflation of his 1945 broadcast "Memories of Christmas" and "Conversation about Christmas," the article he wrote for *Picture Post* in 1947, to *Harper's Bazaar*, which published it as "A Child's Christmas in Wales." Pearl Kazin was highly educated, expert on Thomas's work, attractive, and socially aware. As Brinnin commented, she was "precisely the sort of woman from whom one would expect Dylan only to flee."[9] Yet they had an intense affair when, having completed his readings, he spent almost two weeks in New York. He described this time, in a letter Caitlin never saw, as "one liquid, libidinous fortnight."[10] This affair was to have serious consequences for his marriage.

Though his letters to Caitlin made the most of hardships, there is no doubt that this first tour had more than its fair share, mainly due to Brinnin's inexperience.[11] Thomas was in poor health (though Brinnin had not known this); his schedule would have taxed the fittest of poets. It committed him to thirty-five performances in ninety-seven days, requiring 12,000 miles of travelling, excluding the 6,000 miles from Laugharne to New York and back. The travelling involved extremes of climate from freezing winter in New York to the warmth of southern California. There were inevitable delays, standbys, and reschedulings. Away from New York, almost all Thomas's appearances were at universities and colleges, so that in addition to official readings he was perforce involved in many faculty functions, unofficial performances, discussions with faculty and students, and general socializing. A Thomas often drained of nervous energy was then devoured by cocktail parties at which spirits—stronger in America than in Britain—were invariably served. He drank recklessly and so was often hung over at his next stop.

Ferris noted from income-tax returns that Thomas earned $7,680, about £2,800, from his first American visit, which lasted three months.[12] In present-day Britain this would be more than £20,000, high earnings. He paid no American tax. A few small amounts had been remitted to Caitlin; Brinnin hid a further £300 in dollars in a handbag she received as a present. Thomas put aside nothing for future tax demands. After day-to-day expenses—which could not have been large, given the amount of hospitality he received—and, presumably, Brinnin's commission, Thomas should have returned to Britain with the best part of £1,500. In the event he returned empty-handed, having once again frittered away every penny that reached him.

He sailed back on the *Queen Elizabeth*. It was 1 June 1950, three months and a week since he had sat in the deserted bar of the airplane to Idlewild, wondering what lay ahead of him. On the return journey he had even more time to reflect. In some ways he must have been pleased with his first visit: his readings had been acclaimed, he had made friends, he had commanded the respect of at least some academics, and he had been loved by at least two women. Perhaps he also wondered why he had so often made a fool of himself, why he had so often been dirty, disreputable, dishonest, and stupid, and why he had nothing, financially speaking, to show for it. He must have recognized that drink was destroying him. It is more doubtful whether he understood fully why he drank and behaved crazily. We see now that the state of his marriage played a part, as did his lack of intellectual confidence consequent upon the habitual mental laziness that was the demoralizing legacy of poor schooling, and the abiding sensitivity to the world that he often could not bear. There is no doubt that he was taken advantage of, that as his scandalous reputation went before him, some sought to egg him on to more excesses. There is no doubt that committing himself to a tour of intellectual places was not a wise move for a man who, outside his work, was the arch anti-intellectual. There is no doubt that a man who could not handle money should not have embarked on a tour awash with uncontrolled payouts. But when all is said and done, we must recall that a thirty-five-year-old adult of seemingly sound mind must be held responsible for his own actions.

On 18 June he wrote from the Boat House to Margaret Taylor. It is a careful piece of writing, designed to placate a patron to whom he had not written since leaving for America. The opening, describing his visit, is determined to provide a literary money's worth: "I was floored by my florid and stentorian spouting of verses . . . I was giddy agog from the slurred bibble babble, over cocktails bold enough to snap one's braces, of academic alcoholics anything but anonymous." Thomas was broke again, and much of the long letter waxed lyrical about, in Thomas's opinion, the high salaries and small responsibilities of American poets in residence. He wondered whether Margaret could arrange something similar for him in a British university. The letter ends, inevitably, with a list of his debts (which included Llewelyn's school fees), a reference to him writing articles for *Vogue*, and a sudden glimpse of his real feelings about the academia he vainly wished to enter: "I shall write again, & not all about Poets-in-Bloody-Residence and Work-Bloody-Shops."[13]

His articles for *Vogue* were never written. He thought of writing on his American experiences for the BBC, but nothing came of that until 1953. He struggled to complete "In The White Giant's Thigh," which he had begun the previous year, managing to do so only in late summer. He read it on the air on 25 September 1950; two months later Princess Caetani published it in *Botteghe Oscure*. So far as his literary career was concerned, it was business as usual, as if the American visit had never happened.

It was a different matter so far as his private life was concerned. While Thomas roared around America, Caitlin stayed in Laugharne with Aeronwy and the infant Colm. She was also, as Thomas put it in one of his letters with facile facetiousness, "wailed at by old ill Thomases,"[14] his aged parents at the Pelican. Thomas's bank had been instructed to send her £10 a week during his absence; as has been noted, he sent a few small sums. Caitlin had not reacted well to being left for three months. She had been unfaithful. She had also run up a bill for £150 for groceries and alcohol. Financially profligate, Thomas was very angry. There was mutual suspicion and much alcohol-induced violence; it was said that on one occasion Thomas kicked her in the eye.

He continued to visit London, where Pearl Kazin wrote to him at the Savage Club. When Caitlin found her letters, Thomas laughed them off as those from an overexcited fan. But Caitlin was upset and wrote to Pearl, warning her off. Caitlin Thomas, who had once dreamed of artistic or neoartistic fulfillment, mainly linked to dance, now felt that her life had been wasted. She felt increasingly that she was not even sacrificing herself for what she called his "special work" but for his "public money-making work,"[15] and few of the benefits of the latter had come her way. She remained convinced of the value of what she still regarded as Thomas's only worthwhile vocation: during one violent quarrel she tore up the manuscript of "In the White Giant's Thigh" and threw the pieces out of the Boat House window. Later that night she crept out on to the mudflats and retrieved what she could. But she had become embittered.

Pearl Kazin came to London in September 1950. She and Thomas spent some days together visiting pubs, meeting friends, and staying in Brighton, with little pretence at concealment. Margaret Taylor learned of the affair, went immediately to Laugharne, and told Caitlin. It was almost as if Thomas wished to precipitate a crisis. He was in a quandary: he told Brinnin, who was in London, that he was in love with both and didn't know what to do. Pearl departed for France, and Thomas made his decision by not going with her. He returned to Laugharne and Caitlin's violent acrimony.

She was humiliated and suicidal. Though both had been unfaithful, Caitlin recognized, as had Thomas, that the relationship with Pearl Kazin was sufficiently serious to shatter what was left of their marriage. She felt some guilt about her husband's predicament because, as Ferris noted, "the poetry was waning, and Caitlin knew that 'the tyranny of the family' had something to do with it."[16] Thomas had needed a stable center, someone to control his wild excesses. In this she had failed him. Presumably high-powered, assured, cultured Pearl was what he needed. So why did he reject her? Perhaps he felt irretrievable, unable to stop drinking and knowing that his lyric gift was fading. Perhaps he was afraid—of her, of radical change. When he let her go, we are vividly reminded of that other occasion, long ago in another life, when he drifted away from organized, determined, ambitious, cultured Pamela. Why did he return to Caitlin? The easy answers are that he had nowhere else to go, was still in love with Caitlin, and was a moral coward. We might also feel that he was strangely drawn to the chaos she helped provide. Thomas's fatherly feelings were such that most would consider it unlikely that his children played a major part in drawing him back.

Thomas spent eighteen tempestuous months with Caitlin before returning to America. Their drinking continued, the violence got worse, and financial problems once again burgeoned. He turned once more to the Royal Literary Fund. Harold Nicolson agreed to write on his behalf to the fund secretary. He did so in a way that suggests that Thomas's friends and acquaintances saw him as hurtling downhill:

I should of course have to disclose to the Committee that he is a very heavy drinker. . . . I gather that his wife is almost equally unreliable. On the other hand, he is one of our best poets, and if the Literary Fund exists for anything, it exists to enable such people to write a few more poems before they go completely to pieces.[17]

The fund awarded him £300 but wisely sent most of it direct to Thomas's creditors. They included Magdalen College School, where Llewelyn still survived by the skin of his parents' financial teeth, and the Savage Club, that essential institution for the penniless, where Thomas owed £15.

In January 1951 Thomas escaped for a few days on his last filmscripting jaunt: the Green Park film company sent him to Iran, accompanied by the producer, Ralph Keene. For £250 plus expenses he was commissioned to write a documentary about the Anglo-Iranian Oil Company. He disliked being in Iran and said so loudly, clearly, and pathetically to Caitlin. The overstated anguish of the letter is perhaps a hangover from the affair with Pearl, to whom his remarks on "puking Abadan on . . . the foul blue boiling Persian buggering Gulf" are probably addressed.[18] Apparently there was no reply: "I haven't heard from her since she went away," he told Brinnin in April 1951.[19]

Though Caitlin had threatened to leave him, she was still at the Boat House when he returned, and there was a temporary reconciliation of sorts. He was hardly back in Laugharne when Iran nationalized foreign oil companies and the project was abandoned. Thomas's Persian material was recycled as a short broadcast, for he was still working regularly for the BBC. This provided his main source of income, which he sought to augment by writing a radio comedy series with Ted Kavanagh, the writer of "ITMA." Thomas was optimistic and even began to hope that such work would take him back to London. He intended, he told John Davenport, to keep the Boat House and hoped to take "half a house in Cheyne Walk," adding, "and I have just borrowed 5/-from Ivy Williams to run them both." The wherewithal would, he believed, be provided by "Mad Mags."[20] It all came to nothing.

This was a time of desperate unhappiness. "I am so deadly sick of it here," he told Brinnin.[21] Even Laugharne, to which he had returned so eagerly, was now the site of a "general hell of sickness, children, excruciating worry, the eternal yellow-grey drizzle outside and [Caitlin's] own slowly accumulated loathing for the place in which we live."[22] Caitlin was pregnant again; she later had an illicit and difficult abortion. This was paid for by a new person in Thomas's life, yet another wealthy female admirer. She was Marged Howard-Stepney, a twice-divorced and alcoholic Carmarthenshire heiress. Her tendency to monopolize Thomas made Caitlin furious and sometimes violent, but she was quite willing to benefit from his successful sponging.

Thomas had begun angling for a second visit to America, and during the summer of 1951 Brinnin, with his friend Bill Read, later one of Thomas's biographers, visited the Boat House. They experienced at first hand the state of the marriage: Caitlin contradicted statements by her husband, and an altercation followed that led to fighting and the breakup of the evening. The visitors left the following day, much shaken.

Perhaps surprisingly, amid all the violence and despair, during 1951 Thomas wrote three new poems. One was "Poem on his Birthday," a difficult poem straining after an optimistic conclusion in a manner reminiscent (given the differences of genre) of his scripts for feature films. Its final line, "As I sailed out to die," was to prove sadly prophetic. The second was "Lament," a savagely humorous and explicit poem about declining sexual powers that may have been an indirect reflection of his declining, drink-ravaged physical state amid the ruins of his marriage. Its "jaunty style, sprinkled with naughtiness," has been linked to the "consciously comic manner that Thomas was developing for *Under Milk Wood*."[23] The third, "Do not go gentle into that good night," is one of Thomas's masterpieces, his sadly fierce response to D. J.'s loss of vitality. As a literary bonus, Thomas also made some progress with his radio play, still entitled "The Town That Was Mad," which, of course, became *Under Milk Wood*. The BBC's Douglas Cleverdon, who was to be the first to produce the play on radio, hoped in vain to broadcast it during 1951. An index of waning powers is Thomas's worksheets, which show that he considered returning to *Adventures in the Skin Trade* (he never did) or even, stories from the *Portrait* period (he managed only one). But, comparatively speaking, 1951 was an annus mirabilis. It was his last.

Debts pressed more heavily. Thomas gave readings at small venues. He argued with Caitlin about going to America. She grew increasingly discontented with her lot in Laugharne. Margaret Taylor, recognizing at least the financial crisis, bought 54 Delancey Street in Camden Town. She believed that if the family returned to London, Thomas could increase his BBC earnings and so would not need to return to America. The Thomases kept the Boat House and moved to Camden Town in October, into, as Thomas put it, unhappily, "our new London house or horror on bus and nightlorry route and opposite railway bridge and shunting station. No herons here."[24] They were there for three months, during which time Thomas made five broadcasts. David Higham obtained a contract for him from the publishers Allen Wingate for a travel diary of his next American visit. The advance was £100; the diary was never written. Arrangements for the visit, however, continued to progress. Caitlin, previously hostile to going, now agreed to accompany him. On 20 January 1952, with Llewelyn away at boarding school, Aeronwy left with Margaret Taylor, and Colm with the Laugharne daily help, Dolly Long, they sailed to New York on the *Queen Mary*.

Like the first visit, the second was both a triumph and a disaster. During their four-month stay there were forty or so readings, a more manageable number and a more sensible itinerary: the whole of February, for example, was spent mainly in the Northeast. Thomas was now much more assured in his handling of the public performances, with some possible loss of spontaneity but a considerable reduction in nervous tension. A few days after their arrival, they moved into the Chelsea Hotel, which, despite the name, was an apartment block near Greenwich Village. This became their base. They drank in pubs in the "village," particularly in the White Horse Tavern in Hudson Street, which became Thomas's favorite. He felt at home in that part of New York where buildings were on a more human scale. Ferris made the shrewd point that this riverside area of New York, had similarities with prewar dockland Swansea.[25] Thomas was now well known and moved towards fame when, shortly after he arrived in New York, James Laughlin's New Directions published *In Country Sleep and Other Poems*. It contained six poems, all he had written since *Deaths and Entrances*. The growing reputation attracted those who grasped its possibilities. He was approached by Barbara Holdridge and Marianne Mantell and began recording his poems for their new company, Caedmon Records. He met Rollie McKenna, the photographer, who was a friend of Brinnin's. When they stayed at her Millbrook home, she took the celebrated series of photographs of Thomas—anguished, trapped—entwined in a vine. Chelsea Hotel, White Horse Tavern, recordings, photographs: the legend's props were being assembled.

This new status as a desirable literary property did not increase Thomas's confidence when he was in academic company or being interviewed in a serious way. He was still inclined to deflect questions rudely or facetiously. The main problem was Caitlin. Her presence ensured that all Thomas's earnings would be spent. She had accompanied her husband in a spirit of revenge for previous neglect and was determined to have her share of his income. At times she shopped and spent so extravagantly that Brinnin had to borrow money to keep them going. Despite this, she railed at Thomas's financial fecklessness. When the couple were in San Francisco, a final demand for Llewelyn's fees arrived from Magdalen College School. Thomas had failed to make the necessary arrangements for payment. Caitlin, having been told by him that all was in order, was understandably furious. He promised that he would ask David Higham to arrange payment. In May, with the couple still in America, Llewelyn was required to leave Magdalen School because no fees had been paid. Thomas had done nothing, caring little, it seemed, or being drunk too often to care much, that his young son was humiliated. Money was scraped together; Llewelyn was reinstated. To Caitlin this seemed the end: she told Thomas that she was leaving him and asked Brinnin to book a passage home. But once again the storm blew over.

Money was not the only problem. In public she was often bitterly vindictive towards her husband, ridiculing or contradicting him to such an infuriating extent that they came to blows. An interview with *Time* magazine was ruined by her constant interruptions. She was often contemptuous of the way he dressed, of his too-frequent inability to refuse drinks or invitations, and of the way he could allow himself to be set up, this last usually by journalists or hosts who encouraged him to drink foolishly to get a good story or scandalous incident. Thomas rarely failed to oblige, and this cannot always be explained in terms of him being already too drunk to refuse. We can only agree with Ferris that Thomas was developing a carelessness verging on self-loathing; he was, he told one audience, "a fat little fool."[26] For her husband's loss of self-esteem Caitlin, though at times provoked almost beyond endurance, was partly to blame.

At the end of May 1952 Dylan and Caitlin were back at the Boat House, still penniless, still quarrelling. Visitors to the Boat House found constant tension and dreadful scenes between husband and wife. Meanwhile, the Inland Revenue was still pursuing him relentlessly for tax owed on his now-considerable American earnings. National Insurance contributions had not been paid; £50 of back stamps were required to evade prosecution. He sought David Higham's help, then behaved shabbily by circumventing him—and so avoiding commission—when arranging work for the BBC. His two patrons, Margaret Taylor and Marged Howard-Stepney, still helped out, though, on Margaret Taylor's part, with increasing difficulty. He gave readings here and there, at small venues, that brought in a few pounds.

The first half of *Under Milk Wood*, entitled *Llareggub*, all he had completed, was published in *Botteghe Oscure* in May 1952. Douglas Cleverdon's efforts to induce Thomas to finish the play were only slowly successful. Before Thomas's second American visit Dent had decided to publish a *Collected Poems* to try to boost a reputation that in Britain was suffering from the lack of new poems. When Thomas returned from America, the proofs were waiting for him. Dent had asked for a preface, but Thomas failed to write one. He suggested a prologue in verse and struggled with it through 1952, constantly taking time off to give readings or to broadcast. Caitlin, piercingly shrewd, saw the latter activities as excuses to avoid writing poetry. But he did finish "Prologue," a strange affair with its sense of awful personal vulnerability, its difficult rhyme scheme,[27] and a second half that reads like self-parody, determinedly exhibitionist and seemingly optimistic.

This was his last completed poem. He dragged on with *Under Milk Wood*. He completed a short story, "The Followers," which was published in *World Review* in October 1952. The story is significant and disturbing, not so much for its quality—it is an attempt to return to the *Portrait* manner—as for its handling of place. In those *Portrait* stories set in prewar Swansea, though Thomas sometimes made up names of streets and pubs, the topography was always precise. "The Followers," also set in prewar Swansea, is topographically confused, possibly reflecting the impact of the wartime bombing. Thomas seemed increasingly unable to focus on previously clear points of reference.

Collected Poems, 1934–1952 was published on 10 November 1952 and was generally acclaimed. It won the William Foyle Poetry Prize for 1952 and the Etna-Taormina International Prize in Poetry for 1953. It also sold well, 30,000 copies in the first two years, though Thomas was not alive long enough to reap the rewards.

Such pleasure as Thomas may have felt at the reception of what proved to be his life's work in poetry was short-lived, overwhelmed by the problems of his personal life. During the summer of 1952 his sister Nancy, ill with cancer, had visited from India. He saw her for the last time. In December 1952 D. J., who had at least lived long enough to see his son's poetry acclaimed, died, aged seventy-six. Thomas wrote to Alfred Janes:

He was in awful pain at the end and nearly blind. The day before he died, he wanted to get out of bed & go into the kitchen where his mother was making onion soup for him. Then, a few hours afterwards, he suddenly remembered everything, & where he was, & he said, "It's full circle now."[28]

The family obeyed D. J.'s instructions that there should be no religious service. He was cremated and his ashes buried with those of his brother, Arthur, who had died in 1947. Thomas was much affected by the cremation, unable to enter the crematorium, made ill by a friend's ghoulish tales of corpses' heads exploding in the fire and of the smoke from burned remains being breathed in by the mourners. None of this entered "Elegy," the beautiful fragment that Thomas was working on when he died, in which D. J.'s interment is remembered in terms of pastoral myth and literary reference.

Caitlin had become almost obsessively promiscuous. Effectively, despite Thomas's ignoring of her behavior and protestations of continuing love, she had turned against him. Once again she was pregnant; by whom, she was not certain. Early in 1953 Marged Howard-Stepney paid for a further "back-street" abortion. It was her last philanthropic gesture: she was found dead in her London home, suffocated in a cushion following an overdose. She left nothing to Thomas. He, predictably, was indignant. He was sleeping badly, was drinking and smoking heavily, and had developed gout. The children got on his nerves, so he avoided them as much as possible, to such an extent that when they travelled by train he would sit in a separate carriage.

His money troubles continued; his attempts to solve them now found the literary world less sympathetic. David Higham again tried to impose financial order by arranging a repayment program for his debts by setting aside part of his earnings from the BBC and the *Collected Poems*, the American edition of which came out in March 1953 and sold well. Higham's scheme, though essential, tended to reduce whatever prosperity was beginning to come the family's way. Thomas, ever anxious to fritter cash, protested frequently.

Charles Fry of Allen Wingate wrote about the promised travel book. The firm was increasingly uneasy about its £100 advance. In a letter to Fry Thomas made excuses and then, more openly, tried to explain his continued failure to write any poetry beyond

one tangled sentimental poem as preface to a collection of poems written years ago. . . . Endless booming of poems didn't sour or stale words for me, but made me more conscious of my obsessive interest in them and my horror that I would never again be innocent enough to touch and use them. I came home fearful and jangled. There was my hut on a cliff, full of pencil and paper, things to stare at, room to breathe and feel and think. But I couldn't write a word. I tried then to write a poem, dreading it beforehand, a few obscure lines every dumb day, and the printed result shook and battered me in any faith in myself and workman's pride left to me. I couldn't write a word after that.[29]

Reading in public and the associated role playing had been too easy, he continued. Now he couldn't settle to difficult work.

Caitlin put it more directly and harshly: "[Dylan] has, as good as, given up writing, for the actor's ranting boom, and lisping mimicry."[30] Both Thomas's and Caitlin's are revealing comments. But what Thomas certainly did not state or face in print was that drink had sapped his will for hard intellectual work and devoured his time and money. It had also destroyed much of his marriage.

In response to a decision by Dent to publish his filmscript *The Doctor and the Devils*, he began to look at the material. Dent also suggested a *Collected Prose*, for which the firm was to advance £250. On 9 April Thomas made a disastrous debut on BBC TV, misreading his notes and repeating himself until the program had to be wound up.

The following week, on 21 April 1953, he went back to America. This was a shorter visit, six weeks only as a gesture to Caitlin, with whom he had quarrelled even more bitterly about leaving. He promised to return with sufficient money for a winter holiday in Portugal, "where all, I hear, is cheap and sunny."[31] She no longer believed anything he said. His letters were even more devoted and hysterical.

He was, of course, eager to escape, even for a mere six weeks. But there were some good reasons for going. It was a chance to promote *Collected Poems*, and the centerpiece of the tour was to be readings of *Under Milk Wood*, with one scheduled for Brinnin's Poetry Center on 14 May. There was the usual round of campus readings, mainly in the Northeast, most within fairly easy reach of New York. But *Under Milk Wood* was still unfinished; the need to complete it imposed at least some order and purpose on Thomas's arrangements.

He was now famous in intellectual circles, pointed out, talked about. Before his arrival *Time* magazine had attacked him as a sponger and waster. Thomas sued for libel, and *Time* hired a private detective to follow Thomas and collect evidence—of drunkenness, immorality, irresponsible behavior—for any necessary defence. The article increased his notoriety.

He was installed at the Chelsea Hotel and renewed his acquaintance with the White Horse Tavern. On the evening of his first day Brinnin took him for drinks at the Algonquin Hotel. There he met Brinnin's assistant, Elizabeth Reitell. She was in her early thirties, a striking woman with sharp features and a powerful personality who had been educated at expensive Bennington College. She had been an army officer, an artist, and a dancer and had been twice married. Though Thomas had met Pearl Kazin in Cambridge, the relationship appears to have ended after one night together. In any case Thomas was busy working on *Under Milk Wood*. At Harvard's Fogg Museum he gave a one-man reading of what he had written, and this was so well received that he was encouraged to work further on the text. This he did in New York, in Rollie McKenna's apartment and in that of his old London friend Ruthven Todd. Todd recalled a reinvigorated Thomas who worked for long stretches on the play and hardly drank anything. He also commented that Liz Reitell was very good at settling him to work.[32] This, of course, was her job. She fostered his work and kept callers at bay. Like Pamela Hansford Johnson and Pearl Kazin, Liz Reitell was an efficient, assured, ambitious woman with a substantial life of her own. Part of Thomas's tragedy lies in the fact that he lost the first two and the third arrived too late. She imposed some order on his work, but his physical problems were too far advanced: he had severe gout, gastric problems, and deteriorating organs. Liz Reitell worried about his drinking and believed him to be an alcoholic, but she probably did not recognize the seriousness of his physical predicament or the extent of his psychological despair. Nevertheless, they fell in love with each other.

Thomas scribbled until curtain call, concocting the play's ending at the last moment. He told the cast to "love the words. . . . *Love* the words."[33] Then he, with three actors and two actresses, walked onto the stage of the Poetry Center, and they sat in a flat semicircle, each on a high stool behind a lighted lectern. Thomas read 1st Voice, 2nd Drowned, 5th Drowned, and the Reverend Eli Jenkins; each of the others was allocated a group of parts. Expecting seriousness, the audience was quiet until they discovered they were listening to a comedy. They then responded with laughter and empathetic enthusiasm. Brinnin counted fourteen curtain calls until Thomas, boyishly pleased, took the last one on his own.

Collected Poems, 1934–1952 had been acclaimed; *Under Milk Wood* promised to be a triumph; he was in love with a woman who could order his life. As he stepped out to take his bow, Thomas must have felt that out of the collapse of his career as a poet, the near-perpetual haze of his drunken life, and the ashes of his marriage, new light shone, new hope quivered. Such feelings must have intensified when he received a message from Igor Stravinsky.

Stravinsky's regard and respect for the poet are a measure of Thomas's stature as a writer and an indication that as a man, despite his faults, he possessed to the end the capacity to arouse affection and respect in the truly discerning. Robert Craft has stated that he introduced Stravinsky to Thomas's work as early as 1948, and that Stravinsky's wife had heard Thomas read at the Urbana campus of the University of Illinois in 1950.[34] "In my craft or sullen art" had been used by Craft (not, presumably, to make a point about eponymous puns) to teach Stravinsky the pronunciation of English words when he wrote *The Rake's Progress*. Stravinsky was planning a new opera; Aldous Huxley had suggested Dylan Thomas as the librettist.

Stravinsky was in Boston to conduct a performance of *The Rake's Progress* at Boston University. A meeting with Thomas was arranged, which went smoothly despite Stravinsky being ill in bed. Craft noted that Thomas looked unwell, showing obvious signs of drinking too much.[35] However, he was sober on arrival, and the meeting began nervously on both sides until whisky loosened them up.

Thomas was not wholly unprepared for this meeting with a famous composer. Indeed, the extent of his knowledge of music is, perhaps, surprising, though less so when it is recalled that Daniel Jones became a professional composer of some distinction. In addition, the composer Elizabeth Lutyens became a close friend. Fellow guests at John Davenport's Marshfield home during 1940 included the composers Lennox Berkeley and Arnold Cooke, and, of course, Caitlin's would-be seducer, the music critic William Glock. Throughout Thomas's letters are knowledgeable comments not only on J. S. Bach, Debussy, Mozart, and Wagner, but also on modernists such as Samuel Barber, Honegger, and Milhaud. Further, he knew something of Stravinsky's work, having heard *The Rake's Progress*, with Auden's libretto. The latter was rather wordy, he told Stravinsky. He and the composer then discussed Thomas's idea for a subject:

"His" opera was to be about the rediscovery of our planet following an atomic misadventure. There would be a recreation of language, only the new one would have no abstractions; there would only be people, objects, and words.[36]

In the few poems he wrote after Hiroshima and Nagasaki Thomas's fear of a nuclear holocaust is a recurring idea, replacing the concern with World War II (and before that the Great War) that haunts the earlier work. Such fear even enters "Fern Hill"; it is a more central presence in "In Country Heaven" and its accompanying note, and, implicitly, in the use of the Noah myth in "Prologue."

Despite the doom-laden subject, Thomas was excited by the idea of collaborating with a great musician, and Stravinsky took to Thomas. As he told Craft, "As soon as I saw him I knew that the only thing to do was to love him."[37] He invited the poet to stay with him in California so that they could work on the project. Once it was under way, there would be a large advance. Thomas then wrote to Caitlin:

You and me must, at the beginning of July, go together to Hollywood. We can get a boat from London, direct but slow, to San Francisco, & then fly to Los Angeles in an hour or so. Outside Hollywood, in a huge easy house in the hills, we're to stay for the month with Stravinsky. . . . We'll go back from Hollywood to Laugharne, &, in the winter, we'll go to Majorca. There'll be plenty of money. This time it's working.[38]

When Brinnin met him after the meeting with Stravinsky, Thomas was in a state of great excitement, bursting with ideas, some serious, some wildly humorous versions of opera plots: "Smoking one cigarette after another, circling the room as if it were a cage, Dylan seemed imagination afire."[39] So late in his life, through all the self-abuse and waste, we catch another glimpse of the young man at Pamela Hansford Johnson's door and, perhaps, the merest golden hint—a surviving outline amid the ruins—of the schoolboy in Dan Jones's bedroom, bursting with creative energy, full of life, hope, and talent. So much had been wasted, as Stravinsky realized. He felt, Craft recalled, that in a fatherly way he could save Thomas, could rescue him. Though as yet there was no formal commission, when Stravinsky returned to California, he enlarged his house to accommodate the Thomases when they came.

Despite all these new hopes and the developing relationship with Liz Reitell, Thomas did not stop drinking. When he recorded more poems for Caedmon Records, both Barbara Holdridge and Marianne Mantell thought that he looked dreadful: bloated features, a cut eye, vomit on his clothes. He made a hash of some readings, and the tapes were erased. His gout was increasingly painful. He fell downstairs during a dinner and broke his arm, which brought into his life Liz Reitell's doctor, Milton Feltenstein. Unavailingly, he lectured Thomas about his drinking. Whether Thomas was now so addicted to alcohol that he could not stop is not clear. Whether he drank because he was afraid of the expectations generated by these fresh opportunities or because, as the writing of the letter to Caitlin, following the meeting with Stravinsky, suggests, he was caught between absent fondness for her, mixed with fear of the absolute break, and strong feelings for a woman who might yet save him from himself is also, at this distance, partly speculative. We can only keep in mind that hard drinking is inimical to clear thinking.

Dylan Thomas flew back to London on 2 June 1953, Coronation Day, with a number of good reasons for feeling buoyant. But once he was back at the Boat House, the high promise seemed to fade away. Boston University had not yet managed to raise money for the opera project, though Stravinsky wrote renewing the invitation to stay at his home in Hollywood. Thomas did some work for radio, read "A Story" on television, tried to write "Elegy," and worked further on *Under Milk Wood*.

Visitors to the Boat House during the summer of 1953 were disturbed by the state of the Thomases' marriage. Vernon Watkins recalled a dispute over the pronunciation of "tear" in "Over Sir John's Hill." Thomas rhymed it with "tare," Caitlin with "tier." They screamed at each other, with the children upset and the visitors shaken.[40] Brinnin visited with Rollie McKenna. They found the atmosphere at the Boat House almost impossible to bear. Thomas had a deep cut over his eye that, he later admitted—though not to Brinnin or Mc-Kenna—had been caused by Caitlin striking him with a coffeepot. "Isn't life awful?" he wrote to Daniel Jones. "Last week I hit Caitlin with a plate of beetroot, and I'm still bleeding."[41] He may not have lost his sense of humor, but Brinnin knew that he was looking for any excuse to return to America to escape from his marriage, from a work shed full of discarded jottings, from the attentions of the Inland Revenue and National Insurance, and to a waiting Liz Reitell. Brinnin wrote sadly:

While he perhaps did not know the way toward his creative salvation, he did know ways in which creative exercise could be postponed or superseded. It was sadly apparent that Dylan's energies were directed not toward fighting through to freedom but toward escape from drudgery and the inadmissible thought of failure.[42]

He felt strongly that Thomas should not return to America in the near future but should direct his energies towards his writing. But Stravinsky beckoned, wanting to proceed with the opera in the hope that funding could be found. Thomas had also been contacted by an American agent who had suggested a reading circuit of women's groups and professional organizations that would be far more lucrative than the academic round. He hoped to meet the agent in New York. Thomas was determined to go again. Brinnin guessed shrewdly that he wished to go without Caitlin. She guessed the same and did not want to go.

In September 1953 Aeronwy was sent away to the Arts Educational School at Tring in Hertfordshire. Llewelyn was still at Magdalen College School. The penniless pair now had two children at expensive fee-paying schools. Though Thomas finished a complete draft of *Under Milk Wood* in 1953, it is not surprising that during 1953 he also did much lucrative work for the BBC, and that he spent more and more time writing increasingly despairing begging letters.

His last radio work before leaving for America was a short talk about Laugharne: slick, humorous hackwork that conveyed some of the affection he often, though not always, felt for the place. On 8 October 1953 his old friend Alfred Janes came to the Boat House with Ceri Richards, the distinguished Welsh painter many of whose later works were inspired by Thomas poems. Fierce marital quarrels terminated the visit. That evening Thomas and Caitlin went to the cinema in Carmarthen.

On 9 October Thomas said goodbye to his mother and left Laugharne with Caitlin. She was fiercely opposed to the trip but anxious to enjoy herself in London. She believed that the marriage was over. Young Colm was left with a local family. The couple went first to Swansea and forced a reluctant Daniel Jones into a three-day binge. They then borrowed to get to London, where they spent a few days with Harry and Cordelia Locke, their friends from South Leigh, who now lived in Hammersmith. Thomas delivered the text of *Under Milk Wood* to Douglas Cleverdon at the BBC, obtaining copies for his trip. He was drinking a lot but seemed more sad than drunken. He told Constantine FitzGibbon that he didn't really want to leave. FitzGibbon wondered whether he was frightened by the project with Stravinsky.[43] He seemed in poor health. Shortly before he left Laugharne, he had complained of severe headaches. He may well have suffered blackouts and may have had one in a Carmarthen cinema before he left Laugharne.

After having to rearrange a flight following a mix-up over tickets, Dylan Thomas flew to America on 19 October 1953. The visit was to be of no more than eight weeks. There would be a few poetry readings and performances of *Under Milk Wood* to raise money, but its main purpose was to visit Stravinsky.

Liz Reitell met him off the plane in New York, and they travelled together to the Chelsea Hotel. He told her that the previous week had been dreadful because of Caitlin's hostility. Reitell was concerned to keep Thomas away from well-wishers and hangers-on, partly to see more of him herself, partly to protect him against opportunities for excessive drinking. For three days he drank less and talked with relief of having escaped. They were, said his lover, "the loveliest days I had with him."[44]

Then he took part in a heavy drinking session in his room with members of the Cinema 16 organization and was ill at a rehearsal of *Under Milk Wood*, vomiting onto the green-room floor. Herb Hannum, a friend of Liz Reitell, helped him to a couch, and Thomas whispered to him, "I've seen the gates of hell tonight."[45] His lover took him back to Milton Feltenstein, who again lectured Thomas on his lifestyle, then injected him with ACTH, the cortisone-based drug that served both to counter his gout and act as a stimulant.

Brinnin did not meet Thomas until five days after his arrival:

I was so shocked by his appearance. . . . His face was lime-white, his lips loose and twisted, his eyes dulled, gelid, and sunk in his head. He showed the countenance of a man who has been appalled by something beyond comprehension.[46]

Liz Reitell, much in love, saw that he needed constant watching. She was troubled not only by his health but by his "ineffable loneliness."[47] The sad final sequence was about to begin.

That sequence is hardly edifying. Details were taken by FitzGibbon from the notebook of the detective employed by *Time* to follow Thomas. The latter quarrelled irrationally with Brinnin about finance, believing that returns from this visit's performances would be low, and then had a sentimental and tearful reconciliation. On 26 October he embarked on a drinking binge from which he was rescued by the ever-loyal and loving Liz. He began taking Benzedrine and behaving more irrationally. He made faces at passers-by, swore at them, and could not walk without staggering. Brinnin reported that at a party Thomas leaped at a girl whom he fancied and seriously injured her.

Thomas seemed deranged, but on 28 October he took part, with Arthur Miller and others, in a symposium on "Poetry and the Film" organized by Cinema 16. His contributions had their usual anti-intellectual edge: he did his best to make fools of the other contributors but succeeded only in seeming silly. He made a rare good point about a visual notion of the poetic, having learned, it seems, that film was not a literary medium. What is surprisingly absent from the transcript of the discussion is any reference to his own considerable experience as a film scriptwriter.[48] The following day, 29 October, he gave a lunchtime reading at the City College of New York. He drank moderately and seemed in control of himself.

On 3 November he met Felix Gerstman, the agent who wished to arrange more lucrative tours. Thomas was calmer and looked more respectable. The preliminary discussion went well. But later another extreme mood swing took place: he became suicidal and wept uncontrollably. After sleeping badly until 2 A.M. he got out of bed, ignored his lover's protests, and went out to have a drink. An hour and a half later he returned and said to her, "I've had eighteen straight whiskies. I think that's the record." This was mere bravado. He then said to Liz Reitell, "I love you . . . but I'm alone," and went to sleep.[49]

Thomas awoke late on the morning of 4 November. He complained about a lack of air, and so he and Liz walked to the White Horse Tavern, where he had two beers. He still felt unwell, so they returned to the Chelsea. Gastritis and gout were giving him great pain. Feltenstein was called; when he arrived, he administered some unspecified medication. Later he came again and injected more ACTH. During the evening Thomas had delirium tremens. Feltenstein came once more and because Thomas was in pain injected him with half a grain of morphine sulphate, far more than a normal dose. Why he did this is not clear, but that treatment was to prove catastrophic, given Thomas's intake of alcohol and his long-standing asthmatic condition aggravated by heavy smoking. The horrors continued. A frightened Liz Reitell summoned a friend, the painter Jack Heliker. Thomas woke for a while, said a few words to both, then gripped Liz Reitell's hand tightly as his face turned blue. According to Heliker, his last words before he passed out were "After thirty-nine years, this is all I've done."[50] Feltenstein came quickly and called an ambulance. Thomas was admitted to St. Vincent's, a Roman Catholic private hospital, at 1:58 A.M., New York time, on Thursday, 5 November. Thousands of miles away, his townsfolk, including his wife, were preparing to listen to his broadcast talk on Laugharne.

Thomas lay in a coma for four and a half days. When he was admitted, the hospital noted that he had a "history of heavy alcoholic intake. Received ½ grain of M.S. shortly before admission." The hospital suspected "alcoholic encephalopathy,"[51] though this was never confirmed. Liz Reitell was joined at the hospital by Ruthven Todd and then by Brinnin, summoned from out of town. Following a newspaper report, a stream of visitors began to call.

When the telegram arrived, Caitlin was in Laugharne's Memorial Hall listening to Thomas's broadcast. The telegram stated that her husband had been hospitalized. Her reaction was to ignore the news and go on from the broadcast to a dance. The following day she went to London and stayed overnight with the Lockes. Her friends gave her a send-off lunch at Wheeler's, the famous fish restaurant. Caitlin later recalled drinking a lot of wine: "My strange memory of it is that it felt like a celebration lunch."[52] On the plane she drank a lot of whisky and was very drunk on arrival in New York. She was met by Dave and Rose Slivka, friends from her earlier visit.

At the hospital her first words to Brinnin were "Why didn't you write to me? Is the bloody man dead or alive?"[53] She then tried to throw herself onto Thomas's inert body; according to Rose Slivka, who egged her on, she also tried to pull out the tubes that kept him alive. She swung from the curtain rails, broke a statue of the Virgin and a crucifix, and attacked those near her, including Brinnin and a nun. A straitjacket was brought, and she was taken off to a private clinic on Long Island. There she remained until after Thomas was dead. As a voluntary patient, this would have been her decision. She was probably sleeping off the effects of her drinking.

Thomas never regained consciousness. On Friday, 6 November, he had difficulty breathing, and a tracheotomy was performed. Back in Swansea two old friends, Daniel Jones and Vernon Watkins, learned that nothing could be done. On Monday, 9 November, at 12.40 P.M., with Liz Reitell and Brinnin having withdrawn to the waiting room, only the poet John Berryman was present as Thomas was washed by a nurse. Berryman wrote later to Vernon Watkins: "His body died utterly quiet, and he looked so tired that you might once more have burst into tears too but your grief would have been general, for the whole catastrophe not for the moment. . . . He was one of the greatest poets who ever lived."[54] Thomas gave a small gasp and died. Before his body was removed, Brinnin touched the feet, Liz Reitell kissed its face.

Four-year-old Colm was at the Boat House, looked after by Dolly Long. Llewelyn, at Magdalen College School, was told the news by his headmaster; Aeronwy, at boarding school in Hertfordshire, was told by Caitlin's sister Nicolette. Their mother seemed, for the moment, to have forgotten about them. In California, Igor Stravinsky, that giant of twentieth-century music, who had even enlarged his house in preparation for Thomas's coming, wept bitterly. He wrote later, in words that refer directly to the lost opera libretto and, implicitly, to much else about Thomas's literary career, of "the great sadness of a beautiful dream which could not be born to life."[55] *In Memoriam Dylan Thomas*, Stravinsky's moving setting for trombones and voice of "Do not go gentle," is an enduring tribute.

In the famous phrase, Thomas died "from an insult to the brain," a reference to pressure on the brain that had built up during his last weeks. The main thrust of the postmortem report was that Thomas had died from drink. Doubtless his condition was aggravated by Feltenstein's injection.[56]

He was buried at Laugharne on 24 November, a day of wild drinking and Caitlin's uncontrolled behavior.[57] He died intestate and virtually penniless, but his family was soon to reap considerable financial rewards. Even those who reacted against Thomas's writing and influence felt that death's importance. "I can't believe D. T. is truly dead," wrote Philip Larkin. "It seems absurd. Three people who've altered the face of poetry, & the *youngest* has to die."[58]

NOTES

1. Constantine FitzGibbon, *The Life of Dylan Thomas* (London: Dent, 1965), 321.
2. Jonathan Fryer, *Dylan: The Nine Lives of Dylan Thomas* (London: Kyle Cathie, 1993), 196.
3. Quoted in Fryer, *Dylan*, 198.
4. Paul Ferris, *Dylan Thomas*, (1977; Harmondsworth: Penguin Books, 1978), 250.
5. John Malcolm Brinnin, *Dylan Thomas in America* (London: Dent, 1956), 10. Unless otherwise indicated, I have drawn on both Brinnin and Ferris, *Dylan Thomas*, for basic details of Thomas's visits to North America.
6. *CL*, 751. Letter to Caitlin Thomas, dated [c. 11 March 1950].
7. Quoted in George Tremlett, *Dylan Thomas: In the Mercy of His Means* (London: Constable, 1991), 138.
8. Brinnin, *Dylan Thomas in America*, 63.
9. Ibid., 64.
10. *CL*, 766. Letter to John F. Nims and Mrs. Nims, 17 July 1950.
11. I have drawn on Martin E. Gingerich, "Dylan Thomas and America," in *Dylan Thomas Remembered* (Swansea: Dylan Thomas Society, Wales Branch, 1978), 26–34, an invaluable assessment of the logistics of Thomas's first reading tour. Gingerich is less reliable about Thomas's earnings.

12. Ferris, *Dylan Thomas*, 274.

13. *CL*, 762, 766. Letter to Margaret Taylor, dated 18 June 1950.

14. *CL*, 760. Letter to Caitlin Thomas, 7 May 1950.

15. Quoted in Ferris, *Dylan Thomas*, 278.

16. Paul Ferris, *Caitlin: The Life of Caitlin Thomas* (London: Hutchinson, 1993), 115.

17. Quoted in *CL*, 775n.

18. *CL*, 785. Letter to a Woman Friend, [c. 17 January 1951].

19. *CL*, 795. Letter to John Malcolm Brinnin, dated 12 April 1951.

20. *CL*, 793. Letter to John Davenport, dated 12 April 1951.

21. *CL*, 796. Letter to John Malcolm Brinnin, dated 12 April 1951.

22. *CL*, 791. Letter to Princess Caetani, 20 March 1951.

23. Ferris, *Caitlin*, 118.

24. *CL*, 818. Letter to John Malcolm Brinnin, 3 December 1951.

25. Ferris, *Dylan Thomas*, 398.

26. Quoted in Ferris, *Dylan Thomas*, 302.

27. The poem has 106 lines. The first rhymes with the last, the second with the penultimate, and so on, until the middle two lines form a rhyming couplet.

28. *CL*, 860. Letter to Alfred Janes, dated 5 January [1953].

29. *CL*, 869. Letter to Charles Fry, dated 16 February 1953.

30. Quoted in Ferris, *Caitlin*, 135.

31. *CL*, 879. Letter to John Malcolm Brinnin, 18 March 1953.

32. Ruthven Todd, "Dylan Thomas: A Personal Account," typescript, Todd, R., Works, HRHRC, 6–8.

33. Rollie McKenna, *Portrait of Dylan* (London: Dent, 1982) 71.

34. Robert Craft, in "The Dying of the Light," BBC Radio 3, London, 23 May 1993.

35. Igor Stravinsky and Robert Craft, *Conversations with Igor Stravinsky* (London: Faber & Faber, 1959), 78.

36. Ibid.

37. Ibid.

38. *CL*, 889–90. Letter to Caitlin Thomas, dated [c. 23 May 1953].

39. Brinnin, *Dylan Thomas in America*, 181.

40. Gwen Watkins, *Portrait of a Friend* (Llandysul: Gomer Press, 1983), 138.

41. *CL*, 910. Letter to Daniel Jones, dated 24 August 1953.

42. Brinnin, *Dylan Thomas in America*, 193–94.

43. FitzGibbon, *Life of Dylan Thomas*, 355–56.

44. Quoted in Ferris, *Dylan Thomas*, 329.

45. Brinnin, *Dylan Thomas in America*, 211.

46. Ibid., 213–14.

47. Fryer, *Dylan*, 251.

48. See Dylan Thomas, "Poetry and the Film: A Symposium," in *The Filmscripts*, ed. John Ackerman (London: Dent, 1995), 406–408.

49. Brinnin, *Dylan Thomas in America*, 227–28.

50. Quoted sceptically by Rob Gittins, *The Last Days of Dylan Thomas* (London: Macdonald, 1986), 161.

51. Hospital notes quoted in Ferris, *Dylan Thomas*, 338n.

52. Caitlin Thomas with George Tremlett, *Caitlin: A Warring Absence* (London: Secker & Warburg, 1986), 182.

53. Brinnin, *Dylan Thomas in America*, 239.

54. Quoted in Gwen Watkins, *Portrait of a Friend*, 152.

55. Igor Stravinsky, "The Opera That Might Have Been." in *Our Dylan Thomas Memorial Number*, ed. Miron Grindea, special issue of *Adam International Review* 238 (1953): 8.

56. James Nashold and George Tremlett, *The Death of Dylan Thomas* (Edinburgh and London: Mainstream Publishing, 1997) is the most recent account of Thomas's death. The authors, of whom Nashold is a North Carolina neurosurgeon, have consulted all surviving doctors, medical attendants, and medical documents in what is, to date, the most thorough medically informed investigation into the circumstances of Thomas's death. Their conclusions are that Thomas did not die from alcoholic poisoning aggravated by incorrect medical treatment; nor was he in decline as a poet. Rather, the extent of his drinking has been exaggerated; the effect of what he did drink was intensified because he was a longstanding undiagnosed diabetic. As such, he received fatally inappropriate treatment from Dr. Feltenstein in a hospital that failed to carry out adequate emergency procedures. A medical cover-up followed. Had Thomas's condition been known it could have been easily corrected, thus improving his health, mitigating the effects of his social drinking, lengthening his life, and preventing the perceived decline in his literary career.

That Thomas may have been a diabetic is not a new suggestion, and certainly Nashold and Tremlett amass a large amount of circumstantial evidence. But at this distance in time much is conjectural, particularly so given that, as the authors admit, no diabetes was diagnosed when Thomas was tested in 1946 when he spent four days in St. Stephens's Hospital, Westminster, for alcoholic gastritis (Nashold and Tremlett, 71). Further, at least one doctor's response to their theory points to a similarity between a symptom of alcoholism and that of diabetes: "it is just possible that . . . the discovery of raised blood sugar was not related to diabetes but to alcoholic ketoacidosis" (Thomas Stuttaford, "Did drink kill Dylan Thomas?" *The Times*, 16 October 1997: 14). As for the matter of Thomas's literary decline: he wrote very few poems from 1946 until his death, during which time, irrespective of whether he was technically an alcoholic, there is much evidence that he drank too much. There is an obvious relationship between these two facts. Whether all would have been different and better had Thomas's alleged diabetes been corrected at an early stage we will never know. But since Thomas's excessive drinking can be understood as a response to a complex of psychological factors—bravado, insecurity, unhappiness, and fear amongst them—there are still grounds for reasonable doubt that his life would have been much changed.

57. Daniel Jones, *My Friend Dylan Thomas*, (London: Dent, 1977), 6.

58. Philip Larkin, *Selected Letters, 1940–1985*, ed. Anthony Thwaite (paperback ed., London: Faber & Faber, 1993), 218. The other two poets were T. S. Eliot and W. H. Auden.

II

WORKS

5

Juvenilia and the Notebooks

As has been noted, Dylan Thomas's first published poem is in his school magazine and is entitled "The Song of the Mischievous Dog." It begins:

> There are many who say that a dog has his day,
> And a cat has a number of lives,
> There are others who think that a lobster is pink,
> And that bees never work in their hives.

and ends:

> But my greatest delight is to take a good bite
> At a calf that is plump and delicious;
> And if I indulge in a bite at a bulge,
> Let's hope you won't think me too vicious.[1]

In being so determinedly and derivatively humorous—the poem owes much to the Chesterbelloc school of comic verse—"Song" is typical "school-mag" writing. It is anything but typical in the technical assurance evident in its clever rhymes, particularly the internal ones, and lively anapests. From the first Thomas shows the technical mastery that was never to leave him.

His contributions to the school magazine are varied. They include further humorous verses similar to "Song" and parodies of contemporary writers, such as his imitation of early Yeats in "Little Miss Muffet."[2] Other poems, such as "Best of All" and "In Dreams,"[3] are strongly influenced by 1890s writing and Rupert Brooke the Georgian. Most important of all, of course, are Thomas's three poems about the Great War. "The Watchers" is about the "mighty dead . . . who rest by Ypres and Posières by Vimy and Cambrai,"[4] listening to the armies advance and the attacks succeed. "Missing," the poem written for the tenth anniversary of the Armistice, though using what was in the 1920s still a charged word, encouraged even more emollient responses. In its first two quatrains the sun caresses the face of a soldier dead on the "dread wilderness" of the battlefield; the wind is heard to "whisper a benediction for the dead." The third and final quatrain adds:

> Softly, thou rain—and for his mother's sake,
> Shed thou thy tears on him; he will not wake,
> No weeping through that deep repose can break.[5]

"Wilfred Owen without his bitterness perhaps" has been one response.[6] But though Owen, as will be seen, was particularly important to Thomas, here he is only part of an amalgam of influential aesthetes, Georgians, and war poets of the Laurence Binyon school. An earlier reference to the soldier's "dreamless sleep" echoes *The Prelude* to confirm the poem's predictable literariness. In its skilled rhyming, use of the pentameter line, and alliterative patterns, it is an assured piece of writing, and not only for a thirteen-year-old. Two years later, in 1930, the magazine published "Armistice," a further venture into sentimental but technically assured lyricism that ended:

> But a wise, new love shall ascend,
>   From the dust to the clouds of the sky;
> It shall never grow weary, nor end,
>   Nor, like us who are left, shall it die.[7]

Thomas had certainly read his war poets, as these more direct suggestions of Binyon and his school continue to show, and as he had demonstrated in the same publication during 1929 in that assured essay on "Modern Poetry." In this he asserted that though the Great War had changed English poetry, its brutality had "failed to warp man's outlook and ideals. . . . Out of the darkness came the clear light of genius . . . Wilfred Owen, Robert Graves, Julian Grenfell, and the other heroes who built towers of beauty upon the ashes of their lives."[8]

These precocious public statements, the poems and such sentences from the essay, are of the optimistic-sentimental kind. Out of disaster comes consolation. In "Missing," for example, the dead soldier, beyond grief in death's "repose," is embraced by a benevolent nature; in his essay Thomas stresses that terrible events bring out the best in the poet-participants. To repeat a point made in the account of Thomas's schooldays, all four contributions are consoling gestures towards grammar-school boys and their parents, of whom many would have been bereaved by the war.

Memories of that war haunted the decade in a personal way—through the memories of survivors and bereaved—and, in what was still a predominantly literary culture, by what was written about those recent events. The extent to which this latter occurred has been brilliantly documented and explored by Paul Fussell.[9] Valentine Cunningham reminded us that though the first and most famous modernist response to the Great War occurred in the early 1920s—in

The Waste Land, for instance, in *Mrs. Dalloway*, and in *Kangaroo*—towards the end of the decade "the blocked-up dam of bad memories, nightmares, trauma had burst and memoirs, volumes of letters, novels, autobiographies, and other troops-(rather than generals-) centred books started to pour torrentially forth."[10]

But even before that torrent and the first modernist response the combatant-poets had begun their own assault on conventional ideas of war. Though Ivor Gurney's work began appearing from 1917, and an edition of Isaac Rosenberg's war poetry was published in 1922, their reputations developed slowly. Through the 1920s and the early 1930s the two poets who loomed largest in the general sensibility were Wilfred Owen, whose work had been in print since 1920, and Siegfried Sassoon, who became a war poet in 1917. Owen's influence on the poets of the 1930s was increased greatly by Edmund Blunden's edition of his poems, published, with an important memoir, in 1931.[11] Almost certainly this is the "collected poems" referred to by Thomas when he listed his library in 1933. The list also included a volume by Sassoon.[12] Two points can be stressed. First, as Cunningham insisted, acknowledging Fussell, "much of '30s experience and literature is undertaken in an atmosphere of danger, adventure, conflict, and violence programmed by the Great War."[13] Because of such programming the literature, and particularly the poetry, of the early 1930s has many familiar images of that conflict and its consequences.[14] Second, while Owen was a central figure for early 1930s writers, he was particularly so for Thomas. As late as 1946 Thomas broadcast a talk on Wilfred Owen, the hero-worshipping tone of which almost certainly looks back to teenage enthusiasm. He cited Blunden's edition and emphasized the poems' enduring qualities: "their anguish unabated, their beauty for ever, their truth manifest, their warning unheeded." He pointed also to the qualities of Owen's work that attracted him: "dark, grave, assonant rhythms, vocabulary purged and sinewed, wrathful pity and prophetic utterance."[15] He could have added half-rhymes, much used in Thomas's early work and, though Yeats may be a presence here, certainly reflecting Owen's influence. Technical influences apart, Owen, bitterly opposed to the events that were to destroy him, dying young like Keats, was surely an inspiring high-romantic example for a youthful Dylan Thomas obsessed with being a poet, particularly given basic similarities of background: both were creations of the provinces and from the lower middle class. Owen was brought up in Shropshire and Cheshire, attended local schools, had a father who was a minor railway official, and experienced a family life that was far from affluent.

When Thomas wrote for the school magazine, much of this lay in the future. He was also writing prose, including short stories and essays, the one on poetry already mentioned and another on films. The supernatural short stories "Brember," "Jarley's," and "In the Garden" are strange and atmospheric. The first two depend on surprise endings; the last is far more subtle and is about the imagination's transforming power. They look forward to his early neosurrealistic fiction that eventually found its way into *The Map of Love*, and they are the only magazine contributions that move beyond the conventional.

The two essays insist that both art forms stand on the brink of change. The films are silent ones; the intelligent and knowledgeable essay discusses the difficulty in adjusting from stage to silent screen and from silence to sound. New methods and techniques are required. As for modern poetry in general, Thomas declares confidently that "the most important element that characterises our poetical modernity is freedom—essential and unlimited—freedom of form, of structure, of imagery and of idea." Such freedom, Thomas believes, was a result of the Great War: its poetry rejected conventional responses; we see even its brutality producing "some of the bitterest and the loveliest poetry in the language." He ends by declaring that "to-day is a transitional period" in which poets were hunting for "sure ground" and "laying the foundations of a new art."[16] These remarks belong to December 1929, when Thomas was fifteen. They can be read ironically when we think of the "school-mag" poems. With hindsight we realize that he was sensing his own true beginnings. Barely four months after Thomas published the essay on poetry, in April 1930, he began to fill the famous notebooks.

But before that beginning there was the friendship with Daniel Jones, with whom, as has been seen, Thomas collaborated in writing poems and came under the influence of his friend's wider reading and broader intellectual interests. In the collaborations he invariably followed Jones's leadership. Though very occasionally, as Jones has recorded, he and Thomas wrote lines of poetry in advance and compiled poems by drawing alternate lines out of two hats, usually they composed extempore with, as has also been noted, Jones writing the odd-numbered lines and so beginning each poem.[17]

Such a collaborative method makes for strangeness, particularly given Jones's surrealistic tendencies—perhaps indicating a precocious knowledge of the movement—evident in such an opening line as "The moon is wired to the ceilings of steeple," which encouraged from Thomas a similar exotic response. Further, because Jones wrote the odd-numbered lines, Thomas was always required to complete couplets and thus had imposed upon him the formal discipline of rhyme that, even here, included half-rhyme that sometimes verged on the consonantal, reflecting the influence of Yeats and Wilfred Owen. A sixteen-line collaboration entitled "Alternatives" successfully rhymes each line on "ade" or sound versions of it ("ayed" and "aid"), anticipating the technical skill of his mature work.

Sometimes the results of collaboration can be very beautiful, revealing a strange and exotic world inhabited by two highly imaginative boys fascinated by words and by the mechanics of poetry:

> They had come from the place high on the coral hills
> Where the light from the white sea fills the soil with ascending grace.[18]

Such lines also reveal the difference between the two writers: Jones's opening line is assured but literary; Thomas's is equally assured but original in having light fill the soil with grace. Both, throughout the collaborations, draw on the same kind of reading that can be detected in Thomas's magazine poems: poets of the 1890s, Ernest Dowson perhaps, certainly early Yeats; echoes of Fitzgerald's *Omar Khayyam*; the Song of Solomon; the Georgians, imagism, surrealism, and T. S. Eliot. Thomas probably owed his interest in the romantic Middle East and in Egyptology to his intellectual friend, though the latter concern may have been a legacy of the general interest in Egyptology sparked by the Tutankhamen discoveries of 1922. Very occasionally we encounter adolescent lines of revealing sexual intensity, one example being a poem in which Daniel Jones's lines—such as "This tongue that seared love" and "Burning through your body"—drew from Thomas intense, erotically charged, yet tightly controlled responses that look forward to the best work of the next phase of his development.

From 1930 onwards Thomas began to write his notebook poems. He told Henry Treece that he had "about 10 exercise books full of poems,"[19] but only four have survived, covering the period from 27 April 1930 to 30 April 1934, apart from a gap from 2 July 1932 to February 1933. They contain fair copies, as Thomas told Charles Fisher:

My method is this: I write a poem on innumerable sheets of scrap paper, write it on both sides of the paper, often upside down and criss cross ways, unpunctuated, surrounded by drawings of lamp posts and boiled eggs, in a very dirty mess; bit by bit I copy out the slowly developing poem into an exercise book.[20]

Sometimes he made a fair copy elsewhere before transferring it into his notebooks.

The extant notebooks—which contain drafts or first published texts of forty published poems, as well as many pieces that got no further—enable us to follow the development of the young poet from age fifteen to almost twenty. This has been persuasively described by Ralph Maud, who began by describing the drafts in the "1930 Notebook" as being heavily influenced by the Bible, Shakespeare, Donne, Blake, early Yeats and other poets of the 1890s, and such contemporary writers as Sacheverell Sitwell and the imagist Richard Aldington. Maud stressed Thomas's fascination for the obscure and his tendency to convey meaning wholly through imagery. The "1930–1932 Notebook" then shows Thomas experimenting with automatic or quasi-automatic writing, which may well be a consequence of the abrupt and instant juxtaposing collaborations with Daniel Jones. Maud singled out poem "XXV," which begins,

Through sober to the truth when
All hold out their aequeous hands (*PM*, 125),

as sounding a new, "sober" (*PM*, 17), not to say depressing, note in these writings. He related this to Thomas's leaving school and beginning as a local journalist. His views are seen to mature: conventional responses are replaced by a "personal religion of the organic processes" (*PM*, 25), which, as will be seen, has centrally important implications for his first published volumes. The later poems in the "1930–1932 Notebook" explore another theme of similar importance: the desperate asserting of self against a world that seems more and more restricting.

The "February 1933 Notebook" begins after Thomas had left the *South Wales Evening Post* and continues through the period when Bert Trick's influence was strong. Thus there is more social concern and an even stronger sense of a world pressing in upon the young poet. In the final extant volume, the "August 1933 Notebook," Thomas drafts "process" poems in which the body is used as a cosmic, certainly global metaphor. Maud argued that the two later notebooks are dominated by oppositions: "faith vs. despair, love vs. sexual waste, waking action vs. dream world . . . all . . . part of a universal antithesis of growth vs. decay" (*PM*, 33). All are subsumed in the self-and-world opposition already noted.

John Ackerman has also written on the notebooks as part of general developments in Thomas's work during the 1930–34 period. Like Maud, he stressed influences, adding Thomas Beddoes and Francis Thompson to Maud's list. Ackerman noted erotic themes and the "ironic romanticism" of much of Thomas's writing. He pointed to Thomas's early interest in syllabics and suggested that his style was well formed by the summer of 1933. Thomas, argued Ackerman, turned away from public poetry to a concern with the interpenetration of man and nature and with the body as organic metaphor that led, as Maud indicated, to the "process" poems.[21]

Both Maud and Ackerman offered important accounts, but neither stressed sufficiently the tensions fuelling the notebook poems. Such tensions include not only that between these private writings and the very different poems in the school magazine, but also, within the notebooks, the tension between reaction to the restrictive bourgeois hegemony and the way that hegemony permeated and controlled Thomas's responses.

The inevitable intertextuality of such early writings by a book-soaked young man, together with the exotic, book-learned material in many of these drafts—classical allusions, Egyptian references, echoes of *The Arabian Nights*—creates a wild world of the imagination within prosaic Cwmdonkin. Even the language leaps away from normal Uplands diction as the young man ransacks the dictionary for such new verbal sensations as "sadr," "parhelion," "sistrum," "scalecophidian," "teredo," and others (*PM*, 47, 49, 188, 207).

Further, given that rhyme and other formal and structural devices, as ordering elements, are expressions of the bourgeois hegemony from which Thomas sought to escape, experiments with partial or consonantal rhyming and departures from rhyming are rebellious gestures. "Osiris, Come to Isis" (*PM*, 47–

50), the first draft poem in the "1930 Notebook," shifts from rhyme to half-rhyme ("him ... anemone ... stem"). A later poem in the same notebook opens:

> And so the new love came at length
> Healing and giving strength,
> And made the pure love go.
> She echoed my laughter
> And placed my love upon her,
> Bearing the voluptuous burden,
> With the pure love coming after. (*PM*, 55)

Here the rhyme scheme is *aabccdc*, with one half-rhyme. It is followed by *beefghf* and then by lines that resist any formal pattern. The gradual overwhelming of a fairly formal rhyme scheme by increasingly free verse helps dramatize the poem's subject, which is the superseding of "pure love" by "new love." In the "February 1933 Notebook," in an interesting anticipation of the famous "Once it was the colour of saying," poem "Eleven" is an attempt at a sonnet that rhymes *aabbcdcefeghij*, thus abandoning the strict rhyme scheme of the opening lines. In each of these two poems the change reflects the conflict between authority and rebellion that the notebook writing represents, and that would soon be resolved in favor of the former. On the one hand is free verse, sometimes handled well:

> To be encompassed by the brilliant earth
> Breathing on all sides pungently
> Into her vegetation's lapping mouths
> Must feel like such encroachment
> As edges off your nerves to mine,
> The hemming contact that's so trammeled
> By love or look. (*PM*, 116),

but more often lacking grace, force, and rhythmic tension and thus falling lifeless from the page:

> Cool, oh no cool,
> Sharp, oh no sharp,
> The hillock of the thoughts you think
> With that half-moulded mind I said was yours,
> But cooler when I take it back. (*PM*, 88–89)

Linked to this "free" impulse is a shift into chaotic syntax, a particular feature, as Maud has noted, of the "1930–1932 Notebook." For example:

The natural day and night
Are full enough to drown my melancholy
Of sound and sight,
Vigour and harmony in light to none,
One hour spend my time for me
In tuning impulses to calls. (*PM*, 117–18)

At the extreme is automatic writing. Though Thomas was always opposed to this, as he was always opposed to the surrealism of which such writing was a technique, and could write, tongue-in-cheek, "Sweet, automatic me knows best"(*PM*, 88), the same notebook contains experiments:

if the lady from the casino
will stop the flacillating roof
de paris and many women from my thinking
over the running bannisters. (*PM*, 122)

are the first lines of a long, incomprehensible sequence.

Thus, when Thomas subtitled his first two notebooks "Mainly Free Verse Poems," he was, in a sense, making a literary-political statement. Further, the subtitles are not accurate, which Thomas may well have realized when he deleted that of the second notebook. Some poems, even in the earliest notebook, adopt rhyme schemes, either exact or consonantal. Examples include poem "LII" ("There in her tears were laughter and tears again") in the "1930–1932 Notebook" and poem "Twenty Eight" in the "February 1933 Notebook." Poem "Twelve" in the latter is structured on a contrast between August and winter; poem "Seventeen" ("See, on gravel paths under the harpstrung [leaves]"), more loosely structured, is ordered through repetition, the first line being repeated in the final verse paragraph. Thomas's explorations of form are as much psychological and social as aesthetic.

The notebook poems have four central concerns. The first is the Great War, which provides one angry element of this early writing. In the privacy of the notebooks references to that conflict are more direct, more frank than in the school magazine's popular derivatives, in what is said of the carnage of the recent past, of death, wounding, lasting disfigurement and psychological distress. A poem in the "1930–1932 Notebook" begins:

They are the only dead who did not love,
Lipless and tongueless in the sour earth. (*PM*, 130)

The first line has the emotionally indulgent cadences of a Rupert Brooke; the second purveys harsh realities. In the "February 1933 Notebook" the harsh becomes the compulsively brutal as Thomas writes of the war's all-too-apparent lasting consequences:

Exsoldiers with horrors for a face,
A pig's snout for a nose,
The lost in doubt, the nearly mad, the young
Who, undeserving, have suffered the earth's wrong,
The living dead left over from the war,
The living after, the filled with fear. (*PM*, 170)

Such appalled fascination is a world away from the public sentimentality of the school magazine. The shift had much to do with the influence of Bert Trick, evident in the harder-edged, at times cynical tone of reference to the Great War in both letters and notebooks from February 1933 onwards. It is conveniently demonstrated in a letter of January 1934 from Thomas to Pamela Hansford Johnson: "You know that the Great War was purposely protracted in order for financiers to make more money; that had it not been for the shares in the armament firms the War would have ended in three weeks."[22]

From 1933 onwards the Great War is a recurring and varying presence in Thomas's notebook poems. It is, for example, used illustratively, as the contents of a dream, in "Sweet as the comet's kiss night sealed":

Night's music crept through the tunnels
Of sleep. . . .
Dark messages, terrors before waking,
Of the terrors of men, of men broken,
Maimed men and men killed by smiles. (*PM*, 163–64)

Again, "The Woman Speaks" describes a dead soldier who was once the woman's lover:

A sniper laid him low and strew [*sic*] his brains;
One would not think the greeness [*sic*] of this valley
Could in a day be sick with so much blood;
What were young limbs are faggots on the land,
And young guts dry beneath the sickened sun.

She concludes despairingly that because of steel and bullet,

Since the first flesh of man was riven . . .
Grief, like an open wound, has cried to heaven. (*PM*, 217–8)

Such thoughts—and the creation of this important early symbol, that of a dead body lying on open ground—are deeply felt, which may well explain why Thomas filters them through a female narrator, so it is not surprising that similar feelings are expressed in the next two notebook entries, numbered by Thomas "Fifty" and "Fifty One." "Fifty" is a draft poem concerned with the need to assert oneself against a hostile world:

> Let not the hands garotte,
>   The bullet wing, the bayonet gut. (*PM*, 219)

Here usage is different: the Great War becomes a source of metaphor for the world's inroads upon the individual's capacity for independent assertion. Similarly, in "Fifty One" the heart is a "sentinel," dying truth is a body lying on grass (*PM*, 220). The draft poem "It is death though I have died," written earlier in 1933, utilizes a similar procedure in exploring the poet's survival of adversities. Though he has "died/Many deaths," he is still able to rise, as it were, on the stepping-stones of his dead selves, even though the new self may also be one

> Who, too, has been wounded, has shown fight,
> Has been killed, raised with a cracked heart.

The battlefield metaphor ends with the old selves left like bodies "Staring into the cracked sky" (*PM*, 164–65).

To state that Thomas writes of the Great War with relish would be to exaggerate; nonetheless, he is drawn to that violent world. Such a line as "the mouth that ate the gas" in "I dreamed my genesis," included in *18 Poems*, is terrible in its evocation of death by gassing and troubling in the desirous pleasure implicit in "ate"; hard-stressed statements elsewhere in the poem, such as "young guts dry" and "the bayonet gut," have similar empathetic emphasis. A related point is made by the notebook poem "Out of a war of wits," about writing poetry and experiencing friendship. Out of that war poetry is created, and despite his suffering, the poet is thankful

> that my body be whole, I've limbs,
> Not stumps after the hour of battle . . .
> Praise that only the wits are hurt after the wits' fight.

His "torn brain," he continues, "came crying into the fresh light,/Called for confessor," only to encounter "the perils of friends' talk," the "volley of questions and replies." These comprise a further assault on his "wit-hurt head" and so another battle from which the poet emerges to "Reach asking arms up to the milky sky . . ./And be struck dumb, if only for a time" (*PM*, 171–72). The battle, the relentlessly inquiring friends, the desperate desire for solitude in the sunshine, the compulsion to return to the fight implicit in the last line: here is a familiar Great War sequence, used here to dramatize the process of creativity and its aftermath. As will be seen, at least two of Thomas's well-known poems—"And death shall have no dominion" and "When once the twilight locks no longer"—are shaped and given meaning by the haunting horrors of the war, the realities of which Thomas first confronted in the notebook drafts.[23]

Second, we have the implications of poem "Eighteen" in the "August 1933

Notebook,'' which begins, ''Jack my father, let the knaves,'' and continues in
stanza 2:

> Jack my father, let the thieves
> Share their fool spoil with their sad brood of sneaks,
> No silver whistles chase them down the weeks'
> Daybouldered peaks into the iron van.

This is witty writing; Thomas's use of wit is a much-neglected aspect of his
poetry. Here the ''thieves'' are escaping with life's material rewards, and doing
so in the absence of police who—chasing, blowing whistles, and bundling the
arrested into a police van—resemble the Keystone Kops of Thomas's beloved
silent films.[24]

More important—and perhaps pointing to the use of wit as a means of controlling emotion—this draft was finished on 26 September 1933, during the
period when Thomas's father was having radium treatment for cancer of the
mouth. There is little doubt that the poem is addressed to Jack Thomas. His
son, now eighteen, confronts the possibility that his father might die and urges
him to let the world, with its ''knaves'' and ''thieves,'' go its own sad way.
His father should concern himself only with ''lust and love'' and

> When the knave of death arrives,
> Yield the lost flesh to him and give your ghost;
> All shall remain, and on the cloudy coast
> Walk the blithe host
> Of god and ghost with you, their newborn son. (*PM*, 244–45)

The poem's reference to ''lust and love'' brings together the father's fault and
need, thus saying, essentially, ''be yourself,'' before challenging Jack Thomas's
agnosticism and advocating compliance with death as a prelude to walking with
God as a son with a father.

This associating of Jack Thomas with a Christlike role (that is, as son of God
and the Holy Ghost) during his encounter with cancer may well help explain
why Thomas has a propensity to link his father's name with ''Christ.'' ''Jack
Christ'' and ''Jack of Christ'' occur elsewhere in the notebooks, as they do in
finished poems, and Thomas considered ''Jack of Christ'' as the title of a group
of early poems and stories. The association with Christ is also an assertion of
the son's sense of his father as a worthy man wronged by the world.

The notebooks show a man responding to a crucial historical event, such as
the Great War with its lingering emotional and psychological debris, and to
crucial personal circumstances, such as his relationship with his father, which
was also a response to what his father represented in terms of class tension and
social mobility during the first thirty years of the century. This is not to say that
Thomas sought to be a *social* poet in, say, the Auden manner. Certainly the

direct political gesture is rare—"The hand that signed the paper" is the best-known exception—but perhaps not as rare as is sometimes suggested. Maud drew attention to the notebook poem "Praise to the architects" as suggesting the shallowness of the period's poetry of social immediacy, a poem that can be linked to a letter to Trevor Hughes that argues for "a tearing away from the old heart of the things that have clogged it," an attempt, that is, to recapture the power of language shorn of social accretion.[25] Yet Thomas's own practice makes it clear that though his approach was very different from the "Mac-Spaunday" poets (MacNeice, Spender, Auden, Day-Lewis), his work necessarily could not escape "the impress of the moving age."

Here is the notebooks' third main concern, expressed in the "1930–1932 Notebook" in the suggestive line "Jesus was a social poem" (*PM*, 122) and, more directly, in the reference to man being

> obsessed . . .
> With drink and work, the tame machines,
> Money, graft, lust and incest. . . .
> Men in disease and women made in hospitals. (*PM*, 153)

Poem "Four" in the "February 1933 Notebook" develops the attack on modern living:

> [And the state falls to bits,
> And is fed to the cats,]
>   . . .
> The hunger of living, the oven and gun
> That turned on and lifted in anger
> Make the hunger for living
> When the purse is empty,
> The harder to bear and the stronger. (*PM*, 166; brackets indicate Thomas's deletions)

In the same notebook, poem "Seven," which is continued in "Nine," not only is a poem about the Great War but also—doubtless demonstrating the further influence of Bert Trick—includes a catalog of contemporary social ills:

> Young men with fallen chests and old men's breath,
> Women with cancer at their sides
> And cancerous speaking dripping from their mouths,
> And lovers turning on the gas . . .
> . . . the back street drunks. (*PM*, 170–71)

The key moment in these quotations is the reference to "tame machines": essentially Thomas is attacking machine society and its collapse into the economic depression of the 1930s. Thus in poem "Twenty"

Man toils now on an iron saddle, riding
In sun and rain over the dry shires. (*PM*, 183)

"Twenty Six" ("The first ten years in school and park") reviews Thomas's own life up to April 1933 in the context of the general social predicament of that troubled year. The period imagery carries a potent economic and political charge:

   dole for no work's
No turnip ghost now I'm no minor. . . .
Brother spare a dime sounds louder
Than the academicians' thunder; sooner
Be fed with food than dreams. . . .
And I, as you, was caught between
The field and the machine.

The poem's use of topical imagery—other examples are "factory whistles but dischords [*sic*] . . . Pansy and piston, klaxon horn" (*PM*, 193–94)—is repeated in the later notebooks. For example, poem "Eight" of the "August 1933 Notebook" is compassionate about those hopelessly trapped in uncongenial work: "the wretched/Wheel-winders and fixers of bolts" (*PM*, 233). The well-known final stanza of "Light breaks where no sun shines," reflecting the influence of T. S. Eliot and Stephen Spender, refers to "secret lots" and "waste allotments" (*PM*, 258).

This bleak social vision, focussing on the decade's despairers, the casualties of economic forces, darkens even further in poem "Thirteen" of the "February 1933 Notebook," an impressively moving early poem describing the momentary happiness of young lovers, sadly transformed in the chilling final line: "The suicides parade again, now ripe for dying" (*PM*, 174). All is more poignant because Thomas so obviously includes himself among the lost.

He is not a trapped factory hand; his is a more subtle prison. Recognizing "The music of turbine and lawn mower" (*PM*, 194), he is only too aware that the latter controls him as much as the former controls others. The lawn mower here represents suburban life in between-wars Swansea that is so often evoked in detail and with some affection.

We are taken into the middle-class home in its ordered world with its pianola, ticking clock, goldfish bowl, tethered parrot, caged bird and

   the bells . . . ,
The sideboard fruit, the ferns, the picture houses
And the pack of cards (*PM*, 158)

and the young Thomas

> Leaning from windows over a length of lawns,
> On level hills admiring the sea. (*PM*, 180)

We enter gardens and note the "rich and airy soil," the "green arbutus," the dahlias, the hydrangeas, hearing, in what is surely a memory of evenings at Warmley, the sound of "Chopin in our summer garden" and glimpsing the sun:

> when I catch your rays
> Upon the garden fork,
> The beds aren't bathed in light,
> And the crocus does not cry for shade. (*PM*, 70, 169, 111)

Nearby is the park, with the trees that the poet can see and count from his home, with hothouse plants, lake, railings, and the gardener pushing his barrow along gravel paths. The first draft of "The hunchback in the park" belongs to this period and evokes, with more precision, the Cwmdonkin Park of Thomas's childhood with its swans and rockeries and gravel paths. Beyond the park are the institutions and activities of the provincial middle class: the pantomime, the circus,[26] Guy Fawkes night, this last evoked in the lines

> It was November there were whizzbangs hopping,
> But now there are the but-ends [*sic*] of spent squibs,

the cigarette ends and glasses of the local pubs, and the fascinating socially distanced crazes of the time, such as "non-stop dancing" and "all-in wrestling" (*PM*, 189).

Thomas's is hardly a blind affection: he is well aware of the hypocritical core of some suburban respectability. Thus he writes of "princesses"

> Who with gay coats surrender
> Love to the postman or the clown.

More darkly still, he points to what is, for some, a worse prison within the prison, "the new asylum on the hill" that "leers down the valley like a fool" (*PM*, 52, 158).

Further, he knows and is afraid of the bourgeois hegemony, the power of that suburban world:

> Before the gas fades with a harsh last bubble,
> And the hunt in the hatstand discovers no coppers,
> Before the last fag and the shirt sleeves and slippers,
> The century's trap will have snapped round your middle,
> Before the allotment is weeded and sown. (*PM*, 165)

These Audenesque lines, dramatizing the tension between Thomas's aspiring self and a hostile world, comprise one instance of the recurring motif of personal frustration and fear:

> Upon your held-out hand
> Count the endless days until they end. (*PM*, 157)

The same fierce desperation, at times stemming in part from erotic longing, is more fully realized in the compelling drafts of what became famous poems: "Ears in the turrets hear," "Make me a mask," "How shall the animal," "I have longed to move away," "Why east wind chills," "Before I knocked," and "I see the boys of summer." At the center of each is reaction against oppressive social narrowness.

In the "February 1933 Notebook" two poems about relatives show Thomas's deepening sense of a hostile and limiting world. The first is poem "Six," the early version of "After the funeral" and so not strictly suburban. Yet this piece, probably written on the day on which his Aunt Ann was buried, reveals Thomas's general attitude towards the life he knew. Faced with his aunt's death, Thomas refuses to mourn because, as he puts it, "death has rewarded him or her for living"; the moment of death is "yet another long woe broken," and in any case neither that life nor that death can be taken too seriously. The second is poem "Sixteen," a response to his sister Nancy's first marriage. This draft, which eventually became "On the Marriage of a Virgin" and was written when Thomas was eighteen, is an uncertain attempt to deal with mature ideas. The poem shifts oddly from cynicism—"Her [legal honour] sold to one man for good"—to a compassionate and perceptive grasp of what was in 1933 a sudden change from the virginal bedroom to the realities of sharing a bed with, sexually at least, a virtual stranger. Both poems show Thomas troubled, even appalled, by the only life he then knew.

Thomas is a suburban poet; his work draws its strength from the tension between self and limiting world. He also draws much of his poetic language from that world, retaining, throughout his career, the ability to suggest the colloquial and everyday even when his rhetoric is at its highest. His subtext is invariably the language really used by suburbanites. One example must suffice here: he writes, in a notebook draft, "I knelt to drink the water dry as sticks." The line is a rhetorical flourish in which "dry" is at once an adverb ("to drink dry") and, as part of "dry as sticks," the adjectival clause relating to "I" that was also a colloquial phrase (*PM*, 242).

The relationship between self and world in Thomas's poetry is, in its social manifestation, intensely political. The stance is anticapitalist, left-wing, oppositional. Yet in the later notebooks Thomas was writing what Maud and others have taught us to call "process" poems, in which he uses the body as a metaphor for cosmic process. Here is his fourth main concern. A key poem is "A process in the weather of the heart" in the "August 1933 Notebook," in which bodily processes or functions mirror those in the external world. Useful here is Thomas's comment in a letter to Glyn Jones that he was using a "pre-conceived symbolism derived . . . from the cosmic significance of the human anatomy."[27] Through such a metaphor the "process poems" explore the duality of all natural life, the interlinked processes of creation and destruction both in man and in nature. As Thomas put it to Trevor Hughes: "The flesh that covers me is the flesh that covers the sun . . . the blood in my lungs is the blood that goes up and down in a tree."[28] More will be said of this in due course. The fact that the "August 1933 Notebook" contains twelve of what became *18 Poems*, a number of which examine "process," shows that the young Thomas, still only eighteen, had already found a central preoccupation.

In these notebooks Thomas was developing one of his abiding strengths: the ability to strike off marvellous phrases, superb lines, and memorable words without which no writer can rise above the ordinary. Examples include "The boughs stand symbolic/ In their stiff truculence," "Lift up this seed; life from its circle/Spins towards light," "drink and work, the tame machines," "such cerebral sodomy," "deft and aphrodisiac," "Night's music crept through the tunnels/Of sleep," "Night, careful of topography," "Grief, like an open wound," "good and bed," and "*cistern sex*."[29] These are not only examples of phrase making; they are suggestive, concentrated, and occasionally witty uses of language, pointers towards the nature of Thomas's mature work.

That said, we keep in mind that the notebooks are apprentice work: much is slack, wordy, and overwritten as the young writer tried out ideas and styles. Though there are ambition and confidence aplenty, there is also concern about the difficulty and worth of his poetry:

> How can the knotted root
> Be trapped in a snare of syllables,

he asks despairingly. At times he considers that

> Here is a beauty on a bough I can't translate
> Through words or love.

"Christ, let me write from the heart," he prays desperately (*PM*, 146, 156, 120).

The fact that worry is never far away contributes to the generally sombre tone of this early writing. Thomas is preoccupied with death and with a sex that shifts from impossible romanticism to masturbation. Two positives can, however, be stressed. The first is romantic love, however briefly sustained:

> Their faces shone under some radiance
> Of mingled moonlight and lamplight
> That turned the empty kisses into meaning. (*PM*, 174)

The second is a plea for the consolations of the imagination, asserted fiercely and sincerely against the church (the "bishop's hat") and the rat race ("the juggernaut,/And the great wheels' rut") (*PM*, 212–13).

In these beginnings Thomas reveals the tensions, problems, and complex ideas that fuelled his work. As we know, even as late as *Deaths and Entrances* (1946) he was still turning to early drafts and fashioning them into finished and often famous poems.

NOTES

1. Dylan Thomas, "Song of the Mischievous Dog," *Swansea Grammar School Magazine* 22, no. 3 (December 1925): 74.

2. Dylan Thomas, "Little Miss Muffet," *Swansea Grammar School Magazine* 27, no. 1 (April 1930): 25–26.

3. Respectively, Dylan Thomas, "Best of All," *Swansea Grammar School Magazine* 24, no. 2 (July 1927): 64; "In Dreams," 25, no. 4 (December 1928): 77. The opening of "In Dreams" provides a flavor of this kind of writing:

> And in her garden grow the fleur de lys,
>   The tall mauve iris of a sleeping clime.
> Their pale, ethereal beauty seems to be
>   The frail and delicate breath of even-time.

4. Dylan Thomas, "The Watchers," *Swansea Grammar School Magazine* 24, no. 1 (March 1927): 16–17.

5. Dylan Thomas, "Missing," *Swansea Grammar School Magazine* 25, no. 2 (July 1928): 43. The poem is reprinted in Dylan Thomas, *The Poems*, ed. Daniel Jones (London: Dent, 1971), 222.

6. John Ackerman, *A Dylan Thomas Companion* (Basingstoke: Macmillan, 1991), 59.

7. Dylan Thomas, "Armistice," *Swansea Grammar School Magazine* 27, no. 3 (December 1930): 75.

8. Dylan Thomas, "Modern Poetry," *Swansea Grammar School Magazine* 26, no. 3 (December 1929): 84. The essay is reprinted in Dylan Thomas, *Early Prose Writings*, ed. Walford Davies (London: Dent, 1971), 83–86.

9. Paul Fussell, *The Great War and Modern Memory* (New York and London: Oxford University Press, 1975).

10. Valentine Cunningham, *British Writers of the Thirties* (Oxford and New York: Oxford University Press, 1988), 44–45. Cunningham offers a useful list of the most important relevant publications from 1928 onwards. They include R. C. Sherriff's long-running play *Journey's End*, which opened in London in December 1928; Edmund Blunden, *Undertones of War* (1928); Robert Graves, Goodbye to All That (1929); and Siegfried Sassoon's three volumes of memoirs (1928 to 1936).

11. See Cunningham, *British Writers of the Thirties*, 54, 209, and throughout the volume, for suggestive comments on what Wilfred Owen meant to such central 1930s poets as Cecil Day-Lewis and W. H. Auden.

12. *CL*, 76. Letter to Pamela Hansford Johnson [25 December 1933].

13. Cunningham, *British Writers of the Thirties*, 44.

14. See, e.g., Cunningham, *British Writers of the Thirties*, particularly chapter 3 and page 154; and Fussell, *Great War and Modern Memory*. Also useful is Robin Skelton (ed.), *Poetry of the Thirties* (Harmondsworth: Penguin Books, 1964).

15. Dylan Thomas, "Wilfred Owen," in *The Broadcasts*, ed. Ralph Maud (London: Dent, 1991), 94.

16. Dylan Thomas, "Modern Poetry," *Early Prose Writings*, 83–86.

17. Daniel Jones, *My Friend Dylan Thomas* (London: Dent, 1977), 28.

18. Quoted in Daniel Jones, *My Friend Dylan Thomas*, 26, and, more accurately, in Paul Ferris, *Dylan Thomas* (1977; Harmondsworth: Penguin Books, 1978), 48. Both Jones and Ferris quote other examples, as does Ralph Maud (ed.), *Poet in the Making* (London: Dent, 1968), 338–40. There are many more in Dylan Thomas and Daniel Jones, notebooks containing collaborative juvenilia, manuscripts, Dylan Thomas Collection, HRHRC, the source of other lines by Daniel Jones quoted in this section.

19. *CL*, 298. Letter to Henry Treece, dated 16 May 1938.

20. *CL*, 182. Letter to Charles Fisher, dated [early 1935]. The date of this letter suggests that among those notebooks that are lost are some from the period after April 1934.

21. Ackerman, *Dylan Thomas Companion*, 59–74.

22. *CL*, 88. Letter to Pamela Hansford Johnson, dated [?early January 1934].

23. For a full account of this aspect of Thomas's work, see James A. Davies, " 'A Mental Militarist': Dylan Thomas and the Great War," *Welsh Writing in English: A Yearbook of Critical Essays* 2 (1996): 62–81.

24. Thomas has affinities with the metaphysical poets. His use of wit is a large subject. Such usage often creates grotesque visual effects, as in "All that I owe the fellows of the grave" (*PM*, 253–54), particularly the lines

> All night and day I eye the ragged globe
> Through periscopes rightsighted from the grave.

The dead and buried narrator continues to view the world through a precisely focussed periscope—there may well be a reference here to the Great War—pushed up through the earth.

25. *PM*, 23–24, 209–10. The letter to Trevor Hughes is in *CL*, 93, dated January 1934.

26. I refer here to the mention of "Sanger's show" (*PM*, 189), Robert Sanger's travelling circus, a visit from which was a feature of provincial life before and after World War II.

27. *CL*, 98. Letter to Glyn Jones, dated [c. 14 March 1934].

28. *CL*, 90. Letter to Trevor Hughes, dated [early January 1934].

29. Respectively, *PM*, 51, 145, 153, 113, 123, 163–64, 175, 218, 182, 196.

6

From Notebooks to Final Text: Three Examples

"WHY EAST WIND CHILLS"

On 12 September 1931, when Dylan Thomas was sixteen, he copied twenty lines into his "1930–1932 Notebook" (*PM* 138–39). They begin:

> Why is the blood red and the grass green
> Shant be answered till the voice is still
> That dryeth the veins with its moan
> Of man and his meaning.

These and the lines that follow are in the freest of free verse; the occasional rhyme ("green . . . seen," "won . . . begun") seems fortuitous. There is no clear narrative line: the "voice," we learn, "shall be Job's . . . or Israel's . . . / Or the voice from the wilderness." But there is some sense of structure, for even this early draft expresses Thomas's main ideas, given poetic life in the opposition between, on the one hand, "meaning" and "reason" and, on the other, the implication of "He has no meaning but the blood's," a line that Thomas repeats. Basic questions about existence, such as those asked in the draft's first line, resist reasoned answers, as do other questions about existence, about, say, the nature of "love and the passing of time." "Knowing" and "meaning," intellectual grasp, seem inapplicable concepts; the instinctive response is the only meaningful one. The poem ends with an image from the schoolroom that suggests futile inquiry:

> he lifteth his hand
> But he is not seen.

Two years later, on 23 April 1933, in the "February 1933 Notebook," futility was again on Thomas's mind as he drafted a poem on "*whips and stools and cistern sex*," that is, on perverted sex and masturbation as sterile activities.[1] They create no children for a mother to nurture and, as they grow,

> Sees cool get cold and childmind darker
> As time on time sea ribbon rounds
> Parched shires in dry lands. (*PM*, 196)

Typically, Thomas thinks in terms of opposites: wet versus dry, youth versus time and old age.

Two months later, on 1 July 1933, Thomas wrote the first full version of "Why east wind chills and south wind cools" (*PM*, 204–6). In this he brought together from the two earlier poems the asking of questions about the nature of existence, and the concern with children and with time passing.

This new draft, loosely structured, originally consisted of fifty lines from which Thomas made some deletions. In 1936 he revised this version, reducing the length to twenty-six lines before publishing it in *New English Weekly* (16 July 1936) and subsequently, with only one small revision—"the towers of the sky" for "houses of the sky"—in *Twenty-five Poems* and *Collected Poems*. What follows compares these two versions.

The first five lines of the notebook version are an assured and rhythmic first sentence using the wet-dry opposition to raise questions that cannot be answered until after death. This version continues with lines about horses: a mare and its colt receiving no reply to such questions as "Why grass is sweet and thistles prick." Aspects of equine life—manuring, enduring the seasons' weather, the cruelty of whip and spur—are then described, the point being, it seems, that in the absence of replies life goes on. Children then ask, "What colour is glory?" only to be answered with further questions—"Shall they clasp a comet in their fists?" and "When cometh Jack Frost?"—that imply the impossibility of there being answers. This ends the first section of twenty lines.

The second section, originally thirteen lines long, asserts more directly that answers to the children's questions will not be forthcoming until after death. The extended metaphor of the next four lines, representing the destruction of innocence in terms of a vulture seizing a lamb, is deleted by Thomas. The second section ends with two further assertions that only after death will basic questions be answered. A separate section of three lines then repeats the last three lines of the notebook's first section:

> What colour is glory? the children ask.
> Shall they clasp a comet in their fists?
> When cometh Jack Frost?

The final section of the notebook version gestures, confusingly, in different directions. The "stars' advice"—"heard but little till the stars go out"—is generally ignored until the final catastrophe. Meanwhile, "through the country of the air," which may mean that of the stars but might mean the earthbound world,

I hear content, and Be content . . .
And, Walk content, and walk content
Though famine strips [the valley big with war],

the bracketed phrase deleted by Thomas. The same ambiguous source states "Know no answer," which might be a command but is certainly a description of how things are both for the narrator and for the children who raise fists towards "ghostly comets."

This final section shows Thomas's uncertainty about resolving his theme. The deleted phrase shows this clearly in suggesting economically depressed parts of South Wales on the verge of violent protest, a wholly new idea. Further, though the stars certainly represent external authority, it is not clear whether that authority is to be regarded as offering acceptable advice or as urging compliant acceptance. The line, in its 1930s context, suggests the hostility of the children to that which cannot be attained. It also refers back to the deleted phrase in suggesting, also, the Communist salute and so a general political protest.

Stanza 1 of the published version has only nine lines (*CP*, 46–47). The first five lines are identical to the notebook version except for the only punctuation: in the published poem a semicolon replaces a full stop to close the fifth line. The horses are jettisoned; the questions are now of human, specifically a child's, concern. They comprise three sets of oppositions between the comforting and the troubling. The main thrust of the opening stanza, utilizing the wet-dry contrast, is that basic questions about existence will not be answered until after death. Such questions receive only "a black reply," that is, in an instance of Thomas's suggestive rhetoric being underpinned by colloquial association, disapproval, a "black look."

The second stanza, now of six lines, implies that the children's desire to grasp exceeds their reach. It opens with a modified version of the last three lines of the notebook version's first section. The striking but highly abstract question "What colour is glory?" originally asked by the young daughter of a friend, is omitted and replaced by the more concrete "When cometh Jack Frost?" meaning death, given more prominence than in the earlier version. The Grand Guignol moments of the notebook version—the "whip cut weal" and bloody spur, the vulture seizing a lamb, the moon falling, the worms feeding at the poet's face—are ruthlessly expunged to leave only the more socialized details: Jack Frost, children, fists, eyes, and winter rooftops. These combine to suggest death, but recognizably so. Stanzas 3 and 4 continue the final version's clear narrative line and sharper focus. Since the stress is on what cannot be known in this life, the role of the stars as authoritative sources of knowledge is reduced accordingly. They now "ask" rather than "say"; they are no longer "on their business / Of rounding time on time the shires of sky," but "round / Time upon time the towers of the skies,'' seemingly excluded by a source of greater power. The stars have their own questions and represent time passing; they do no more.

The focus has shifted. Whereas the insistence on contentment emanated from the region of the stars (''the country of the air''), in the final version

> I hear content, and ''Be content''
> Ring like a handbell through the corridors.

The school image—perhaps derived associatively from the raised hand in the early source material—is that of socialized institutional authority in action. That the poem regards the limiting of knowledge as undesirable is implied by the structural contrast between the narrowness of ''corridors'' as opposed to the openness of the blowing winds, rooftops, and skies of the earlier stanzas. Though questions cannot be answered in this life, yet they should still be asked, the poem asserts. It is a protest against social restriction, emphasized in political terms by the final line, retained from the notebook version: ''And ghostly comets over the raised fists.'' The poem links a general desire for knowledge—a desire that should be instilled into children—and, from the 1930s left-wing perspective that Thomas adopted, the freed masses reaching for the stars and hostile to limitations. However, he qualifies these positives by stressing the unknown consequences of such gestures, the poem ending with the uncertainty about the future all too characteristic and understandable in 1933, let alone in 1936.

The relationship of the earlier material to the final version shows Thomas, though concentrating effect and structuring tightly, much concerned to focus and to clarify. He is also concerned to preserve or include recognizable social detail, an element of realism furthered by his preference for the concrete over the abstract. Further, whereas the notebook version offers a series of instinctive gestures, the final version insists on the need to ask questions, to reject socially authorized complacency. We see Thomas move through his various drafts to an engagement with the self-versus-oppressive-world theme that was always a central preoccupation.

''AND DEATH SHALL HAVE NO DOMINION''

One of Thomas's most famous poems, ''And death shall have no dominion,'' has a different history of composition. It began its known life as poem ''Twenty Three'' in the ''February 1933 Notebook.'' Here it is closely linked to its context, the notebook poems immediately preceding and succeeding it (*PM*, 183–86, 188–91). Of these, poem ''Twenty'' is about social change: the old way, that of the ploughman and the hansom-cab driver, has been replaced by the ''iron saddle'' and the ''engines.'' In itself this is a hackneyed theme. But the old way's passing, in which both the ploughman and the hansom driver ''lie cold, with their horses, for raven and kite,'' should remind us of Thomas's school-magazine poems about the Great War. ''Missing,'' for example, as has been seen, describes a soldier lying dead on the battlefield. Poem "Twenty One" is equally dark though less specific; its theme is the child's need to master "night's terrors." "Twenty Two," "My body knows its wants," is about the difficulty of achieving ambitions. It ends with lines on friendship. "A friend is but an enemy on stilts," asserts a cynical Thomas, meaning that a seeming friend may exist on a plane so far above objective scrutiny that he may well turn out to be an enemy. That plane is one

> Where war moves not the planets in their course
> An inch more than armistice, signed with a cross.

Having moved, readily, into language redolent of World War I, so often used by Thomas, he concludes:

> Man's wants remain unsatisfied till death.
> Then, when his soul is naked, is he one
> With the man in the wind, and the west moon,
> With the harmonious thunder of the sun.

"Twenty Two" is dated "April 2, '33." These four concluding lines were deleted, three of them to be reused immediately, with only a minor variation, in stanza 1 of the very next poem, "Twenty Three" ("And death shall have no dominion"), dated "April '33" (*PM*, 186–88).

Poem "Twenty Four," following "And death shall have no dominion," concerns a madman. It opens:

> Within his head revolved a little world
> Where wheels, confusing music, confused doubts,
> Rolled down all images into the pits
> Where half dead vanities were sleeping curcled [*sic*]
> Like cats, and lusts lay half hot in the cold.
>
> Within his head the engines made their hell,
> The veins at either temple whipped him mad.

Psychological confusion is rendered in terms of wagons tipping loads into pits that fill with human attributes, perhaps with bodies, and of the hellish noise of engines. As the madman wanders through a grotesque world, he observes "man to engine, battling, / Bruising," a November in which "there were whizzbangs hopping"—a reference to Guy Fawkes celebrations but using Great War slang for high-velocity shells—and confesses to having "waved flags to every fife and drum" of jingoistic patriotism. His is a search for God in a world the hostility of which is in part conveyed, once again, through Great War imagery.

In such a sequence—linked tightly to it via the lines deleted and transposed from poem "Twenty Two," lines that themselves follow specific war references—is ''Twenty Three,'' the first published version of ''And death shall have no dominion.'' In part, as has been noted, it owes its existence to a competition between Thomas and A. E. Trick for the best poem about ''Immortality.'' Trick's poem was published locally and opens:

> For death is not the end!
> Though soul turns sour
> And faith dry-rots,
> Let maggots feed on flesh . . .
> And memory sink
> Beneath the dust of falling years.

It continues with lines already quoted:

> Lungs chewed by poison gas
> Attempt to sing.[2]

The poem demonstrates Trick's own obsession with the Great War. ''And death shall have no dominion'' not only emerges from the notebook matrix of war-dominated associative thought, but was also written when Trick's influence on Thomas was at its strongest. Our expectations of the poem are colored by these two facts.

The notebook version was published, without alteration, in *New English Weekly* during May 1933.[3] The first of its four stanzas opens with the familiar image of a body lying on open ground: ''Man'' lies dead in the wind, through the night and under the sun, preyed on by birds or rats until even his bones are taken. Though, with ''soul naked,'' his spiritual being is especially vulnerable, and in a clause that allows the verb's military meaning, ''Though he fall mad'' or drown, Thomas insists that Man will achieve resurrection. His finer human qualities will also survive: in a line recalling tragic casualties Thomas asserts that ''Though lovers be lost, love shall not.''

Stanza 2 asserts that ''Man'' will survive drowning. But the line ''Under green shiftings of the sea'' also hints at rippling grass and combines with a line describing ''Man'' lying under the snow to sustain the sense of the battlefield setting where he lives and dies courageously:

> Twisting on racks when sinews give way,
> Strapped to a wheel, yet he shall not break.

The lines dramatize indomitable spirit in the face of general suffering. The second line allows for harrowing World War I connotations. ''Field Punishment No. 1,'' for a soldier convicted of indiscipline, meant being fastened to a fixed object for a specified time. The punishment was often known as ''Crucifixion,'' for the offender was usually strapped to the wheel of a wagon or gun carriage with his arms outstretched.⁴ The lines that follow,

> Faith, in his hands, shall snap in two,
> And all the swords of evil run him through;
> Split all ends up, he shan't crack;

describing the apparent vulnerability of Man's religious faith, bayonetting, and the effect of explosions, nevertheless insist on a basic invincibility.

Stanza 3 asserts that beyond death's desolation and the seeming destruction of beauty, "Beauty may blossom in pain," a sentiment that recalls Thomas's view of the war poets in his schoolboy essay on "Modern Poetry." The final stanza develops this optimism with thoughts of resurrection: through death

> Man shall discover all he thought lost,
> And hold his little soul within his fist;
> Knowing that now can he never be dust,
> He waits in the sun till the sun goes out;
> Now he knows what he had but guessed
> Of living and dying and all the rest;
> He knows his soul.

This published writing moves away from the explicitness of other notebook poems about the Great War. Overall, it tends to mythologize the body on the field and the suffering of the soldier, leaving the reader to infer a harsher subtext. The quoted ending is affirmative, a version of *per ardua ad astra*, Christian immortality intended to console.

Few now read it, for the version published in 1933 has long been superseded by the revised version in three shorter stanzas (*CP*, 56) that is one of Thomas's most famous poems. This final text has important differences, two of which are in stanza 1. Though the final version begins with the same battlefield scene, "Man, with soul naked" is replaced by the bleaker "Dead men naked." The soul, it seems, is no longer a consideration. Second, "Though he fall mad" becomes "Though they go mad": in the former the man is mad at the moment of death in battle; in the latter the men, no longer the "fallen," may well have been mad before that. In stanza 2 the deletion of "green shiftings" means that the sea is now simply the sea. Thomas replaces "Man . . . shall not die" with "They . . . shall not die windily," playing on the "cowardly" meaning of the last word to infer courage in death. He preserves most of the remainder of the stanza, including the reference to field punishment. But the Great War connections are slightly more difficult to make: the battlefield references—the "green shiftings" and the snow—have gone; "swords of evil" becomes "unicorn evils," still suggestive of bayonets, but more obliquely, more mythologically.

The new stanza 3 replaces stanzas 3 and 4 of the first version. Though it retains some of the original lines, the differences are fundamental. All suggestions that "Beauty may blossom in pain" and all references to achieving religious awareness through death and Judgment Day resurrection have been deleted. Instead, the poem ends pantheistically. Life after death means that life continues as part of nature:

> Though they be mad and dead as nails,
> Heads of the characters hammer through daisies.

The dead possess a continuing and strangely violent power that, in enabling them to "Break in the sun," can even control the main source of natural energy. This power is in direct contrast to the helplessness of the living and the dying.

Critics of Thomas's poetry are in general agreement about "And death shall have no dominion." William York Tindall, for example, considered that "Thomas is conducting a service for all the dead in certain hope of glorious resurrection." Clark Emery stressed its affirmative quality: "Death is not an end of living but a metamorphosis." For William Moynihan, the "poem is simply . . . a . . . statement . . . that matter cannot be destroyed." Walford Davies considered that the poem illustrates a central theme in Thomas's work, that death is to an extent overcome by the dead person entering the natural cycle.[5] The consensus is that this is a straightforward poem of simple affirmation. Yet if we begin with the notebook version and register its emergence from that matrix of Great War associations and from A. E. Trick's influence, we see what has never before been noticed: that both versions can also be read as war poems.

Further, the relationship between the two published versions is anything but simple. The absence of the Christian ending and the compressing of the poem that concentrates attention on the dead of stanza 1 and, in stanza 2, on the violence done to soldiers seem, on the face of it, to make the final version darker. But in this version the emotional effect of the Great War material is countered by two factors. One is the tight form of the poem, achieved almost wholly by a rhythmic energy that surges in support of the recurring optimistic refrain. The other is what might be called a domesticating subtext: the pun on "windily," the use of the common Welsh phrase for "raining" (*bwrw gwlaw*, literally the "blows of the rain"), phrases that suggest "dead as a doornail" and "pushing up daisies," the "daisies" reference also creating a homely version of the Adonis myth, and the witty link between "nails" and "hammer." We might wish to say that form and subtext are essentially deconstructive; we might also wish to say, with more certainty, that they impose on the poem sufficient control of the darker Great War material to enable the reader to respond very directly to the optimistic repetition. In this sense the final version is a poem demonstrating Thomas's increased concern for his readers—increased social awareness—that was to increase further in the later part of his career: "And death shall have no dominion" resembles the school-magazine poems in that it has become a poem for bereaved survivors still desperately clinging to consoling ideas of triumphant heroism.

"WHEN ONCE THE TWILIGHT LOCKS NO LONGER"

Whereas "And death shall have no dominion" emerged from a poetry competition with a friend, the initial impetus for "When once the twilight locks no longer" was a letter to Pamela Hansford Johnson:

This is written on Armistice Day, 1933, when the war is no more than a memory of privations and the cutting down of the young. There was panic in the streets, we remember, and the food was bad; there were women who had "lost" their sons, though where they had lost them and why they could [not] find them, we, who were children born out of blood into blood, could never tell. The state was a murderer, and every country in this rumour-ridden world, peopled by the unsuccessful suicides left over by the four mad years, is branded like Cain across the forehead. What was Christ in us was stuck with a bayonet to the sky, and what was Judas we fed and sheltered, rewarding, at the end, with thirty hanks of flesh. Civilization is a murderer. We, with the cross of a castrated Saviour cut on our brows, sink deeper and deeper with the days into the pit of the West.[6]

The war was fifteen years into the past, when both writer and reader had only a child's partial understanding. Yet the coolly distanced, slightly cynical tone of this passage's opening soon gives way, with the reference to "children born out of blood into blood," to a more violent reaction, disturbing in its intensity, against those "four mad years." That was a time of legalized murder; among the victims were not only those cut down and those whose subsequent lives were ruined, but also man's very capacity for Christlike goodness, which was betrayed and destroyed. The result, writes Thomas, is despair and frustration for his own generation. What is evident in the imagery of branding, bayoneting, and mutilating is the depth of Thomas's hatred of what the Great War did and continued to do, and the extent to which it seized his sympathetic and fascinated imagination. With this letter Thomas enclosed the first draft, dated "November 11, 33," of "When once the twilight locks no longer" (*PM*, 255–57).

It begins with the narrator observing himself about to be born, as a locked-in fetus in the womb about to pass through the "twilight locks" into the outside world. In that world he sleeps and dreams, and the nature of the dream, dominating the central part of the poem, reminds us of its Armistice Day origins. The opening line of the dream sequence, "Some dead upon a slab of wind," Thomas's recurring symbol of bodies lying dead on open ground, already encountered in "And death shall have no dominion," is the prelude to a series of horrors in this and subsequent stanzas: the gangrenous "redhaired cancer," the dead man's "stuff [to give the troops?]," flies, rats, and general rottenness and infection, which "did crow upon my heap" and so include the narrator among the dead. Rotting bodies, dying men,

> violet fungus still alive
> And winking eyes that catch the eye of death

are at the center of the sleeper's dreadful vision. So too are the growing poppy ("The seed of dreams that showed a bud"), the narrator's continued exposure to all possible horrors, and his persisting sense of himself as a victim.

The lurid dream sequence, in particular, is very much a first draft, not always controlled or clear. It contains echoes of earlier notebook references to the Great War, such as the phrase "O living deaths," which recalls "The living dead left over from the war" in the appallingly direct "We who are young are old." "Some dead upon a slab of wind" and "as age knocks down the flowers" are strong reminders of "the man in the wind" and "Where blew a flower may a flower no more" in "And death shall have no dominion," all of which is further evidence of Thomas's associative use of the notebook drafts. Above all, the poem, like "And death shall have no dominion," moves to pantheistic affirmation:

> A sweet shrub rises from the wrecks
> And sprouts between the coffins [sic] crack;
> The dead are singing in the cypress yard.

Less than four months later, "When once the twilight locks no longer" was extensively revised and extended for publication.[7] The structure, though clarified, remains essentially the same: the narrator is precisely placed as a nonphysical, perhaps spiritual consciousness that observes the fetus being born and weaned only to see it succumb to life as "dream," to be "drowned" in lurid imaginings. Three stanzas then describe the contents of the dream: rotting bodies with falling jaws, flies, the "shades" of the buried dead who observe "the working sea" of life as though through periscopes, hanged men whose limbs protrude from lime pits, and dead men in "sleep's acres" who are alive only in dreams. The poem ends with an exhortation that the "sleeper" should awake and seize through action what in one sense are the world's opportunities.

For Tindall "the theme of this poem is creation," the dream stanzas comprise a poem within a poem parodying Thomas's own work, and the final stanza is Thomas exhorting himself to move from the lurid to the real. Korg considered that the narrator is God, whose son, the born Christ, becomes no more than a dreamer. Walford Davies's detailed and illuminating analysis develops Tindall's point in arguing that in the poem's "main statement . . . The creature ('my sleeper') is urged to commit himself not to the morbid world of adolescent dreams and fears but to the waking everyday world of reality." Davies concluded that "at least in terms of developing statement," together with its element of "self-scrutiny and self-appraisal," the poem advances from the "relatively static quality" of much of Thomas's early work.[8]

Though there is no interpretive consensus, commentators are united in their failure to appreciate the significance of the poem's Armistice Day origins, even though there are explicit references to the Great War in the final version. For example, the fetus's birth is described in terms of an exploding land mine:

> My fuses timed to charge his heart,
> He blew like powder to the light.

After the birth, says the narrator, "I sent my creature scouting on the globe." The dream itself retains horrific physical description and adds two more significant images. One is "the Christ-cross-row of death" that, while it retains other possible meanings, certainly evokes the Flanders war cemetery. Second is the reference to "the shades / Who periscope through flowers to the sky," this example of Thomas's grotesque wit—the dead in their graves peering at the living—drawing on the periscopic scanning of no-man's-land from the safety of a trench. In the new sixth stanza limbs protruding from lime suggest propeller blades; the dead in "sleep's acres," brought back to a kind of life through dark but deluded imaginings, "snipe the fools of vision in the back." The final apostrophe to "my sleeper" urges him to "leave the poppied pickthank where he lies" in favor of a cavalry charge over flattened fences that only the "briskest" survive. The stanza translates without strain into a Great War scenario. Its final line, "And worlds hang on the trees," supplies an ambiguous ending, at once optimistic in its sense of prizes to be won and pessimistic (we recall the "hanged" in the lime pits) in suggesting the death of hopes and opportunities.

Though this is a more explicit war poem than the notebook version, as with "And death shall have no dominion" Thomas is careful to control the emotional impact. The rhyme scheme is *aabccb*, the rhymes themselves all consonantal but sufficiently stressed—helped by the two couplets in each stanza, plus the echoing *b* rhyme—for a controlling structure to register. It is supported by the syllable counts in each stanza—8, 8, 10, 8, 8, 10—which are strictly maintained,[9] with the exception of the poem's final line of 6 emphatic syllables. The ending also counters horror. The penultimate stanza not only sums up the effect of Thomas's Great War imaginings, which "conjured up a carcass shape / To rob me of my fluids in his heart," but also, through recapitulation, imposes logical sequence on emotional impact. The final stanza then provides a possible positive conclusion to the poem. In allowing, as the whole poem does, for a Great War interpretation, the ending develops Walford Davies's perceptive observation that the poem is a distinct step forward in Thomas's poetic development. That is, the final positive possibilities indicate Thomas's desire to free himself from the recent war's persisting nightmare scenario. "I dreamed my genesis" exhibits a similar desire in a similar ending. The poet escapes dreaming's "sweat of death"

> until, vision
> Of new man strength, I seek the sun.

Significantly, this poem also was mainly written during the same period (May–June 1934) in which Thomas completed "When once the twilight."

NOTES

1. *PM*, 196. Maud commented that part of this poem is missing (the notebook pages were torn out), and he has substituted a typescript copy now in the British Library. Part of this copy is in italics, presumably Thomas's own.

2. See *CP*, 209, where the poem is quoted in full.

3. Dylan Thomas, "Death shall have no dominion," *New English Weekly* 3, No. 5 (18 May 1933): 118.

4. See the official *Manual of Military Law*, 6th edition (February 1914), which was based on the Army Act of 1881. Quoted in John Baynes, *Morale* (London: Cassell, 1967), 188–89.

"Strapped to a wheel, yet they shall not break" has been interpreted very differently by Walford Davies as suggesting "the death of martyrs (St Catherine was tortured and killed on a spiked wheel)" (Dylan Thomas, *Selected Poems*, ed. Walford Davies, revised Everyman ed. [London: Dent, 1993], 88). My intention, here and elsewhere, is not to displace other readings but to add to them. What may be arguable, of course, is the comparative importance of various possibilities. In my opinion there is as strong a case for regarding "And death shall have no dominion" as a war poem as there is for a specifically religious reading. The former does not, of course, invalidate the latter.

5. Respectively, William York Tindall, *A Reader's Guide to Dylan Thomas* (1962; New York: Octagon Books, 1981), 122; Clark Emery, *The World of Dylan Thomas* (Coral Gables, FL: University of Miami Press, 1962), 211; William T. Moynihan, *The Craft and Art of Dylan Thomas* (1966; Ithaca, NY: Cornell University Press, 1968), 205; Walford Davies, *Dylan Thomas*, Open Guides to Literature (Milton Keynes: Open UP, 1986) 92.

6. *CL*, 54. Letter to Pamela Hansford Johnson, dated [week of 11 November 1933].

7. The poem was first published in *18 Poems* (London: *Sunday Referee* and Parton Bookshop, 1934). The version in Dylan Thomas, *Collected Poems, 1934–1952* (London: Dent, 1952), omits stanza 6 ("The hanged who lever from the limes"). *CP*, 9–10, restores it. The present discussion is of the *CP* (and *18 Poems*) version. See *CP*, 166–67 and 179–80, for a full discussion of the textual history.

8. Respectively, Tindall, *Reader's Guide to Dylan Thomas*, 34; Jacob Korg, *Dylan Thomas* (New York: Twayne, 1965), 62; Davies, *Dylan Thomas*, Open Guides to Literature, 38.

9. The first lines of stanzas 1 and 2, and lines 4 and 5 of stanza 6, have 9 syllables, but these seeming deviations are probably explained in terms of the oral value Thomas accorded to "longer," "finger," "wither," and "acres."

7

18 Poems

When Thomas prepared *18 Poems* (1934) for publication, he included only eleven previously published poems.[1] Others had been available, only to be omitted. Yet all the exclusions are not without interest or merit. "That sanity be kept," for example, which Pamela Hansford Johnson read with such interest when it first appeared, describes a solitary and detached figure—surely the young Thomas—hearing "sweet suburban music from a hundred lawns,"[2] a distanced observer of the suburban scene and especially of passing lovers who struggle with feelings of "grief" and "vague bewilderment." The similarly titled "That the sum sanity might add to naught," included in Thomas's first list of poems to be included,[3] has a priestlike narrator who wishes to offer inadequate counsel to what appear to be victims of 1930s deprivation. "Greek Play in a Garden" engages with an outdoor performance of Sophocles' *Electra*, in part contrasting indifferent, thoughtless nature to the play's horrific events. All three poems reflect the narrator's uneasy, neovoyeuristic apartness from the social mainstream. A related unease is found in two other uncollected poems: "No man believes," which argues, interestingly, for doubt as a necessary precursor of faith, and "Song," which begins, "Love me, not as the dreaming nurses," an elegant short lyric on love's contradictory complexities.[4] Thomas also omitted two poems permeated with references to the Great War: "The Woman Speaks," also on Thomas's short list, and "Within his head revolved a little world," published with the title "Out of the pit," both of which have already been discussed, the latter as a poem in which the narrator searches for God in a hostile world.

All these poems focus on central ideas and themes: the outsider stance, the dualism of life, the Great War. Thomas may well have felt that they reflected influences too blatantly—that of T. S. Eliot, for instance, in "That sanity be kept"—that one or two were untypical, or that others were structured too slackly. Certainly it is hard to argue that any except possibly "Song," which, though untypical in its echoes of "cavalier" lyricism, is beautifully made, should have replaced any of Thomas's final eighteen. Here, at least, he showed good judgment.

Thomas always arranged his volumes carefully. He decided at an early stage that *18 Poems* should begin with "I see the boys of summer in their ruin."[5] This is now a famous poem with an opening that reminds us that one of Thomas's enduring strengths was his ability to compose striking single lines. One of the sources of the poem was his comment to Bert Trick when walking on the beach at Swansea that "middle-aged men in Corporation bathing suits [were] 'boys of summer in their ruin,' "[6] a characteristic connecting of the semisatirical and the more universal and seriously suggestive. The line could be seen as descriptive of the dead and maimed survivors of that Great War so often on Thomas's mind; it has, perhaps, even more direct applicability to the economic casualties of the 1930s. But, as the source comment indicates, at the heart of the poem is the suburban predicament: the poem is a product both of Thomas's heightened sense of the restrictive narrowness of his Swansea upbringing, and of his relationship with his father.

The poem's first section, narrated by an older man, begins with futile sexual hope: out of the heat of intercourse comes only "frozen love." The boys' members are "jacks of frost" inserted like fatal fingers into the female "hives." The phrase "jacks of frost" echoes the vulgar "jacking off" in suggesting fruitless masturbation. It also, via the colloquialism and the idea of creative failure, reminds us of Jack Thomas.

Stanza 2 explains the "boys' " predicament. The physical life is frozen or soured by the puritanically moral restrictions of life in the provincial suburbs;

> There in the sun the frigid threads
> Of doubt and dark they feed their nerves.

When conception and birth do occur, only "men of nothing" come from such "seedy shifting." Yet potential and possibility persist, even though they may amount to no more than "the dogdayed pulse / Of love and light." That the "pulse of summer" survives even such a frozen world is one possible reading of the final line of section 1.

Section 2 is the boys' reply. They know that they are "dark deniers" and that their sexual energy is deathly or, at best, enables the birth of a "man of straw." They also know that

> seasons must be challenged or they totter
> Into a chiming quarter
> Where, punctual as death, we ring the stars;

that is, something must be done before time passes and lives end. Such recognition preserves phallic potential: "O see the poles of promise in the boys."

The poem's single-stanza final section is best read as a dialogue between the older narrator and the boys. The latter recognize themselves as the products of corrupting circumstances: they are "the sons of flint and pitch." The narrator tells the boys, "I am the man your father was," a line effecting a subtextual link with the futile aspirations of the younger D. J. Yet the final line, in which the verb "cross" preserves some ambivalence, suggests the creative link between sex and love, thus ending the poem with an optimistic gesture.

"I see the boys of summer" is a poem typical of Thomas in that it generates great tension. This last is partly derived from the boys' frustrations, the extent to which social context and the passing of time limit sexual efficacy, and partly from the dialogue between the observing, commenting, older narrator and the boys who reply to him. The narrator's language is, in the main, lyrically regretful; the boys' reply at first echoes the narrator's constructions, then becomes more vehement; the syntax becomes more tortuous, the language more polyphonic. When this is combined with the dialogic force of the two main sections, plus the internal dialogue of section 3 and the neoapostrophic final lines of each section, with their counterpointing ambiguity, the effect is of a tendency towards fragmentation indicative of social strain—different languages, different worlds—countered by a narrative thrust towards reconciliation and by imposed structural devices.

These last include controlling repetition, one example of which is the placing of a verb at the beginning of the second line of each stanza in section 1. Another is the use of "There" to begin the fourth line of each of the first four stanzas in order to state what the boys do as a consequence of what they have become. This is repeated in the fifth stanza, the first of section 2, spoken by the boys, as one way of dramatizing how, initially in this section, the boys have difficulty in freeing themselves from the world that is destroying them. We perceive a decrease in repetitive patterning from section 1 to section 2, reflecting the boys' attempts to break free. We also perceive that though all is subsumed within the rhyme scheme of *aabccb* in each stanza, the rhymes invariably consonantal/assonantal, that scheme, though always a presence, is never blatantly authoritarian. As with the limited use of rhetorical patterning, this seems appropriate in a poem that never wholly denies the possibility of escaping from repressive social control.

As has been suggested, the "boys of summer in their ruin" could be a description of the Great War's victims. The explosion imagery of stanza 4—"love and light bursts in their throats"—could be a similar connection. Here is one way in which this opening poem serves as an introduction to a volume in which, as in the notebooks, the Great War is a recurring motif.

Indeed, the collection is haunted by those "four mad years"[7] that even in the early 1930s, as has been shown, were still a terrible presence in many minds. We understand why Thomas reaches so readily for the military image, even in poems with different central themes. Korg reminded us that the fourth stanza of "Before I knocked," a poem at once about the Incarnation and about secular suffering, renders what is both the Flagellation and Thorn Crowning of Christ,

or the tortured imaginings of the secular fetus, in a manner that suggests cutting
wire to penetrate enemy defences:

> And flesh was snipped to cross the lines
> Of gallow crosses on the liver
> And brambles in the wringing brains.[8]

In the same poem the shadowy subtext of the line "And I was struck down by
death's feather," and the repeated "death's feather" references throughout this
volume, may well reflect the wartime practice of handing a white feather to
civilians suspected of being reluctant to fight. The "shot" in stanza 1 of "A
process in the weather of the heart" and the famous central figure of the "fuse"
and the (implied) mine in "The force that through the green fuse" are similar
examples.

Three poems have substantial links with the Great War. One, discussed in
detail elsewhere, is "When once the twilight locks no longer," the war poem
written on Armistice Day 1933. The second is "I dreamed my genesis," which
reflects Thomas's awareness of his own wartime birth during the first Battle of
Ypres. In the opening stanza a "rotating shell" drives "Through vision and the
girdered nerve," an image of wartime violence developed in key lines in stanza
4:

> I dreamed my genesis and died again, shrapnel
> Rammed in the marching heart, hole
> In the stitched wound and clotted wind, muzzled
> Death on the mouth that ate the gas.

The third poem is "My world is pyramid," in which the Austrian uprising of
1934 is described in terms more appropriate to the Somme:

> the riddled lads
> Strewing their bowels from a hill of bones,
> Cry Eloi to the guns.

"Who blows death's feather?" is a later chilling line in the same poem. Thomas
was fascinated by the Great War and drawn to its violence and horror. He was
to preserve a propensity for violent imagery throughout his career. Here is one
source.

"I dreamed my genesis" also relates back to another main concern of "I see
the boys of summer," that with the role of the male in the sexual act. As the
title indicates, this concern is linked to his own conception; it is also linked to
the obsession with his father, the tension between "D. J. Thomas" and "Jack
Thomas" that impels much of his poetry. "Jacks of frost" of that opening poem
is echoed in "Jack of Christ" in "If I were tickled by the rub of love." Both

"Before I knocked" and "I dreamed my genesis" stress the father's contribution to the procreative sexual act, represented, respectively, by "the rainy hammer / Swung" and "the scalding veins that hold love's drop." Both "hammer" and "veins" suggest power that is more destructive than sexually creative, indicating, on Thomas's part, a fascination akin to that for the Great War, another instance of the attraction of violence.

Further, in each of these poems, as in, for example, "My world is pyramid,"[9] the prebirth state is one of knowledge, even wisdom, and, comparatively speaking, security. That state is, so to speak, destroyed by the father, whose copulation results in the birth that, in "Before I knocked," means entry into a hostile and ultimately disappointing world:

> And time cast forth my mortal creature
> To drift or drown upon the seas
> Acquainted with the salt adventure
> Of tides that never touch the shores.

Similarly, in "I dreamed my genesis" the narrator, about to be born, "marked the hills, harvest / Of hemlock and the blades" of the cruel world he is about to experience.

Hence the stress on reenactment: "I am the man your father was," the poet-narrator tells each ruined boy of summer. In insisting, in these early fatherly poems, on a creative power that, inhibited by circumstances, results only in the destruction of happiness and in a lack of fulfillment, Thomas's poetic expression of his relationship with his father and his own initial ventures into the world, his poetry reenacts his father's relationship with his own early promise and subsequent disappointment. It can also be said that the poems themselves, the tight, disciplined structures containing sexual and natal material daring in its time and burgeoning in suggestiveness, figure the tension between D. J. Thomas the fastidious suburbanite and Jack Thomas his rougher, fouler-mouthed alter ego.

One other aspect of Dylan Thomas's fatherly obsession is echoes of *Hamlet*, that archetypal study of a son haunted by a father's posthumous desires, an early instance of which is in "I dreamed my genesis" when the narrator states that "From limbs that had the measure of the worm, [I] shuffled / Off from the creasing flesh." Tindall suggested that the word "rub," and particularly the phrase "And that's the rub," in "If I were tickled by the rub of love," also refer to the famous soliloquy.[10] A further reference is in "I fellowed sleep," the poem in which parents compete for their son, and in which the son, having risen above his mother, is still followed by "My father's ghost."

The violence of conception linked to the tension and consequent familial unease generated by his father's class-bound predicament—the failure of working-class Jack wholly to become middle-class D. J.—the complications of the middle-class son's paternal relationship, and the ramifications of the Great War contribute to the strong social dimension within these eighteen poems. The substantial amount of social detail also helps anchor these poems firmly to the 1930s. Among allusions, direct or indirect, to contemporary domestic and industrial life are the "doubt and dark" and "quarry" images in "I see the boys of summer" that once again introduce a series of references that include, in succeeding poems, "propellers," "workers in the morning town," the overhead cisterns of old lavatories, a liner's screws propelling it through the sea, the cinema, the park, the "pot of ferns" and "wagging clock," and the constant use of industrial or mechanical imagery—pumping, gushing, drilling—and the "secret lots . . . tips . . . [and] . . . waste allotments" of the between-wars urban landscape.

At the center of such a world is the individual. Yet, despite such centrality, our sense of his power is undermined by the body's metaphorical role. Here again we encounter Thomas the "process" poet, who has often received disproportionate attention at the expense of his other characteristics, notably the social ones. That said, his "processive" proclivities cannot be denied.

The classic account is Ralph Maud's.[11] He defined "process poems" as those that explore "the duality of the world," the "struggle between black and white." This leads, as Maud noted, to the use of a vocabulary that seeks to unite opposing meanings. Thus "worm" suggests death, of course, but also "sperm," which is a life force. "Tide," another example, is used as part of the conventional sea of life to suggest the life force, which seems positive, but can also connote the destructive or inhibiting, as in "Tides that never touch the shores," the line in "Before I knocked" that points to life's failure to fulfil or to satisfy.

But "process" is not simply duality; it also involves, to put it grandly, metaphoricizing existence, the processes of life represented by the processes of the body. Thomas found his authority in John Donne. The key passage is worth quoting in full:

Nearly all my images, coming, as they do, from my solid and fluid world of flesh and blood, are set out in terms of their progenitors. To contrast a superficial beauty with a superficial ugliness, I do not contrast a tree with a pylon, or a bird with a weasel, but rather the human limbs with the human tripes. . . . The body . . . has its roots in the same earth as the tree. The greatest description I know of our own "earthiness" is to be found in John Donne's Devotions, where he describes man as earth of the earth, his body earth, his hair a wild shrub growing out of the land. All thoughts and actions emanate from the body. Therefore the description of a thought or action—however abstruse it may be—can be beaten home by bringing it onto a physical level. Every idea, intuitive or intellectual, can be imaged and translated in terms of the body, its flesh, skin, blood, sinews, veins, glands, organs, cells, or senses. Through my small, bonebound island I have learnt all I know, experienced all, and sensed all. All I write is inseparable from the island. As much as possible, therefore, I employ the scenery of the island to describe the scenery of my thoughts, the earthquakes of the body to describe the earthquakes of the heart.[12]

Here are two important ideas: the self-sufficiency of the body through which the physical illustrates the emotional, and the relationship between the body and the external world, the processes of the former serving as metaphors for those of the latter, or, to repeat another phrase of Thomas's, "the cosmic significance of the human anatomy."[13] From this passage we begin to understand why, in thus harmonizing self and world, Thomas is sometimes regarded as a romantic survivor. We also see that such harmonizing is in terms of *natural* processes, heightening, not contradicting, the tension between self and world that, as we have seen, is expressed elsewhere in Thomas in social terms.

So far as "process" in *18 Poems* is concerned, the key poems are "A process in the weather of the heart" and "The force that through the green fuse drives the flower." In the former the "process" of the first line is mirrored by that which "blows the moon into the sun"; in the latter the same forces are recognized, yet here man's separation from nature—the consequence of his being "dumb to tell"—becomes a predicament with tragic potential.

Thomas worried lest his obsession with "process" become a damaging, because limiting, solipsism, explaining his use of "imagery almost totally anatomical" and continuing:

But I defend the diction, the perhaps wearisome succession of blood and bones, the neverending similes of the streams in the veins and the lights in the eyes, by saying that, for the time at least, I realise that it is impossible for me to raise myself to the altitude of the stars, and that I am forced, therefore, to bring down the stars to my own level and to incorporate them in my own physical universe.[14]

This smacks of significantly defensive special pleading. It also seems unnecessary, for in the best poems in this volume, which include "Before I knocked," "The force that through the green fuse," and "Light breaks where no sun shines," the body does take on the "cosmic significance" he sought; here, at least, the implications of "Man be my metaphor" are triumphantly realized. But it is surely true to say that even in these avowedly "process" pieces, "cosmic" is a familiar abstract distraction from the poems' more important concern with self and world.

In this early volume, despite the importance of "process," we invariably return to four other themes, two of which, the effect of the Great War on the sensibility of Thomas's generation, and his relations with a father who struggled with the problems of being a first-generation member of the professional middle class, have already been discussed. Of the third, his own provincial predicament first encountered in "I see the boys of summer," there is more to say.

In so doing we can return to "process," for in one sense its link between the body and the world, the former controlled by the same forces as charge the latter, implies the former's helplessness. Indeed, these poems are full of the helpless and the failures. For example, as has been noted, to enter the world, like the newly born who may also be Christ in "Before I knocked," is to encounter disappointment and frustration. To be in the world, like the "boys of summer," is to be ruined, seemingly by circumstances; positive possibilities remain in the future. As befits the adolescent poet (Thomas was twenty when *18 Poems* appeared) of "If I were tickled by the rub of love," though he hopes for satisfying sex he can only

> sit and watch the worm beneath my nail
> Wearing the quick away.

The pun on "quick," life itself, not simply the skin beneath the nail, makes its own point. The poet's world is dominated by the tyranny of the temporal, by the "tides of time," "clocking tides," blood-sucking time, reproving time, time cruelly seizing the fetus to "cast [it] forth . . . To drift or drown upon the seas." It is the "wagging clock" shaking an admonitory finger at the vulnerable individual.

Yet despite the combined power of social circumstance and implacable time, positive possibilities—possible positive readings—often persist. Once again "I see the boys of summer" serves as an introduction to the volume. The optimistic thrust that is one reading of those three section endings, the contrasting, in characteristic structural maneuvers, of endings that stress assertive and hopeful sensual/sexual action with preceding pessimism, recurs in later poems. Thus the conclusion of "When once the twilight locks no longer" urges, "Awake, my sleeper, to the sun" and to seizable opportunities as "worlds hang on the trees." "A process in the weather of the heart" ends by echoing the positive side of Judgment Day, when "the heart gives up its dead." "Our eunuch dreams" concludes:

> And we shall be fit fellows for a life,
> And who remain shall flower as they love,
> Praise to our faring hearts.

In "From love's first fever," after life's vicissitudes "the tears of spring / Dissolved in summer" so that one's life becomes "One sun, one manna, warmed and fed." The narrator of "I dreamed my genesis" emerges from horrors to "seek the sun." "Light breaks where no sun shines" ends by greeting a perpetual sun. Even "Where once the waters of your face," concerned as it is with the loss of childhood wonder, closes with an attempt at retrieval. We reach for such words as "resilient" and "indomitable," qualities also evident in Thomas's grotesque wit: a personified "love" tickling, the mouth of the womb like a canal or harbor "lock," "time" represented as a "running grave" chasing after the poet. The vision is strange, sometimes bizarre, but, in being witty, often reassuring, as are the endings in insisting on survival.

This chapter has argued for "I see the boys of summer" as an introduction to the volume, treating themes and ideas that recur in succeeding poems. In one respect it does not fulfil this function: except in the most general way, if the second part is read as the narrator's statement of what poetry should and should not do, it does not engage with the fourth central subject, the theme of writing. Nevertheless, this theme becomes for Thomas a near obsession.

We see it emerging even in poems mainly concerned with other matters. For example, the opening of "When once the twilight locks no longer," which is essentially a war poem, in such references as "locked in the long worm of my finger" and "the sea that sped around my fist," suggests the writer's not-altogether-controllable power and the way that power is set free when the twilight locks are opened. Similarly, "The force that through the green fuse" can be interpreted as the failure of the creative imagination to deal with what is experienced. The poet imagines his own "mouthing streams" turning to "wax," which is an image of despair. An alternative reading states that though nature's "mouthing streams" dry up, yet his ability to preserve them in poetry burgeons. That the former is truer to the poem is evident not only in its recurring concern with dumbness, but also because of the poem's final line. To the poet's "sheet" is applied only a "crooked worm": the dishonest pen creates nothing that will survive. In any case, he remains "dumb."

"My hero bares his nerves," deeply felt, though set with scabrous humor in a lavatory, compares writing to masturbation in particular and emotional catharsis in general. It anticipates "Especially when the October wind," which also, in another use of "process" metaphor, links writing to bodily draining. This last-mentioned poem is about writing, its demands, and what it might achieve. Thomas's sense of the compositional activity is brought out in two early lines,

Caught by the crabbing sun I walk on fire
And cast a shadow crab upon the land,

in which "fire" may well mean poetic inspiration, the "crabbing sun" a visual image of the shadow of the walking man cast by the fire that is also the low October sun, and the "shadow crab" a reference to the status of his writing—a "shadow" of real life—as well as to his handwriting and possibly to the cramped nature of his poetic vision.

In this poem inspiration, perhaps the act of writing itself, is like a wound, draining the heart of "syllabic blood." Fisher-king–like, the wounded writer is imprisoned in his "tower of words," staring out of his source material and offering (readers? God?) to make "wordy shapes" of the landscape he sees. The winds of autumn presage the storms of winter, the words are "heartless," the "heart is drained," worse is to come.

None of the other poems in this volume are as disturbing as "Especially when the October wind" in what it tells us of the creative demon controlling the young man and in its intimations of forthcoming disaster. It tells us, further, of Thomas's paradoxical struggle to find words that will enable him to move beyond rendering experience as merely words to instinctive emotional effect, stressing the heart. He returns to this struggle in later poems. In *18 Poems* he insists that the emotional, physical life is more valuable than the intellectual. "When, like a running grave," for example, celebrates that insistence. More negatively, "From love's first fever" describes intellectuality as one of the dangers threatening poetic development:

> And from the first declension of the flesh
> I learnt man's tongue, to twist the shapes of thoughts
> Into the stony idiom of the brain.

Here Thomas conveys what for him was always the aridity of concept and abstraction. In this poem it is only one danger, the other being the problem of originality when faced with the power of the poetic past, "the dead . . . in their moonless acre." "From love's first fever" is a "shades of the prison-house" poem, but only up to a point; Thomas survives and escapes through heroic determination, writing in secret to celebrate, eventually, "One sun, one manna, warmed and fed," the instinctive, emotional life newly achieved. This poem can be coupled with "In the beginning," in which Thomas describes beginnings: Genesis, the example of Christ, the creative sexuality of natural life. Also, "In the beginning was the word," not only in the religious sense suggested by this allusion to St. John's Gospel, but also in terms of literary creativity far removed from the intellectual:

> The word flowed up, translating to the heart
> First characters of birth and death.

The brain, Thomas considers, "celled and soldered in the thought," imprisoning, making rigid. The poetic impulse—we recall the drained heart and bleeding syllables—is

> Blood [that] shot and scattered to the winds of light
> The ribbed original of love.

The poem, like Adam's rib and therefore feminine, is given to the world.

One other poem, "I fellowed sleep," links writing to the practicalities of Thomas's world and returns us to Thomas's social concerns:

> Then all the matter of the living air
> Raised up a voice, and, climbing on the words,
> I spelt my vision with a hand and hair.

Through poetry, through "climbing on the words," Thomas escapes from and rises above the provincial, socially limited world that in this poem is represented by his mother. What he cannot escape is the "fathers' ghost" of paternal literary influence.

Thomas's view of the poem as feminine, created by the male, introduces us to two other related elements of this first volume. The first is Thomas's treatment of women. From the first this is disturbing: "I see the boys of summer" is a stridently male poem, aggressively phallocentric, in which women are regarded as sexual and maternal objects. Essentially passive, they wait for the boys to "fetch" them "frozen loves," to "plant" stunted life in their wombs, or, in summoning death, to take life from them. They are "hives" in which "jacks of frost" are inserted to make them carriers of the unborn. Even in their maternal role they seem powerless: the boys they carry make decisions about the course of their pregnancies.

Such attitudes are typical of the volume. On Thomas's part they represent wish fulfillment consequent upon fear. As it is put in "Our eunuch dreams," girls (in these poems they are rarely women) are "the dark brides, the widows of the night." In "If I were tickled by the rub of love" the man is seized by lust, made "daft with the drug that's smoking in the girl." This to some extent results from masturbatory fantasy, "rehearsing heat upon a raw-edged nerve." In such imaginings, in "My hero bares his nerves," he sees

> his heart
> Tread, like a naked Venus,
> The beach of flesh, and wind her bloodred plait.

These girls, these "dark brides" of "Our eunuch dreams," have "hollow hulks" that the boys make pregnant. At full term they submit passively to a "Time" that "cast[s] forth" the fetus from the womb or sucks it out into the world, as occurs in, respectively, "Before I knocked" and "The force that through the green fuse." Elsewhere, birth is animalistic, hence the "boy she dropped" when one "womb . . . spewed out the matter, / One breast gave suck." Masturbatory fantasy is one instance of the concern with dreams and imaginings that permeates this volume and links the various themes. Thomas dreams of his genesis and of the horrors of the Great War; he thinks of the act of writing as physical maiming. Through re-creating the Austrian uprising in terms of the Great War, Thomas imagines his own death and sees his own grave. All is linked through the imagination; and at the center of each of his main preoccupations is the violent moment.

"I see the boys of summer in their ruin" was placed first in *18 Poems* because, as has been seen, it embodies a number of the volume's main themes. "All all and all," built on half-rhymes that suggest but do not impose a pattern, is the final poem because it serves as a conclusion. Section 1 describes a world saved by what Tindall described as "phallic renewal,"[15] expressed sexuality lifting or "levering" up a dry world, renewed also by political effort and inspired by poetry (this last conveyed by allusions to *The Merchant of Venice* and

King Lear). Section 2 is addressed to the world's workers, Thomas's contemporaries. Because of the assertions of section 1, the worker should not fear the "working world," the industrial life of the 1930s. The worker should not be afraid of succumbing to indirect human experience, symbolized here by the gramophone, because he can turn to the world of section 1.

The final section states that even out of the "dry worlds" and "mechanical flesh," sexual force, the instinctive, physical life, will "square ... the mortal circle." Here is the promise of a new social order, "the people's fusion," recalling the new politics of section 1. The poem and the volume end with a positive apostrophe celebrating a life force ("the drive of oil ... the brassy blood"), instinctive physical power that will "Flower, flower, all all and all." This final optimistic poem relates to the volume in the same way as optimistic conclusions counterpoint individual poems. We end in uncertainty, not wholly sure whether we are encountering an indomitable spirit or hearing whistling in the dark.

NOTES

1. All quotations from *18 Poems* are taken from *CP*, 7–30.

2. Dylan Thomas, *Selected Poems*, ed. Walford Davies, Rev. Everyman ed. (London: Dent, 1993), 13.

3. *CL*, 125. Letter to Pamela Hansford Johnson, 2 May [1934].

4. These poems are included in Dylan Thomas, *The Poems*, ed. Daniel Jones (London: Dent, 1971).

5. *CL*, 125. Letter to Pamela Hansford Johnson, 2 May [1934].

6. Quoted in *CP*, 178.

7. *CL*, 54. Letter to Pamela Hansford Johnson, [week of 11 November 1933]. As has been noted, the words were written on Armistice Day, 11 November.

8. Jacob Korg, *Dylan Thomas* (New York: Twayne, 1965), 47.

9. In which "the fellow-father ... doubles / His sea-sucked Adam in the hollow hulk," that is, creates a version of himself in the womb.

10. William York Tindall, *A Reader's Guide to Dylan Thomas* (1962; New York: Octagon Books, 1981), 48. Tindall is less convincing when suggesting that "crabs" in stanza 4 of the same poem refers to one of Hamlet's speeches to Polonius ("for you yourself, sir, shall grow old as I am, if, like a crab, you could go backward," 2. 2. 203). Though Thomas refers to old age, his own use of "crabs" is more likely to echo the slang of the period and mean "venereal disease."

11. Ralph Maud, *Entrances to Dylan Thomas' Poetry* (Pittsburgh: University of Pittsburgh Press, 1963), 57–80.

12. *CL*, 38–39. Letter to Pamela Hansford Johnson, [early November 1933].

13. *CL*, 98. Letter to Glyn Jones, [c. 14 March 1934].

14. *CL*, 90. Letter to Trevor Hughes, [early January 1934].

15. Tindall, *Reader's Guide to Dylan Thomas*, 75.

8

Twenty-five Poems

Second volumes can be difficult.[1] The volume of *18 Poems* was the product of a prolific period in Thomas's career as a poet, whereas the two years before the publication of *Twenty-five Poems* saw a marked decline in Thomas's output. Indeed, he included in the new volume all but two of the poems he had published between *18 Poems* (1934) and September 1936. The exceptions are "Before we mothernaked fall" and "Poet: 1935." The former is about the nature of the newly born being determined before birth; it is notable for describing the moment of conception, seemingly from the male point of view, as a "raid,"[2] an image that links even sex with war. "Poet: 1935" is an overdiscursive poem about suburban alienation, as has been noted (years later, Thomas was to quote part of it in "Reminiscences of Childhood"), but the former poem is tight and suggestive. It is difficult to see why Thomas omitted it, particularly given one or two of his inclusions.

Both the omissions are revisions of notebook poems, as are sixteen of the inclusions. Four of the latter revisions were published for the first time in *Twenty-five Poems*. Of the nine recently written poems, two—"Now" and "Then was my neophyte"—were also published for the first time. Two of the notebook poems, "Ears in the turrets hear" and "And death shall have no dominion," had been published in 1934 and 1933, respectively, but not included in *18 Poems*. The latter poem was heavily revised for the later volume, but the former was not. Such complications emphasize what has long been realized: because Thomas drew upon earlier material for each volume, there is no clear chronology of composition from *18 Poems* to *Twenty-five Poems*. That chronology has to be established independently of the published volumes, and not only of the first two.

More important, even at this early stage in Thomas's literary career he had some difficulty in collecting twenty-five poems of sufficient quality. Evidence for this is found in Thomas's uncertainty about several of his poems. Thus in a letter to Pamela Hansford Johnson he described "Ears in the turrets hear," now regarded as an important early poem, as "a terribly weak, watery little thing.''[3] He wrote to Desmond Hawkins, then editing the magazine *Purpose*: ''Do for sweet Christ's sake use the one beginning Foster the Light, nor veil the cunt-shaped moon,''[4] surely the language of implicit disparagement. Little wonder that Hawkins did not accept it. Elsewhere there was bravado: when Vernon Watkins tried to persuade him to exclude ''Now'' and ''How soon the servant sun'' because of their ''unwarrantable obscurity,'' Thomas refused, even though he ''remarked of one of them that so far as he knew it had no meaning at all.'' He also told Watkins that ''I, in my intricate image'' was not a successful poem.[5] The ''Altarwise by owl-light'' sequence also caused him concern: he described it in the letter to Hawkins already quoted as ''Altarwise by owl light in the bleeding house.'' Writing to Glyn Jones after the latter had reviewed *Twenty-five Poems* in *Adelphi*, he agreed that the sequence took ''certain features to their logical conclusion'' and that one of the results was ''mad parody.'' Among these ''certain features'' were ''rhythmic and thematic dead ends, that physical blank wall, those wombs, and full-stop worms.''[6] We may, with Davies and Maud,[7] be doubtful about the parodic element, but the disparagement is revealing. There is no doubt that Thomas felt trapped in a style. During the summer of 1935 he confessed uneasily to Bert Trick: ''My own eyes, I know, squint inwards; when, and if, I look at the exterior world I see nothing or me.''[8] In April 1936 he wrote to Vernon Watkins:

I should stop writing altogether for some time; now I'm almost afraid of all the once-necessary artifices and obscurities, and can't, for the life or the death of me, get any real liberation, any diffusion or dilution or anything, into the churning bulk of the words; I seem, more than ever, to be tightly packing away everything I have and know into a mad-doctor's bag, and then locking it up. . . . what I do fear is an ingrowing, the impulse growing like a toenail into the artifice.[9]

This unease at his aesthetic solipsism did not, however, stop him writing; neither did his uncertainty about individual poems prevent him including them in his second volume. Such attitudes did, however, affect the volume's general shape, in one important way so different from that of *18 Poems*: it divides more sharply into two groups of poems, the difficult and at times obscure, and the comparatively clear and straightforward.

Because of such dualism it is appropriate that the volume opens with ''I, in my intricate image,'' a difficult poem about the poet's conflicting personae. It is a new poem, but with strong roots in that earlier division of Thomas's own writing life into a public presence of acceptable ''school-mag'' verse and the anarchic secret life of his notebook poems. Significantly, whereas the first poem of *18 Poems* was about repression, its counterpart in *Twenty-five Poems* is about the related theme of the divided self.

This opening poem seeks to reconcile poet and person. It struggles to do so, the narrative line too often overwhelmed by clotted imagery that generates numerous and often confusing subthemes and ideas. Thomas explores the idea of writing as a haunting that can only be exorcised by print ("Laying my ghost in metal"), or as a form of masturbation ("The natural parallel"). His view of the literary task is a disturbing one: though his "images stalk the trees," yet he remains

> with the wooden insect in the tree of nettles,
> In the glass bed of grapes with snail and flower,
> Hearing the weather fall.

Here, pen in hand, is the writer in the hostile world. His world is earth-bound—linked to nature in an echo of "process"—slow to achieve beauty, though aware of it. In a piercing intimation of future disaster we learn of the bottle's comforts, while the fragility of "glass" preserves, as yet, the possibility of breaking free.

Perhaps the darkest moments of this vision are found in two instances of dark wit. In the first the man and his poetic alter ego are

> invalid rivals . . .
> On the consumptives' terrace taking their two farewells

before embarking on a voyage that, given the sanatorium setting in a tubercular age, can only be doomed and short. The second is the neosurrealistic conceit of life as a gramophone record and so a limited "circular world." Thomas's poetic exploration of that world is uselessly self-centered, as the allusion to masturbation makes plain:

> Let the wax disc babble
> Shames and the damp dishonours, the relic scraping.
> These are your years' recorders.

Such themes and ideas, plus Thomas's general vision of life as "death's corridor," restricted and institutionalized, hardly reassure. The pessimism is intensified by the fact that "I, in my intricate image" is the most intricately formal of all the poems published by Thomas up to this point. Seventy-five of the poem's one hundred and eight lines end with a variation on the letter *l*, the patterning (lines one, three, four, and six) being particularly strict in the first two sections. The spreading pessimism, the accumulating images and conceits, and the thrusting energy of the narrative are controlled, trapped, even, by the strict poetic patterns, to dramatize, as so often, the power of bourgeois suburban control of rebellious creative force.

Like "I see the boys of summer" in *18 Poems*, "I, in my intricate image" is placed first because it introduces a number of this new volume's main concerns. They are essentially the same themes and devices as in *18 Poems*. Thus even in this opening poem Thomas continues his obsession with the Great War. Section 2 of the poem offers an account of the dual personality drowning in the

sea of life. Within this account is a parenthesis containing two socialized metaphors to illustrate the power of death. One is death as a surgeon, performing at
the "antiseptic funeral"; the other is death as war, the "black patrol" with its
"monstrous officers and the decaying army," and

> The sexton sentinel, garrisoned under thistles,
> A cock-on-a-dunghill
> Crowing to Lazarus the morning is vanity.

The imagery of the Great War reinforces the idea of death as finality, as the
"sexton sentinel" echoing the period's trenches-induced loss of faith in mocking
even Lazarus's hopes of resurrection.

Elsewhere in *Twenty-five Poems*, "And death shall have no dominion," discussed elsewhere, stands as one of Thomas's key responses to the conflict, an
attempt to reconcile his increased sense of the horrors of violence with the
susceptibilities of his readers. Two other poems with central concerns linked to
World War I are "The seed-at-zero," with its developed conceit of bombarding
a town, and "Out of the sighs," with its moving image of the protagonist
"leaving woman waiting / For her soldier" that echoes similar lines in the
notebook poem "The Woman Speaks." W. S. Merwin was later to describe this
poem, Thomas's first published poem in the free verse that he rarely adopted,
as his "first genuinely personal poem."[10] It is significant—because it is indicative of the depth of feeling generated by Thomas in relation to that conflict—
that this new venture is, to a large extent, conceived of in a warring context. A
similar and related point concerns a single image in the important poem "I have
longed to move away":

> Some life, yet unspent, might explode
> Out of the old lie burning on the ground,
> And, crackling into the air, leave me half-blind.[11]

Thomas describes the feared power of provincial compromise in terms of a land
mine or unexploded shell and Great War mutilation. Again and again, even
personal problems were explored in terms of that warring discourse.

In section 3 of "I, in my intricate image" the person-poet narrator struggling
through the sea of life encounters an authoritarian figure, represented by the
"pointed ferrule" and linked to the ghost that is poetic inspiration. "Ghost"
and "bodiless image" are also linked to the *Hamlet* reference later in the stanza
and so to specifically paternal authority, hence the key quotation:

> And the five-fathomed Hamlet on his father's coral,
> Thrusting the tom-thumb vision up the iron mile.

The first line, of course, brings together *The Tempest*, that play of death by water as a prelude to new life, as well as *Hamlet*. The lines are complex: the son is submerged in his father's world but not drowned. He is supported by what his father's bones have become, and in that second line, with its suggestion of hands reaching above the surface, he thrusts imaginatively (the vision as yet is limited) beyond restricting paternal influence and the prison of the familial past (the "iron mile" that suggestively recalls the railway antecedents of Jack Thomas's family). But the son is still Hamlet grieving for what his father once was, well aware of his father's continuing power, condemned by his father to a tense, unhappy life.

In *Twenty-five Poems* Hamlet reappears in "Today, this insect" as one of a series of literary references grouped together as "fibs of vision," persisting but vulnerable to the application of reason. The *Hamlet* references encourage us to recognize the fatherly source of much of the poetry's drama and complex power. "Find meat on bones," for example, is a dialogue in which the father urges the son to make hay before it is too late, only for the son to reply despairingly that he cannot because time and nature have already mastered him.

Much of Thomas's poetic relationship with his father is summed up in "Do you not father me." The lines "the erected arm / For my tall tower's sake cast in her stone" are a phallic paternal reference that, like earlier ones, suggests power that is more destructive than sexually creative. This idea of destructive power, let alone of authoritarian force, is doubly emphasized by the political suggestiveness of that "erected arm," the fascist salute used by too many during the troubled 1930s. The "tall tower" of "stone," though in one sense revealing of Thomas's sense of female passivity, also represents his other idea of prefetal wisdom and seeming security. It is stormed, "felled by a timeless stroke," by the copulating father, another imagistic link between war and sex. The result, as always, is entry into a hostile and ultimately disappointing world.

The violent copulating father is, of course, Jack Thomas rather than "D. J." The name "Jack," which could never, for Thomas, escape its fatherly association and scatological links, is used three times in this volume. In "Jack Frost" in "Why east wind chills," one of Thomas's finest early poems and already examined in detail, it is part of a figure representing death and may well create a masturbatory subtext with "night-time rain" and clasping the comet. In "Grief thief of time," an early example of the "Do not go gentle" theme, Thomas appeals to "Jack my fathers," one of whom was his own and a disappointed man in poor health, to "shape [up]" to Time the thief. Don't go quietly, the son insists. Finally, in the eighth sonnet of the "Altarwise by owl-light" sequence, the narrator addresses "Jack Christ" as part of a response to the Crucifixion. The name, harking back, as has been seen, to the earlier notion of Thomas's father, believed dying, walking with God as God's son, is a union of opposites that include tensions between irreverence and reverence, unconventional and conventional, and ordinary and special that permeate the poetic fatherly encounters.

At the center of the fatherly theme in this volume are further lines from "Do you not father me":

> Am I not father, too, and the ascending boy,
> The boy of woman and the wanton starer
> Marking the flesh and summer in the bay?

The famous second line can refer wholly to the poet (he is the boy of woman, and he is "the wanton starer") but can also refer to him as the offspring of woman and of "the wanton starer," the latter thus referring to Thomas's father. "Wanton" is a loaded word: its several meanings include "irresponsible, unrestrained, motiveless, purposeless," all contained within a general sense of lewd wildness. "Starer" is, of course, more passive, an observer, not a participator, which is what his father became. The two words amalgamate into a paradox that brilliantly combines and characterizes the father who was both Jack and D. J.

The exploration of the narrator's writerly role, part, as has been noted, of the central theme of "I, in my intricate image," also begins another recurring preoccupation. The latter is a substantial presence in four other poems. "Today, this insect" describes a fall from an Eden of poetic achievement that occurs through a dissociation of sensibility: "In trust and tale have I divided sense." The "insect" is what the poem has become as a consequence of allowing reason too much power. In "Here in this spring" the poem is a "timeless insect" inclined to speak mysteriously, a contrast to the clear meaning of the natural world and seasonal cycle from which, nonetheless, it draws its symbols. "Out of the sighs" stresses the inadequacy of "hollow words." All in all, Thomas's exploration of his role as poet harrows rather than reassures. He is increasingly disturbed by his controlling obsession. His doubts about his task are intensified through a contrast with "The hand that signed the paper," a poem that insists on the power of the written word. That hand, with its "goose's quill," wields absolute power, but political, not poetic.

As in *18 Poems*, Thomas here uses much detail from 1930s suburban life. Even a selective list is long and begins with the two conceits already quoted—the invalids on the sanatorium terrace and the gramophone—in the opening poem. Seaweed on the shore, the hunt riding through Glamorgan, the circus, the handbell ringing through a school corridor, ships, sea, rain, playing ball in the park, fireworks, and memories of Keystone Kops and other cinematic imagery are examples from the other poems. The suburban mentality, that marvellous ability to express universals in terms of everyday metaphor that is one of Thomas's great strengths and one reason why a "difficult" poet can still command a popular response, is clearly seen in the short lyric "Incarnate devil." This poem begins with the Fall and uses it as a metaphor for birth to express what is now a familiar idea in these early poems of the newly born entering a threatening world. Thomas writes of Eden:

And God walked there who was a fiddling warden
And played down pardon from the heavens' hill.

Eden becomes a park and God the park-warden who neglects his duties and is reluctant to help those in trouble. Such imagery, archetypally suburban in expressing grand themes in terms of the everyday, not only prevents abstraction or disembodied mythologizing but strengthens the myth through contrast and relevance.

"Incarnate devil" is one of Thomas's more immediately understandable poems, a fact that returns us to the division of *Twenty-five Poems* into the difficult and the (sometimes seemingly) more straightforward. The latter group includes "This bread I break," "Why east wind chills," "Ears in the turrets hear," "The hand that signed the paper," "Should lanterns shine," "I have longed to move away," and "And death shall have no dominion."

"This bread I break" uses the setting of the Eucharist—its bread and wine having once been corn and grapes—to make a general point about the reduction of the natural to the man-made, and a more personal point about society's effect on the instinctive physical life, the "desolation in the vein" he feels consequent upon being separated from "the sensual root and sap." "Why east wind chills," in some ways a key poem of this period, focusses, to repeat a point, on the restricted world of socialized authority, the thought police ordering complacency and limiting response. The beleaguered narrator does not quite bring himself to have faith in the "raised fists" of left-wing demonstrations against the intellectual fascism at the heart of the poem. (This poem links interestingly with "Was there a time," especially with the line "What's never known is safest in this life.")

In the generally powerful "Ears in the turrets hear" the young Thomas is again beleaguered. He is a fortified house, an island, that is at once a prison within and a refuge from the incursions of an unwelcoming provincial world from which he considers escaping. The poem juxtaposes two languages: the realist detail of wind, rain, ships, and bay, used to describe what is obviously the Swansea setting, and the romantic medievalism in the references to "turrets" and in the incongruous refrain of "poison and grapes." The latter discourse may have been the source of Thomas's uncertainty about the poem: the presence of two languages not only dramatizes the separation of poetic self and provincial world, but also suggests the poet's youthful literary pretensions. "Should lanterns shine" is about the competing claims of heart and head. "I have longed to move away" is another poem about Thomas's need to escape the provincial world of his upbringing—described as a fallen Eden in which he hears "the hissing of the spent lie"—and his fear that he might not manage to escape intact. The poem dramatizes the dilemma by juxtaposing realist detail and the near melodramatic. In "And death shall have no dominion" the assertive optimism is subverted by the much darker subtext, but the presence of such assertion suggests that Thomas was as anxious to escape from his preoccupation with those "four mad years" as from his suburban roots.

All these poems explore the relationship between self and world, between Thomas and his social context. Even the remaining poem in the group, "The hand that signed the paper," well known as Thomas's only overtly political poem, through its concern with ruthless authority can be linked to Thomas's feeling of entrapment. The need to reach outside himself enables him to write with greater directness and clarity, whereas when, as in "I, in my intricate image," he explores complex internal relationships—here, himself as person and as poet—his syntax becomes difficult, his imagery clotted, and his narrative line difficult to sustain. This distinction, linked to understanding, has implications for his later work.

Thomas's clear understanding of the self/Swansea-world relationship is also evident in the interest in religion that is a new element in his published poetry. Though there is some religious longing in "Foster the light" in such a line as "O who is glory in the shapeless maps," Thomas's is essentially an antireligious stance, touched on in "I, in my intricate image" in the secular finality of his rejection of the Lazarus story. "This bread I break" and "Incarnate devil," the second and third poems in this volume, are further hostile statements. One reading of the former opposes the Eucharist to the sensual world; the latter, as has been suggested, posits tension between an Eden neglected by God and the fallen world that awaits the newly born. The very next poem, "Today, this insect," explores the similar theme of the "Murder of Eden and green genesis." The concern with a fallen world that permeates the volume may well be, like all Thomas's work, a reflection of its social context: the Eden of his childhood may well have been replaced by problematic provinciality, but London's debauching tendencies and the need to make his literary way were the worrying preoccupations of this time. "Find meat on bones" and "Grief thief of time" are both antireligious in their carpe diem insistence. So, too, in their differently indirect ways, are "Shall gods be said," which insists shamelessly on pagan explanations of natural phenomena, "And death shall have no dominion," with its pantheistic thrust, and "Do you not father me," with its puritan flourish at sex as sinful. "Then was my neophyte" is more directly hostile in stressing the inadequacy of Christian faith and of Christ's power in the face of adult reality. The poem concludes bleakly that though Christ promises salvation, yet "I saw time murder me." Most antagonistic of all these poems is "The hand that signed the paper," in which the ruthless ruler signs a murderous and repressive treaty. Thomas's comment—"A hand rules pity as a hand rules heaven"—points unambiguously to the cruelty of God.

The importance of the religious theme in *Twenty-five Poems*, together with those constituents of faith, the limitations of knowledge and the desire to know, make it appropriate that the volume should close with the sonnet sequence "Altarwise by owl-light." This consists of ten sonnets based on the Christian story.

The sequence is one of Thomas's most ambitious poetic ventures. Though its main concern is to retell the Christian story, it is also about Thomas's own life. It is another personal poem in which he becomes tangled in his own complexities. The result, in Tindall's phrase, is "obscure magnificence,"[12] highly controversial. "Altarwise by owl-light" describes Thomas growing up, emerging from the womb—wittily described as "the wrinkled undertaker's van"—asking questions, playing cowboys, experiencing his first sexual feelings,

> Till tallow I blew from the wax's tower
> The fats of midnight when the salt was singing,

his beginnings as a writer, and doubts about his work. He becomes aware of the tyranny of time and, interestingly, given the antireligious sentiment in this volume, comes to recognize Christ's sufferings. Indeed, in the eighth sonnet he recognizes the crucified Jesus as "all glory's sawbones" curing the world's ills and links his own suffering as a writer—again a chilling point—with that of Christ at Calvary. As the final line of this sonnet has it, "Suffer the heaven's children through my heartbeat."

Sonnet 9 uses Egyptian burial imagery to present his writing as resurrected through being published, though Thomas cannot help worrying that his work may be like a "World in the sand." The tenth and final sonnet ends positively. The poet is the "rhubarb man" because he is growing palely in darkness and will hope to create a desirable world in his work that will

> Soar . . .   to that Day
> When the worm builds with the gold straws of venom
> My nest of mercies in the rude, red tree.

That is, not only will the poems flourish into virtual permanence, but the worm that combines the literary and the sexual, pen and penis, will also reconcile the hostile world with his writing and God's mercy with the fallen world and, with "red," its political aspirations.

This complex ending provides this volume with an affirmative conclusion, a reminder of other affirmative endings to individual poems, such as "And my images roared and rose on heaven's hill," "Your sport is summer as the spring runs angrily," and, of course, "And death shall have no dominion." But these are exceptions. More characteristic are endings framed as questions close to despair, such as

> What shall it tell me if a timeless insect
> Says the world wears away?

and statements chilling in their categorical darkness, such as "Hands have no tears to flow" and "I saw time murder me."

We also encounter a trope that becomes fundamental to important later poems:

the use of the closing apostrophe. Examples include the endings of "Foster the light," "O who is glory . . . ," of "Find meat on bones," "Before death takes you, O take back this," and the final lines of "Then was my neophyte":

> "Who could hack out your unsucked heart,
> O green and unborn and undead?"
> I saw time murder me.

To agree with Jonathan Culler that all apostrophes are deconstructive is to recognize that their presence turns the poem back on itself.[13] They introduce a new kind of discourse, change the tone, break down unity. They disturb the argument by refusing a definite conclusion. In a sense they are postmodernist elements, literary and disconcerting, adding to the darkness that spreads through this volume.

Twenty-five Poems, as might be expected given the chronology of composition, has much in common with Thomas's first volume. But, as might also be expected, his choice of poems makes for different emphases. It is significant that that choice created a volume darker in tone, perhaps more tormented, than its predecessor as Thomas worried about his poetic development, found himself able to write fewer poems, and became more preoccupied with his personal predicament and social context. When the volume appeared, he was still only twenty-one, a small age for prison-house shades to begin to close in, let alone for clouds to appear on a literary horizon that was never to be distant.

NOTES

1. All quotations from *Twenty-five Poems* are taken from *CP*, 33–63.
2. Dylan Thomas, *The Poems*, ed. Daniel Jones (London: Dent, 1971), 73.
3. *CL*, 131. Letter to Pamela Hansford Johnson, 9 May 1934.
4. *CL*, 203. Letter to Desmond Hawkins, dated 1 November 1935.
5. Dylan Thomas, *Letters to Vernon Watkins* ed. Vernon Watkins (London: Dent and Faber & Faber, 1957), 15, 16.
6. *CL*, 243. Letter to Glyn Jones, dated [December 1936].
7. *CP*, 211.
8. *CL*, 192. Letter to Bert Trick, dated [summer 1935].
9. *CL*, 223. Letter to Vernon Watkins, dated [c. 20 April 1936].
10. W. S. Merwin, "The Religious Poet," *Adam International Review* 238 (1953): 75.
11. The notebook version of this poem has

> Some life, yet unspent, might explode
> Out of the lie hissing on the ground
> Like some sulphurous reminder of November,
> And, cracking into the air, leave me half blind. (*PM*, 175)

The removal of that third line still allows the "firework" reading but, by rendering the lines less explicit, makes possible a "Great War" interpretation.

12. William York Tindall, *A Reader's Guide to Dylan Thomas* (1962; New York: Octagon Books, 1981), 128.

13. Jonathan Culler, ''Apostrophe,'' *The Pursuit of Signs* (London: Routledge & Kegan Paul, 1981), 135–144.

9

The Map of Love

The Map of Love was published on 24 August 1939. On 3 September 1939 Britain declared war on Germany, and the 1930s effectively ended. In this volume, particularly (and in *Portrait of the Artist as a Young Dog*, published the following year), Thomas makes his major response to the decade, especially to its closing years. The contents began life during the period 1933 through 1939; *The Map of Love* looks back, consolidates, and considers how to proceed.

The volume is very different from the first two in consisting of sixteen poems, followed by seven short stories.[1] A simple chronology of composition is again defied, for eight of the poems are known to have notebook antecedents; one other may well have had them.[2] In the three years, 1936 to 1939, following *Twenty-five Poems* Thomas wrote only seven new poems. As for the stories, five began life in the "Red Notebook" Thomas reserved for prose. The other two, "The Map of Love" and "The Mouse and the Woman," seem in style and content, such as surrealistic tendencies and references to the mythical land of Jarvis, to belong with the others and so to the period 1933–34. All except the title story were published before *Twenty-five Poems*. "The Map of Love" was the only one of the eight stories published by Thomas between *Twenty-five Poems* and *The Map of Love* to be included.

The rejected stories, written before and after *Twenty-five Poems*, include explorations of incest and illegal cremation ("The Burning Baby"), sexual initiation ("A Prospect of the Sea"), clergymen caricatured as vices ("The Holy Six"), madness, sex, and violence ("The True Story" and "The Vest"), and, particularly in "Prologue to an Adventure," what appear to be ventures into surrealism. They are, generally speaking, sexually more explicit, at times more violent, and occasionally more blasphemous than the stories Thomas chose for his third volume. They seem also more experimental. That their content and approach may well explain their omission may indicate, once again, Thomas's bourgeois pragmatism. The choice may also point to the transitional status of *The Map of Love* and Thomas's concern to move on from what he considered to be the stylistic traps of his early writing. He wrote to Vernon Watkins, "I think it will be good for me to write some short poems, not bothering about them too much, between my long exhausters."[3] Watkins coined the term "opossums,"[4] a term his friend adopted,[5] for the short poems. Thomas was continuing his personal argument about moving from difficult, at times tortuous writing to clearer poetic statements, which we see reflected in *Twenty-five Poems*. To mix a metaphor, his poetry was at a crossroads.

The Map of Love begins disturbingly with Thomas's societal—we keep in mind that he was now married with a son and living in Laugharne—as well as aesthetic predicament. The volume opens with "Because the pleasure-bird whistles," a poem for the New Year of 1939. Untypically but significantly, the volume thus begins with blank verse, the significance being that the absence of a strict formal structure in itself suggests incipient chaos. The poem is about wild living in London and about the problems of writing. It is a poem presaging disaster. It opens:

> Because the pleasure-bird whistles after the hot wires,
> Shall the blind horse sing sweeter?

The first line refers to the barbaric practice of blinding birds in the belief that if they were blind, they would sing better. The key word, of course, is "after," meaning both "because of" and "attracted to." Whether Thomas identified with "pleasure-bird" or "blind horse," or both, the point is one with dreadful personal relevance: the singer sings because of self-destructive activities to which he is irresistibly drawn.

The new year, described as a tongue, with January as its tip, dramatizes Thomas's sense of an uncontrollable present (and future) by tearing itself free from the dead past: "the wild tongue breaks its tombs." Despite the example of Lot's wife—turned into a pillar of salt when she looked back at Sodom— Thomas is determined to examine that past and, in "furnish[ing himself] with the meat of a fable," draw a lesson from it. The (and his) past and world are being devastated:

> an old year
> Toppling and burning in the muddle of towers and galleries

The sense is not only of a personal crisis—Thomas drunk and confused in London—but of a collapsing world already in flames. The background to the writing of *The Map of Love* includes Italy invading Abyssinia, the Spanish civil war, and German annexations in Europe. Thomas will escape to Laugharne, he tells us, that place seemingly furthest from London, with its sustaining sea, to become

> An upright man in the antipodes
> Or spray-based and rock-chested sea.

Here, at least, is praiseworthy intention.

The combination of personal predicament with general disaster makes "Because the pleasure-bird whistles" a suitable opening. A major element of the former is Thomas's continued concern about his writing. The uneasy self-awareness of those first two lines of the opening poem can be linked to "When all my five and country senses":

> The whispering ears will watch love drummed away
> Down breeze and shell to a discordant beach,
> And, lashed to syllables, the lynx tongue cry
> That her fond wounds are mended bitterly.

The quoted lines lament real emotions, here "love," being reduced to words. The depth of Thomas's desire to write poems that re-create the form of such emotions is evident from the central metaphor: "love drummed away . . . And, lashed to syllables." We return disturbingly to "And death shall have no dominion" and the Great War: "love" is subjected to Field Punishment Number One. The implication is that writing can perform atrocities upon life. The harking back to 1914–18 is all the more telling for its rarity in a third volume in which the new nightmares of the late 1930s take over.

The lines are also part of a sonnet, the choice of which traditional formal structure draws attention to the literary task and to the poet's unease. Though Thomas chooses a traditional form, he uses it in a personal way. The sonnet divides unusually into a ten-line group followed by a quatrain; the rhyme scheme is *abcbcdecae fgfg*. The effect is both to suggest and reject a traditional scheme, and so to dramatize the crucial moment as Thomas considers how to proceed, given his reservations about his current poetic practice.

"How shall my animal" is another worried, insecure poem dealing in part with the similar theme of how to preserve in his words the dynamic essence of the life his words describe:

> How shall my animal . . .
> Endure burial under the spelling wall.

As Tindall put it, "How can a poem endure the confinement of printing?"[6] though Thomas's question is, more precisely, how can *my* poem deal with real life? The poem contrasts Thomas's own internalized work with that of other poets who "creep and harp on the tide"; their equipment may be inadequate, but theirs is at least a less subjective approach. The final stanza is dominated by the story of Delilah destroying Samson's strength, offered as an analogy of what the poem does to dynamic life.

A related poem is "The spire cranes," which raises questions about solipsistic attention. The spire stands for the poet. The poems are either the stone birds carved on the spire, representing the failure to free themselves from life-denying subjectivity, or the chimes of the bells inside the spire, these last being poems that resonate widely, that "plunge from the spire's hook."

In this volume Thomas does not worry only about what his poems may be doing to the life they explore. Two new elements enter the argument. First, a far cry from earlier fluency, is his concern about his ability to write at all. "On no work of words" is a desperate response to "three lean months" in which, as he puts it, "I bitterly take to task my poverty and craft" as "The lovely gift of the gab bangs back on a blind shaft." Second, his work was now well known, a consequence of which was greater critical attention. Some of this was hostile and troubled him. Hence "O make me a mask" is in a sense a counter to Thomas's general shift towards a simpler style. Suddenly he wished to thwart spying critics by writing in a manner that would "shield the glistening brain and blunt the examiners."

Two of Thomas's finest and most famous poems, the one in part, the other centrally, are shaped by his interrogation of his own poetic development. One is "After the funeral," his final response to the death of his Aunt Annie of Fernhill farm. As well as portraying his aunt as a virtuous woman in tune with the natural environment and as a victim of a life of unremitting toil in a narrowly Nonconformist world, Thomas considers appropriate style. He praises the dead woman in a grandly public rhetorical manner, only to conclude that the result is a "monstrous image blindly / Magnified out of praise." He turns to a smaller-scale, more domestic alternative—"Ann's bard on a raised hearth"—and, noticeably, struggles to lower his voice. The struggle, as invariably in Thomas's work, is class based, part of a typically bourgeois reluctance to raise the voice: the poem's abrupt transition from the extravagant gesture to the deeply felt yet tightly controlled and intended simpler response to Ann's life ("Her flesh was meek as milk") is a move, not altogether convincing in its difference, into a different social register. It is also, of course, expressive of Thomas's poetic dilemma, his need to find an approachable style that could connect public and private, great events and the personal life. "After the funeral" is a superb dramatizing of that dilemma. As will be seen, later poems in this volume and in *Deaths and Entrances* respond to the crisis-laden second half of their decade by effecting such connections.

The second poem, placed to follow "After the funeral," is "Once it was the colour of saying," Thomas's most explicit statement of how things were and what needed to be done. It begins with Thomas when young at his writing table in 5 Cwmdonkin Drive. Outside is real, developing life: the girls growing as they played in the private school seen from his window, and, earlier, truancy and mischief in the park, gestures against authority and adulthood. Then the "colour of saying," the aesthetic effect, was enough, and even now, Thomas considers, his work purveys a general aestheticism, indulgent cadences—"gentle seaslides of saying"—a concern to charm, and, on his part, a lack of real involvement. The result is that instead of life being re-created, it is turned into words. There may be brief moments of illumination, but invariably his readers are "the poor in the dark."

The poem offers an odd description of Thomas's early poetry; such deprecation flies in the face of readerly response, much of which prizes the strangely compelling, at times piercing, effects of his 1930s writing. But Thomas was always concerned about the worth of his work, as he confessed to Pamela Hansford Johnson:

My lines, *all* my lines, are of the tenth intensity. They are not the words that express what I want to express; they are the only words I can find that come near to expressing a half. And that's no good. I'm a freak user of words, not a poet.[7]

Thomas had high standards. The important point, however, is not one about accurate description but about professional dissatisfaction with both his prolificity, or lack of it, and with the quality of what he produced.

The poem was completed in December 1938; from this time forth, Thomas insisted, he would strive for deeper effect, "That all the charmingly drowned arise to cockcrow and kill," the subject no longer drowned in words but lancing directly into the reader's sensibility. Thomas, who had long regarded writing as a wound draining his blood, accepted the sacrificial difficulty of the writing to come:

> Now my saying shall be my undoing,
> And every stone I wind off like a reel.

He will fish in the sea of life, his poems stones brought up from the seabed and so requiring arduous shaping. The shape of this poem in itself supports this point brilliantly, for at first glance it seems to be a sonnet. Certainly it begins like one, with an *abba* quatrain. The second quatrain, however, though preserving some shape, is short of one rhyme; its definition is further eroded by the sentence running on into what should be the third quatrain. Here shape is subverted by the sentence continuing its progress beyond the four lines; the rhyme scheme is abandoned. The sentence, though running on, pauses on a semicolon at the end of line 11, suggesting that a final couplet follows. In fact, the penultimate line of the poem belongs to the third quatrain, even though it is syntactically linked to the poem's final line. That final line is the thirteenth. What seemed to begin as a sonnet turns out not to be; the traditional form collapses into irregularity. Thomas rejects the old and searches for the new. His dissatisfaction with what has been achieved, the searching and fishing for the new, and the acceptance of arduous shaping all perhaps constitute positive thinking, but they cannot escape a tinge of despair. We should not be surprised that "Because the pleasure-bird whistles" also belongs to the period from December 1938 to January 1939.

It is a cliché that in *The Map of Love* Thomas began writing poems about other people, turning from inward contemplation to outward engagement. Like most clichés, this is only partly true: in this volume he is certainly more concerned with other individuals, but, as this study seeks to show, in part via Thomas's fatherly writing and obsession with the Great War, he was always alive and responsive to events around him. The poetry in *The Map of Love* responds to the outside world in two ways. It responds to the storm clouds of the late 1930s—the rise of fascism, Spain, the depression—and to the changed circumstances of Thomas's personal life: marriage to Caitlin, the birth of their first child, and the continuing relationship with his father.

What fades is Thomas's concern with the Great War. Apart from a few brief references, such as that already noted in "When all my five and country senses," the unexpected and isolated military image of "her wits drilled hollow" in "After the funeral," and his description of "I make this in a warring absence," that response to a fierce quarrel with Caitlin, as a "narrative, of all the emotional events . . . between the war of her absence and the armistice of her presence,"[8] that concern is displaced by new wars and rumors of them.

These last foster the apocalyptic sense of "Toppling and burning in the muddle of towers and galleries" that was noted in the discussion of this volume's opening poem. That sense can also be found in stanza 5 of "I make this in a warring absence" in the nihilism of the estranged husband as doomed Samson eager to destroy. It is present again in the fire-gutted cathedral of "It is the sinner's dust-tongued bell," a poem of 1936 that may well be a response to the opening months of the Spanish civil war. The insertion of "the bayonet tongue" and "the sweetly blown trumpet of lies" in "O make me a mask" is a further response to conflict. The same point can be made about the increased amount of violent imagery throughout this volume.

That Thomas was able successfully to fuse his response to the troubled 1930s with personal concerns is evident from the fact that his most profound responses to the events leading to World War II are found in poems about familial relations. Five of these last are important explorations of relations with aunt, wife, and first child.

The first is "After the funeral," that poem reflecting Thomas's uneasiness about appropriate style. It is influenced in part by the Welsh short-story writer Caradoc Evans, whom Thomas admired and visited. Evans's stories are fiercely critical of "the Peasantry of West Wales,"[9] an influence particularly evident in the opening lines of the poem, for it begins by stressing how alien rural and Nonconformist Carmarthenshire is for the boy visiting from urban Swansea. In Walford Davies's words, there is "a recognition of the wilder inheritance that lay behind the suburban tidiness of his parents' home."[10] It is also physically and morally ugly: these opening lines describe a group of hypocritical grotesques. Though the poem celebrates his aunt's Christian and natural virtues and enduring fortitude, it is fiercely and movingly critical of what her way of life has done to her:

I know her scrubbed and sour humble hands
Lie with religion in their cramp, her threadbare
Whisper in a damp word, her wits drilled hollow,
Her fist of a face died clenched on a round pain.

That life was one of hard manual work, of knowing her place, of narrow, life-denying religion, and of dreadfully monotonous subsistence living. She took it all on—that chilling "fist of a face" image not only expresses pain but also links her, in suggesting the Communist salute, to the aggressive defiance of lowly people—but her final achievement was mainly the pain that was the prelude to her death from, as Thomas knew, cancer of the womb. The nature of that life and the tragic helplessness of its victim are what affect him. They "storm"—that image so suggestive of his reluctance to be conquered—even his distancing suburban defences. Here is a major example of "saying" as "undoing": his aunt's life and death have changed him utterly. The significance is profound: his aunt lived and died in a world in which general love would only return on some far-off Judgment Day when all things dead would come back to life. The poem allows the personal relationship to remind the reader—via this sense of a hostile world and gesture towards Armageddon—that it was rewritten in 1938.

The second poem is "We lying by seasand," the beautiful love poem in which two lovers are beyond the tide line on a stretch of marine estuary of the kind found on the Welsh coast and at Laugharne, there on "the dry tide-master / Ribbed between desert and water storm." The poem dramatizes a moment of calm and love that modulates into the threatening and the ominous.

The third is "I make this in a warring absence," the poem about quarrelling with Caitlin written disconcertingly soon after their marriage. The poem belongs to the "exhausters" group, one of the persisting sequence of difficult, at times obscure, poems. As with, for example, "I, in my intricate image," in which Thomas's attempt to clarify his profound personal relationship between self and muse results in the clotted complexities of imagery and syntax, so this later poem, through its doggedly accumulating clauses and thinning narrative line, points to the difficulties Thomas had in clarifying his feelings for Caitlin. The other two poems, both of which belong more to the "exhausters" group than to that of the "opossums," are "A saint about to fall" and "If my head hurt a hair's foot." The former anticipates Llewelyn's birth in 1939; the latter is a response to the birth itself.

As has already been noted, "After the funeral" effects an indirect link between personal and general-historical, the darkening world of the late 1930s. All five personal poems are impressive and important because of that link. For example, "I make this in a warring absence," a poem of 1937–38, moves from a couple's quarrel to threatened aggression to reconsideration to the desire for reconciliation, a movement very apt for that time of appeasement. Thomas's initial exclusion from Caitlin's world, the way the relationship—both the companionship and the sexual life—is reduced to nothing, and his puzzled sense of her contradictory nature, at once open and unattainable ("In the molested rocks the shell of virgins") are all simply pushed aside at the close when reconciliation comes and he can return to comfortable married life ("in the cloud's big breast lie quiet countries"). The parallels with contemporary governmental reaction are suggestive. This is not to say that the poem is a political or historical allegory, but, rather, that Thomas's work is influenced by his inevitable consciousness of external events.

Again, "A saint about to fall," the poem about Llewelyn's imminent birth, describes it as a version of the Fall, as a violent disaster, with the breaking of the waters as a new Deluge: "the sour floods / That bury the sweet street slowly." Though the father hopes that this birth will enable him to see the world freshly, joyously, he is forced to tell his child that "The skull of the earth is barbed with a war of burning brains and hair." The world is a place of violence and atrocity in which time, like a 1930s dictator, bullies the gentle newborn, though even this, Thomas asserts, not altogether convincingly, cannot destroy his sense of joy in creation.

The final stanza, beginning, "Strike in the time-bomb town," offers imagery that ranges from the womb as refuge or asylum to Herod's massacre of the innocents, modern atrocities against children, life after the Deluge, the physical stress of childbirth, a rifle being cocked or a jail being opened, birth and the entrance of a bullet, and the bullring with its reminder of the Spanish war. The mode is baroque, with violent shifts and changes of language and a rhyme scheme that functions only at the borders of control. The effect is Guernican, fragmentary, polyphonic; the grand-scale rhetorical gestures are constantly undermined by language—"eardrum," "parcel," "dishrag," "sponge"—that reminds us of ordinary, individual suffering. Once again we are made to move from personal to public, from small to great.

"If my head hurt a hair's foot" is a dialogue, written, of course, by a male poet, between the child about to be born and the mother. The child grieves for the pain it may cause; the mother states that there is no other way:

> "No. Not for Christ's dazzling bed
> Or a nacreous sleep among soft particles and charms
> My dear would I change my tears or your iron head."

A single word links this event to the historical moment. In both this poem and in "A saint about to fall," only Thomas would link birth to the firing of a bullet ("a stranger enter like iron") and, with the reference to "your iron head," to what might be either bullet or bomb. This sense of the new arrival as disruptive, even destructive, is an interesting reversal of Thomas's understanding of his own birth as an entry into a hostile and frustrating world. To put this another way, in this poem Thomas's relationship with his father gives way to his own fatherly concerns.

If this volume's sixteen poems and seven short stories are considered together, Llewelyn, like his father before him, was entering an unashamedly middle-class or bourgeois world. A topographical composite makes this clear. In the short story "The Enemies," for example, the Reverend Mr. Davies reaches the Owens' bungalow, their "little house with a garden," and

saw a young man with a beard bent industriously over the garden soil; he saw that the house was a pretty picture, with the face of a pale young woman pressed up against the window. And, removing his black hat, he introduced himself as the rector of a village some ten miles away. (*CS*, 18)

This scene is a surprising combination of 1930s country-cottage life, latter-day Trollopiana, even a domesticated Pre-Raphaelitism. It is also part of a world that includes suburban gardens and men in deck chairs listening to the wireless, while from a first-floor bedroom window a young man sitting at his desk stares at a private girls' school close to a park. The asylum in "The Mouse and the Woman" has grounds like that very park, with flowers and gravel walks, where "children in print dresses might be expected to play, not noisily, upon the lawns." Even the asylum building "had a sweet expression, as though it knew only the kind things of life and the polite emotions" (*CS*, 74). Elsewhere the houses are grander, as in "The Tree," with its gardener, potting shed, and tower. Within such a house is, doubtless, "the clean glittering of the kitchen, among the white boards, the oleographs of old women, the brass candlesticks, the plates on the shelves, and the sounds of kettle and clock" (*CS*, 76), and the front parlors where stuffed animals rehearse the pastimes of the gentry. Elsewhere, in the poems, lovers lie on the sand, part of the bourgeois world of "a white child in the dark-skinned summer" (*CP*, 71), released from "nurseries" (*CP*, 72) in (to return to the fiction) homes visited by clergymen who are invariably and surprisingly Anglican. There is also the picnic, that genteel between-wars occasion, such as that in "The Orchards" (*CS*, 42–49).

Indeed, this story, written in 1934 and placed last in the volume, is fundamental to our understanding of Thomas's middle-class suburban sensibility. The story has powerful biographical elements: the central character, Marlais, has Thomas's middle name and is described as "Marlais the poet" (*CS*, 48). He steps from his "top-storey room in the house on a slope over the black-housed town" (*CS*, 43) where "cloud . . . bursts in cold rain on the suburban drives" (*CS*, 45), leaves "the great stack forests" (*CS*, 45) and the "long dead of the stacked south" (*CS*, 46) of the country, the scenes of industrial waste, and journeys over the "water-dipping hills" (*CS*, 4) to where he

laid himself down in the grass, and noon fell back bruised to the sun; and he slept till a handbell rang over the fields. It was a windless afternoon in the sisters' orchards, and the fair-headed sister was ringing the bell for tea.

. . . The fair girl, in a field sloping seaward three fields and a stile from Marlais, laid out a white cloth on a flat stone. Into one of a number of cups she poured milk and tea, and cut the bread so thin she could see London through the white pieces. She stared hard at the stile and the pruned, transparent hedge, and as Marlais climbed over, ragged and unshaven, his stripped breast burned by the sun, she rose from the grass and smiled and poured tea for him. (*CS*, 48)

The whole story translates without strain into autobiography: Thomas turns away from suburban Uplands, from industrial Swansea and the smoky south, to head west into rural Wales, only to discover that, as always in Thomas's life, despite his journey and changed, disreputable appearance, in his end is his beginning. The picnic in the orchard refers us back to the Uplands of authoritative, scholastic handbells, clipped hedges, unfulfilled sexual promise and maternal/domestic comfort, sandwiches cut with ineffable gentility, and glimpses of wider, metropolitan horizons. A bourgeois upbringing is re-created in a field.

The story penetrates to the heart of that upbringing, the bourgeois world that shaped Thomas's work. Into that world come strange intruders: Callaghan in "The Visitor," who may well represent death, battles with Rhianon for the dead or dying Peter, then carries him off into the "corrupting night" on the Jarvis hills (*CS*, 29); the good but bewildered clergyman in "The Enemies," whom Thomas styles the Reverend Mr. Davies, stumbles into a world whose respectable facade conceals "the secrets of darkness" (*CS*, 19); the girl and boy in "The Map of Love," initially embarrassed by a world of tropical fecundity and uninhibited sexuality, move shyly yet eagerly into the aqueous world of sensual pleasure, this being a story about a world governed by basic and often joyous instincts existing outside social limits. The idiot in "The Tree," the woman's lover and the writer himself in "The Mouse and the Woman," and the madman in "The Dress" have similar roles: all seven stories in this volume are structured in terms of intrusion, of what can be called invasive difference. We understand why "The Visitor," suggestively titled, opens the section entitled "Prose." Recurring intrusion is also found in the poems: the young narrator enters the harsh peasant world of "After the funeral"; Thomas's first child, Llewelyn, is the "saint about to fall" into the murderous world from a heaven of sorts; the compassionate fetus of "If my head hurt a hair's foot" worries about entering life; Thomas himself, in "Twenty-four years," crouches "in the groin of the natural doorway" (*CP*, 81), preparing to advance—or decline—through life.

The entered worlds are, to say the least, unwelcoming and sometimes hostile. Callaghan, in "The Visitor," battles with the caring Rhianon for Peter's dead or dying consciousness; the Reverend Mr. Davies is afraid and feels like "an old god beset by his enemies" (*CS*, 20); the idiot in "The Tree" is crucified by the boy in the garden; Beth Rib and Reuben are drawn by and submerged in a sensual world dominated by the old and seductively virile; in "The Mouse and the Woman" the lover goes mad possibly through sexual guilt, while the writer is an all-powerful destroyer; the madman in "The Dress" returns to his mutilated wife and asks, it seems, for affection and/or forgiveness; in "The

Orchards'' Marlais finds only a burned landscape, sexual disappointment, and the world he thought he had left. Though, to be sure, in these worlds there is some sexual joy, some love, as is evident in Peter's feelings for Rhianon in ''The Visitor,'' in the surrendering to each other of the boy and the girl in ''The Map of Love,'' or in the initial exchanges between the lovers in ''The Mouse and the Woman,'' it has to be said that the relationships in Thomas's work are often destroyed by death or socially induced inhibitions, or lead to jealousy and sexual failure. This is the case both in the stories and in such poems as ''Not from this anger'' or ''I make this in a warring absence.''

Throughout this volume intrusion, invasive difference, is the main structural principle. It is a reflection of the most significant activities of those troubled times: the invasions, intrusions, and penetrations carried out by successful fascists, bewildered refugees, and the mobile unemployed desperate for work. This volume is permeated by the period, shaped by its social and political tensions and structures.

These tensions and structures are also responsible for the recurring apocalyptic note. It is first heard in ''Because the pleasure-bird whistles,'' in the burned cathedral overwhelmed by a new Deluge in ''It is the sinners' dust-tongued bell,'' and in the general violence of the volume's imagery. It is heard again in the fires that burn in ''The Orchards,'' in the massacre of the cattle and sheep in ''The Visitor,'' and in the chillingly prophetic sentence in ''The Map of Love,'' the title story, written during 1937: ''There was a spirit in the valley that would roll on when all the hills and trees, all the rocks and streams, had been buried under the West death'' (*CS*, 112). It is even heard in ''We lying by seasand,'' in which the lovers hope in vain that sand will ''drown red rock'' and are unable to ''fend off rock arrival'' (*CP*, 71). Tindall perceptively recognized this poem as a reaction to T. S. Eliot, as a poem in which the beach becomes a waste land.[11] But whereas in *The Waste Land* the ''red rock'' is a mainly, probably wholly, spiritual refuge, in Thomas's poem it is a disturbing and persisting intrusion. In Thomas's poem ''red'' and the lovers' reaction suggest middle-class fears of communism. Here is a crucial instance of invasive difference. External circumstances break in as the lovers lie together until, inevitably, the ''golden weather / Breaks.'' Even that love is intensely vulnerable, a sadly pessimistic comment possibly on the Thomases' young marriage, certainly on the decade.

NOTES

1. *CP*, 67–81, prints the poems from *The Map of Love* in the order they appear in that volume. Quotations from the poems are taken from this edition. The stories, also in order, are ''The Visitor,'' ''The Enemies,'' ''The Tree,'' ''The Map of Love,'' ''The Mouse and the Woman,'' ''The Dress,'' ''The Orchards.'' Quotations from the stories are taken from *CS*.

2. The one ''possible'' is ''When all my five and country senses.'' Davies and Maud

(*CP*, 220) ''conjecture that it was a revised early poem (perhaps from a missing note-book), since it was submitted with three other revised poems to *Poetry*, and published there, August 1938.''

3. *CL*, 264. Letter to Vernon Watkins, dated 13 November 1937.

4. Dylan Thomas, *Letters to Vernon Watkins*, ed. Vernon Watkins (London: Dent and Faber & Faber, 1957), 40.

5. *CL*, 287. Letter to Vernon Watkins, 1 April 1938.

6. William York Tindall, *A Reader's Guide to Dylan Thomas* (1962; New York: Octagon Books, 1981), 165.

7. *CL*, 130. Letter to Pamela Hansford Johnson, dated 9 May [1934].

8. *CL*, 269. Letter to Hermann Peschmann, 1 February 1938.

9. See Caradoc Evans, *My People*, ed. John Harris (1915; Bridgend, Seren Books, 1987). The subtitle is *Stories of the Peasantry of West Wales*, the term ''peasant'' being a calculated insult.

10. Walford Davies, *Dylan Thomas* (1972; rev. ed., Cardiff: University of Wales Press, 1990), 36.

11. Tindall, *Reader's Guide to Dylan Thomas*, 153.

10

Portrait of the Artist as a Young Dog

Thomas's most famous volume of short fiction is another instance of the willingness to compromise with popular literary conventions that points to his underlying suburbanism. The volume was a response to a suggestion made by Richard Church, who was still at Dent's, still one of the most respectable and traditional of publisher's editors, and increasingly nervous about, and out of sympathy with, the heavily symbolic, sensual, neosurrealism represented by the stories in *The Map of Love*. He suggested that Thomas try autobiographical fiction; Thomas was immediately interested.[1] Two years later the first of the *Portrait* stories, "A Visit to Grandpa's," was published in *New English Weekly*. It was part, Thomas wrote later, of "a provincial autobiography" consisting of "short, straightforward stories about Swansea."[2] With his fiction as with his poetry, the late 1930s saw Thomas concerned about appropriate style, the shift from the difficult, sometimes obscure, stories to the immediately approachable.

The shift worried him. In a letter to Vernon Watkins he described the *Portrait* stories as no more than "illuminated reporting."[3] They were "mostly potboilers," he told Bert Trick. "They may be amusing eventually, but the writing of them means the writing of a number of poems less."[4] On this occasion his guilt was misplaced.

The title was simply "flippant," Thomas considered, used for "moneymaking reasons."[5] As always, such statements must be received cautiously. Certainly there have been attempts to relate Thomas's volume to James Joyce's *Portrait of the Artist as a Young Man*: Warren French, for example, wrote interestingly of the concern of both volumes with "tragic losses."[6] In 1951 Thomas himself wrote of the relationship with Joyce:

As you know, the name given to innumerable portrait paintings by their artists is, "Portrait of the Artist as a Young Man"—a perfectly straightforward title. Joyce used the painting title for the first time as the title of a literary work. I myself made a bit of doggish fun of the *painting*-title and, of course, intended no possible reference to Joyce. I do not think Joyce has had any hand at all in my writing; certainly his *Ulysses* has not. On the other hand, I cannot deny that the shaping of some of my *Portrait* stories might owe something to Joyce's stories in the volume, *Dubliners*. But then *Dubliners* was a pioneering work in the world of the short story, and no good storywriter since can have failed, in some way, however little, to have benefited by it.[7]

The comparison with *Dubliners* places Thomas's volume. It is a much funnier book than Joyce's, but, in important ways, it lacks Joyce's range. The political and religious dimensions of *Dubliners*, for example, are almost wholly absent from *Young Dog*. Characterization is more narrowly conceived, mainly because Thomas's autobiographical framework restricts the age range of his main characters. Thomas tends to hint where Joyce explores, an instance being the treatment of deviance, as a comparison of, say, the effeminate Ted Williams in "Old Garbo"—the volume's fleeting encounter with homosexuality—and the pervert in "The Encounter" makes all too clear. However, there are similarities between the two books: they include elements of the bildungsroman, the combination of first-person and third-person stories, the use of dreams, and, particularly, the symbolic use of place. There are occasional echoes, such as the echo of "Araby" in "One Warm Saturday" when the narrator sighs, "Oh love! O love!"

Portrait of the Artist as a Young Dog was published in April 1940.[8] The ten stories were written during 1938 and 1939, though not in the order in which they appear in the volume. "A Visit to Grandpa's" was written first; "Where Tawe Flows" and "Who Do You Wish Was with Us?" were last. They are stories of the late 1930s and, like all Thomas's work, reflect and explore the historical context. Thus, like the fiction—and some of the poems—in *The Map of Love*, the *Portrait* stories are all structured in terms of invasive difference, the significance of which has already been explained. The main character, whether as narrator or protagonist, enters a series of new worlds in which he is bewildered, uneasy, or befriended. The historical events that help shape the stories are encountered, in passing, in "Where Tawe Flows": references to anti-Semitism, fascist links with Welsh nationalism, Oswald Mosley, and what Mr. Evans describes as the "uniformication of the individual" (*CS*, 189) suggest very directly the gathering darkness of the time.

The economic depression of the period also enters a number of the stories. For example, in nocturnal activities in "Just like Little Dogs,"

little quick scarecrows had bent and picked at the trackline and a solitary dignified scavenger wandered three miles by the edge with a crumpled coal sack and a park-keeper's steel-tipped stick. Now they were tucked up in sacks, asleep in a siding . . . in coal-trucks thinking of fires, or lying beyond pickings on Jack Stiff's slab. (*CS*, 179)

The references here are to the desperate unemployed, the homeless, and the houseless dead. In "Old Garbo" we learn of "the silent, shabby men at the corners of the packed streets, standing in isolation in the rain" (*CS*, 212), and "the poor and the sick and the ugly, unwanted people" (*CS*, 217) ignored by

Mr. Farr. On the summer beach in "One Warm Saturday" are "valley children, with sunken, impudent eyes, quick tongues and singing voices, chests thin as shells" (CS, 225). Thomas's compassion is evident in imagery that is at times— the "little quick scarecrows," for instance—reminiscent of Dickens. All such descriptions of poor working-class South Wales, in the story and often in themselves, are also invasions of essentially bourgeois spaces.

Drastic and impoverishing social change is not always an urban phenomenon. In its rural version it is an important element of the opening story, "The Peaches." This and the volume's second story, "A Visit to Grandpa's," constitute an introduction to the whole sequence. Both stories explore family origins: the first, the world of his mother's relations on their small farms in Dyfed, the second, that of his father's family in Johnstown, Carmarthen.

"The Peaches" opens with a journey from town to country in spring, at night. As such, it is a useful introduction, given that Thomas structures the sequence partly in terms of a town/country antithesis, makes some use of the seasonal cycle—what begins in spring ends, in "One Warm Saturday," in high summer—and, significantly, sets much of the action in darkness. The journey, almost certainly from Carmarthen to Fernhill Farm (the "Gorsehill" of this story), begins in a "narrow passage" outside a pub. Symbols of restriction and confinement, such as passages, arches, and alleys, are found throughout the stories, dramatizing the limitations, psychological as well as physical, of the world in which the protagonist grows up.

The boy from the town enters a strange rural world. At times, as when he plays with his Swansea friend, Jack, he feels at one with his surroundings: "all my young body like an excited animal surrounding me" (CS, 137). More often the boy registers its alien quality. He has journeyed from a warm, safe, urban world to a world in ruins:

The ramshackle outhouses had tumbling, rotten roofs, jagged holes in their sides, broken shutters, and peeling whitewash; rusty screws ripped out from the dangling, crooked boards. . . . There was nowhere like that farm-yard in all the slapdash county, nowhere so poor and grand and dirty as that square of mud and rubbish and bad wood and falling stone. (CS, 132)

In his personal way Thomas is responding to the economic plight of Welsh rural areas during the 1930s. This passage is a gloss on official reports, typical of which is a survey of prewar conditions published in 1944: "Farm buildings were neglected through poverty, improvements went unmade, the land itself was sadly neglected."[9] Further, as a distinguished Welsh historian has pointed out, rural decline "had shattering effects on that native culture which the country areas had so largely kept alive."[10] This effect is also one of this story's concerns. Uncle Jim has become a drunkard who takes the farmstock to pay for beer, though this, in itself, seems hardly the only cause of the farm's decline. Rather, the drunkenness is one manifestation of a general cultural decline that Thomas suggests brilliantly. Uncle Jim's chair is "the broken throne of a bankrupt bard" (*CS*, 130), thus pointing to the collapse of once-vibrant eisteddfodic traditions. Religion is suffering the same fate. Jim's son, Gwilym, is purportedly training for the ministry. In an edged gesture towards Caradoc Evans, scourge of Non-conformity, Thomas characterizes Gwilym as infantile, preaching to terrorize and exploit young Dylan and his friend Jack, and as a sexual fantasizer and masturbator. He is the archhypocrite. Auntie Annie is a pathetic and ineffectual figure.

The combined economic and cultural disaster is summed up in a description of the front parlor at Gorsehill. This is the dusty best room, with "stale, sour air," rarely used. On its old-fashioned furniture are old photographs of Annie and family and of herself when young and a sexual being, trinkets, vases and a Bible lying together, pictures, brass fire irons, and a harmonium, deteriorating and neglected reminders of more prosperous days. Through the window we glimpse a garden choked with weeds, a traditional symbol of a fallen world.

The story's title, suggesting luscious fruit, refers, of course, to the tinned variety, a further implied contrast with the old ways, living off the land, and a decadent version of traditional Welsh rural hospitality. But tinned peaches were then a luxury, so that, as such, they are saved for the important visitor. In this is a point about social class, or, more precisely, social inferiority. The rural world is confronted and rejected not simply by the urbanized sensibility but by a different social class. Young Dylan is "a royal nephew in smart town clothes, embraced and welcomed" (*CS*, 130). His aunt takes off his shoes and fusses over him. He feels superior to and distances himself from this ruined rural outpost. His affiliations are with genteel Swansea that is middle-class, suburban Wales. This last, as the story demonstrates, has its own hierarchy, evident in the boys' games:

Jack cried: "I see you! I see you!" He scampered after me. "Bang! bang! you're dead!"
    But I was young and loud and alive, though I lay down obediently.
    "Now you try and kill me," said Jack. "Count a hundred." . . . I counted fifty . . . and killed him as he climbed. "You fall down," I said.
    He refused to fall, so I climbed too. (*CS*, 138)

Jack is the son of a wealthier family than Dylan's and so dictates the rules with which Dylan complies. Indeed, compliance, together with class rather than fa-milial loyalty, is one of the story's themes. The ending makes this clear. Jack, frightened by Uncle Jim's drunken threats, telephones his mother to take him home:

Mrs Williams sent the chauffeur for Jack's luggage. Annie came to the door, trying to smile and curtsey, tidying her hair, wiping her hands on her pinafore.
    Mrs Williams said, "Good afternoon," and sat with Jack in the back of the car and stared at the ruin of Gorsehill.

The chauffeur came back. The car drove off, scattering the hens. I ran out of the stable to wave to Jack. He sat stiff and still by his mother's side. I waved my handkerchief. (*CS*, 142)

The farewells are carefully differentiated. Annie reacts with ingrained servility; Mrs. Williams is a disliked but superior stranger. Dylan's only concern is to retain friendly contact with his suburban friend and his socially powerful mother.

In "A Visit to Grandpa's" the world of his father's family is equally strange when judged by the young narrator on his first visit. Grandpa rides horses in his dreams; awake, he tries to walk to nearby Llangadock to be buried because there "the ground is comfy." When his neighbors find him, he refuses to return home, but stands "like a prophet who has no doubt" (*CS*, 148). The world is made even stranger through constant simile: for example, "Dan Tailor . . . like an Indian priest but wearing a derby hat . . . an old woman by the gate of a cottage . . . ran inside like a pelted hen."

After the two-story introduction, effecting young Dylan's rejection, through class distance and transforming simile, of the worlds that produced his parents, eight stories of Swansea life follow chronologically. They explore aspects of the protagonist's life from childhood to late adolescence. All but three of the stories are in the first person. The exceptions are the first of this sequence, "Patricia, Edith, and Arnold," "Where Tawe Flows," and the final story, "One Warm Saturday," each marking a crucial point in the boy's development: glimpses of a heartless adult world through the maid's romantic entanglements, a provincial literary evening with local writers, and a final disillusionment.

It has to be said that the stories are of variable quality. "The Fight" tends to sprawl; "Just like Little Dogs" relies too much, and too neatly, on the inserted story about sexual exchange; "Where Tawe Flows," with its deliberately trite story within a story, is open to much the same objection. But the best stories are considerable literary achievements. "The Peaches" moves with assurance from individual actions to wider cultural statements. The two urban stories that end the volume, stories of a young man growing up in betweenwars Swansea, are superb.

"Old Garbo" is set in the weeks up to Christmas Eve (*CS*, 211–23). Old Garbo is Mrs. Prothero's nickname. She is an old working-class woman who believes that her daughter and new grandchild have died in childbirth. "We call her Old Garbo because she isn't like her, see," an acquaintance tells the narrator. But she is in one respect. After a collection is made for her, the daughter is found to be alive; the mother, drunk, spent out, and unable to face the friends who had subscribed, throws herself into the river. Garbo's famous catchphrase, "I want to be alone," takes on a sadly ironic meaning. Its ironic resonance extends beyond the one character to highlight the story's concern with loneliness: hardbitten Mr. Farr, the senior reporter, fears being drawn into the world of "silent, shabby men" whom he ignores in the crowded street, and his apartness and, paradoxically, good reason for that fear are vividly dramatized when we learn that "he swore, violently and privately, like a collier used to thinking in the dark"; effeminate Ted Williams visits sleazy pubs; the young narrator longs for romance.

"Old Garbo" begins in a Swansea newspaper office. The narrator works as a journalist, then has morning coffee with his friends in a nearby café. The story then becomes a rite of passage for the young Thomas, an evening's pub-crawl with hard-drinking Mr. Farr. It begins among respectable professional men in the Three Lamps pub, which was in actuality, as Thomas places it, at the heart of prewar Swansea's business district, and continues in the Fishguard and the Lord Jersey, in a sleazy part of the city. In this sense we see the story structured in terms of the invasive difference noticed elsewhere. Young Thomas becomes drunk and remains fascinated by the low life he has suddenly glimpsed. On Christmas Eve he returns alone to the Fishguard and learns what has happened to Mrs. Prothero. Later he writes about it all, but is confused about what happened where.

The important sequence, for this story as for the volume and for much of Thomas's other work, is the first transition from pub to pub. In the Three Lamps Mr. Farr and Thomas are "safe in a prosperous house," drinking "lazily in the company of business and professional men"; after only a short walk and a brief call at the lower-class Carlton Hotel—where they watch young men from the valleys having a night out in the big town—they "crawled down Strand alleys by the side of the mortuary, through a gas-lit lane where hidden babies cried together," to reach the Fishguard Arms. To understand the symbolism, we need to know that in prewar Swansea the respectable bourgeois heart of shops and offices backed onto a very different district of disreputable pubs, slums, cheap lodging houses, and the sexual promise of a busy seaport. Thomas's main concern is with the narrowness of the dividing line between two such different worlds. This story begins in the familiar, precisely located, and reassuring surroundings of middle-class Swansea, with its controlled patterns of behavior, only to slide swiftly into darkness, chaos, and confusion. That new world is disturbing: it confronts the narrator with loss, disorientation, and even death. (We can note in passing the strange similarity between such a contrast and Thomas's own life: his frequent abrupt, increasingly irrevocable, and eventually fatal sliding from a kind of order to a terrible chaos.)

The same kind of juxtaposition is found in other stories. For example, in "Who Do You Wish Was with Us?" the narrator's friend, Ray Price, during a summer excursion to the seaside, talks graphically of the deaths through tuberculosis of his father and his brother. In "Patricia, Edith, and Arnold" the child glimpses an adult world of sexual anarchy and unhappiness; there are similar effects in "Just like Little Dogs" and in the inserted story in "Where Tawe Flows." Such glimpses and juxtapositioning can also be found in the poems, as three examples demonstrate: "Why east wind chills" charts a shift from an adult's acceptance of the limitations of knowledge—a limited but controlled position—to a sense of inadequacy and the beginnings of confusion; "Once it was the colour of saying'' describes the transition from the reassuring certainties of Thomas's early career as a poet to a present disturbed by a desire to change direction; "The hunchback in the park" contrasts days in the park with nights in the dreadful and unlocated "kennel in the dark."

"One Warm Saturday," the story that not only ends but concludes the sequence, has a very similar structure to "Old Garbo" (CS, 224–43). It begins with the narrator, now examined more dispassionately via the third person, alone on August Bank Holiday Saturday, then at the beginning of August. His friends have gone in various hedonistic directions; he has decided to keep his own company. He is now a writer: "He thought: Poets live and walk with their poems; a man with visions needs no other company. . . . But he was not a poet living and walking, he was a young man in a sea town on a warm bank holiday." He sees a girl named Lou in a park, meets her with her friends in a pub, and goes with them all back to her flat somewhere on the other side of the city. Sexual promise beckons, but he leaves the flat for the lavatory, loses his way in the tenement building, fails to find his way back to the flat, and ends walking home across a demolition site.

To use the word of the period, Lou is "fast," perhaps a prostitute, and encourages the young man. In her apartment, in response to a chance remark she produces a volume of Tennyson, and the young man, encouraged, reads "Come into the garden Maud." It is not the first suggestion of Tennyson's poetry in this volume: "Go to bed plain Maud, thought young Thomas" of Mr. Evans's wife in "Where Tawe Flows"; in "The Fight" young Thomas's outrageous modern poem is immediately assimilated into the Tennysonian tradition. Nor is the reading the only reference in "One Warm Saturday." The story sets up a series of parallels with *Maud*, the most important being that at the heart of both story and poem is a walled and gated garden, and that both narrators are lonely, introspective, set apart from society. These similarities are supported by a large number of allusions and echoes, such as references to dancing and being buried alive, and the use in both works of overblown romantic responses.[11]

The poem exists as the story's subtext; we are constantly made aware of the former as we read the latter. But, as with most subtexts, we are reminded of it; we are not involved in it; as we are in the story. The poem remains a world of words; the story is our actuality. The relationship between the two works offers a metaphor for the young man's transforming propensity. The poem provides a paradigm for the "dark interior world" of the young man's imagination. It is also one of three instances of different worlds juxtaposed. The second concerns a drunken, deformed collier from what was then the economically depressed valley town of Dowlais, a sudden glimpse of a harsh alternative existence. The third returns us to the topographical contrast between western, middle-class, ordered Swansea, where the action begins, and its eastern, down-market counterpart:

The young man, on Lou's knee, saw the town in a daze spin by them, the funnelled and masted smoke-blue outline of the still, droning docks, the lightning lines of the poor streets growing longer, and the winking shops that were snapped out one by one. . . . On through the night, towards Lou's bed, towards the unbelievable end of the dying holiday, they tore past black houses and bridges. (*CS*, 237)

Topographically this appears to describe a journey to Swansea's working-class dockland suburbs. More important than simple accuracy of setting is the symbolism of lights going out as the group enters a morally as well as physically disorienting world. That chaos beckons; the young man responds eagerly.

Portrait of the Artist as a Young Dog, then, is a volume of juxtapositions, of differences apparent not only in the abrupt changes of place but also in the modulating language. As we might expect, this polyphony reflects the growth of the young Dylan. Becoming a writer is a process of distancing himself from the town. We see this, for example, reflected in musings that are moments of romantic expression. In "Just like Little Dogs" he tells us:

I was a lonely nightwalker and a steady stander-at-corners. I liked to walk through the wet town after midnight, when the streets were deserted and the window lights out, alone and alive on the glistening tramlines in dead and empty High Street under the moon, gigantically sad in the damp streets by ghostly Ebenezer Chapel. And I never felt more a part of the remote and overpressing world, or more full of love and arrogance and pity and humility, not for myself alone, but for the living earth I suffered on and for the unfeeling systems in the upper air. (*CS*, 182)

In "Who Do You Wish Was With Us?" we learn:

Instead of becoming small on the great rock poised between sky and sea, I felt myself the size of a breathing building . . . as I said: "Why don't we live here always? Always and always. Build a bloody house and live like bloody kings!" (*CS*, 206)

From "One Warm Saturday":

In the safe centre of his own identity, the familiar world about him like another flesh, he sat sad and content in the plain room of the undistinguished hotel at the sea-end of the shabby, spreading town where everything was happening. He had no need of the dark interior world when Tawe pressed in upon him and the eccentric ordinary people came bursting and crawling, with noise and colours, out of their houses, out of the graceless buildings, the factories and avenues, the shining shops and blaspheming chapels, the terminuses and the meeting-halls, the falling alleys and brick lanes, from the arches and shelters and holes behind the hoardings, out of the common, wild intelligence of the town. (*CS*, 230)

In the first passage the young man's sense of identity is derived from separation. When alone and self-communing he feels at one with the world because, paradoxically, he feels, alone at night in the dead town, that he has floated free from that world. The second quotation tries desperately for confident assertion. In the third, the interior life is not enough; the more objective, third-person stance allows empathetic response to the world outside himself. The third engages in sad dialogue with each of the others, as the young man feels at one with the living town and its people, rather than with a dead, deserted world. This is momentary empathy and, as such, points to the volume's main themes.

One, as has been stated, is intrusion, or invasion, which links these stories with Thomas's poetry of the period and, of course, with the period itself. Further, as the boy and then the young man enters various worlds, his desire to belong intensifies while his ability to belong decreases due to unease, confusion, hostility, or disappointment. Alienation is the key word, reaching a climax in the final two stories. Even though the vigor and humor of these stories convey youthful energy and life, and despite the moments of contextual harmony, they invariably end in disappointment, the feeling that is at its most intense in the volume's final lines, the conclusion to "One Warm Saturday," the lost young man stumbling out of the tenement into a ruined world.

Polyphony fragments further what is necessarily a volume of fragments. Even the potentially unifying effect of a common protagonist is subverted, first by the departure from chronology in the first three stories, and second, by the insertion of three third-person stories into the otherwise first-person sequence, thus casting doubt on the identity of the narrator and reminding us of authorial presence. This impulse towards disintegration overwhelms the gestures towards unity. Oddly, perhaps, the recurring idea of disappointment is one of the latter. So, too, is the recurring "ruins" motif: Gorsehill farm in "The Peaches," the derelict house with its smashed windows and the "half-built house, with the sky stuck in the roof" (*CS*, 182), through which the solitary nightwalker wanders in "Just like Little Dogs," "the ruins of fine brown eyes" (*CS*, 190) possessed by Mrs. Evans in "Where Tawe Flows," the "dark, stunted room" of the Fishguard Arms in "Old Garbo," and, of course, the final sequence of "One Warm Saturday" in which the lost young man wanders across the demolition site "that had been houses once." The counterpointing of realist narrative to inset stories, films, literary references (of which Tennyson is the major example), songs, dreams, and reveries suggests a different, perhaps better, and certainly more glamorous life away from the seedy town. The young man's desire for that glamour is reflected in his frequent journeys, his constant restlessness. Those dreams and reveries point, further, to the transforming power of the imagination.

A certain unity is achieved through Thomas's use of the Swansea setting, present, directly or indirectly, in all the stories. That sense of unity is countered once again by our changing sense of the place. Swansea as approachable symbol has already been discussed; it also exists as a private place, understandable only to the initiated. Two examples make the point. In "The Fight," when Dan suggests *The Warmley Magazine* as the title of their joint production, Thomas replies, "No . . . I live in Glanrhyd." This was a large house on the way from

Cwmdonkin Drive to Daniel Jones's home in Sketty and thus a private joke and revealingly pretentious. Even more private is the topographical sequence in "Old Garbo." When young Thomas leaves the Café Royal to return to the newspaper office, he "took the short cut down Chapel Street." The Café Royal was based on the Kardomah, which, in prewar Swansea, was in Castle Street; the newspaper office was on the opposite side of the street. Chapel Street was the long way round; Thomas's friends would understand the joke. The effect of such jokiness is to blur our sense of Swansea's presence by suggesting its dual identity. The same is achieved via the presentation of the city as a site of class- and gender-based difference and tension. Certainly a sense of community is countered by misogyny: in the world of the *Portrait* woman are either ridiculous or objects of desire. The urban monolith is subverted, and dialogic fragmentation asserts itself further. Meanwhile, in the wider world of the late 1930s monolithic Europe itself began to disintegrate.

NOTES

1. *CL*, 227. Letter to Richard Church, 1 May 1936.

2. *CL*, 279, 375. Letters to Vernon Watkins, postmarked 21 March 1938, and to David Higham, 11 May 1939.

3. *CL*, 333. Letter to Vernon Watkins, postmarked 19 October 1938.

4. *CL*, 416. Letter to Bert Trick, dated 29 September 1939.

5. *CL*, 437. Letter to Vernon Watkins, postmarked 30 January 1940.

6. Warren French, "Two Portraits of the Artist: James Joyce's *Young Man*; Dylan Thomas's *Young Dog*," *University Review of Kansas City* 33 (1967): 263.

7. Dylan Thomas, "Poetic Manifesto," in *Early Prose Writings*, ed. Walford Davies (London: Dent, 1971), 157.

8. All quotations are taken from *CS*, 127–243.

9. Welsh Reconstruction Advisory Council, *First Interim Report* (London: Office of the Minister of Reconstruction; HMSO, 1944), 6–7. Quoted in Dennis Thomas, "Economic Decline," in *Wales between the Wars*, ed. Trevor Herbert and Gareth Elwyn Jones (Cardiff: University of Wales Press, 1988), 33.

10. Kenneth O. Morgan, *Rebirth of a Nation: Wales, 1880–1980* (New York and Cardiff: Oxford University Press and University of Wales Press, 1981), 220.

11. See James A. Davies, "Dylan Thomas' 'One Warm Saturday' and Tennyson's 'Maud'," *Studies in Short Fiction* 14 (1977): 284–86, for a detailed account of the relationship.

11

Minor Prose

THE DEATH OF THE KING'S CANARY

All his life Thomas read detective stories; at times he gave the impression that he read nothing else. This enthusiasm was shared by a number of his friends. It is thus not surprising that the combination of reading interest, iconoclastic edge, and, no doubt, the hope of making some easy money should make him consider contributing a spoof to the genre. He discussed the possibility with Desmond Hawkins as early as 1935. In 1938 the proposed collaborator was his Swansea friend Charles Fisher:

I'd like to make it, with you, into a novel, make it the detective story to end detective stories, introduce blatantly every character & situation . . . that no respectable writer would dare use now . . . make many chapters deliberate parodies . . . It could be the best fun.[1]

But nothing was done until 1940, when, with the Battle of Britain at its height, Thomas stayed with John Davenport at the Malting House in Marshfield. Between them, the spoof was written.

The text as we have it is almost certainly not the complete work.[2] It ends where most detective novels begin, with the death of the poet laureate ("the king's canary"). The interest, therefore, cannot be in the skill with which Thomas and Davenport handle the form's conventions. Such interest as this work still possesses stems from its role as a roman à clef and, in particular, from its eleven parodies of poets of the period.

The novel begins in the prime minister's study at Chequers. He becomes steadily drunker as he reads through files on the candidates for poet laureate. He has samples of each poet's work, hence the parodies. The prime minister chooses the least likely and most disliked candidate. He is Hilary Byrd, based on Cecil Day-Lewis. The new laureate celebrates by inviting all his beaten competitors to dinner at his country home, Dymmock Hall, and makes a speech in which he insults his guests. All then attend a fair set up in the hall grounds. Hilary Byrd is found stabbed to death.

The work has not worn well, particularly when considered as a roman à clef. Thomas and Davenport possessed an intimate and detailed knowledge of the contemporary literary scene; at this distance in time many references cannot be appreciated. Certainly the frisson of the book cannot be recaptured. Further, not all the parodies can be identified with certainty. For example, "Lamentable Ode" by "Albert Ponting," Essex born and Polytechnic educated, may be a parody of George Barker or possibly of David Gascoyne. Less plausibly it is sometimes suggested that this parodies Thomas's own work.

A further problem is that we do not know which parts were written by which of the collaborators. Davenport himself said that he wrote chapter 1, a view supported by Diana Davenport, his widow.[3] He also stated that he wrote most of the poetry parodies, except for that of William Empson, which Thomas later published. We also know that Thomas wrote the Stephen Spender parody, "The Parachutist," which was intended for *Horizon*. We can be certain about little else.

The parodies are very skillful. There are some good scenes, in particular, that in a boat off the Cardigan coast in which Tom Agard and Owen Tudor—Davenport and Thomas—drink freely from a bobbing keg of Irish whiskey. But much is labored, even, surprisingly, the later scatological sequences. All that can really be said is that Thomas, in aligning himself with Davenport in such a venture, placed himself outside and at odds with the London literary establishment of the period. More sadly, in spending time at what is essentially a trivial and abortive gesture, Thomas grasped too readily at distractions from the increasingly difficult task of writing poems.

ADVENTURES IN THE SKIN TRADE

"My prosebook's going well," Thomas wrote to Vernon Watkins in 1941, "but I dislike it. It's the only really dashed-off piece of work I remember doing. I've done 10,000 words already. It's indecent and trivial, sometimes funny, sometimes mawkish, and always badly written which I do not mind so much."[4] A later letter commented further: "My novel blathers on. It's a mixture of Oliver Twist, Little Dorrit, Kafka, Beachcomber, and good old 3-adjectives-a-penny belly-churning Thomas, the Rimbaud of Cwmdonkin Drive."[5]

In 1941, when he tried the early chapters on Dent's, its readers reacted so unfavorably—"more coprolitic than ever, and seems to be quite without intellectual control"[6]—that the firm decided against proceeding. Thomas then published the first chapter, "A Fine Beginning," in *Folios of New Writing* later that year. The rest did not appear until shortly before his death, at the height of his fame, in the American magazine *New World Writing*.

Despite his satirical comments about himself, Thomas had begun the project with serious intentions. His four literary references are not thoughtless name-dropping but considered. They point to his main concerns: his protagonist, Samuel Bennet, asking for more of life than his upbringing seemed to offer, the innocent at risk in the great city, life as a nightmare, and a surrealistic edge to experience. Thomas also began the work with a clear plan, which Watkins has described:

It would be an extended story, not strictly autobiographical, but bearing a relation to the two parts of his experience, his own actions and the actions of his dramatised self. . . . The central character, Samuel Bennet, would attract adventures to him by his own un-adventurous stillness and natural acceptance of every situation. . . . Then, at a certain point, an unpredictable point in time, he would look back and find that he had shed a skin. In Dylan's first plan . . . there were to be seven skins. At the end of the story the character would be naked at last.[7]

Such a statement, of course, raises questions about intention vis-à-vis achievement that the unfinished state of the work is unable to answer. It also demonstrates Thomas's persisting interest in split personality or the dual self; we are reminded of the dichotomy between his school-mag poems and the private outpourings in the notebooks, and of such a poem as "I, in my intricate image," in which the poetic self is, as it were, separated from the core being.

The story begins in 42 Mortimer Street, near Stanley's Grove, which is obviously Cwmdonkin Drive near the Grove, Uplands, Swansea. Samuel Bennet, so obviously based on the young Dylan Thomas, leaves home for London, but not before vandalizing his home. He defaces his schoolmaster father's essays, ruins his sister's crochet work, breaks his mother's china, and tears up photographs. On the train to London he destroys all the contact addresses he has been given except one, the name of Lucille Harris, known as an obliging girl, given him by an acquaintance. On arriving in London he meets a Mr. Allingham in Paddington Station buffet, jams his finger in a bottle of beer, and embarks on a series of adventures. These include an attempted seduction by a girl in a bath, which involves him in drinking eau de cologne, and visits to sleazy clubs. All the while he fails to remove his finger from the bottle.

Though this is intended as a rite of passage, the sequence turns back upon itself in familiar fashion. In London he hopes to escape from the suburban, bourgeois world he professes to hate. What George Ring, his new London acquaintance, says of his own feelings when he arrived, "I felt there was something I must find, I can't explain it. Something just round the corner" (AST, 60), applies also to Samuel. Yet the more he tries to escape, the more he seems to encounter what he believed he had left behind, a recurring idea in Thomas, as has been seen, for example, in "The Orchards." Thus, when he arrives in Paddington Station buffet, the first person he meets is Ronald Bishop, who lived near him in Swansea. Even the strangers are transformed into characters from his home milieu: the chapel deacon on a spree in the big city, the shop assistants, the cold women. It is, indeed, "A Fine Beginning," as Samuel realizes: "If I go out of the station and turn round the corner I'll be back in 42. The little Proberts will be playing doctors outside the Load of Hay" (*AST*, 37).[8] As Annis Pratt has pointed out, the sister, mother, and father from whom he has escaped are immediately replaced by those he meets in London, respectively, Polly, Mrs. Dacey, and Allingham. Pratt saw this as a part of a reversion to childhood that continues with "the tepid bathwater and rubber duck" in the bathroom where the attempted seduction occurs. She wittily observed that the scene suggests "amniotic rather than seminal fluids."[9]

Even London streets are dull, so that "It's like the streets at home" (*AST*, 52). The first room Samuel enters in the house in Sewell Street is piled high with furniture and house fittings that offer reminders of the cluttered rooms of the home he has left. Whereas in the opening Mortimer Street scene, while "the family breathed and snored securely" (*AST*, 18), he opens pantries and cup-boards to destroy the contents, now, in Sewell Street, matters are much the same: he imagines lying in the dark, "opening cupboards and putting my hand in" (*AST*, 63), with "the invisible dead breathing and snoring all around me, making love in the cupboards, drunk as tailors in the dry baths" (*AST*, 64). Even the women in the louche clubs "might have lurched in from Llanelly on a football night, on the arms of short men with leeks," and are, as Samuel puts it, "dull as sisters" (*AST*, 105). More important, Samuel has not escaped his upbringing, as we see, for example, in his all-too-suburban fear of sex: of Polly, naked in the bathroom, and of Mrs. Dacey's hand on his thigh.

Adventures in the Skin Trade asserts fiercely that "In my end is my begin-ning," thus indicating the strong influence on—and possibly the strong attrac-tion for—Thomas of suburban middle-class values. These values are made even more attractive when they are contrasted with the book's stress on drowning, on being "drownded" (*AST*, 86), as it is put, in Dickensian fashion, in the sleazily amoral world of Mr. Allingham's metropolis. One example is when Samuel recovers from drinking cologne and falling into the bath: he feels as though he "sank into the ragged green water for a second time and . . . saw the whole of his dead life standing trembling before him" (*AST*, 83). Later, in the Cheerioh Club, the effect is much the same: the dancers have "deep green faces, dipped in a sea dye, with painted cockles for mouths and lichenous hair" (*AST*, 114).

Thomas underestimated this work, as did Dent. To be sure, there are moments of slack writing. An example is such a sentence as "His eyes were still heavy from a dream of untouchable city women and falling, but he could see that" (*AST*, 17–18), where "falling" could be an unrelated participle. A good editor could easily have dealt with this and other lapses and so furthered the structural expression of serious ideas. One such is the role of dreams. Samuel's parents are so permeated by their suburban lifestyle that his father dreams of bills and his mother of housework. For them, even the imagination is circumscribed, whereas for their son, in his own dream "the lights of a city spun and shone through the eyes of women walking" (*AST*, 28). Again, when he wakes on his last morning in Mortimer Street, it is like rising from the sea's depths; in London, as we have seen, his waking life is a series of drownings. This unfinished work is full of such effective contrasts and, of course, links. The sea is another point of similarity between London and his Swansea home. The London scenes are far from negligible, touching on fear of women, self-absorption, and the attraction of repulsion. For Thomas, as for Shelley, "Hell is a city just like London"; the nightclub scenes in the final section, with their neosurrealistic vigor and humor, edged with disgust, are reminders of book 7 of *The Prelude*, of Wordsworth's troubled encounter with London and his use of the Bartholomew Day fair, with its freaks and perversions, as a symbol of city life.

Adventures in the Skin Trade is as much an attack on London as on Mortimer Street. Whereas that on the latter protests slightly too much, that on the former may well reflect Thomas's idealist disappointment at what the city offered him. Years earlier he had sat with Pamela Hansford Johnson in Chelsea pubs, talked of literature, and dreamed of literary London. We catch the remnants of those expectations in the brief exchanges between Samuel and the homosexual George Ring on Sir Henry Newbolt and Walter de la Mare. In reality, Thomas's visits to London meant visits to drinking clubs, scatological chat, and anarchic escapes into alcohol and sex. In *Adventures in the Skin Trade* we catch another appealing subtextual glimpse of the young man on Johnson's doorstep.

The Death of the King's Canary and *Adventures in the Skin Trade* are slight, unrealized works. Yet, like all Thomas's prose, neither is without moments of interest and humor. That they are wartime pieces is also evident in their sense of a world without certainties, careering towards chaos. With hindsight, that sense is all too sadly prescient, so far as his personal life was concerned.

REVIEWS

Most of Dylan Thomas's reviewing took place between 1934 and 1939, during his early years in London. Much of this was for the *Morning Post*, work secured for him by Geoffrey Grigson when the two were still friends. From January 1935 to September 1936 Thomas reviewed batches of detective novels and thrillers—usually three or four at a time—almost on a weekly basis.[10] This was hackwork. Thomas retained a liking for such reading but, in general, took a jaundiced view of the state of the genres, of "those dull but sterling spy stories that always begin in a Scotch mist" and of the detective story that needed to liberate itself from "rules and good taste" that had made it "smug and self-satisfied."[11]

His serious reviewing was initially for *Adelphi, New Verse*, and the *Bookman* during 1934 and 1935. Two years later he reviewed Djuna Barnes's *Nightwood* for *Light and Dark* and volumes by Emily Dickinson and Edna St. Vincent Millay for *Time and Tide*. In 1938 and 1939 he contributed nine notices to *New English Weekly*. They were the last until 1951 and 1952, when he reviewed Roy

Campbell's autobiography, *Light on a Dark Horse*, and, with a gruesome appropriateness, Amos Tutuola's *The Palm-Wine Drinkard*, both for the *Observer* newspaper.

Thomas's reviews are entertaining, often revealing, but not impressive. One reason for this is that he is too eager to succumb to the attractions of his own wit. For example, noting the influence of Blake on Alfred Haffenden's *Dictator in Freedom*, he comments: "Much of the Prophetic Books reads like Tupper after absinthe" (*EPW*, 177). In a review of Gandhi's *Songs from Prison* he refers to "the Tory solutions of life, the heaven for the good and the hell for the bad, of the Rig Veda" (*EPW*, 173). "This is just the book to give to your sister," he writes of Flann O'Brien's *At Swim-Two-Birds*, "if she's a loud, dirty, boozy girl" (*EPW*, 197). Inevitably, he can slide into schoolboyish attempts at humor, describing H. G. Wells as "the boy who never grows up; a sort of Peter Bedpan" (*EPW*, 191).

Another reason is that Thomas cast a decidedly drooping eye on the left-wing attitudes of drawing-room intellectuals and tended to judge poetry accordingly. Thus in Stephen Spender's *Vienna* "the propaganda is bad, to be condemned, and even despised, by the real communist" (*EPW*, 170). As for John Pudney, he was "the gifted retailer of second-hand ideologies" (*EPW*, 168), a member of the Auden group of writers self-consciously aligning themselves with the left. As for John Lehmann, whose poems *The Noise of History* Thomas reviewed in two magazines, though he attempted to be "a poet of the masses . . . he is more concerned with the tinglings of his delicate nerves than with the percussions of his own loud generation." His poems merely "leave in the mouth the faint, contradictory flavours of aerated water and marzipan" (*EPW*, 172, 175).

Thomas also sought evidence that poets were proceeding in a manner similar to that in which he believed himself to proceed. He repeats, mantralike, one principle, that the true poet should be working from words and not from ideas towards words. Neglect of this principle was all too apparent:

Too much poetry to-day is flat on the page, a black and white thing of words created by intelligences that no longer think it necessary for a poem to be read and understood by anything but the eyes. (*EPW*, 166)

Thus William Soutar is criticized for being "too content to *incline* towards words and not to work *out* of them." Spender's *Vienna*, attacked for placing political ends before poetical means, fails because he is no longer "sensitively working from words." As for long-dead John Clare, "Though words were his active medium, Clare worked towards them, not out of them," as did Emily Dickinson, who was "primarily interested not in words, but in ideas" (*EPW*, 166, 169, 180, 185). Of course, we understand Thomas's concern for the sound of poetry and his detestation of poetry as primarily propaganda, but it is a narrow way to proceed.

Thomas reserved his greatest enthusiasm for Djuna Barnes's *Nightwood*—

"one of the three great prose books ever written by a woman" (*EPW*, 183)—which he reviewed almost wholly through quotation. His strongest criticism of a writer of standing was of Spender's *Vienna*, which represented much of what he disliked about the committed poetry of his contemporaries. He did not much like the poetry of John Clare, Emily Dickinson, and Edna St. Vincent Millay ("negligible"), Beckett's *Murphy* ("Freudian blarney: Sodom and Begorrah"), and William Carlos Williams's "slang-strung, hard boiled" short stories, seizing on Williams's medical background to describe them as "like contributions to the Gangsters' Lancet" (*EPW*, 186, 187, 188). Roy Campbell's autobiography is praised for its vivid descriptions of Campbell's South African upbringing, but the account of the 1930s, when Campbell supported Franco and had other fascist sympathies, "throws rather a bad light on an old war-horse" (*EPW*, 203).

Thomas emerges from these reviews alive to his time, particularly in the troubled 1930s, and determinedly iconoclastic. We may have reservations about some of his literary judgments, but we remain impressed by his unabashed youthful confidence.

NOTES

1. *CL*, 275–76. Letter to Charles Fisher, dated 16 March 1938.

2. See Diana Davenport, "The Malting House Summer," *New Review* 3, no. 31 (1976–77): 66–70. I have used the following edition: Dylan Thomas and John Davenport, *The Death of the King's Canary* (1976; Harmondsworth: Penguin Books, 1978).

3. Diana Davenport, "The Malting House Summer," 67.

4. *CL*, 485. Letter to Vernon Watkins, dated 22 May 1941.

5. *CL*, 487. Letter to Vernon Watkins, 28 May 1941.

6. Quoted in *CL*, 488n. Letter from Dent's editor to Laurence Pollinger, 10 July 1941.

7. Vernon Watkins, foreword to *Adventures in the Skin Trade*, by Dylan Thomas, Aldine paperback ed. (1955; London: Dent, 1965), 11–12. References to this edition, abbreviated as *AST*, are included in the text.

8. The Load of Hay was a pub outside Paddington Station well known to visitors from South Wales. It no longer exists. The Proberts are next-door neighbors in Mortimer Street.

9. Annis Pratt, *Dylan Thomas' Early Prose: A Study in Creative Mythology* (Pittsburgh: University of Pittsburgh Press, 1970), 156.

10. Full details are in Ralph Maud, *Dylan Thomas in Print: A Bibliographical History (with Appendix)* (London: Dent, 1970), 98–100.

11. Dylan Thomas, "Recent Novels," *New English Weekly*, 21 April 1938: 34 (*EPW*, 188–90). Almost all Thomas's reviews—the main exceptions are those in the *Morning Post*—are reprinted in Dylan Thomas, *Early Prose Writings*, ed. Walford Davies (London: Dent, 1971). For convenience my references will be to this volume, abbreviated as *EPW*, and will be included in the text.

12

Deaths and Entrances

DEATHS AND ENTRANCES

Deaths and Entrances is Dylan Thomas's finest volume.[1] It is the culmination of the clarifying tendency detected in the volumes of the 1930s. As has been noted, of the volume's twenty-four poems, only two—"The hunchback in the park" and "On the Marriage of a Virgin"—are revisions of notebook drafts, and three others have slighter notebook connections. We are reminded that Thomas had sold the notebooks in April 1941; the other poems, so far as is known, were new. They divide into two groups: those written or completed during the period from 1939 to 1941, and those from 1944 and 1945. During the three years between groups Thomas was preoccupied with filmscript writing and thus with the demands of immediacy and popular appeal.

The first poem is "The conversation of prayers," a technically brilliant poem based on a pattern of internal and line-end rhyming. The poem links a child's bedside prayers and those of a man who prays for his "dying love." Thomas's view of the child's future is bleak: he too, like the man, will soon learn of "grief as deep as his true grave." But though this poem dwells on personal problems, when we learn that the child prays for "sleep in a safe land," we feel the presence of World War II.

In this volume the war is never far away, this second catastrophe having displaced Thomas's sense of the first. A number of poems are specifically on the war; they are about the London blitz and from a civilian's point of view. One is "A Refusal to Mourn the Death, by Fire, of a Child in London," always regarded as a war poem even though no specific conflagration is mentioned. The carefully punctuated, unemotional title in itself indicates a refusal to mourn that is part of the poet's determination to put the child's death in a wider, consoling context. The poem can seem callous, particularly in its reference to the "majesty and burning of the child's death," or, at the very least, open to accusations of reducing the terrible to abstractions. Both reactions ignore the deep feelings generated by the tension of long sentences winding through rhymed stanzas. These stanzas, in which full rhymes dominate, impose a pattern on the poem that reflects the natural order in which the girl's death is placed and in which she will remain until the end of the world, until

> the last light breaking
> And the still hour
> Is come of the sea tumbling in harness.

Thomas refuses to mourn because the dead child becomes a part of living nature, resurrected through the natural cycle. Yet in responding to tension-generated feeling and to tone, we recognize that the poem is not so much a refusal to mourn as a refusal to mourn in a conventional way with either "a grave truth" or with "any further / Elegy of innocence and youth." On offer is a less direct but no less sincere kind of mourning, a way of controlling grief that avoids tears and seeks reassurance in the positive possibilities of the ambiguous final line: "After the first death, there is no other." We contrast that response with the paradoxical indifference of friendly Nature, represented by "the unmourning water / Of the riding Thames."

This poem, like, for example, "After the funeral," is about the appropriate poetic response to the sufferings of others. In its concern with writing it has links with a second war poem, the eponymous "Deaths and Entrances." In what is one of Thomas's finest war poems he makes a disturbing connection between the bomber pilot striking fear into the populace below and the poet penetrating to his reader's heart. The poet, as much as the airman, is

> One enemy, of many, who knows well
>   Your heart is luminous
> In the watched dark, quivering through locks and caves,
>   Will pull the thunderbolts
> To shut the sun.

That the airman has located and even seems able to see those who hide from imminent bombs behind locked doors and in underground shelters speaks to the worst fears of the blitzed Londoner. The poem is equally striking as a heroic assertion of the value of poetry in defying war: the poet will "load the throats of shells / With every cry." Further, as has been seen, in "Once it was the colour of saying" Thomas wrote of poetry's deep demands, knowing that "my saying shall be my undoing"; in "Deaths and Entrances" those demands "wound," requiring him to "bathe his raining blood in the male sea." The poem ends with the poet as Samson: for his readers, who may well wish, ultimately, to avoid what he has to say—and, as the poem as a whole implies, for himself—a source of strength and support *and* of disturbance and destruction. Poetry is powerful but does not necessarily order or reassure: it is no accident that a rhyme scheme does no more than flicker through these stanzas, hardly insisting on pattern and arrangement.

"Ceremony After a Fire Raid" is less successful. It is in three parts. The first grieves for the victims of an air raid, in particular, a child and its mother burned to death, the former linking the poem with "A Refusal to Mourn." The burned child, symbolizing outrages against civilians in World War II, displaces, in Thomas's haunted mind, the dead body on open ground that dominates his responses to the 1914–18 conflict. The second part makes further reference to that child to lament the death of innocence and the loss of all Edenic possibilities. Part 3 celebrates natural force and magnificence even in a world become "garden of wilderness." Here Thomas uses the language of religious ceremony to make a pantheistic point. But in relation to the powerfully moving references to that burned child, to

> its kneading mouth
> Charred on the black breast of the grave
> The mother dug,

in which the puns on "kneading" and "dug" create an emotional subtext of maternal love and loss, and to "the cinder of the little skull," the celebratory third part seems both glib and overinsistent.

The strangest of these war poems is "Among Those Killed in the Dawn Raid was a Man Aged a Hundred." Of the old man we are told that "he died," suggesting the consequence of age rather than of the dropped bomb. The bomb itself, described as "a sun," and the man's death, "When all the keys shot from the locks, and rang," have positive connotations. The death is deprived further of serious emotional effect by the final line, in which the idea of the old man's resurrection is expressed humorously by "a hundred storks." The seeming implication is that one so old should not be mourned.

But elements of the poem disturb, an example being the reappearance of the dead body lying in the open that, as has been seen, marks Thomas's obsession with the Great War. Indeed, some of the poem's details—plants growing through eyeball sockets (a disturbing version of the Adonis myth), the spade, the "common cart"—suggest the first war more than the second, affording a glimpse of persisting nightmare. The poem's form points to further serious concern. Its fourteen lines are sonnetlike, with a recognizable division between octet and sestet, but lacking a sonnet's rhyme scheme. Though the *abbc* of the first four lines hints at a quatrain, thereafter in the octet there are very few rhymes and no discernible pattern. We are reminded of Thomas's use of the slightly truncated sonnet form of "Once it was the colour of saying," made to disintegrate in support of the rejection of old ways of writing. "Among those Killed" seems to abandon the form, then retrieves the suggestion of it by means of the defined sestet and the reappearance of rhymes. The chaos of war threatens and is to some extent countered by this retrieval and by the strange humor that distances emotion, reflecting the poem's central meaning. This last is yet another restatement of "A Refusal to Mourn": we need not mourn for the old man's death because it is part of the natural course of events for one so old, and seemingly he is reabsorbed into the natural cycle. The "heavenly ambulance" that is the "common cart" of conventional religious thinking (the old man taken to heaven) is rejected in favor of continuing existence as part of nature.

"Holy Spring" is also a war poem. Its origins can be discerned, albeit dimly, in the notebook draft, "Out of a war of wits." As such, it is an interesting example of a response to the Great War being revised into a poem about World War II.[2] The Great War imagery in the former is replaced by references to bombing ("the god stoning night") and by Thomas's existential despair: "I climb to greet the war in which I have no heart." He derives no solace from spring or from the morning that emerges "out of the woebegone pyre" that is blitzed London. His only comfort is that such "hail and upheaval" lead to poems.

The beautiful "Lie still, sleep becalmed" may also be a war poem. Its central image of a wounded man in a boat floating on the sea suggests this. But the wound "in the throat, burning and turning," as Walford Davies and Ralph Maud point out,[3] may well be a reference to D. J. Thomas and his cancer, Thomas's father a heroic casualty of his own war, sailing to his death as Arthur to Avalon. Since, to repeat, Thomas so often referred to his poetic impulsion as his "wound," the poem can also be understood as a metaphor for his struggles to write. "Lie still, sleep becalmed" links the group of war poems with two other groups in this volume: familial poems and poems about writing.

The opening poem, "The conversation of prayers," is about family life: the child, the man, the loved woman dying in the "high room." The man, expecting the worst, finds his love still "alive and warm"; the uncaring child about to say his prayers will soon experience grief and death. Somewhere in the subtext is Thomas's own marriage, under great strain by 1945 but still alive despite expectations. The pessimism about the child's future is echoed in "This side of the truth," which is for Llewelyn, then aged six. He has the naïve vitality of youth; in what in some ways is a precursor of "Fern Hill," he does not realize that ignorance is bliss. He does not yet know that the world is morally indifferent and all is doom-laden and predestined. He will proceed to his death—the "truth" of the title—through life's "grinding sea." That life is stripped of moral certainty, which is consigned to an apocalyptic chaos:

> Good and bad . . .
> Blow away like breath . . .
> Into the innocent
> Dark, and the guilty dark . . .
>   . . . and then
> . . .
> Fly like the stars' blood.

In this there may be echoes of Eliot's *East Coker*; certainly such annihilation owes much to Thomas's experience of the blitz. The ambiguous final line, with its notion of "unjudging love" that can only come from the very young, hardly counters the poet's bleak vision.

"Vision and Prayer," the poem reminiscent of George Herbert's "Easter Wings" in its use of shape, and probably begun in response to Aeronwy's birth in 1943, is no happier. The child is born into darkness; the hourglass shape of the stanzas in the second part stresses time already ebbing away; in the final lines Thomas's attempts to affirm an orienting Christian faith are to some extent subverted by desperate vehemence.

Though Thomas's marriage survived a few more years, there is little doubt that his pessimism about his children's future was linked to his tempestuous and often violent marital state. Hence "Unluckily for a death," in which "the brawl of the kiss" could well describe the Thomases' marriage even in 1939, when the poem was written, and which also points to a longed-for morality always "honoured" in the breach:

> All love but for the full assemblage in flower
> Of the living flesh is monstrous or immortal,
> And the grave its daughters.

That "full assemblage" is true love, perhaps within marriage; all other kinds are "monstrous" or unworldly, bringing forth only deathliness. That true love is his "fate got luckily," yet the desperate appeal of Thomas's characteristic final apostrophe, "O my true love, hold me," all the more compelling in the dark days of 1939, forces the poem to end with hope rather than marital achievement.

"Unluckily for a death" and "Into her lying down head," another troubled marriage poem about Caitlin's infidelities and his own sense of exclusion, can be linked to the earlier "I make this in a warring absence." They form a sequence of poems made difficult through contorted syntax, long accumulative sentences, and compressed imagery as Thomas tries to make sense of a marriage always too close to "libidinous betrayal." Such a sequence parallels that of clearer, more approachable work, the latter dominating this volume. Yet part of the latter is "On a Wedding Anniversary," written for Thomas's third in 1940, which is a short, clear, and bitter statement, almost as if, for the first time, he saw clearly—or, at least, admitted to himself—how marital matters stood between them: "Now their love lies a loss" and "Death strikes their house":

> Too late in the wrong rain
> They come together whom their love parted:
> The windows pour into their heart
> And the doors burn in their brain.

That sense of beckoning life beyond the relationship, conveyed by the "windows" and "doors," was one that, sadly, they both indulged but never properly heeded.

In part because of Thomas's tormented feelings about wife and children, *Deaths and Entrances* is a troubled volume. Though we could argue that a positive element is the continued concern shown by Thomas about his writing, that group of poems is, ultimately, equally troubling. His stress in "Deaths and Entrances" and "Lie still, sleep becalmed" on poetic inspiration as a wound has already been noted. If, as Tindall suggested,[4] "the winged trees flying my name" in "Poem in October" refers to Thomas's poems, then that "wound" reappears in the final stanza as inspiration and experience intersect and "the town below lay leaved with October blood" flowing from that wound. Thomas, not for the first time, makes a literary pun out of "leaved."

But he is not only disturbed about the personal cost of writing poems; he also worries about what he has achieved and the purpose of it all. The former leads to "Once below a time," a sad poem that sketches his own literary career that took off when

> Up through the lubber crust of Wales
> I rocketed to astonish,

only for disappointment to follow. Though he once felt that he would "never . . . regret the bugle I wore / On my cleaving arm," he now wishes only to "lie down and live / As quiet as a bone." What saddens most is the tone: Thomas's self-mockery points to self-doubt. The poem implies questions: was it all worth it, what has been achieved? It also suggests a writer trapped by literary obsessions and lifestyle and so generates a tragic interest. "When I woke" is even more troubling. It is another poem of 1939 and so intimates disaster. In particular, Thomas feels time running out. In the first section Old Father Time, scythe replaced by billhook, decapitates the morning. Thereafter the narrator hears Time

> Cry my sea town was breaking.
> No Time, spoke the clocks, no God, rang the bells,
> I drew the white sheet over the islands
> And the coins on my eyelids sang like shells.

Though short of time and lacking faith (the latter a recurring idea in this volume), even in the face of death, the imminence of which is chillingly suggested via the "coins" and the dreary sea sound of shells, Thomas has recourse to the "white sheet" of paper. This poem movingly dramatizes his despair as war came; it also dramatizes what in 1939 was still heroic determination. This determination, as has been seen, is found in "Holy Spring," where "hail and upheaval" lead to literary creativity.

Heroism is also present in "In my craft or sullen art," which presents the poet as solitary, disdaining material reward, wondering about the permanence of his work, and writing for its own sake. This poem may be a reflection of some cultural anxiety about the poet's role: Thomas rejects traditional Welsh bardic roles of poetic remembrancer and court poet and places himself squarely in the English romantic tradition of altruism and apartness. We can, however, detect in the whole shape of the poem sadness that this is how matters are or might be.

The other main group of poems in this volume consists of those about Thomas's own childhood. Three are among the most famous of those he wrote. In "Poem in October" the poet describes walking out of Laugharne on his thirtieth birthday and enjoying a vision of childhood in which, interestingly and unusually in Thomas's poems about childhood, a parent appears, in this case his mother. The poem re-creates rather than simply recollects not only the moment of intense happiness when the young boy "walked with his mother" but also the sense of wonder in the boy's intense affinity with the natural world. Hence the emotional force of Thomas's marvellous phrase "the listening / Summertime of the dead," which comments sadly on his near-wintry life—in 1945 he was still only thirty-one—in the early 1940s.

In the final stanza the poem's style changes. In the first five stanzas the syntax flows, enjambement dominates: stanzas 1 and 3 each consist of a single sentence, and there are only six sentences in stanzas 1 through 4. Stanza 5 has only one sentence, which runs over to take in the first two lines of stanza 6. Such compelling lyricism dramatizes reverie. But from line 3 of stanza 6 to the poem's end lyrical flow is checked by periods to effect a tonal change. The poem darkens as

> the true
> Joy of the long dead child sang burning
> In the sun.

The memory still gleams, but in registering the ambiguity of "burning," we know that time is destroying it. In recognizing, also, the recurrence of the burning child, the death of that memory is linked to war's violent destruction, suggested again by the reference to "October blood" that in another reading refers to the creative act. All changes, all fades and dies. In the face of this we have another characteristic final apostrophe:

> O may my heart's truth
> Still be sung
> On this high hill in a year's turning.

The poem thus ends with a plea rather than a prayer. The addressee is unnamed and could be either self or God. Thomas hopes for the best, for himself and for his work, and is close to despair.

"The hunchback in the park," that final flourish of notebook drafts, is also about Thomas when young. In the notebook version the hunchback's imagined "woman figure without fault" is a poem, but this idea does not survive in the final version, which is a study of loneliness and sexual longing. That this should be so is understandable in a poem of adolescence—the early draft is dated 1932, when Thomas was seventeen—less so, or perhaps more sadly so, in the 1941 version, four years after he married Caitlin. We are reminded that versions of loneliness, whether sexual, literary, or physical, are recurring ideas in *Deaths and Entrances* and can take the force of Tindall's comment, specifically on "A Winter's Tale," that this fine poem, in which a lonely man prays for love and has his prayers answered, has elements of autobiographical allegory.[5] The third poem on childhood is "Fern Hill," which, as Thomas's most famous poem, is considered in detail and in its literary and historical contexts.

"FERN HILL": INTERSTITIAL PERSPECTIVES

"Fern Hill" (*CP*, 134–35) is the final poem in *Deaths and Entrances* and the last of that volume's poems to be written. Two letters, one to David Tennant,[6] the other to Edith Sitwell, tell us that it was composed during August 1945 and "in September, in Carmarthenshire, near the farm where it happened."[7]

These dates are important: they place the writing of "Fern Hill" at a crucial point in history. The war in Europe had ended on 8 May 1945; a left-wing Labour government had been swept to power in Britain, with a large majority, on 26 July. On 6 August the first atom bomb was dropped on Hiroshima; three days later the second bomb destroyed Nagasaki. Japan surrendered on 15 August.

Thomas's position as the war ended, already described, can be restated briefly. Since 1944, after a barren and distracted two years, he had begun writing poems again. This, together with the end of the war and the arrival of the new government, instilled in him—as in millions of others—a great sense of freedom, of new beginnings, and doubtless, given his long-professed left-wing sympathies, of welcome social change. His correspondence with Oscar Williams has much on his hopes of moving to work in America. But though literary prospects seemingly had improved, the war's end did not solve his problems. In one sense it made no difference: he wrote to Williams that for a poet, the essential war never ended; a poet was only "at peace with everything except words."[8] More immediately and problematically, the Allied victory ended lucrative and regular work scripting propaganda films for Gryphon. Despite his leftist sympathies, the arrival of a Labour government was to arouse in him, as Ferris put it, "middle-class fears of rampaging socialism,"[9] which meant state interference. Thomas wrote to Oscar Williams: "The rain has stopped, thank Jesus. Have the Socialists-in-power-now stopped it? An incometax form flops through the window. . . . Let's get out, let's get out."[10]

He was also profoundly troubled by the atrocities discovered during the liberation of Europe and by the final acts of the war against Japan. The death camps were much on his mind: Belsen, for example, became a ready figure for disturbance and horror, as when he referred in letters to "nature serene as Fats Waller in Belsen" and, less ambiguously, to "worse-than-Belsen London" and the "boiling black Belsen" of Oscar Williams's darker poems.[11] The destruction of Hiroshima and Nagasaki was even more traumatic, causing a further darkening of his apocalyptic vision.

During the late spring of 1945 Thomas, Caitlin, and the two children left New Quay, Cardiganshire, where they had lived for a year, to spend the summer with Thomas's parents at Blaen Cwm. In some ways, rather like the end of the war, this was a promising move: Thomas was able to keep an eye on aging parents—in particular, on his father, with whom he now had a warm relationship—and, as he told Edith Sitwell, in a place not far from and in countryside similar to the famously eponymous farm and where, far from the dangers of bombing, living expenses were low. Like Fernhill, Blaen Cwm was redolent of happy childhood holiday memories and thus was part of his "never-to-be-buried childhood in heaven or Wales."[12] It was also a place that, from adolescence, Thomas had always found conducive to the writing of poetry.

Yet once again there was a negative side. The Thomases had been forced to leave their bungalow in New Quay when their landlord reclaimed his property, and Thomas, as usual, was harassed by financial problems. They had nowhere else to go except Blaen Cwm, about which, despite the memories and the cheap living, Thomas had strong reservations. It was

. . . a breeding-box in a cabbage valley, in a parlour with a preserved sheepdog, where mothballs fly at night, not moths, where the Bible opens itself at Revelations; and is there money still for tea? . . . the nonstop, probably frog-filled rain . . . this house too full of Thomases, a cottage row of the undeniably mad unpossessed peasantry of the inbred crooked county.[13]

This is, of course, fond and fascinated distaste. But his predicament was real enough: he was cooped up with aging and demanding parents, a tense marital situation, and the unaccustomed proximity of the two young children, in dreadful weather and in an isolated, eccentric, rural world with the values of which, those of toil and narrow Nonconformist religion, he was hardly in sympathy. America seemed more and more attractive.

"Fern Hill" is, to a great extent, a product of such circumstances, a creature of the interstice between British (indeed, international) history and Welsh (which for Thomas meant personal) social history. It was also generated in those internal interstices—within each history, as it were—that are the points where positive feelings are countered by the negative.

The larger historical interstice is reflected disturbingly in the poem, in the first place, generally, by the choice of childhood as a subject, Thomas seeking to flee from both public and private worlds. But flight is not wholly achieved. One of the central ideas of the poem is of nightly annihilation ("the owls were bearing the farm away") and the world beginning again the next morning, at once a metaphor for a child's carefree eagerness and, more deeply, an aspect both of the mentality of the blitzed Londoner,[14] particularly during the final German onslaught of 1944, and of the aftermath of Hiroshima. Indeed, as regards the former, "the horses / Flashing into the dark" may well owe something to visualized recollections of London's guns firing into the night sky. In the final stanza annihilation becomes permanent, the narrator imagining waking after death "to the farm forever fled from the childless land." Here, though, it may be no more than grim prescience that refers to sterility and, in line 2, to the reduction of physical presence to a lingering and chilling shadow, respectively a now realized consequence and an awful immediate effect of Hiroshima and Nagasaki. "Fern Hill" is also a poem about hierarchies (a point to which I shall return); let it suffice here to suggest that in this sense it is a reaction to the advent of a powerful socialist government.

Reflections in the poem of life at Blaen Cwm are more indirect, more redolent of wish fulfillment. It seems no accident that a poem written in the cramped and squalid country cottage should stress outdoor freedom and social power, or that, given the continuing crises of Thomas's adult life, it should seek to celebrate the carefree and the bliss of ignorance. But once again, as will be seen, such positives encounter difficulties.

"Fern Hill" is also a poem of the interstice in the Bhabharian sense of the term, a poem at the point at which one literature meets another.[15] It is a Welsh poem that, like all Welsh poems in English, is held in a matrix of English literary traditions and associations, here to such an extent that it might seem that Thomas deliberately placed his poem—as he did, for example, with the late fatherly poems and with "Prologue"—in relation to influential outside texts or literary movements.[16] Indeed, "Fern Hill" is a traditional poem in many ways, detached as it is to a great extent from the neomodernist gestures of Thomas's earlier work.

It is easy to connect with such traditions, with, say, writings that recall childhood. Examples might include Goldsmith's English/Irish praise of "Sweet Auburn" in *The Deserted Village*,

> Dear lovely bowers of innocence and ease,
> Seats of my youth, when every sport could please,

Keats's lines from *Sleep and Poetry*,

> A laughing schoolboy, without grief or care,
> Riding the springy branches of an elm,

Hopkins's "Spring,"

What is all this juice and all this joy?
    A strain of the earth's sweet being in the beginning
In Eden garden.—Have, get, before it cloy,

and D. H. Lawrence's "Ballad of Another Ophelia," which Thomas read and quoted in a letter during that summer of 1945. This haunting poem on the ending of innocence and the destruction of the idyllic, with its opening orchard of green apples and closing "grey garner," seems a direct influence. Eliot's *East Coker*, first published in 1940 and then again in 1943 as part of *Four Quartets*, reminded all his contemporaries that "In my end is my beginning."

Again, "Fern Hill," because of its rhapsodic quality and occasional shifts into religious language, can be linked—and often is—with poems that conceive of childhood in more spiritual terms. Henry Vaughan, Welsh but, as with the Irish Goldsmith, writing within the English tradition, in "The Retreat" longs for an innocent infancy when he felt closer to God and, he considers, to his soul's preexistence. Thomas Traherne's "The Rapture,"

Sweet Infancy!
. . .
    How great am I,
Whom all the world doth magnifie!

is an ecstatic outpouring stressing the child's God-given and glorious sense of self. Such writing, that of Vaughan in particular, is an obvious precursor of Wordsworth's "Immortality Ode." This later poem probably has a more intimate intertextual relationship to "Fern Hill" than have the metaphysicals, a relationship that has been described in detail by Alistair Fowler.[17] Wordsworth's poem looks forward to John Clare's "Remembrances":

O I never thought that joys would run away from boys,
Or that boys would change their minds and forsake such summer joys . . .
Till I found the pleasure past and a winter come at last.

There are also links between "Fern Hill" and other literary traditions. One is that of the country-house poem, glimpsed through moments of socially inappropriate neoaristocratic suggestiveness: the narrator when young as "prince," "lordly," "huntsman," and "honoured among foxes and pheasants." Another, of course, is the great tradition of rural writing that runs, for example, through Clare, George Eliot, Trollope, and Hardy to such poems as Edward Thomas's "The Manor Farm" and "Two Houses."

Yet, as with Dylan Thomas and modernism, his work can never be wholly absorbed into any of these traditions. "Fern Hill" is not consciously conventional in the manner of Goldsmith's late-Augustan lament, nor does it have the specific social and chronological implications of Keats's schoolboy reference.

Nor does it demonstrate the eye or ear for natural sight and sound, the realist detail of country life, of Hopkins and Lawrence. It certainly lacks T. S. Eliot's philosophical edge.

The experience it describes is not socialized, as in, say, Clare's "Remembrances," with its precise references to childhood games and the details of country life, let alone as in the weighty realism of the nineteenth-century rural novel or in Edward Thomas's work. Dylan Thomas here has no eye for natural phenomena or persisting countryside traditions; his is a generalized, neomythologized rurality. This last might well provide a link with Wordsworth, but even the references to prelapsarian Eden and to childhood as a state of grace lack spiritual force. "Fern Hill" is a poem almost wholly devoid of Wordsworthian mysticism or religious awareness.

Again, though the poem might occasionally seem to nod at the grand places of the country-house tradition, that small farm in Carmarthenshire was no Penshurst, or Appleton House, or even Vaughan's "Priory Grove." Further, the realist element, though present, is sparse when compared to that dominating English farming literature.

"Fern Hill" is at once within the text and in the margin—at the interstice—of mainstream English literature, at once inside and outside. It is different in degree, not in kind. It is not fully absorbed because of its Welshness, part of which is the fact that much of the finest Welsh writing in English is a bourgeois/ suburban creation, alive to the limitations of realism, that bourgeois mode, but rejecting extremes, as, here, those of the mystical or spiritual. It is also about a Welsh place with an English name, a fact that in itself has resonance for its Welsh readers, who would regard it differently if it were entitled, say, "Argoed" or "Nant Ceri."

All of this tells us that this is a poem out of English-speaking, urban South Wales and reflecting the specifically Welsh class structure of its day, one that lacked, for example, a strong upper-middle class. Partly because of this, it valued education so that, to repeat a point, a schoolteacher, say, was accorded higher status than in many parts of England, which, in turn, affected the attitudes of the schoolteacher's son, particularly when among poor rural relations. Hence the poem's edge of social superiority and the way in which, as will be seen, middle-classness is asserted in Welsh terms, in part defined in relation to the odd English usage and potentially comic accents of lower-class Wales. We might also wish to argue that the main language of the poem—what might be described as rhetorical lyricism—reflects the Bible-based preaching style of Welsh nonconformity. This last is certainly present in the lines

> And the sabbath rang slowly
> In the pebbles of the holy streams,

a most un-English and ironic reference in a poem of 1945. Intimations of secular Sabbatarianism, plus more than a dash of pessimism, can be a very Welsh combination.

"Fern Hill" belongs to the English tradition but is also a key text in Welsh Writing in English. As regards the latter, it can be easily related to some of that literature's main themes of memory, childhood, and place. M. Wynn Thomas suggested, for example, that "the trope of the house" has a "centrality to Anglo-Welsh culture"[18] that could be seen to develop from Thomas's poem and Vernon Watkins's "Returning to Goleufryn." Indeed, his choice of founding poems indicates a basic point about Welshness: both houses are transformed, at times rhapsodically, beyond realism into symbolic constructs, neomythological places, though detached from any sense of the mystical. Yet the language of both can remind us of Blake or Wordsworth.

Critical accounts of "Fern Hill" are, in essence, similar and positive. Five examples make the point. For Ralph Maud, the poem is one "in praise of mortality."[19] Walford Davies, though recognizing the duality of Thomas's vision of childhood, placed the stress firmly on "the harmonious *unity* . . . of the child's vision of the world."[20] " 'Fern Hill,' " wrote Tindall, "is Thomas' victory over what he laments."[21] Seamus Heaney, in a brilliant modern essay on Thomas, pointed to the poem's "affirmative strains" and the extent to which it is "buoyant upon memories."[22] Alan Bold's account of "Fern Hill" concerned itself almost wholly with the re-created Eden of childhood.[23]

These accounts and other similar ones are convincingly comprehensive only if they detach the poem from its historical context and avoid precise accounts of interstitial (interfacial) literary relationships. Otherwise, the former's mixture of positive and negative and the latter's tension between the syncretic and its opposite are necessary and profound influences on our interpretive and comparative understandings of the poem.

Interpretation begins by recognizing that in the first delighted rush of memory, the initial surge of remembered childhood happiness, the poem effects only a momentary escape before that surge and effecting are swiftly subverted. "Fern Hill" is, of course, an adult's view of childhood happiness in rural surroundings, an adult who knows all too well that childhood is fleeting and Time conquers. That accepted, childhood in itself is not altogether reassuring. To be sure, it was mainly a "young and easy," "carefree," "heedless," and happy period, yet the ideas forced into the poem by its context, in the lines to which I have already referred,

> As I rode to sleep the owls were bearing the farm away,
> . . . the nightjars
> Flying with the ricks, and the horses
> Flashing into the dark,

are also adult memories of himself when young sensing dislocation and of riding uncontrollably into the powerful (and perhaps sensual) unknown.

The center of the memory is even more troubling. The boy is remembered as invariably climbing, playing, running, and enjoying himself, but this only serves to emphasize the poem's uneasy solipsism: "I," "me," and "my" occur twenty-two times in this fifty-four-line poem. The boy is the sole occupant of remembered childhood; no other human being, neither friend, relation, nor parent, gets a mention. Nor is there any reference to childhood games or other communal activities, or, apart from the hint at helping in "herdsman," to the activities of a child's holiday helping on the farm.

Paradoxically, this solitary world that seems initially to be a desirable alternative to careworn life becomes suggestively and restrictively urban/suburban, with the farm's name one that would not seem inappropriate on the front of a semidetached house, with its "apple towns," the boy always playing near the house and yard, its self-important hierarchies—Time superior to the golden boy, the latter, as prince, lord, huntsman, and herdsman, superior to all else—echoing those of class-conscious Swansea suburbia. Cwmdonkin's middle-class codes can be further detected in the strange sexlessness of the boy's country experience: this is the bourgeois, suburban adult's sanitized prelapsarian Eden of "Little boy blue" and "Adam and maiden" and not a muddily realistic farm where a young boy can delight in having "manure in my shoes and hear it squelch as I walked, to see a cow have calves and a bull on top of a cow" (CS, 135). Much bourgeois confidence is certainly built into the texture of the poem, one example being the two essentially authoritative single-sentence stanzas that open the poem. But there is also an all-too-suburban hint of social uncertainty in the golden boy, the lord and prince, plying "sky blue trades," presumably effected via the tradesman's entrance. Above all, the urban sensibility is reflected in the presentation of childhood almost wholly in terms of a relationship with cultivated nature.

So far as this nature—farmed land—is concerned, the poem has much realist detail: the farm has barns, stables, wagons, orchards, fields of barley and of hay, cattle, horses, sheep perhaps, even pheasants. It seems a fine place. If we know that Fernhill was a delapidated smallholding from which Thomas's aunt and uncle scratched a living, the effect even of this detail is undermined. But it is anyway, because the detail is blurred by metaphor and simile—orchards as "apple towns," the "hay fields high as the house"—and the poem's firm refusal to describe the house or place it in the landscape.

The remembered world—house and farm—is far from being a solid presence, if only because meaning is further destabilized through ambiguity. A few examples make the point. "Easy," in the first line and in the famous finale, suggests attractive existence but also carries a moral (or perhaps amoral) edge in its version of carelessness; "heedless," in stanza 5, has more of the latter (the moral edge) than the former. The meaning of "green," that ubiquitous Thomas word, slides from natural growth to decay and naïveté. Even the line "The sky gathered again," part of Thomas's description of a world restoring itself, has a subtext darkened by a verb the meaning of which can range from coming together to a poisoned eruption. The use of musical imagery contributes to the slippage of precision: the "lilting house," "singing as the farm was home," "the calves / Sang to my horn," "the tunes from the chimneys, it was air / And playing," and Time's "tuneful turning" that limits the "morning songs," are controlled neosurrealistic excursions dramatizing the happy fluidity of childhood but resisting solidifying paraphrase. Though the regular stanza form and some patterned repetition control the material assertively, the absence of a rhyme scheme or even of a half-rhyme scheme—unusual in a Thomas poem—counters the attempts of poetic form to shape the past into a strong and confident presence. Though this might be seen as an intensification of mellifluous flow in what is often regarded as Thomas's most lyrical poem, subversion is present even here, as class-based polyphony. That is, at points in the poem Thomas reverts to what in Wales would be recognized as colloquial language and cadences. Thus the opening, "Now as I was young," meaning "Once, when I was young," is a characteristic South Walian use of "Now," which usually refers to some other time than the present. In stanza 3 a similar usage is the repeated "lovely," meaning "good" or "fine" or emotionally satisfying. The phrases "it was lovely," "lovely and watery," and, to use an example from stanza 4, "it was all / Shining" play on the exaggerated accent of working-class South Wales. At such moments the poem comes closest to dissociating itself completely from mainstream English literature.

In the poem's last two stanzas the dominance of negatives effects a further shift in language and tone. In the final stanza, despite an initial use of reassuringly traditional spatial terms—the idea of rising out of life into the afterlife—death is conceived of in wholly secular and discomforting terms as a "swallow thronged loft" in perpetual night, the moon "always rising," the dispossessed boy riding into darkness. Little wonder that in the famous final lines the poem's lyrical narration is countered by the despairing exclamation, or equally despairing apostrophe, that constitutes the poem's last three lines:

> Oh as I was young and easy in the mercy of his means,
>> Time held me green and dying
> Though I sang in my chains like the sea.

If this is an exclamation, to a great extent it expresses Thomas's fundamental despair. If it is an apostrophe, then, as Jonathan Culler noted, it "resists narrative because its *now* is not a moment in a temporal sequence."[24] Culler insisted that the apostrophe is always a deconstructive trope. At the end of "Fern Hill" we do not know to whom the apostrophe is addressed, whether to self, reader, God, or some spirit of the universe. It is freed from specific dialogic placing; it is also, as recollection, lifted out of time as a final dislocation that checks, perhaps deconstructs, the poem's only internal sense of order, that imposed by Time's authority.

At the poem's heart we sense rootlessness, uncertainty, and a kind of despair as the past blurs and the present darkens; even happy memory ultimately fails to orientate, order, or console. We sense, that is, what awareness of context points us towards. But we should also be reminded that the context was not wholly bleak and that Thomas's response even to the bleakness could be hopeful and often heroic in its humor: we recall the letter describing Blaen Cwm. We should also recall the affirmative interpretations of the poem, some of which I have cited. They may be incomplete, but they certainly stress what are present in the poem: the confident tone and language, the defiant insistence on being "young and easy" and on running "heedless ways," and the determinedly persisting consolation of being "held" by a "Time" that might support as well as trap.

It seems no accident that the most positive accounts of the poem—those by Tindall and Walford Davies, for instance—are by critics most concerned to recognize the poem's place in English literature.[25] Whereas our awareness of context points to the tension in the poem between despair and heroic assertion, what I have called our comparative understanding of the poem—that which proceeds from belonging to a major literature as well as a minor—also places it, reassuringly, within two ordering systems. But there can be little doubt that the poem draws its main positive strength, strength in numbers, as it were, from its links with members of the greater tradition, with *English* literature's version of what T. S. Eliot has described as tradition's "ideal order."[26] To adapt Mikhail Bakhtin: "[The poem] has no sovereign internal territory, [it] is wholly and always on the boundary"; to apply Lynn Pearce: "[The poem exists] *only in relation.*"[27] Its relationship with that glittering and weighty literary past, that past's sense of desirable possibilities, holds the poem "green" as well as "dying," as Time holds the boy, and counters the impulse towards rootlessness and dislocation.

The poem is profoundly shaped by a historical and literary context that is partly British, partly Welsh. It is set firmly in Homi Bhabha's interstice.[28] This is not to say that the poem lies dead or wounded in some desolate no-man's-land. Rather, it lies in what might be called poetical marches, which, like the Welsh Marches themselves, are a place of great beauty and fertility, a site of cultural forces often in tension but that combine as much as compete. The poem retains a sense of otherness that requires careful defining, as well as the inter-textual presence of a directly available great literature. This directness results, of course, from a common language, a common education system, intimate and institutional relationships, and numerous shared cultural assumptions; it poses problems for those seeking to relate the relationship between Welsh Writing in English and mainstream English literature to a colonial or postcolonial model.

Russell Davies once wrote that "Fern Hill" was "about as political as a mountain goat."[29] We know what he meant. We know also that he was wrong. "Fern Hill" is a Unionist document. It reminds us that the Acts of Union with England of 1536 and 1543 should be celebrated, at the very least, for furthering, in Susan Bassnett's words, "the juxtaposing of texts [and circumstances] in order to create new readings."[30]

NOTES

1. Quotations are taken from *CP*, 85–135. This section comprises the contents of *Deaths and Entrances* (1946). See *CP*, 170–71, for a description of minor textual emendations.

2. I discuss "Out of a war of wits" in more detail in James A. Davies, " 'A Mental Militarist': Dylan Thomas and the Great War," *Welsh Writing in English* 2 (1996): 68–69.

3. *CP*, 245.

4. William York Tindall, *A Reader's Guide to Dylan Thomas* (1962; New York: Octagon Books, 1981), 186.

5. Ibid., 197–99.

6. *CL*, 565. Letter to David Tennant, dated 28 August 1945.

7. *CL*, 583. Letter to Edith Sitwell, dated 31 March 1946.

8. *CL*, 561. Letter to Oscar Williams, dated 30 July 1945.

9. *CL*, 560n.

10. *CL*, 559–60. Letter to Oscar Williams, dated 30 July 1945.

11. *CL*, 554, 555, 557. Letters to Unknown Woman, 21 May 1945; to Caitlin Thomas, [24 June 1945]; and to Oscar Williams, 30 July 1945.

12. *CL*, 583. Letter to Edith Sitwell, 31 March 1946.

13. *CL*, 557–58. Letter to Oscar Williams, 30 July 1945.

14. In 1944 Thomas scripted the Strand documentary "Our Country," in which a factory girl describes her fears of the air-raid warning sounding followed by the nightly wartime "black-out":

And suddenly the lights would be out, and then, this is the end of the world I would say to myself, in case the others heard, though they were thinking it too in the dark. This is the end of the world. And you were dead as well.

And then we'd grow alive again, slowly, just like blind people creeping out of a cave into the light at the very beginning of the world. And you were alive. And when the morning came it was like Spring in the middle of the Winter.

Dylan Thomas, *The Filmscripts*, ed. John Ackerman (London: Dent, 1995) 72.

15. Homi K. Bhabha, *The Location of Culture* (London and New York: Routledge, 1994), 3.

16. For the fatherly poems, see James A. Davies " 'Hamlet on his father's coral': Dylan Thomas and Paternal Influence," *Welsh Writing in English: A Yearbook of Critical Essays* 1 (1995): 52–61. For "Prologue," see James A. Davies, "Questions of Identity: Dylan Thomas, the Movement, and After," *Appropriations and Impositions: National, Regional and Sexual Identity in Literature*, ed. Igor Navrátil and Robert B. Pynsent (Bratislava: Národné literárne centrum, 1997), 118–29.

17. Alistair Fowler, "Adder's Tongue on Maiden Hair: Early Stages in Reading 'Fern Hill,' " in *Dylan Thomas: New Critical Essays*, ed. Walford Davies (London: Dent, 1972), 240–41.

18. M. Wynn Thomas, " 'Prints of Wales': Contemporary Welsh Poetry in English," in *Poetry in the British Isles*, ed. Hans-Werner Ludwig and Lothar Fietz (Cardiff: University of Wales Press, 1995), 99.

19. Ralph Maud, *Entrances to Dylan Thomas' Poetry* (Pittsburgh: University of Pittsburgh Press, 1963), 80.

20. Walford Davies, *Dylan Thomas*, Open University Guide (Milton Keynes: Open University Press, 1986), 81.

21. Tindall, *Reader's Guide to Dylan Thomas*, 268.

22. Seamus Heaney, *Dylan the Durable? On Dylan Thomas* (Bennington, VT: Bennington College, 1992), 29–30.

23. Alan Bold, "Young Heaven's Fold: The Second Childhood of Dylan Thomas," in *Dylan Thomas: Craft or Sullen Art*, ed. Alan Bold (London: Vision Press, 1990), 162–65.

24. Jonathan Culler, *The Pursuit of Signs* (London: Routledge & Kegan Paul, 1981) 152.

25. See Tindall, *Reader's Guide to Dylan Thomas*, 268, and Walford Davies (ed.), *Selected Poems* by Dylan Thomas (1974; rev. Everyman ed., London: Dent, 1993), 118.

26. T. S. Eliot "Tradition and the Individual Talent," in *Selected Prose*, ed. Frank Kermode (London: Faber & Faber, 1975), 38.

27. M. Bakhtin, *Problems of Dostoevsky's Poetics*, ed. and trans. C. Emerson (Minneapolis: University of Minnesota Press, 1984), 287; Lynne Pearce, *Reading Dialogics* (London: Edward Arnold, 1994), 93.

28. Bhabha's "interstice" is a useful metaphor. However, its appropriateness to the relationships between British literatures seems questionable, given that it mainly connotes separation. "Interface," offering more stress on merging, though, these days, something of a cliché, may be more precise. The study of such relationships requires its own theoretical apparatus. Colonial discourse and postcolonial theory, in this writer's opinion, have only limited applicability.

29. Russell Davies, "Fibs of Vision," *Review*, Autumn–Winter 1971–72: 75.

30. Susan Bassnett, *Comparative Literature* (Oxford: Blackwell, 1993), 42.

13

Late Poems

In Country Sleep and Other Poems was published in 1952, but only in the United States. It is a very slim volume; its six poems represent all Thomas's completed poems since *Deaths and Entrances* in 1946.[1] "Author's Prologue," later simply entitled "Prologue" and written to preface *Collected Poems, 1934–1952*, is the only other poem completed by Thomas before his death. Two poems remained unfinished: "In Country Heaven" and "Elegy." The former, which Thomas probably began in 1947,[2] he intended to lengthen and place as the first and eponymous poem of a sequence that was also to include "In the White Giant's Thigh," "Over Sir John's Hill," and "In Country Sleep." The lengthening never happened, but Thomas left a detailed description of his intentions that casts light on all his late poems.

"In Country Sleep" was also conceived of as a longer poem. Thomas planned it in three parts, but after two were written, he lost momentum and brought the poem to, seemingly, an adequate conclusion. The poem concerns a sleeping girl who is threatened by a wolf and a prince but need only fear a "Thief as meek as the dew" who represents death and comes in the night to try, unsuccessfully, to conquer her. She hopes that he will come so that she can reject his overtures. Her faith in life survives all such crises.

This poem sets the agenda for these final works: all concern themselves with death and attitudes to death. Here, in such a line as "And you shall wake, from country sleep, this dawn and each first dawn," there is an insistent desire for survival, made more urgent by apocalyptic despair evident in the conclusion to the first part—"As the world falls, silent as the cyclone of silence"—and yet another poetic consequence of the age having become nuclear. But though there is some impressive writing in "In Country Sleep," the main problem with the poem is that, as Thomas put it, he started it "in cold blood."[3] The poem is the result, eight months after completing "Fern Hill," of his desperate need to write a poem, and it shows: the writing is strained and prolix. The essentially simple central narrative is overwhelmed by much natural description—at times a heaping up of detail—that in such lines as

> The sermon
> Of blood! The bird loud vein! The saga from mermen
> To seraphim
> Leaping!

edges the exclamatory Thomas close to unintentional self-parody. Certainly, exclamation is substituted for poetic inventiveness; here is neither the daring neomodernism of the early poems nor the clarified complexity of poems like "Fern Hill."

"Over Sir John's Hill" is a different matter. Narrative drive and a clear line of argument are restored in this Laugharne poem—the hill seen from Thomas's work shed was named after Sir John Perrot, the Elizabethan lord of Laugharne castle who died in the Tower in 1592 while under sentence of death—that deals, as so often in Thomas, with fatal hierarchies of power. The hawk, himself subject to some greater power, kills the small birds. All are doomed. The whole is a moral fable in which the birds are guilty because, in a word used twice in the poem, they are "blithe," uncaring of life and of their fate. Even as the hawk drops fatally upon them, they war, wrangle, and squawk; led astray hedonistically, they go suddenly. The birds are criticized because they do not sufficiently value the life they have and thus do not take sufficient care to preserve it. We can recognize links with "Do not go gentle into that good night."

The poem is permeated with a sad fatalism: the watching heron, itself a killer of fish, watches the killing of the sparrows with helpless stoicism. The poet himself, styled as "young Aesop," offers a disturbing sense of his work's vulnerability to time and chance when he "open[s] the leaves of the water" (perhaps here an allusion to Keats's epitaph).[4] The poem ends, characteristically, with a tonal change, here a shift into melancholy:

> The heron . . .
> Makes all the music; and I who hear the tune of the slow,
> Wear-willow river, grave,
> Before the lunge of the night, the notes on this time-shaken
> Stone for the sake of the souls of the slain birds sailing.

What he records, "[en]grave[d]" on stone, seemingly permanent, is still vulnerable to time's power. What strikes even more deeply is that the engraving is done "Before the lunge of the night," the chilling phrase enacting death's fatal thrust. The narrator, like the heron's fish and the hawk's sparrows, faces a sudden and violent end. Though in the penultimate stanza the narrator hopes that God will show mercy to the sparrows, his sense of his own death, as in "Fern Hill," is as bleakly secular night. These late poems dramatize Thomas's existential despair.

Two other poems offer nothing to relieve such despair. In most of "Poem on his Birthday" a tortuous narrative inches through heaped detail in the manner of earlier unsuccessful "exhausters." That said, an important and significant difference between this and those earlier poems is that "Poem on his Birthday" has some lines that betray a thinness of language. The bathetic "Doing what they are told" in stanza 2 is one example; the hackneyed

> Plenty as blackberries in the woods
> The dead grow for His joy

is another. Such lines and the increasingly desperate optimism weaken the poem's overall effect. But there are deeply felt moments, usually subverting the optimism, as when, in a manner reminiscent of "Over Sir John's Hill," the poet

> In his slant, racking house
> And the hewn coils of his trade.

"toils towards the ambush of his wounds," beleaguered and confined, haunted by death. He "slaves to his crouched, eternal end / Under a serpent cloud" in a world that is now "the earth of the night" and in which

> the rocketing wind will blow
> The bones out of the hills,
> And the scythed boulders bleed, and the last
> Rage shattered waters kick
> Masts and fishes to the still quick stars.

That is, the world may well be destroyed by nuclear catastrophe.

The other poem is "Lament," which Thomas once planned to entitle "The Miner's Lament," a poem of the 1950s. Behind the bluster, exploitation of women, vulgar humor, and energy of the writing is a dark sense of emasculating old age and destruction through marriage, further reflections of Thomas's personal desperation. In addition, its ostensible dislike of succumbing to bourgeois respectability while suggesting the latter's attractions continues a central theme found in all stages of Thomas's literary career. That said, this is a late poem because of its attitude to approaching death. The narrator grieves because he no longer rages.

"In the White Giant's Thigh" can be grouped with "Poem on his Birthday" and "In Country Sleep": all three are, in part or implicitly, responses to Hiroshima and Nagasaki. The "white giant" is that of Cerne Abbas, the huge priapic figure cut into a chalk hill; the poem draws generally on the belief that barren women would conceive if they copulated within the member. The poem mourns generations of barren women longing for pregnancy and children; it mourns the dead who, with their buildings and rural ways, have been utterly extinguished, so that

> The dust of their kettles and clocks swings to and fro
> Where the hay rides now or the bracken kitchens rust.

The poem also celebrates the persistence of the sexual impulse, ''the women of the hill / [who] Love forever meridian,'' but most significant is Thomas's concern with the annihilation of individuals and whole communities. The important fragment ''In Country Heaven,'' intended to be the sequence's title poem, in which Christ weeps, it seems, because of widespread destruction, is part of the same mind-set. Unusually, Thomas was compelled to offer an explanation of what the whole sequence would do. When in 1950 he published ''In the White Giant's Thigh'' in *Botteghe Oscure*, he added a note that explained that the whole sequence, regarded as one poem, would be about the death of the world and the survival of affirmation and possibility:

The Earth has killed itself. It is black, petrified, wizened, poisoned, burst; insanity has blown it rotten; and no creatures at all, joyful, despairing, cruel, kind, dumb, afire, loving, dull, shortly and brutishly hunt their days down like enemies on that corrupted face. And, one by one, these heavenly hedgerow men who once were of the Earth, tell one another, through the long night . . . what they remember . . . of that self-killed place. . . . And the poem becomes, at last, an affirmation of the beautiful and terrible worth of the earth. . . . It is a poem about happiness. (*CP*, 252–53)

The sequence remained unfinished, and ''happiness'' is not what is conveyed by the most forceful and deeply felt lines of the sections Thomas left to us.

To Thomas, in those postwar years, ''Heaven,'' indeed, seemed ''blind and black'' as the Cold War took hold and the nuclear standoff could not yet be perceived as a weapon of peace. The personal problems that found their way into ''Lament,'' for example, compounded his predicament. Against such a background, it is no accident that Thomas's finest poems of this period are the two addressed to his father: ''Do not go gentle into that good night'' and the unfinished ''Elegy.'' The relationship, closer and warmer in the final years of both father and son than it had ever been, was Thomas's only stable, indeed, strengthening, point of reference at that time.

The difference between the two poems has often been noticed: the earlier advocates demonstrating against death, the later ''Elegy'' celebrates dying with pride, dignity, and calm. Together they enact the tensions of his father's life explored by the son throughout his poetry: the thrusting aside of the genteel in order to rage openly, and restrained gentlemanly submission.

''Do not go gentle'' and ''Elegy'' both adopt traditional poetic forms: respectively, the villanelle and terza rima. In the former the strict intricacies of the villanelle contain a deeply emotional subject in, paradoxically, a clamping yet intensifying context. The strict progression of the poem from ''close of day'' to the ''sad height'' that is, in the words of one recent critic, a movement to a ''metaphorical plateau of aloneness and loneliness before death''[5] strengthens the containing. The cause of this containing, the poetic form, is in creative tension with the poem's ostensible purpose: though Thomas's father is urged to reject conventional behavior, to put aside "gentle"-manly conduct and to "rage," the poem's rigid formality insists on the great and continuing power of those very conventions. Second, the special suggestiveness of the diction links a powerful sense of death, the facing of death, and ways of living with reminders of prosaic suburban existence. Line 1 contains "gentle," with, to repeat, its second sense of "gentlemanly" or "genteelly," and "good night," which is both a morally charged euphemism for death and the casual late-evening fare-well of Uplands and other acquaintances. In line 2 "close of day" certainly evokes life's end but can also echo "close of play" to recall Thomas's, and possibly his father's,[6] love of cricket fostered by regular watching at the county ground below Brynmill. In such words and phrases, as in further references to "gentle" and "good night," the poem, as so often in Thomas, excavates a potent subtext that is also exposed in the simple moral insistence of "right" and in the use of "wave," a gesture of farewell and part of sea imagery that, with "green bay," not only symbolizes existence but recalls Swansea's coastal setting. Against the reference to "wild men . . . who caught . . . the sun in flight," that early love of cricket again presses, as does Thomas's implied dis-approval—the pun on "sun"—of his own behavior. The simple, mainly mon-osyllabic diction, the language really used by suburbanites, and the poet's suggestive evasiveness—death is only mentioned once, and that indirectly; it is the "light" that is "dying"—are other strong reminders that to confront his father was, for Thomas, to explore his own deep roots in the middle-class world that, in the deepest sense, he never left. It is also an encounter with the Jack/D. J. tensions of his father's life, the son urging the latter not to forget his former persona.

Further, in this poem, in the literary form and in the echoes and allusions, is a tribute to that other father, the scholarly D. J. Hence the echoes of Yeats, of "I have met them at close of day," the famous line that opens "Easter 1916," of the structure of the fifth section of "Nineteen Hundred and Nineteen," and of the "gay" eyes of the Chinamen in "Lapis Lazuli"; and of Byron's use of "fork'd / His lightnings" in stanza 95 of *Childe Harold's Pilgrimage*,[7] which might also echo *Romeo and Juliet* (5.3.88–90). There is also a possible gesture at Kierkegaard in the cursing father on the "sad height" that Vernon Watkins picked up, and, more probably, links with Old Testament Moses dying on Mount Nebo.

Similar elements recur in "Elegy" in the lines known to be close to Thomas's final version (*CP*, 155–56). Here the basic terza rima form is modified (we keep in mind that the poem is unfinished) and complicated not only by internal rhym-ing in the first two lines of each tercet but by the initial imposing of quatrains on the three-line stanzas. The consequent tension between stanza form and rhyme scheme, and between the sentence, with its emotional momentum driving it past stanza ends, and the stanza form itself, suggests an impulse towards fragmentation but stresses the poet's controlling hand. Patterns of alliteration, internal echoes, near repetitions, and clearly developing symbolism strengthen that hand in mastering grief. As with the villanelle, Thomas's obsessive concern with formal problems, his choice of poetic structures of amazing strictness, are, here as elsewhere, a reflection of the ordered and authoritative structures that sought to shape his formative years.

Unlike "Do not go gentle," the later poem is not at odds with advocated behavior. Though the dying man retains "burning pride," he is urged to "go calm to your crucified hill," where he will, Thomas prays, "be fathered and found." But, as in the villanelle, the urging is achieved, in part, through literary references. The opening hint at *Samson Agonistes* ("broken and blind he died / The darkest way") is followed by a version of the Adonis myth central, for example, to Milton's "Lycidas," Shelley's "Adonais," and the Tennyson of *In Memoriam*:

> Oh, forever may
> He live lightly, at last, on the last, crossed
> Hill, and there grow young, under the grass, in love,
> Among the long flocks.

The fragment ends with an allusion to D. J. Thomas as Christlike in that he goes bravely through suffering to meet God his father.

The most significant reference is to the poem's version of the Adonis myth: the father's body buried, grass growing on his grave, sheep grazing on the grass. The significance is in the fact that D. J. Thomas was cremated, an occasion to which his son reacted with violent distaste.[8] Thomas shapes events to express his sense of his father.

Here Jack Thomas is finally set aside and D. J. Thomas celebrated not only by being associated with gentlemanly behavior, but by being absorbed into a classic literary tradition that pays tribute to him as a gentleman-scholar, the man he had wished to be. D. J. Thomas is further admired for his middle-class virtues of restraint and brave reserve. In the manner of his dying he exhibited qualities different in degree but not in kind from those that sustained respectable life in the suburbs of west Swansea, where folk valued privacy and too often hid tensions and troubles behind a front of normality heroically cultivated.

If, as has been suggested, poetic formality in Thomas's work is expressive of the ordering, conforming impulse essential to middle-classness, then these late works are the most bourgeois of poems. They are all tightly controlled, fiendishly strict. "Poem on his Birthday," for example, alternates lines of six and nine syllables. Strictest of all is Thomas's last completed poem, the "Prologue" to the *Collected Poems*.

This is a work of great technical brilliance and seeming confidence, evident, for instance, in the huge periodical sentence that opens the poem, outdoing Milton, it seems, as it winds through thirty-three lines, and in the strange and difficult rhyme scheme that famously rhymes the first and last lines, the second and penultimate, and so on, until the poem of 102 lines balances on a rhyming couplet. To qualify that confidence with "seeming" is to recognize the sadness of the poem's opening, its sense of all "winding down now," and that the poem conveys the intense vulnerability of Thomas's personal and literary life: his house is "seashaken," the rocks are "breakneck" and "tangled," and in the lines

> the cities of nine
> Days' night whose towers will catch
> In the religious wind
> Like stalks of tall dry straw

we have, in the conflation of "nine days' wonder" and James Thomson's bleak poem *The City of Dreadful Night*, the recognition that the attractions of London and New York were illusory and certainly short-lived and will be destroyed in the Armageddon that stands, once again and ever more menacingly, at the edge of Thomas's world.

In addition, this poem also expressed Thomas's worries, as life slipped away from him, about the nature of his work:

> Seaward the salmon, sucked sun slips,
> And the dumb swans drub blue
> My dabbed bay's dusk, as I hack
> This rumpus of shapes.

Dylan Thomas was the most self-conscious of writers, and what surely strikes us about such lines, as about the opening periodic sentence and the rhyme scheme, is that they are overtly demonstrative, overinsistent, yet, to repeat, supremely confident. It is as if Thomas, in poor health, dragged down by drink, possibly drying up as a poet, is saying to his readers, "Look what I can still do!" Yet such a gesture is at odds with his sense of the inadequacy of his writing, those "sawn, splay sounds," and his despairing sense that his "sea-thumbed leaves"

> will fly and fall
> Like leaves of trees and as soon
> Crumble and undie
> Into the dogdayed night.

The personal apocalypse parallels his sense of general catastrophe. Indeed, both equally dominate the poem as Thomas utilizes the Noah myth and insists, desperately, on his poems as arks.

Though "Prologue" comments on the parlous state of the nuclear world, it is also a Welsh poem, about Thomas *in* Wales, and so we hear it insist, "This is what this *Welsh* poet can do!'' The Welshness is evident in the opening account of Thomas at the Boat House and in Laugharne and, particularly, in the second half in his rendering of ''Wales in his arms'':

> Hoo, there, in castle keep,
> You king singsong owls . . .
> Huloo, on plumbed bryns,
> O my ruffled ring dove
> In the hooting, nearly dark
> With Welsh and reverend rook
> Coo rooing the woods' praise . . .
> Heigh, on horseback hill, jack
> Whisking hare! . . .
> Huloo, my prowed dove with a flute!
> Ahoy, old, sea-legged fox,
> Tom tit and Dai mouse!

Thomas is here deliberately exclamatory. Much of this would be dreadfully quaint—terribly twee in a Disneyish way—if it was not so obviously exhibitionist (''Look what I can still do with sounds!''), deliberately rhapsodic, and wordily and bardically anthropomorphic. The effect is deliberately parodic. Here is stereotypical ''Welsh poetry in English'' of the two decades up to 1950 taken to extremes: rural, rhapsodic, bardic. Here is a version of the carnivalesque that, in a sense, out-Thomases Thomas, for the stereotype, that which is being carnivalized, is Thomas himself. This is the familiar phenomenon of Thomas playing the part expected of him—but with a keen sense of irony—by those who reacted against all he stood for. These last, as will be seen, included F. R. Leavis and the Movement, as postwar poetics changed. The poem's ending readmits deeper feelings: the familiar sense of catastrophe as a modern deluge closes the world's eyes (''The water lidded lands''), and the significance of the final ambiguity:

> My ark sings in the sun
> At God speeded summer's end
> And the flood flowers now.

Here the ark is Thomas's poetic oeuvre. It may conquer the flood with its metaphorical flowers, but, as the syntax and stress pattern more forcefully dictate, it is more likely to succumb to the flood's own flowering. ''Prologue,'' intended as an introduction to Thomas's ''collected'' achievement, certainly demonstrates persisting technical skill, but ultimately succeeds only in revealing his personal problems and uncertainties, exacerbated by his troubled sense of a changing literary world.

NOTES

1. Quotations are taken from *CP*, 139–152.

2. See *CP*, 259–63, for a detailed discussion of the process of composition.

3. Quoted in Paul Ferris, *Dylan Thomas* (1977; Harmondsworth: Penguin Books, 1978), 227.

4. "Here lies one whose words were writ in water." Dylan Thomas may well have known of this through his friendship with Vernon Watkins. Watkins had visited Keats's grave in Rome and, after Thomas's death, published "In the Protestant Cemetery in Rome."

5. Jonathan Westphal, "Thomas's 'Do not go gentle into that good night,' " *Explicator* 52, no. 2 (Winter 1994): 114.

6. See Joan Harding, "At 'Dame' School with Dylan," *New Welsh Review* 7, no. 4 (Spring 1995): 39–40. She stated that she sometimes met the young Dylan when their fathers took them to watch cricket matches. This may have been so, though an earlier suggestion in this article that D. J. Thomas was a regular drinker at a gentlemen's club near his home called the Beechwood cannot be supported by club records and may well make us wonder about the reliability of memory almost seventy years later.

7. For a full discussion of this allusion, see Richard Poole, "Dylan Thomas, Ted Hughes, and Byron: Two Instances of Indebtedness," *Anglo-Welsh Review* 24, no. 54 (Spring 1975): 119–124.

8. D. J. Thomas's ashes were buried with those of his brother Arthur, who had been cremated in 1947. The quoted lines from "Elegy," so suggestive of a traditional burial, may well gain further literary impact from this additional fact.

14

Towards *Under Milk Wood*

The origins of *Under Milk Wood* go back to the 1930s, but the main impetus came during the 1940s from Thomas's work for BBC Radio and for film companies. One other important precursor was his letter writing, which enabled him to develop his gift for humorous observation of everyday life.

BROADCASTS

Much of Thomas's work for radio was of the bread-and-butter variety. As has been noted, it included some nonliterary work, such as hosting the "Country Magazine" series from Witney in 1948, presumably because he was reasonably famous, an experienced broadcaster, and living in nearby South Leigh. But usually, from 1937 until his death, particularly when the Third Programme established itself during the postwar period, he contributed to programs of literary interest, mainly involving reading poetry. These included parts in dramatizations and dramas, thus reviving teenage enthusiasms. The former included the part of Satan in a semidramatized version of *Paradise Lost*, Thomas being a last-minute replacement for Paul Scofield. His eight appearances were criticized by Martin Armstrong in the *Listener* for "outboom[ing] Milton" (*B*, 294), with a consequent loss of articulative clarity. Other notable parts were the Elder Brother in *Comus* and Private Dai Evans in David Jones's *In Parenthesis*, in which the young Richard Burton also appeared. Appearances in dramas included parts in plays by Louis MacNeice.

In 1943 Thomas broadcast the first version of "Reminiscences of Childhood" and so began the series of talks and features about himself, his life, and the places associated with him that ended with "Laugharne," broadcast on the day (5 November 1953) on which he collapsed in New York into the coma from which he was not to recover. These are the famous broadcasts. They led him to examine closely himself, his life, and the places he knew, and, in so doing, to generate much social detail, to write for immediate effect, and to dramatize ordinary life.

The first broadcast version of "Reminiscences of Childhood" illustrates Thomas's main preoccupations.[1] The piece is about Swansea in the 1920s, beginning with a general view of the town, focussing on Cwmdonkin Park, then offering memories of his dame-school, before ending with a fantasy about flying over the district. The piece is structured around two poems: one is "The hunchback in the park," the other lines from the uncollected poem beginning, "See on gravel paths under the harpstrung trees." A number of motifs run through the essay. One is the Great War, the time of Thomas's birth, dealt with in a light and poignantly humorous reference to the Front and linked in thought with the final reference to Swansea's later fate: "war has made a hideous hole in it" (*B*, 8). Another is the sea, to which the piece, like Thomas himself, always returns. A third is a series of small gestures against authority, or the established community: truancy, running on the park grass, wandering the streets "whistling and being rude to strangers" (*B*, 6), fighting with boys from a lower social class, numerous petty crimes in school, the illicit smoking of "butt-ends of cigarettes" (*B*, 7) after school, the final terrorizing of the teacher when the boy imagines flying. A fourth is references to the economic depression of the time: the "old anonymous men, in the tatters and hangovers of a hundred charity suits" (*B*, 3), the "patient men with the seaward eyes of the dockside unemployed" (*B*, 6), the out-of-work observed when flying.

The main theme is the power of the imagination. This is expressed by means of a number of structural devices. One is a succession of moves from the wide or panoramic to the narrow. Thus the first paragraph begins with a general view of Swansea and ends with a preacher on the beach; paragraph 2 moves from a panoramic view of Wales to the boy in bed hearing others play in the park, and the old man on the park bench memorialized as the hunchback. Such shifts from wide to narrow continue through the piece, culminating in the boy's imagined flight over Swansea, a final panoramic view that also dramatizes the imagination's power.

The two poems within the prose in themselves make a similar point about the power of the creative imagination. They also associate the possessor of that power with loneliness. The "hunchback" poem, which began life in 1932, remains a 1930s poem on economic deprivation, sleeping rough, and the mockery of conventional society. At its heart is loneliness and sexual longing. The second poem, written at much the same time, is an overwrought expression of teenage angst, accommodated to the maturer vision by means of self-mockery. Thomas recognizes the overstated rhetoric and laughs at himself when young.

Such tension between how things were and the transforming impulse is mirrored throughout the piece in that between similes and metaphors. The former convey the homely and reassuring vision of the child that was Thomas: enemies in childhood games "like a flock of wild birds" (*B*, 3), a child's "happy heart waiting, like an egg, to be broken" (*B*, 5), a tram shaking "like an iron jelly" (*B*, 6), the flying boy "like a large, stout bird"(*B*, 7) and "like Dracula in a schoolboy cap" (*B*, 7). There are fewer metaphors: Smokey the park-keeper as a "whiskered snake in the Grass one must Keep Off" (B, 5) and memories of childhood as "every-coloured and shifting scented shoals that move below the surface of the moment of recollection" (B, 7) are two examples. The similes struggle to familiarize; the metaphors transform childhood neomythologically into a lost and magical world.

At the close Thomas imagines himself, when a boy, astonishing his friends by flying, first past the school windows to frighten the mistress and then over the town and the dockyards. Valentine Cunningham has shown that during the 1930s flying was an important literary motif.[2] We keep in mind that Thomas was a product of that period. However, in 1943 the use of a flying finale was more probably a consequence of Thomas's experience of the blitz in London and Swansea. Flying is an expression of power: to discomfort authority and to observe not only familiar parts of the town but also, from a moving and secure middle-class aerie, the unknown working-class areas. This recognition of childhood's power is also an expression of wish fulfillment.

The BBC worried about Thomas's disregard of broadcasting conventions. He begins with a long, single-sentence paragraph; thereafter, long sentences are the norm, one extending to over eighteen lines of the standard edition. They accumulate clauses and strings of adjectives, but inventively and with lively rhythms. They sustain tension; they never sag. Such writing is an expression of self-confidence, also implicit in his willingness to laugh at himself and, importantly, in his assumption that his early life and place have perpetual interest. Here is confidence in a Welshness not wholly tailored to an English listener and all the more remarkable given wartime's disturbing circumstances and Thomas's increasingly problematic personal circumstances. But the piece is also, understandably, an escape into memory and the imagination. "Reminiscences of Childhood" is important as marking the beginning of Thomas's humorous—at times, self-reflexively humorous—examination of aspects of Welsh life. This was to lead eventually to *Under Milk Wood*.

Initially, it led to "Quite Early One Morning" (B, 10–14), a direct antecedent of the "play for voices." It was written in 1944 and is set in New Quay, the fishing village in Cardiganshire where the Thomases then lived. It begins on a winter morning after a stormy night. The town is still asleep as the narrator walks through the small streets. He is an outsider—"like a stranger come out of the sea, shrugging off weed and wave and darkness with each step, or like an inquisitive shadow, determined to miss nothing" (B, 11)—observing but not wholly belonging, a familiar Thomas stance evident in the *Portrait* stories and in the early poems. The piece explores a second recurring concern: the difference between a mundane, invariably narrow Nonconformist external world and the riotous imaginative life of dreams: "mild-mannered men and women not yet awake and, for all I could know, terrible and violent in their dreams" (B, 11). These dreams, the narrator suggests, are often worlds of impossible desires floating free of time and place. Such ideas are central to *Under Milk Wood*. Other precursors include early sketches for characters, particularly for Captain Cat,

Mrs. Ogmore-Pritchard (who is named), and the Reverend Eli Jenkins. The piece ends with a sense of the helpless and the ephemeral.

"Memories of Christmas" (*B*, 21–27), which, after later amalgamations and rewritings, became the famous essay "A Child's Christmas in Wales" (*CS*, 304–11), begins by questioning the accuracy of memory. Memories merge or blur into one, and in any case we remember selectively. Here Thomas evokes a secular and essentially tedious Christmas, transformed by his appealing and consciously nostalgic affection, in vividly visual prose. The whole is saved from sentimentality by reminders that beyond bourgeois comfort and assurance was the social deprivation of the 1920s: "We returned home through the desolate poor sea-facing streets where only a few children fumbled with bare red fingers in the thick wheelrutted snow" (*B*, 25–26).

The same element is present in the beautifully written "Holiday Memory" (*B*, 138–44), when "wiry, cocky, bow-legged, coal-scarred, boozed, sportsmen" (*B*, 143) try their luck in fairground boxing booths. Yet overall this radio talk is more sadly nostalgic in its sense of "boys and girls tumbling, moving jewels, who might never be happy again" (*B*, 142). Perhaps because of this, the piece purveys a desperate escapism: into games, days out, magical fairgrounds, and, on the part of the narrator, generally into his past. One reviewer praised the tonal range and suggested that Thomas should write a play for radio.

"The Crumbs of One Man's Year" (*B*, 153–57), however, has thinner material. Broadcast on 27 December 1946, it offers a personal account of the previous year in a rather strained humorous style. But it has a fine paradigmatic ending: when walking home in the rain down a dark and muddy lane, Thomas, all at once and close together, encounters two lovers, a man reading a book, and two dogs fighting. Here is no humorous fantasy or assertion of power but a chastening cameo combining, as it were, the main themes of "In my craft or sullen art" and Auden's "Musée des Beaux Arts."

Such radio work was preparation for Thomas's most successful broadcast feature before *Under Milk Wood*. This is "Return Journey" (*B*, 179–89), in which he revisits bombed Swansea during the dreadful winter of 1947 in search of himself when young. The feature takes the narrator back through Thomas's young life, ending in Cwmdonkin Park. Thomas brings together ideas from earlier pieces, such as the schoolroom scene from "Reminiscences of Childhood" and the music imagery from "Fern Hill," and focusses on one of his persisting preoccupations: the effects of war. Thus the narrator moves through "the blitzed flat graves" (*B*, 179) of shops and "the snow and ruin" (*B*, 183), recalling a young schoolboy becoming "a fierce and many-medalled sergeant-major" (*B*, 185), the bombed grammar school, the intoned names of those whom war had killed, and the cenotaph on the promenade. The journey, as so often in Thomas, is towards loss, darkness, and death: "Dusk was folding the Park around, like another, darker snow" (*B*, 188), as the Park-Keeper recalls all the lost boys demonstrating against restrictions and the demands of the adult suburban world. Then, recalls the Park-Keeper, "I think he was happy all the time," but now he's "Dead . . . Dead." (*B*, 189).

"Living in Wales" (*B*, 202–6) was written in 1949 when Thomas and family left Oxfordshire for the Boat House. It conveys dislike of England and a stereotypical view of Wales: "The primitive, dark promenade of hidden loves after chapel . . . the first tram hissing like a gander to the steelworks . . . men with white mufflers and lean dogs waiting for a miracle outside the pub shut like a tomb" (*B*, 204). The smell of the potboiler permeates much of the prose, though the final paragraphs describe Laugharne and so rehearse material for later, more dramatic use.

"Living in Wales" can be grouped with "Swansea and the Arts" (1949) (*B*, 218–22) and three broadcasts during 1953, "Home Town—Swansea" (*B*, 262–65), "Laugharne" (*B*, 280–81), and "A Visit to America" (*B*, 274–78), as reminiscing broadcasts that show a sad falling-off from the earlier features. Thomas relies far too much on his fatal verbal fluency; clichés abound. He had mined the personal vein for too long. Yet all point to the preoccupation with Welsh life and with memory, imagination, dreams, and the techniques of feature writing that found their most memorable outlet in *Under Milk Wood*.

Two other less personal pieces also contributed. One is "The Londoner" (*B*, 76–91), characterized by Maud as being "like a trial run for *Under Milk Wood*." It describes a day in the life of the Jacksons, a London family, immediately after the ending of World War II. The feature begins and ends with dreams and with a Narrator who, at first, is accompanied by a Questioner, the better to convey contextual information. The feature is strongly influenced by Thomas's work scriptwriting Gryphon's wartime propaganda films: it is much concerned to praise the power of the people, the warmth, bravery, and innate wisdom of a working-class community. The humor is affectionate; the whole piece is reassuring, even escapist, in its contrast between the recent experiences of war and life for the demobilized soldier. It can also be considered as a political piece reflecting the left-wing idealism of the early days of the new Labour government, and as a product of the nuclear age, stressing the helplessness of ordinary people faced with possible annihilation, summed up by Ted's fatalistic comment: "Atom-bombs got everyruddybody's name on 'em" (*B*, 82). "The Londoner" shows Thomas in command of the techniques of radio, experimenting with rhyming verse to convey thought sequences and, on occasion, to distinguish the Narrator from the surrounding dialogue, and keeping a shrewd eye on what will appeal to his audience.

The second is "Margate Past and Present" (*B*, 104–19), written for the BBC to exchange with a New York radio station for a piece about Coney Island, hence the format: an American ex-serviceman returns to Margate to marry his English fiancée. This allows for a shrewd mixture of sentiment and humor in which Thomas utilizes his good ear for ordinary dialogue. This piece, "The Londoner," and "Return Journey" demonstrate his increasing mastery of the radio feature, essentially different from the radio play in that it combines, in

Douglas Cleverdon's words, ''any sound elements—words, music, sound effects—in any form or mixture of forms—documentary, actuality, dramatised, poetic, musico-dramatic. It has no rules determining what can or cannot be done. . . . it has no need of a dramatic plot.''[3]

From ''Quite Early One Morning'' to ''Return Journey'' there is a shift from the talk to what can be described as the talk-inclusive feature, the genre to which *Under Milk Wood* belongs. Thus in the three features—''The Londoner,'' ''Margate Past and Present,'' and ''Return Journey''—Thomas engages with the problems of reconciling drama with what a talk provided directly: background, setting the scene, and establishing, though hardly developing, character. In ''The Londoner'' and ''Margate Past and Present'' we have experiments with double narration. In the former there are a Narrator and a Questioner; in the latter 1st Voice is supported in the opening pages by 2nd voice that is then replaced by a ''Voice of Information'' to convey something of the history of Margate (thus anticipating the Guidebook interpolations in *Under Milk Wood*).[4] At this stage the technical problem of conveying basic information is not solved with complete success: the American, Rick, is clumsily forced to describe the attractions of Margate to a girl who has always lived there; that girl, Molly, is required to make a long closing speech to convey personal and family background.

As well as the personal talks and features, Thomas made numerous broadcasts on literary subjects. Some are revealing. For example, ''Welsh Poetry,'' readings plus comments written just after the war, in including work by Edward Thomas and Wilfred Owen, shows how, even at this late stage in his career, Thomas still had the Great War on his mind, at least to the extent of admiring its Poets. A later talk on Wilfred Owen underlines this last point. So, too, does the fact that in 1949 he wrote a program on Edward Thomas, working through his countryside poems to his death in the Great War, ending with a reading of ''Lights Out.''

Thomas ranges widely in his talks about poetry, but they are in a sense the literary version of his personal reminiscences. That is, they made him examine himself as literary man and the nature of his writing. In ''On Reading One's Own Poems'' (*B*, 214–16) he is self-critical, considering his early poems ''with their vehement beat-pounding black and green rhythms like those of a very young policeman exploding'' (*B*, 214). Elsewhere he has firm views on the nature of poetry. Thus in ''The Poet and His Critic'' (*B*, 171–75) he argues that a poem's ''narrative adventure'' (*B*, 174) goes beyond philosophy, religion, or politics; ''It is the poetry [that] remains.'' In ''What Has Happened to English Poetry?'' (*B*, 128–35), when his cobroadcaster, the Georgian poet Edward Shanks, mounted the traditionalist's attack on modern poetry, Thomas's response was a surprising mixture of the modernist belief that changing times means changing poetry and, mainly, an assertion of conservative poetic virtues: a concern with rhyme and metre and the need to work within a tradition. He also shows, in ''A Dearth of Comic Writers'' (*B*,192–95), a taste for such Edwardian humorists as W. W. Jacobs and Stephen Leacock, both escapists into "*minor* comic worlds." The dearth of modern comic writers, Thomas considered, was because comic writing was now more difficult in the face of dreadful modern problems, not the least of which was "the maniac new Atom."

Despite his belief that where writers were concerned, nationality was not important, and that writers should be considered as "good poets rather than good Welshmen" (*B*, 32), Thomas was much preoccupied with his own position as a Welshman writing English poetry. This was possibly because others were: John Arlott, for example, was inclined to stress Thomas's Welshness, once describing his poems as reflecting "the typical Welsh religious consciousness" (*B*, 49). Certainly Thomas had views on the relationship between Welsh-language poetry and that written in English by Welshmen: the styles and techniques of traditional Welsh poetry "succeeded only in warping, crabbing and obscuring the natural genius of the English language," he wrote of Glyn Jones's verse (*B*, 45). In the same broadcast he considered that there were "not more than half a dozen Welsh poets who wrote in English of any genuine importance" from Henry Vaughan to Alun Lewis, and he tended not to differentiate between poets born in Wales and those such as the Londoner Edward Thomas and Shropshire-born Wilfred Owen (*B*, 32). There is no doubt that he understood the problems of the Welsh-born writer of English. Some he explored in "Swansea and the Arts," insisting that such writers should not "stay in Wales too long, giants in the dark behind the parish pump" (*B*, 220); nor, when moving to England, should they hide their Welshness, change their accents, and stoop to offering stereotypes for the English market.

One other broadcast, of a very different kind, can be mentioned: a program on Edgar Lee Masters, author of *Spoon River Anthology*, published in 1915 (*B*, 255–58). This is a sequence of poems about the inhabitants of a town in midwestern America who, all dead and buried in the local graveyard, speak honest epitaphs. As Cleverdon noted, this approach was one "possibly anticipating Rosie Probert speaking from the bedroom of her dust."[5] He may be right, though Masters writes harsh, bitter poetry attacking small-town repression, hypocrisy, and violence. Something of Masters's essential views of small towns, and certainly the basic idea of the dead speaking, can be found in *Under Milk Wood*, but the latter's spirit of affectionate tolerance is worlds away from Masters's volume.

Thomas's work is a substantial contribution to broadcasting: his marvellous visual sense made him, at his best, a broadcaster of genius. His radio work made him focus on Welshness, in some ways the subject of what is now his most famous work, perhaps ironically, given his professed literary internationalism.[6]

LETTERS

Even what seemed to be Thomas's most anarchically syntactical poems had, as he put it, a structuring "moving column"[7] of narrative. In his often chaotic life letter writing might be seen to have had a similar ordering effect. It provided a series of points of reference, or special correspondents: Pamela Hansford John-son, to whom he—carefully and designedly—opened his heart; Vernon Watkins, with whom he discussed his work and from whom he sought advice; and his wife Caitlin, to whom, during the enforced and the increasingly sought absences of the 1940s and 1950s, particularly those in the United States, he wrote a series of strange letters, some of which may have been expressions of love.

The epistolary "moving column" at times provided links with kindred spirits in times otherwise, despite social brashness, existentially lonely. Examples are the letters to Johnson and to Watkins. In later years, as the world closed its trap upon him, his desperate letters to his wife performed a similar role.

But there were other less consoling uses of the mail: the begging letter, for instance, which became more frequent during the Boat House years, and nu-merous business letters to agents or publishers. The latter often reveal him as shrewd and precise, evidence, we might guess, not only of what could have been an advantageous business sense, but also of a temporary sobriety. Thomas did not retain the letters he received; hardly any have survived. Thus reading his letters is like overhearing a telephone conversation: we know what we hear, can deduce much, but cannot always understand. Yet some aspects of the letters are clear enough. One is the extent to which these letters reveal not only Tho-mas's reading but the manner in which he was alive to his time. He was, in his early days at least, a book-soaked young writer and a young man alive to popular culture. Thus he makes literary jokes, as when, in a letter to Bert Trick, he recalls "something attempted obscenely, something dung,"[8] parodying a line from, of all the poems we might think of him reading, Longfellow's "The Village Blacksmith." "Just a song at twilight," he wrote to Daniel Jones, "when the lights Marlowe and the Flecker Beddoes Bailey Donne and Poe,"[9] a witty transformation of literary names into the lyrics of a popular sentimental ballad. His ear for popular music might surprise us: it emerges again in a letter to Desmond Hawkins, when he echoes Cole Porter in writing of his constant need for money: "night and day in my little room high above the traffic's boom I think of it."[10]

In a letter to Ted Kavanagh during 1951 the reference to "haggisy stone-snaffling Scotch" is to the now-almost-forgotten theft of the Stone of Scone from Westminster Abbey. This reflects an interest in current affairs that, years earlier, he had insisted upon in an indignant response to Henry Treece. Thomas rejected the suggestion that he was "out-of-contact with the society from which I am necessarily outlaw,"[11] then listed a number of events of the time, from gossip column to sport to life-threatening invasion, that remind us of similar lists in "Return Journey," when the young men in the Kardomah Café discuss "music and poetry and painting and politics" (*B*, 183). In later years he re-sponded to the disturbing events of the time: the war, the aftermath, particularly when the liberation of Europe revealed German atrocities and, as has been noted, Belsen became a ready figure for horror and disaster. The dropping of the atom bombs on Japan in August 1945 also sparked off a string of references: "Let's

... drink to the Only Atom,'' he wrote to David Tennant. That December he told Oscar Williams that for two months "there was nothing in my head but a little Nagasaki,"[12] before such references faded out, to be replaced by more profound exploration of atomic catastrophe in his note on "In Country Heaven," in "Poem on his Birthday," and elsewhere. Such references reveal his current preoccupations, the dark wit a desperate need to control the extent to which they disturbed him.

The letters were also a means of working out his poetics, or at least of enabling his reader to deduce them. One source of deduction is the criticism he offered to those who sent him poems. There is much of this in letters to two friends: Trevor Hughes and, particularly, Pamela Hansford Johnson. To both he offered advice with tremendous precocity and confidence: "Spin a lot of sentences out of your guts. . . . I have given up believing in logic long ago. . . . But there's a fountain of clearness in everyone," and, again, "Into the sea of yourself like a young dog, and bring out a pearl."[13] His reactions to Johnson's poems were frank: he criticized her for lack of ambition and for, on occasion, producing work that "hangs between verse & poetry," that was no more than "a talented piece of versifying, facile, ornamental."[14] Years later he was to write more calculatingly and thus less frankly of Margaret Taylor's poetry, at a time when she was his most generous patron. In 1946 a Harry Klopper sent Thomas nine of his poems and received in return a long and kind letter stressing the need to make a poem work as a whole, to work towards a climax, to eliminate abstract words, and to preserve intellectual clarity.[15]

More directly revealing of his poetic principles and aims are his comments on his own work, such as references to his "anatomical imagery" and, to repeat a quotation, his use of a "preconceived symbolism derived . . . from the cosmic significance of the human anatomy."[16] The letters to Henry Treece, written during the late 1930s, when Treece began his book-length study of Thomas, are fascinating though not always helpful. The three most famous comments are, first, that on the need to interpret his poems literally, second, on his use of images,

I make one image, though "make" is not the word; I let, perhaps, an image be made emotionally in me & then apply to it what intellectual and critical forces I possess; let it breed another; let that image contradict the first, make, of the third image bred out of the other two together, a fourth contradictory image, and let them all, within my imposed formal limits, conflict,

and third, on social awareness. As has been noted, Thomas was indignant at accusations that he lacked this last quality. In his letter to Treece already noted he echoed "I, in my intricate image" in insisting that though "I think a squirrel stumbling at least of equal importance as Hitler's invasions," he was just as aware of the latter and numerous other contemporary matters.[17]

The first and second comments pose more problems than they solve. The insistence on literal interpretation can seem mischievous, as when he rejected Edith Sitwell's interpretation of lines 5 and 6 of the ''Altarwise by owl-light'' sonnet: ''She doesn't take the literal meaning: that a world-devouring ghost creature bit out the horror of tomorrow from a gentleman's loins.'' Well, yes, but the reader is still faced with the task of relating that meaning to the real world, a position towards which Thomas, despite himself, appears to move when he explains ''a jaw for news'' as indicating the ability ''to taste already the horror that has not yet come.'' As for ''breeding images,'' though this highlights the complexity of Thomas's poetry, in particular the way his images can suggest opposites, his poetry does not always respond in this schematic way.

We cannot argue about the third comment on social awareness. What are also clear are Thomas's basic principles, the first, in particular, already seen in action in his reviews. Thus ''the structure [of a poem] should rise out of the words and the expression of them.'' There must always be intellectual control of his material; he regarded surrealism and automatic writing as ''worthless as literature.'' He was not a deliberate ''experimentalist,'' but wrote ''in the only way I can write.''[18]

The letters are also important for Thomas's self-examination and sense of where he was from and where he was living. The letters to Pamela Hansford Johnson are particularly valuable in this regard. Considering himself, as he also put it to Geoffrey Grigson, to have ''developed, intellectually at least, in the smug darkness of a provincial town,'' he was fortunate in that his first affair was with a Londoner of similar ambitions, widening his horizons and indicating possibilities. It was a chance to project himself, to construct a persona, as in the letter to Wyn Henderson, in which we have seen him describing himself as ''moping over his papers in a mortgaged villa in an upper-class professional row.'' Class bothered him: years later, in 1938, he told Treece, when inviting him to stay at Gosport Street, in Laugharne, that he would find him '' 'lower middle class' in attitude and reaction.''[19]

Thomas is a fine letter writer, often sharp, gifted in phrase making, invariably entertaining, and sometimes very funny. ''I'm trying hard to think of respected gentry to get testimonials from,'' he wrote to Desmond Hawkins. ''I know one defrocked bard.'' During World War II he wrote to Clement Davenport essentially about his long-held pacifist views in language always sharp, alive, and darkly humorous:

I think that unless I'm careful and lucky the boys of the Government will get me making munitions. I wish I could get a real job and avoid that. Clocking in, turning a screw, winding a wheel, doing something to a cog, lunching in the canteen, every cartridge case means one less Jerry, bless all the sergeants the short and the tall bless em all blast em all. . . . deary me I'd rather be a poet anyday and live on guile and beer.

''I hear John Arlott's voice every weekend, describing cricket matches,'' he wrote nostalgically from Italy. ''He sounds like Uncle Tom Cobleigh reading

Neville Cardus to the Indians.''[20] Any account of the letters runs the risk of becoming simply a list of witty lines and comic vignettes. However, three other important aspects require consideration.

The first relates to Thomas the sponger, the writer of begging letters. Alec Waugh once remarked, to Thomas's intense irritation, that he should be advised ''to write more stories and fewer letters.''[21] He was right, given the great expense of time and energy Thomas devoted to letters designed to prize money from the generous or unwary.

In 1951, with his finances in chaos and his life in its usual mess, he wrote to Princess Caetani, the generous owner of *Botteghe Oscure*, a letter that opens:

I have been ill with almost everything from gastric influenza to ingrowing misery. And only now my wife Caitlin has given me a letter that Davenport had forwarded from you nearly six weeks ago. She didn't know who the letter came from, and had half-mislaid and half-forgotten it in the general hell of sickness, children, excruciating worry, the eternal yellow-grey drizzle outside and her own slowly accumulated loathing for the place in which we live.

The first sentence opens directly and forcefully before modulating into a play on words that suggests brave humor amid despair. It is followed by an excuse: Caitlin is to blame. But Caitlin herself must be excused because of the dreadful psychological pressures on her life. That life is also his, as the sentence insists through the quiet change of person from third singular to the collusive ''we.'' The pressures, now on Thomas, are impressed vividly upon the reader through the general energy of the language and through considered rhetorical effects that include a stress on ''excruciating worry'' and the extended emphasis of ''her own slowly accumulated loathing.'' The ''worry'' in the second sentence, which includes worry about his writing—he was then completing ''Lament''—becomes, as the letter continues, the ''nervous hag that rides me, biting and scratching into insomnia, nightmare and the long anxious daylight,'' and then domestic handwork, a tangible object, as it were, at which he is compelled to work ''day & night with a hundred crochet hooks.'' But Thomas, typically and slyly, shifts from worrying about himself to seemingly selfless apologies for worrying his patron: and the crochet work of ''worry'' becomes, in a play on words, ''his crotchety poem'' on which he is, nonetheless, working ''very hard.'' His final paragraph is as follows:

I wish I knew what to do. I wish I cd get a job. I wish I wish I wish. And I wish you a happy Easter, with all my heart. The sun came out this morning, took one look at wet Wales, and shot back.[22]

Emphasized concern for himself shifts again to what he wishes for the princess, so that the letter ends by once again suggesting a selfless Thomas and does so with a defiant humor that makes him attractive to his patron—and so worth patronizing—but that also ensures that a rich woman in sunny Italy will not forget a sad life in rainy Laugharne.

Of course, letters are not like more formal works of literature; that is, they must seem to their immediate reader to be spontaneous responses to specific situations and correspondents. Thomas's great achievement, in these fund-raising performances as well as in his most intimate letters to Caitlin, is to seem artless while manipulating reader response. Even to his agent, David Higham, to whom he writes brisk and competent business letters, he is anything but unconsidered. Thus in 1953:

I don't know how my account stands with you, but you should have received, from the BBC over £100 for four Personal Anthologies I recorded . . . on the Welsh Region, week by week. Also, I recorded a Childhood Reminiscences sketch for the Welsh Region, from Swansea, last week, for £20 (twenty pounds) and this coming Friday . . . I need £50 for various small bills here which simply *must* be paid this week. I have no money at all.[23]

The hint of financial innocence is followed by precise and detailed awareness of how things were. The lapidary finality of the last sentence, with its sequence of heavy stresses, seems far from accidental.

About the same time Thomas drafted, but probably never sent, a letter to Marged Howard-Stepney, the wealthy Welsh eccentric who briefly became one of his benefactors. It begins with a rhythmic prose that is then rearranged as the opening of a poem:

You told me, once, to call on you
When I was beaten down.[24]

This, in turn, is abandoned for three stanzas of vigorous light verse appealing for money.

Some months later he drafted a letter to Princess Caetani that opened:

What can I say?
Why do I bind myself always into these imbecile grief-knots, blindfold my eyes with lies, wind my brass music around me, sew myself in a sack, weight it with guilt and pig-iron, then pitch me squealing to sea, so that time and time again I must wrestle out and unravel in a panic, like a seaslugged windy Houdini, and ooze and eel up wheezily, babbling and blowing black bubbles, from all the claws and bars and breasts of the mantrapping seabed?

The "Houdini" motif is linked to the notion of drowning, of finally giving up the fight to stay clear of the "spongy dives" or "down and out on the sea's ape-blue bottom."[25] At the heart of such a passage is self-loathing made worse by self-awareness and the recognition that he is unable to rescue himself from a lifestyle inimical to his literary ambitions. The letter belongs to Thomas's last months; almost certainly death prevented completion. What is remarkable is the care lavished upon it: the phrasing, the rhythms, the balancing of clauses. Here is evidence both of psychological need to make sense to himself of what was happening to him, and, it seems, of the distancing comforts of metaphor. It is a sad, disturbing piece of writing that in the end did not help at all.

Second, a series of intimate letters to Caitlin tells us much—often through omission, as Thomas shows little interest or involvement in the day-by-day minutiae of married life, or in his children—about Thomas's passionate and tormented marriage. Two letters are typical. The first was written before 1943 from Thomas in London to Caitlin in Cardiganshire:

God, Catly, if only I could see you now. I want to touch you, to see you, you are beautiful, I love you. . . . tell me if you want me to come down. . . . I want to see you terribly terribly soon. . . . Please. . . . tell me that you want me to come down. . . . tell me when I can. . . . I want to come as soon, as soon as I can. . . . I could come to you now.[26]

The repetition is surely calculated; it dramatizes not only desperation but also fear, dependence, and a chilling sense of subservience. It appears to have been persuasive.

The second was written shortly after his first arrival in the United States. It opens frantically:

Caitlin my own own own dearest love whom God and *my* love and *your* love for me protect, my sweet wife, my dear one, my Irish heart, my wonderful wonderful girl who is with me invisibly every second of these dreadful days, awake or sleepless, who is forever and forever with me and is my own true beloved amen—I love you, I need you, I want, want you, we have never been apart as long as this, never, never, and we will never be again.[27]

Yet what can—and doubtless did, to the waiting wife—seem a passionate, uncontrolled outpouring is carefully constructed for maximum effect. The long and complex sentence is beautifully taut and balanced. The use of repetition, the accumulation of compliments and responses, the balancing of phrases (''*my* love and *your* love''); the clever ''awake or sleepless,'' the removal of punctuation to hurry the lines along, the ripples of alliteration, and the conscious stress on key words (''I love you, I need you, I want, want you''; ''never, never, and we will never be again'') all contribute to the sentence's driving rhythm, to the fierce energy of the language.

As the long letter proceeds, it makes abrupt shifts from the language of love to that of the chatty and newsy, the latter a reassuring context for the former. The shifts also emphasize further the recurring impression that, with the objectivity of hindsight, we gain of Thomas's letters, that of their carefully ''composed'' nature. The very next letter in the series, written from Brinnin's Connecticut home and opening with a sentence (''You're mine for always as for always I am yours'') that immediately involves the reader in its rhythmic poignancy, is a further example. A letter from San Francisco ends less success-fully: "I will come back alive & as deep in love with you as a cormorant dives, as an anemone grows, as Neptune breathes, as the sea is deep."[28] Thomas strains for effect and lapses into cliché.

Ferris suggested (*CL*, xi) that these contrivances can indicate insincerity. Though Thomas's marriage was falling apart in his final years, one can only respond to Ferris with "Not necessarily," given that care can indicate concern. Further, he wrote differently to other women, even to his last mistress, Elizabeth Reitell:

Liz love,
   I miss you terribly much.
   This plane rode high and rocky, and over Newfoundland it swung into lightning and billiard-ball hail, and the old deaf woman next to me, on her way to Algiers via Man-chester, got sick in a bag of biscuits, and the bar—a real, tiny bar—stayed open all the bourbon way. London was still glassy from Coronation Day, and for all the custom-men cared I could have packed my bags with cocaine and bits of chopped women.[29]

This is hardly a love letter: Thomas is preoccupied with re-creating in prose his own separate experiences and hardly at all with his feelings for Liz. Yet in his letters to Caitlin he tries desperately, perhaps too desperately, to convey how he feels. "Sincerity" is always a slippery concept; the letters to Caitlin move us—or, at least, trouble us—precisely because Thomas deploys literary skills. That he did so with such care and intensity in the midst of an anarchically crowded life in which, of course, he was frequently unfaithful should make us believe that he took trouble *because* he was concerned about the relationship, though whether because of fear or love is difficult to say.

   We might also wish to say with equal certainty what can be said of the begging letters: despite his despairing and potentially suicidal self-awareness that he could not stop himself sliding into the depths, he retained an obsession with words, with experiments with prose, with capturing experience in patterns of language. Caitlin Thomas put matters at their bleakest in her letter to Oscar Williams and his wife in February 1953: "The trouble is our lives are perma-nently in need of being saved, and I doubt, very forcibly, that they are worth it."[30] Yet all who read these letters have abundant evidence to the contrary. Three late extracts begin to make the point. The first is to Margaret Taylor, thanking her for money: "I'm writing this in the heaven of my hut. Wild day, big seas for Laugharne & the boats of the Williamses lurching exactly like Williamses." "Things are appalling here," he wrote from Laugharne to John Davenport.

Temporary insolvency goes the glad rounds as swift as a miscarriage. . . . Yesterday I broke a tooth on a minto. . . . There are rats in the lavatory, tittering while you shit. . . . the biggest prig in Wales, is coming to see me Saturday . . . looking about him, prigbrows lifted, in my fuggy room like an unloved woman sniffing at the maid's linen on the maid's day out. . . . If you see anyone likely, pinch his boots for me. . . . I'm sorry to write you such mournings. See you at the barracudas.

The third is from another letter to Margaret Taylor, also sent from the Boat House in late 1951:

Lizzie came into the Pelican yesterday afternoon, raving drunk, and gave my father a heart attack. . . . Caitlin's black eye has just faded; a boy fell from a tree where he was picking conkers . . . and his shoulderblade broke & pierced his lung, and at the post-mortem in Carmarthen Infirmary they found he had been eating stamps; a white owl breathes on a branch right outside Phil the Cross's bedroom window, like a hundred people making love, and inflamed Phil so much he ran, for the first time in years, to his wife's bed and set about her so fiercely he nearly died of a fit of silicotic coughing and couldn't go to work next day. . . . Ivy's teeth fell out one evening while she was playing skittles, and yesterday she told me she had been blind in one eye for twenty years.[31]

Common to all three passages, and to numerous similar ones, is a never-fading delight in the sound and movement of words and in the minutiae—comic moments, miniature dramas—of day-to-day living in small houses in small places by a Welsh sea. Such delight, particularly in wordy humour, persisted to the end: in probably his last communication, a telegram from New York to Ellen Stevenson in Chicago, he agreed to perform *Under Milk Wood* "with or without cast but not without cash."[32]

The letters are a series of heroic gestures, conclusive evidence of Thomas's indomitable spirit, his marvellous ability, to quote Berowne, "to move wild laughter in the throat of death."[33] In his letters, as in his life generally, he can be a less-than-attractive figure. But he is invariably redeemed not only by the indomitable qualities already described, but also by, to echo Charles Lamb, a kind of tragic interest.

Further, and third in the list of major concerns, the reference to *Under Milk Wood* reminds us that, as with the broadcasts, letter writing prepared him for the creation of that unique drama. The letters and the drama savor the same kind of material: both celebrate the comic possibilities of small-town life. In addition, and finally, the letters suggest, in a manner only partly speculative, the way Thomas's writing might have proceeded. The draft letter to Princess Caetani, already quoted in part, also contains the following:

Deep dark down there, where I chuck the sad sack of myself . . . time and time again I cry to myself as I kick clear of the cling of my stuntman's sacking, "Oh, one time the last time will come and I'll never struggle, I'll sway down here forever handcuffed and blindfold, sliding my woundaround music, my sack trailed in the slime, with all the rest of the self-destroyed escapologists in their cages, drowned in the sorrows they drown and in my piercing own, alone and one with the coarse and cosy damned seahorsey dead, weeping my tons.[34] (*CL*, 915)

Though we can catch in this something of Captain Cat's plunge into the sea of memory, here are deeper notes, darker tones, and more complex and strangely compelling psychological explorations than are dreamt of in Captain Cat's Llareggub. *Under Milk Wood* refuses the neosurrealism of some of the letters' descriptions of life in Laugharne and certainly stops short of the deeper, profounder engagements of the Caetani letter. The psychological promise of the latter continues to tantalize.

FILMSCRIPTS

Thomas's work for films was of two kinds: he wrote voice-over commentary for numerous documentaries and dialogue for feature films.[35] Together this was ideal preparation for *Under Milk Wood*, certainly in terms of technique. For example, in at least two of the feature-film scripts—those for *No Room at the Inn* and *Twenty Years A-Growing*—one of the characters sets the scene in a manner similar to "First Voice."

In the context of Dylan Thomas's short and turbulent life, his career as a film writer is surprisingly substantial. FitzGibbon estimated that "he probably put more words on paper in this professional capacity than in any other."[36] Caitlin Thomas despised Thomas's scriptwriting, one reason being that she believed that it wasted a great poetic talent. She was right.

During 1942–45 Thomas scripted at least fourteen documentaries. Much is hackwork, including *This Is Colour*, a documentary made for Imperial Chemical Industries about dyeing processes, *New Towns for Old*, about urban planning, and *Young Farmers*, which publicized rural activities. This last has an interesting voice-over: the teacher in an urban school introduces his children to a country village with a brief overview, yet another precursor of "First Voice." But generally this was work Thomas did with his left hand and very quickly.

The wartime propaganda is more interesting. The high points, from a literary and possibly also from a filmic point of view, are Thomas's voice-over commentaries in *Wales—Green Mountain, Black Mountain* (1942) and *Our Country* (1944). The former was designed to inspire the war effort in Wales. It suggests values of work and community and a sense of Welsh traditions combined with a new—war-induced, of course—industrial vigor that are carefully weighted so as to overpower the all-too-obvious effects of the between-wars depression. The script is of variable quality: the film critic David Berry quoted the line describing Rhondda coal miners going down into the pit, "like ghosts in black, only their smiles are white" (F, 29), and called it "excruciating," presumably because of its cosy (and racist?) sentimentality.[37] It is also confusingly inaccurate, given that miners were black when returning from work. Elsewhere, windy rhetoric, such as "Wales is a mountain of strength" and "the world shall never deny [Welsh workers] again," is too often the order of the day. Yet when Thomas moves into an angry poem about the state of the Welsh industrial valleys, real feeling is not wholly subverted by writing that is essentially imitation Auden:

Remember the procession of the old-young men
From dole queue to corner and back again . . .
With a drooping fag and a turned up collar,
Stamping for the cold at the ill-lit corner. (*F*, 29, 31)

Our Country features a sailor on shore leave travelling through Britain and observing the country at war. The film's purpose is to reveal an inspiring "Britishness" that will sustain a tired nation still fighting hard. Scenes are set in Glasgow, London, the English countryside at harvesttime, the Rhondda Valley in South Wales, amid timber felling in Scotland, and in a steelworks in Sheffield. The script's lyricism drew some criticism, one reviewer complaining that the "poetic" commentary suffered from "vagueness and woolliness."[38] To be sure, Thomas sometimes lapses into automatic rhetoric, as when he writes, "Music of the towers and bridges and spires and domes of the island city" (*F*, 68) in a description of London, and "through fat lovely fields all lying green under their flower folds" (*F*, 71). The complaint, of course, was about "literary" films and was eventually accepted by Thomas, to judge from his contribution to the Cinema 16 symposium in 1953, when he made a perceptive point about the essentially visual quality of "poetry" in films. But there are telling moments when the script and the picture combine effectively: for example, the description of Waterloo Station as "the shunting flagged and whistling cluttered cave-hollow other world under glass and steam," or the "explosive the moon-moved man-indifferent capsizing sea" (*F*, 68). On two occasions Thomas enables moments of true filmic penetration. Thus, standing at Dover:

and from this island end white faced over the
    shifting sea-dyes
a man may hear his country's body talking
and be caught in the weathers of her eyes (*F*, 69),

in which the anthropomorphism and the use of "weathers" to suggest a nation's life force—both reminders of early "process" poems—show Thomas's deeper engagement with a neo-Shakespearean patriotism. Second, in the Sheffield scene (*F*, 72) a factory girl speaks of the nightly blackout and fear of air raids in the scene already quoted (see chapter 12, note 14) that resonates in the subtext of "Fern Hill".

Thomas was not always as good as this, as we see from *These Are the Men* (1943), which superimposes self-denouncing speeches onto film of Nazi leaders speaking at a Nuremberg rally. There were reservations about the ending, at least one reviewer believing that the script protested too much and did so with "a suspicion of hysteria rather than with confident determination."[39] Most would now agree with this and, further, with David Berry's opinion that *These Are the Men* is an overwritten piece making all-too-predictable attacks on easy targets.[40]

The scripts for feature films are less interesting. Two of the few actually made into films have been unsuccessful. *The Doctor and the Devils* (1986) failed dismally, even though it starred Jonathan Pryce, the popular and talented actor, and had a subject—the Burke and Hare body snatching in Victorian Edinburgh—that seemed to have popular appeal. Yet Thomas's screenplay has some marvellous visual moments, one of which features Dr. Rock, who dissects the dead bodies in the interests of medical research. Rock tells of accusations against him—"My hands, to him, are red as Macbeth's"—and the script continues: "Rock raises his very white hands in an elegant gesture, and smoothes the palm of one hand along the back of the other." Music, darkness, and laughter follow, "then sudden light, and Fallon's hands, palms downwards, fingers stretched and tautened, murdering down the screen" (*F*, 186). This is superbly filmic. But elsewhere, we see too clearly that the script is far too literary for visual success. One direction reads: "All the inanimate furies of the Close alive suddenly, crying like the wind through telegraph wires, grotesque dancers from the dirt." (*F*, 190). This, to put it mildly, poses obvious problems for any director.

Rebecca's Daughters (1992) also failed, only partly because of Karl Francis's direction. Francis drew a fine performance from Paul Rhys as Anthony Raine, the young and sympathetic aristocrat. But he failed to control Peter O'Toole's overacting or to give the film a clear structure. Thomas's working script has its amusing moments: jokes about Sir Henry's cat, a boy caught eating a sweet in chapel. There is some powerful writing describing the Welsh farmers going to their secret, nocturnal meeting:

Out of the deep dark woods and into open country they ride together through wild wind. Over street cobbles they come, their horses' hooves covered with sacking. (*F*, 392)

This is compelling; only occasionally, as, for example, with Thomas's use of alliteration, are we reminded that he is not thinking in purely visual terms. The dialogue comes to life in the long speeches at Rebecca gatherings and chapel meetings; Thomas is always good at rhetorical outbursts. Elsewhere, the talk can be labored, particularly when the aristocrats joke with each other. More important, the characters are stereotypes: unfeeling landowner, dashing young aristocrat, assorted Welsh peasants. There is little character development. The blatantly romantic ending, in which Anthony Raine and Rhiannon come together, is commercial through and through, and not a lot to do with the film's main theme.

Of Thomas's other scripts for feature films, two can be mentioned. *The Three Weird Sisters* is set in a Welsh valley and is the potboiler to out-boil all pots, an improbable, disjointed, and inconsistent mélange of clichés mainly hostile to Welsh valley life. Much better, though it remains unfilmed, is *The Beach of Falesá*, a screenplay prepared from the Stevenson short story. This tale of lust, violence, and betrayal in the South Seas obviously appealed to Thomas. He writes precisely, controls the lyricism, uses dialogue to forward the action, and creates a good, working script, demonstrating a fine visual sense:

The lantern and the moonlight make the bush all turning shadows that weave to meet him and then spin off, that hover over his head and fly away, huge, birdlike, into deeper inextricable dark. The floor of the bush glimmers with dead wood. (*F*, 377–78)

The treatment of clergymen also has its interest. The Roman Catholic priest, Father Galuchet, is pilloried for having gone native and, consequently, for being unwilling to oppose Case's combination of threats and black magic; the missionary Jenkins, Thomas's own creation, is given an attractive Welshness—a contrast to the anti-Welsh feeling in *The Three Weird Sisters*—and plays a large part in rallying the natives against Case and his exploitation. That said, Thomas does little with Stevenson's exploration of power and the disturbing suggestion that in order to survive in such an alien culture, Wiltshire, the hero, will have to assume Case's evil role. Rather, Thomas simplifies Stevenson's complex text into a romantic story.

Thomas worked hard at his scripts and did his own research. In so doing, he extended his knowledge of Wales, particularly of economically depressed South Wales, of which he had known comparatively little, of current affairs generally, of some of the technicalities of mining, of antibiotic drugs, of dyes, and of agriculture. Little of this was intellectually demanding, but, given the popular view of the man, we can still be surprised at such consistent, objective professionalism. We are probably not surprised to discover that as a scriptwriter, he was very much a child of his time in, for example, his patronizing attitude to women and strong sense of social class.

We can also see that the filmscripts are not completely isolated from Thomas's serious work, even though they were a distraction from it. There is a strong relationship between *Our Country* and Thomas's poems of the blitz; the link with ''Fern Hill'' has already been noted. The unfinished script of *Twenty Years A-Growing*, Maurice O'Sullivan's lyrical account of life on the Blasket Islands, was written contemporaneously with ''Fern Hill'' and ''Poem in October'' and, in Ackerman's fine phrase, anticipated ''the fabled pastoralism of the later verse'' (*F*, 230). So far as *Under Milk Wood* is concerned, the filmscript writing was an important preparation: Thomas learned to manipulate dialogue, to construct scenes, and to use a narrator. *The Unconquerable People*, for instance, is Thomas's first use of numbered narrative voices.

Above all, we must keep in mind that Donald Taylor hired Thomas to script propaganda films, to be a hack. Thomas simplified issues in the interests of popular persuasion, suppressed complications, created stereotypes, cheered up, and encouraged. Later he wrote scripts with happy endings for films designed to be popular. The influence of such writing on his later serious work is there for all to see in the uneasy attempts at a simplifying optimism in a number of his later poems, and in the unjudging tolerance of *Under Milk Wood*. When we recall the young writer of the 1930s working so defiantly against the grain of his time, we recognize the tragic decline and understand Caitlin's anger.

Under Milk Wood

The road to *Under Milk Wood* not only passes through the broadcasts, letters, and filmscripts, it also takes in at least two works of literature. One is Joyce's *Ulysses*: as early as 1932 Thomas and Bert Trick talked vaguely about writing a Welsh version. The "Nighttown" sequence, which Joyce had once entitled "Circe," was influential, particularly on "The Town That Was Mad," the early version of what became *Under Milk Wood*. Both novel and early version use memory to highlight a lost golden age, both have a farcical court scene—in Thomas's piece the townfolk are "tried" by the outside world—and both use lists for comic effect. But the "Circe" section is altogether a much darker piece of writing than either early version or broadcast play: it explores secret, often squalid, sexual fantasies, playing on the Circe theme of human beings turning into swine. It moves effortlessly from realism to magic realism to surrealism, showing great linguistic inventiveness. Beyond having in common the general notion of a set period of time during which a community is revealed, the influence is tenuous at best. Apart from the basic idea of the dead speaking from their graves, much the same could be said of Edgar Lee Masters's *Spoon River Anthology* (1915); Thomas's radio program on the book has already been discussed.

Under Milk Wood, then, is uniquely Thomas's. It is also unfinished. It has been argued that this does not matter and, indeed, that "the gusto of the parts, the burst of human colour, might even have been dulled and diluted by a concern for abstract proportions."[41] But it is the case that the closing pages offer a much thinner and far less arresting prose. It is not always coherent: the last sentence of the play, for instance, is not only far too long and complex for listening, but has central clauses—"that is a God-built garden to Mary Ann Sailors who knows there is a Heaven on earth and the chosen people of His kind fire in Llareggub's land" (*UMW*, 89)—that pose problems of understanding because of the ambiguous status of "fire" as a part of speech and the difficulty of relating the final part of the sentence to the verb "knows." The closing effect is very different from that achieved by the brilliantly taut and clear opening. Further, the work's proportions are far from perfect, as Daniel Jones noted when he wrote that the work had "an abbreviated and makeshift end. . . . [Thomas's] aim was to have a complete evening sequence in the pub, and many more ballads, including one for Bessie Bighead."[42] On one worksheet Thomas drew up a list of characters who would be given further songs or poems.[43] These were to have been contributions to a "celebration of maudlin drunkenness and ribaldry,"[44] but never became more than tantalizing possibilities.

We might wonder whether Thomas would have completed the play in quite this way, given that his treatment of the various drafts reveals a sanitizing tendency. We see this last in two ways. The more overt sexual innuendo was eliminated, for example, "Gossamer Beynon yawns in the middle of her world. If only if only he would goat up the ladders of my legs then his singed beard would sing to me on the last lust-rung"; a reference to condoms, "*Captain Cat* six, seven, eight. Plain, sealed brown envelope from Liverpool for the lodger in Craig-y-Don. Don't stick a pin in it, Willy"; and a suggestive reference to Mrs. Ogmore Pritchard and candles. Mr. Waldo's song, always dependent on double-entendre, in the drafts attaches more specific sexual meaning to the act of sweeping "chimbleys."

The other significant change is the abandonment of material that would have changed the whole mood of the play. Thus on one worksheet Thomas wrote, "What have I missed out?" answering his own question with a list that includes "Incest/Greed/Hate/Envy/Spite/Malice," followed by notes that in emphasizing the churchyard, the dead, and epitaphs, register the influence of *Spoon River Anthology*. Had Thomas incorporated these ideas, the play would have been radically different because it would have been much darker. His other early intention of concentrating on the town during darkness would have had the same effect. A dance in the graveyard, a violent conflict between a tinker and his wife, and an old couple in bed with the man having died, were all rejected. As he put it in the same bundle of worksheets: "This all to show Llareggub no Utopia." Indeed, the theme, as it were, of Thomas's notes and drafts is a reaching beyond or through comedy to darker, more enigmatic and atavistic ideas.[45]

It is no accident that *Under Milk Wood* is Thomas's most popular work. It reflects his shrewd sense of audience gained through broadcasting and the script-writing of propaganda films. He knew what would be popular. This was not simply a question of knowing how to entertain—he knew that already—but also how to work through consoling simplifications and the direct or implied restating of bourgeois values to essentially happy endings. Such ends were achieved because he understood the means: the techniques of radio and, in particular, those, already described, of the radio feature. He knew that features made their own rules, that they could dispense with plot and could combine different discourses. Thomas makes use of lyrical descriptive prose, guidebook pastiche, parodies, allusions, one-liners, comedy sketches, slapstick, and so forth. The use of two narrators is pure radio in that it varies the sound. Thomas is not always consistent in his use of the two voices, but there is little doubt that, as in his earlier features, what interests him is the playing off, one against the other, of different sounds and languages and thus of functions. One critic has argued that the presence of two voices reflects Thomas's ambivalence towards Wales: one loves, the other laughs.[46] There is something in this, even though both voices sometimes laugh. Certainly, in the opening sequence describing the dreaming towns-folk, Thomas effects a clear division of functions: First Voice sets the scene and introduces the characters, while Second Voice describes their dreams. On the first four occasions this is done by Second Voice continuing First Voice's sentence by intensifying the language, adding clause after clause to evoke the associative thrust of dreams.[47] The hypnotic rhythm of this opening depends greatly on the listener's or reader's expectations of this tonal alternation.

What is also effected by the dualism is the reduction of the narrator's authority, fitting for a feature that evokes careless characters in an amoral village. In recognizing this effect, we also recognize that *Under Milk Wood*, like all the best comedy, has a serious purpose. One way of understanding that purpose is to begin with the circumstances out of which the feature emerged, the age of austerity that, through the 1940s, was also the nuclear aftermath to the nightmare of World War II.[48] The extent to which Thomas was haunted by such events can be seen from his ideas for "The Town That Was Mad": the town was to be cordoned off, "barbed wire was strung about it and patrolled by sentries." FitzGibbon commented that such ideas emerged "after the revelations of the German concentration camps."[49] That Thomas regarded the rest of the world, and not the town, as the camp only makes the idea more disturbing. In an important way *Under Milk Wood* resembles "Fern Hill," another product of the fraught 1940s. As has been seen, "Fern Hill" begins as an escapist return to a lost Eden, only for Thomas to discover that escape is not possible. Similarly, through the 1940s Thomas's attempts to withdraw from urban terrors to small places, usually, but not always, in Wales, only made it clear that his troubles were internal. *Under Milk Wood*, developing as it did from "The Town That Was Mad," is centrally about escaping from the world, but, we quickly realize, into what is at best a troubled sanctuary.

Thomas's own reservations about the impossibility of escape are implied by the dismissive reversal of the town's name.[50] We attempt, with Thomas, to escape from the real world of that present day into a place seemingly isolated from social upheaval and economic pressures, a place of tolerated, indeed cherished, eccentricity far from the drably surging uniformity of Labour Britain in the late 1940s. Once there, we discover that the townsfolk are themselves seeking to escape from the "present" of the play.

That escape is invariably into that strange world referred to by Thomas in his description of Mog Edwards, the lovelorn draper, who

bellows to himself in the darkness behind his eye

MR EDWARDS (*Whispers*) I love Miss Price. (*UMW*, 40)

Thomas is fascinated by the darkness behind all their eyes: again and again he contrasts intense imaginings with controlled—sometimes relatively—public behavior. Here is a not wholly unexpected reminder of life in suburban Uplands. Mog Edwards is also typical in that his darkness is shot through with longing, for this feeling dominates the imaginings of many of the characters. They long for the lost and happier past, the golden age of Polly Garter's Willy Wee, Captain Cat's Rosie Probert and dead seamen, Bessie Bighead's Gomer Owen, and Mary Ann Sailors's childhood. Dreams and imaginings are always to be preferred to moralistic actuality. Happiness is always somewhere else. Even childhood in Llareggub, with its rashes, fighting, and cruel games, offers little consolation. For most, the present is only bearable when viewed through an alcoholic haze or with unreal naïveté.

This naïveté is personified by the Reverend Eli Jenkins, one of Thomas's most interesting and misunderstood creations. Eli Jenkins constantly misses reality's point. As the last of a series of clergymen or would-be clergymen from the early stories to Gwilym in "The Peaches," this is the most devastating portrait. Thomas's thrusts against kinds of Welshness and Welsh Nonconformity are all the more piercing because they are seemingly affectionate. Jenkins is a simple-minded Welsh romantic who in his morning poem celebrates a land seemingly uninhabited in the stale language of late-Victorian romanticism, of which "And boskier woods more blithe with spring" (*UMW*, 26) is only one example, and mindless listing of insignificant natural phenomena. His sunset prayer, with its clichéd generalizations and, in context, lifeless South Wales slang—"touch-and-go," "just for now" (*UMW*, 82)—sums up a moribund religious tradition out of touch not only with real life but with true spirituality.

Under Milk Wood's often subtextual seriousness does not, of course, hide the humor and warmth that fuels the popular appeal. But the characters' gleeful daring does not go very far. It helps raise a number of thematic ideas, among them, in addition to the abiding contrast between the external life and the world of dreams, reveries, and the imagination, the notion of unjudging love, the power of the past, the relationship between love and hostile or repressive social forces, and even a basic and not-always-distressing failure to communicate. This radio feature is full of undeveloped ideas. The consequent suggestiveness, particularly when considered with the "Houdini" letter, probably points to Thomas's potential as a dramatist. It is, though, a sad contrast to the perfectionist polishing of his finest poems. In his work, as in his life, we end with unfinished business.

DYLAN THOMAS AS A READER

Almost half a century after Thomas's death, it is hard to understand the reactions to Thomas's public poetry readings. Aneirin Talfan Davies, who produced many of Thomas's readings for the BBC, described Thomas's voice as "warm, rich, dark, soothing. . . . [It] brought one as near as possible to the ecstasy of the creative act. . . . His technical skill in reading the most amazing variety of poetry was astounding."[51] The public readings, especially those in America, were regarded as sensational. No doubt they were: sufficient testimony exists to put even the greatest sceptic to flight. Shortly before Thomas's death Cid Corman wrote:

Anyone who has heard him read (and who hasn't? and who hasn't, should) remembers the strong syllabic drunkenness (something of an orgy), the craze of sound sometimes running against the flow and the clear sense.[52]

In 1955 Karl Shapiro recalled that Thomas

did the impossible in modern poetry. He made a jump to an audience which, we have been taught to believe, does not exist. . . . they hear the extraordinary vibrato, a voice of elation and anguish singing over their heads like a wind that tears all the blossoms off the trees. They know this is poetry and they know it is for them.[53]

Later reactions, however, relying on recordings, are more likely to be like that of the Welsh poet Leslie Norris:

> In the evening I thought
> Of Dylan, how he had read
> In Seattle. "The little slob,"
> My friend said, marvelling,
> "He read Eliot so beautifully,
> Jesus, I cried." I did not answer.[54]

Neither can we in the way his live listeners did. We hear a heavy, sometimes booming voice that tends to impose a sameness on much of his own work, the voice of high rhetoric in an age attuned to quieter, more intimate renderings that his work makes possible, but never received, either from Thomas or from Richard Burton, his most famous professional reader, or receives now.

The partial exceptions are Thomas's readings of "Fern Hill" and "Do not go gentle." Thomas enunciates these with clarity and power, without being overemphatic, and, for example, in the final lines of "Do not go gentle," with a more personal tone. In both instances Thomas lets the words do the work; they move us in part because we sense a necessary control.

Thomas's recordings of his own prose are more compelling. Their essential quality has been brilliantly (and racistly) summed up by Philip Larkin: "Like many Welsh voices, Thomas's has a rich fraudulence that sets you chuckling even before—perhaps I should say even after—the adjectival combination-punching begins."[55] This quality makes Thomas's recording of First Voice in *Under Milk Wood* far more in tune with the essential playfulness of the drama than, say, Richard Burton's beautifully sounding but too "earnest" and "reverential" rendering.[56]

Again, to judge from recordings, Thomas also read the work of other poets with variable success. In the character of the aged speaker in Alun Lewis's monologue "Sacco Writes to His Son," Thomas achieves the necessary dignified feeling. The combination of the poetic and the colloquial in Lawrence's "Ship of Death" defeats him. He destroys Wilfred Owen's "Strange Meeting" by adopting a too-declamatory and slightly hectoring style all too reminiscent of a latter-day Wolfitish actor-manager. To Thomas's credit, it can be said that his choice of poems publicized Welsh writers such as Idris Davies and John

Ormond. Unfortunately, too often we are conscious of poems being enunciated rather than being explored aloud and are left unmoved.

NOTES

1. Dylan Thomas, *The Broadcasts*, ed. Ralph Maud (London: Dent, 1991), 3–8. Subsequent quotations are from this edition, abbreviated as *B*, and are included in the text.

2. Valentine Cunningham, *British Writers of the Thirties* (Oxford and New York: Oxford University Press,), 1988. 167–71 and passim.

3. Douglas Cleverdon, *The Growth of "Milk Wood"* (London: Dent, 1969), 17.

4. Thomas's liking for two narrators is seen, of course, in his own text of *Under Milk Wood*. This makes incomprehensible—it will always be unscholarly—the editorial decision to conflate the two narrators in Dylan Thomas, *Under Milk Wood*, ed. Walford Davies and Ralph Maud, "The Definitive Edition" (London: Dent, 1995). This edition is reviewed by James A. Davies in *New Welsh Review* 9, no. 1 (Summer 1996): 98–99.

5. Cleverdon, *Growth of "Milk Wood,"* 18.

6. Thomas died in the early days of television as a popular medium in Britain. Daniel Jones, *My Friend Dylan Thomas* (London: Dent, 1977), 79–81, commented shrewdly on Thomas as a television performer. He appeared only a few times and never mastered the medium, mainly because he talked too much and in the style of the stage actor or public performer. This may not have been his fault: producers were also learning their trade. Thomas died before he could learn his.

7. Dylan Thomas, "Answers to an Enquiry," in *Early Prose Writings*, ed. Walford Davies (London: Dent, 1971), 150.

8. *CL*, 184. Letter to Bert Trick, dated [c. February 1935].

9. *CL*, 196, Letter to Daniel Jones, dated 14 August 1935.

10. *CL*, 236. Letter to Desmond Hawkins, dated 21 August 1936.

11. *CL*, 790, 310. Letters to Ted Kavanagh, dated [1951], and to Henry Treece, 6 or 7 July [1938].

12. *CL*, 565, 576. Letters to David Tennant, dated 28 August 1945, and to Oscar Williams, 5 December 1945.

13. *CL*, 9–10, 17. Letters to Trevor Hughes and to Pamela Hansford Johnson, dated [late 1932/early 1933] and [May 1933].

14. *CL*, 51. Letter to Pamela Hansford Johnson, written during the week of 11 November 1933.

15. *CL*, 591–2. Letter to Harry Klopper, dated 30 May 1946.

16. *CL*, 72, 98. Letters to Pamela Hansford Johnson, [c. 21 December 1933], and to Glyn Jones, [c. 14 March 1934].

17. The three comments can be found, respectively, in *CL*, 301, 397, 310. Letters to Henry Treece, 1 June [1938]; to Desmond Hawkins (quoting from an earlier letter to Treece), 14 August 1939; and to Henry Treece, 6 or 7 July [1938].

18. These basic principles can be found, respectively, in *CL*, 25, 51, 134. Letters to Pamela Hansford Johnson, [15 October 1933], [week of 11 November 1933], 9 May 1934.

19. *CL*, 19, 216, 304. Letters to Geoffrey Grigson, dated [Summer 1933]; to Wyn Henderson, 9 March 1936; and to Henry Treece, 26 June 1938.

20. *CL*, 421, 478, 651. Letters to Desmond Hawkins, dated 14 October 1939; to Clement Davenport, 2 April [1941]; and to Margaret Taylor, 11 July 1947.

21. *CL*, 476. Letter to John Davenport, 27 January 1941. See also Paul Ferris, *Dylan Thomas* (1977; Harmondsworth: Penguin Books, 1978), 182.

22. *CL*, 790–91. Letter to Princess Caetani, dated 20 March 1951.

23. *CL*, 876–77. Letter to David Higham, dated 17 March 1953.

24. *CL*, 835–36. Letter to Marged Howard-Stepney, probably drafted during 1952.

25. *CL*, 915–16. Letter to Princess Caetani, probably drafted during 1953.

26. *CL*, 499. Undated letter to Caitlin Thomas, probably 1942 or 1943.

27. *CL*, 751. Letter to Caitlin Thomas, dated [c. 11 March 1950].

28. *CL*, 753, 755. Letters to Caitlin Thomas, [15 March 1950], [c. 5 April 1950].

29. *CL*, 891. Letter to Elizabeth Reitell, 16 June 1953.

30. Caitlin Thomas to Oscar Williams and his wife, quoted in *CL*, 865.

31. *CL*, 716, 722–23, 816. Letters to Margaret Taylor, dated 5 August 1949; to John Davenport, 13 October 1949; and to Margaret Taylor, [?October 1951].

32. *CL*, 918. Telegram to Ellen Stevenson, dated 25 October 1953.

33. *Love's Labour's Lost*, 5.2.843.

34. *CL*, 915. Letter to Princess Caetani, probably drafted during 1953.

35. See Dylan Thomas, *The Filmscripts*, ed. John Ackerman (London: Dent, 1995). All quotations are from this edition, abbreviated as *F*, and are included in the text.

36. Constantine FitzGibbon, *The Life of Dylan Thomas* (London: Dent, 1965), 62.

37. David Berry, *Wales and Cinema* (Cardiff: University of Wales Press, 1994), 188.

38. Quoted in Ralph Maud, *Dylan Thomas in Print: A Bibliographical History (with Appendix)* (London: Dent, 1970), 139.

39. Quoted in Maud, *Dylan Thomas in Print*, 138.

40. Berry, *Wales and Cinema*, 189.

41. Walford Davies, Introduction to *Under Milk Wood*, by Dylan Thomas, ed. Walford Davies and Ralph Maud, "The Definitive Edition" (London: Dent, 1995), xl.

42. Daniel Jones, letter to Jacob Schwartz, 9 May 1955, typescript, Dylan Thomas Collection, HRHRC.

43. "Notes, Suggestions, Outlines" for *Under Milk Wood*, manuscript, Dylan Thomas Collection, HRHRC.

44. Daniel Jones, Second Preface to *Under Milk Wood*, by Dylan Thomas (1954; London: Dent / Everyman, 1992), xiii. Quotations are from this edition, abbreviated as *UMW*, and are included in the text.

45. For the quotations from the worksheets and drafts, see Cleverdon, *Growth of Milk Wood*, and Walford Davies, introduction to *Under Milk Wood*, "The Definitive Edition," xxxviii–xl. All can be found in Dylan Thomas, work-sheets for *Under Milk Wood*, manuscripts and typescripts, Dylan Thomas Collection, HRHRC.

46. Peter Lewis, "Return Journey to Milk Wood," *Poetry Wales* 9 (1973): 34. The conflation of the two voices in Davies and Maud's "Definitive Edition" has no authorial authority whatsoever.

47. The relationship between the two narrative voices during this part of the piece is an interesting reminder of Daniel Jones and Thomas, when they were boys, writing alternate lines of poems. This is a further indication of Thomas's lifelong interest in dual response.

48. This is a point also made by Walford Davies. See his introduction to *Under Milk Wood* by Dylan Thomas, "The Definitive Edition," xxx–xxxii.

49. FitzGibbon, *Life of Dylan Thomas*, 248.

50. That is, "Llareggub," which looks and sounds Welsh, is, reversed, "buggerall."

51. Ancirin Talfan Davies, quoted in Dylan Thomas, *Broadcasts*, 301.

52. Cid Corman, "Dylan Thomas: Rhetorician in Mid-Career," *Accent*, Winter 1953: 58; reprinted in E. W. Tedlock (ed.), *Dylan Thomas: The Legend and the Poet* (London: William Heinemann, 1960), 225.

53. Karl Shapiro, "Comment: Dylan Thomas," *Poetry* 87 (1955): 109.

54. Leslie Norris, *Collected Poems* (Bridgend: Seren, 1996), 141. The poem was included in *Water Voices* (London: Chatto & Windus and Hogarth Press, 1980).

55. Philip Larkin, *Required Writing: Miscellaneous Pieces, 1955–1982* (London: Faber & Faber, 1983), 141.

56. Peter Stead, *Richard Burton: So Much, So Little* (Bridgend: Seren, 1991), 113–15.

III

CRITICAL HISTORY

15

Dylan Thomas and the *Times Literary Supplement*

The *Times Literary Supplement* (*TLS*) was founded in 1902. By 1934, when Dylan Thomas published *18 Poems*, it had become "an institution, a collective, in the best sense a civil service," one of the central pillars of what one of its editors described as the "English literary establishment."[1] This establishment, based in "smoky London paved with poems" (*CS*, 164), was, for almost all of Thomas's lifetime, the only one that counted. Through its reviews and its readers' letters the *TLS* was the "official" voice of a world that Thomas sought to conquer. Until 1974 its reviewing was anonymous, which tended to emphasize the institutional effect. It was (and is) read by the general reader as well as by the literature specialist. Certainly during Thomas's literary career a *TLS* review was a sine qua non for the serious writer. Thomas received many.

During his lifetime the *TLS* reviewed all his British publications, plus Henry Treece's *Dylan Thomas: "Dog among the Fairies"* (1949), the first book-length critical study. It published letters on Thomas from readers; it published two of his poems. Since his death, with the strange exception of Walford Davies and Ralph Maud's edition of *Collected Poems, 1934–1953* (1988), it has noticed all editions of his writings, on occasion in lead reviews, as well as much of the biographical and critical work of the past forty years. The *TLS* has done much to sustain Thomas as a strong literary presence. In so doing, its notices embody attitudes and approaches to Thomas and his work that can be found elsewhere, at times in more developed form, throughout Thomas's critical history.

During Thomas's lifetime the *TLS* was not slow to recognize Thomas's quality. The very first *TLS* review, of *18 Poems*, seized perceptively on the "process" element in the poems:

Mr. Thomas's habit of translating human experience into the terms of physiology and the machine, and his vivid sense of the correspondence between the forces informing the macrocosm and the microcosm result in some powerful as well as surprising imaginative audacities.[2]

Two years later, the notice of *Twenty-five Poems* referred to "the highly original quality of his idiom and of his vision" and praised the volume's group of more direct poems, including "the magnificent triumph song"[3] that is "And death shall have no dominion." "Of his extraordinary imaginative endowment there can be no doubt," asserted the reviewer of *The Map of Love*.[4] These three volumes of the 1930s were recalled in the notice of Treece's critical study as "visionary, memorable" work.[5] Though the reviewer of *Portrait of the Artist as a Young Dog* could find little more to praise than "lingering accuracy" and "snatches of dialogue as clever as paint,"[6] that of *Deaths and Entrances* praised the volume for demonstrating "much more clarity and fervid observation with a picturesqueness of language and imagery."[7] In 1951 the *TLS* reprinted two of Thomas's poems, "Over Sir John's Hill" and "In the White Giant's Thigh,"[8] both first published in *Botteghe Oscure*. This was ideal advance publicity for *Collected Poems, 1934–1952*, which received star treatment. The full-page review contained its share of superlatives: "the complete truth of vision," "the incomparable 'Fern Hill' " and the "piercing simplicity" of "Do not go gentle into that good night," together with an insistence on the approachability of many of his best poems. Many recent hopes about poetry had been disappointed, stated the review, so that "in this critical situation . . . *Collected Poems 1934–1952* is a delightful event."[9]

Taken all in all, such praise may well hint at hedging bets. There is little doubt that the reviewers were not wholly comfortable with Thomas's work; they sensed a great talent but were not quite sure they fully understood it. This is evident in the eager praise for Thomas's simpler poems seen in the notices of *Twenty-five Poems* and *Collected Poems, 1934–1952*. The thinking it reflects is implicit in the reference already quoted to "the highly original quality of his idiom," which is, however, best appreciated in the more immediately approachable poems of Thomas's second volume. For "highly original" read "often obscure," or, as the review of *Twenty-five Poems* put it, there is "much . . . that is baffling."[10] This echoes the earlier review of *18 Poems*: "Mr Thomas's idiom is certainly entirely his own, even if it is often too 'private' to be easily intelligible."[11] The reviewer was more forthright in a notice of the first number of *Wales*, the literary magazine edited by Keidrych Rhys, to which Thomas contributed "Prologue to an Adventure," described as "a short story by Dylan Thomas, in which a young poet of undoubted but wilful talent wastes his strength to achieve obscurity."[12] Despite some general compliments, forthrightness persisted in the review of *The Map of Love*: the stories and poems are often "baffling" and "the vision is still excessively subjective." Thomas's story "The Dress," however, is "magically simple and complete."[13]

In the two postwar reviews of *Deaths and Entrances* and *Collected Poems, 1934–1952* obscurity is consigned to the past. Thus in the 1946 volume, though the "earlier symbolism and 'surrealism' . . . still remain . . . there is much more clarity and fervid observation."[14] The quotation, significantly, is from "Fern Hill." The difficult work in *Collected Poems, 1934–1952* belonged to a far-off and best-forgotten past when Thomas, following T. S. Eliot, was, as it were, fashionably obscure. The "Altarwise by owl-light" sequence, singled out as "a Golgotha of the poetry of that time,"[15] was considered an aberration surprisingly reprinted. The reviewer knew that Thomas's strengths lay in such poems as "Poem in October," "A Refusal to Mourn," and "Do not go gentle." We are reassured that many of his best poems are not obscure at all.

That obscurity was never simply a matter of following the modernist trend; it stemmed from a fundamental aspect of Thomas's approach. As the reviewer of *The Map of Love* put it: it is because Thomas has "a naked imagination which refuses to temper its power by accepting the assistance of less exalted faculties." That is, there is insufficient "reason" in the work "to order the spate of his metaphor." Hence the "clotted," difficult style evident, for example, in such a poem as "Because the pleasure-bird whistles."[16] This poses problems for the reader, as described by the reviewer of *Twenty-five Poems*: "[Thomas] writes in images peculiar to himself, but so intensely conceived that it is only when we cease trying to explain them to the reason that we begin to grasp the quality of experience they communicate."[17] Here begins what develops into one of the main charges against Thomas: that his poems say little or nothing but only create emotional and sensational effects.

The "obscurity" accusation, linked as it is in these early reviews to Thomas's so-called private or foreign language, leads to what may at times be a subconscious concern with Thomas's Welshness. This last was a new consideration both for metropolitan critics and, within Wales, for the Welsh-language literary community: Thomas was the first important Welsh poet writing in English to emerge since Henry Vaughan. Hence the double-voiced nature of the concern. One is the voice of Welsh-speaking Wales unable at times to accept that writing in English, like speaking English, is a Celtic activity of long standing and of worth in itself. Thus a substantial part of the long review of *Collected Poems, 1934–1952* sought to claim him for the Welsh language. It discussed Thomas's debt to "the Welsh poetic tradition. It is said that he does not speak Welsh: it is certain that he thinks Welsh." In fact, the reviewer continued, Thomas's work has been saved by the Welsh language: the discipline he has gained from "the study of Welsh metrics . . . saved [him] from a Swinburnian facility" and has given him "his feeling for strict pattern." Thus we need to establish "how much the rhythm and structure of his poems owe to traditional Welsh forms" and to understand that much of his seeming obscurity stems from the fact that he works within an unfamiliar tradition.[18] This last comment is not explained, but if it refers to Thomas's use of the sound patterning of Welsh strict-meter poetry, it may well be a Welsh restatement of the canard that Thomas's poems sound rather than mean. As such, this is a rather backhanded compliment. Claiming him for or rejecting him from the Welsh-language poetic tradition remains a recurring theme in Thomas criticism.

The second voice has the edged and, at times, patronizing tones of one element of the English literary establishment to which the *TLS* belonged and that has already been described in all its narrowness.[19] It can be detected in the implied and barbed reference to Welshness in the review of *Twenty-five Poems*, when Thomas's language is regarded as "often as difficult to interpret as a foreign tongue."[20] It is more overtly present in criticism of *Portrait of the Artist as a Young Dog*, that "somewhat random series of Welsh scenes and incidents . . . often vivid enough in their drab and depressing detail." In the same review it can certainly be distinguished in the stereotyping of Thomas as Celt, offering "verbal adventurousness or the flash of fancy" but lacking "something more substantial,"[21] which, with its suggestion of impetuous inspiration, can be linked to the description, in the review of Treece's critical study, of the author of *Deaths and Entrances* as having "great but untrained genius."[22] Anti-Welsh prejudice figures prominently elsewhere in Thomas's critical history, as will be seen.

During the 1950s, following Thomas's death in 1953, the *TLS* attended to the deluge of posthumous material. This began with the first publication of Daniel Jones's edition of *Under Milk Wood*. It was not well received. The reviewer accepted that the piece was written to be heard rather than read before referring to Thomas's "conjuring tricks with words" and the way in which he "played in such a masterly way with words," both statements suggesting a degree of deception. This prepared the ground for his main assault:

There remains a question. *Under Milk Wood* is the most gaily gruesome of bawdy rhetorical fancies: is it much more? . . . it must be said that the view of life expressed here, which is implicit also in Thomas's poems, is an adolescent one. To say that the flowers wither and the seasons change, that the respectable are lecherous and young girls eager, is hardly a sufficient philosophy for a great poet. Of such a poet is demanded an essential seriousness (not a solemnity) which Thomas simply did not possess.[23]

The voice of F. R. Leavis is here alive in the land, treating all with the same portentousness and hardly offering evidence from the poems.

This review preceded by only a few months the magazine's main assessment of Thomas's whole career. This appeared in a "Special Autumn Number" of signed articles entitled "Personal Preferences." Stephen Spender wrote on Auden's *Collected Shorter Poems* and Thomas's *Collected Poems, 1934–1952*.[24] His opening sentence, "Today, when several poets seem drawn to writing poems submitted to criteria of correctitude and academic respectability, it may be useful to draw attention to the greatness of aim of two poets as different as Mr. W. H. Auden and Dylan Thomas," places the essay as a reaction to the, in part, Leavis-inspired poetics of the Movement. Spender gave Thomas (and Auden) high praise for "originality," for extending "the possibilities of what can be written out of the 'absolutely modern' life." Thomas is "wonderful with verbs"; in his later poetry his "stanzas spread wings . . . [and] make exalted flights." Yet Spender had substantial reservations about Thomas that were not wholly disguised by the generally supportive tone. Paradoxically, though Spender's approach was more positive, essentially the same points were made as in the earlier *TLS* reviews. Thus he began by stressing Thomas's subjectivity: "The dominating passion of Dylan Thomas was to put as much of his own life as he personally felt it . . . into his poetry." Too often, the poems that emerge "are scrap-heaps of marvellous junk"; his best poems involve "lives beyond him," a sense of dialogue in which he "transcends his own personality." Again, when Spender wrote that Thomas's "collection of symbols always remains a boy's stamp collection of private sensations," we are returned to those earlier charges of an adolescent lack of seriousness.

Further, to Spender, Thomas was "all Celt, writing with dreams and blood, not Greek, writing with mineral made of intellect, like Rimbaud." His symbolism was really "an expressionist technique" substituting the imaginary for the real. His expressionist palette was "not blue or green, but sea-coloured, not grey, but Welsh-village-coloured." His poetic method "might be compared with that of plunging a shaft deeper and deeper into his own unconscious being." What interests here is the combination of clichés: Spender's Wales is at once Arnold's romantic Celtic twilight,[25] the drab village by the sea, and the land of coal miners, presumably singing as they plunge. Little of this conventional composite has much to do with the reality of Thomas's life in Wales, but in thus thoughtlessly stereotyping, Spender again echoed earlier *TLS* reviews.

Spender regarded Auden as the finer poet: his was "much the more considerable achievement" because he "has gone much further in achieving the main task of contemporary poetry, which is to transmute the anti-poetic material of modern life into transparent poetry." Such a conclusion implies agreement with the recurring objection to Thomas's alleged obscurity: Spender considered Thomas and Auden as, respectively, "opaque" and "transparent" writers. They also offered a choice between "the way of intuition or the way of learning," leading him to stress the superiority of Auden's intellectuality, "the way of knowledge, analysis, depersonalization and bringing into the area of poetic symbolism the instruments of science and religion which can dissect the modern world," to Thomas's "way of intensively living the contemporary experience, turning it into the flesh and soul of the poet's own personality, out of which closed world he hammers his romantic poetry." Once again we hear the voice of the metropolitan, university-educated literary establishment.

As Blake Morrison has reminded us, Spender was often attacked by the Movement and by Leavis as "a false metropolitan reputation";[26] his championing of Auden and, despite his reservations, of Thomas was thus provocative. This need to defend is also found in other reviews of that period. One such is of J. Alexander Rolph's *Dylan Thomas: A Bibliography*, revealing, on the part of a reviewer who took Thomas very seriously indeed, a detailed knowledge of Thomas's work and enthusiasm for it. Rolph's volume "revives the excitement of a period which saw the unfolding of this poet's genius." The reviewer echoed earlier notices in insisting that Thomas in his poetry was careful to control his exuberance. He continued: "Dylan Thomas was the very opposite of a careless writer; his poems are not eccentric; his relationship to any one of his poems was not a trance-relationship; it was rather that of a chess master to a piece.''[27]

The ''trance-relationship'' reference seems to look back to the 1930s and concerns about surrealism and automatic writing, attacks long ago repulsed. It was, however, only being used to emphasize the intellectuality implicit in the chess image and so was an attempt to rebut the Movement's main criticism of Thomas's work, its lack of intellectual content. Only a month later the author of ''Experiment in Verse,'' an anonymous essay in ''The Frontiers of Literature,'' another ''Special Autumn Number,'' adopted a more forthright attitude. He attacked the ''great reaction among poets of the new generation against the influence, for instance, of Dylan Thomas since his tragic death.'' Thomas was compared with Donald Davie by means of an examination of lines from ''Deaths and Entrances'':

These lines . . . might seem very intractable to exposition. . . . Yet they have a kind of poetic eloquence which even the most sympathetic of readers does not expect to find exemplified in the work of the younger generation, in the same degree. . . . Taking greater risks, Thomas seems at last to reach at a greater prize.[28]

Here, in a restatement of Spender's ''greatness of aim,'' is the highpoint of the *TLS*'s championing of the dead poet.

The argument for Thomas's intellectuality was made most strongly in studies by Elder Olson, H. H. Kleinman, and, to a lesser extent, Derek Stanford. Both Olson and Kleinman offered extended analyses of the ''Altarwise by owl-light'' sonnets. Olson argued for the overall coherence of the ten-sonnet sequence as a ''meditation on the fate of man''[29] that offers the consolation of Christian resurrection, the poem being clearly structured in terms of biblical, mythological, and astronomical symbolism. Kleinman, too, found coherence in a sequence that shows ''religious perplexity concluding in spiritual certainty,''[30] in his case using Egyptian myths, sermons, and marine biology as unifying devices. Stanford, in a wider-ranging survey, praised Thomas as a poet of ''memory and sensation'' whose work succeeded in ''extending literary technique.''[31] Stanford adopted a low-key and slightly guarded approach to Thomas, placing him, at this time, on a par with Thomas Gray. The *TLS* reviewer praised Stanford's book for its practical approach. The same reviewer was clearly not convinced by Olson: ''He pays less attention to the puzzling verbal details of the poems than to their dramatic plotting as wholes'' and so ''makes Thomas often look tidier than he is.''[32] Ten years later—ten years on from a more reverential approach to Thomas's poetry—G. S. Fraser was much harsher on Kleinman, anticipating later responses to both Olson and Kleinman's work: ''[He] turns the young Thomas into a potential theological student of great brilliance, and a man with an extraordinarily detailed knowledge of medieval iconography.''[33]

For most reviewers, the problem with arguing for Thomas's intellectuality was his perceived behavior stemming from lack of education. This is evident in the review of *Letters to Vernon Watkins*, which exposed "the narrowness of his literary interests," the reviewer adding that Thomas invariably shunned literary conversation because he realized his own "inadequacy and ignorance." Further, he "never questioned as he should have done the basis of [his] art. Borne along on the intoxicating wave of his own words, he never was able to stop long enough to decide the shape or direction of his real talent."[34] Whether he was capable of making such decisions was also an open question, given that, in the opinion of another critic, reviewing biographies by Bill Read and Constantine FitzGibbon, Thomas had, in prose at least, "an innate inability to handle abstract ideas, an inability, in the ordinary sense, to think."[35] *The Colour of Saying*, Ralph Maud and Aneirin Talfan Davies's edition of poems Thomas used in his readings, was another piece of telling evidence: in Fraser's opinion it showed his taste for uncomplicated poems of which he liked the sound, "a good, hearty, old-fashioned school anthology of verses."[36] Such a choice was hardly an intellectual's.

The argument for "poetic eloquence" was a stronger one. Fraser, for example, criticized the painstaking exegesis in the studies by Tindall and Emery, believing that it would be more valuable to have "some quite impressionistic description of what this effect [of a Thomas poem] is—of what the poem does" rather than "the more usual heavy-footed plunging about of expositors into a morass of speculation about what it says." He concluded: "The poems retain their power; and it is part of that power that attempts to 'explicate' them make one revise and perhaps clarify one's notion of the process of poetic explication." That is, they don't say much, but they sound fine. In Fraser's opinion only Ralph Maud in *Entrances to Dylan Thomas' Poetry* perceived the true nature of a Thomas poem: each was "creating an image or a concept which is new and original within the poem."[37] Neil Powell, in a much later review, was close to this in insisting that Thomas was an uncomplicated man with "an essentially simple and primitive poetic imagination."[38]

Both arguments, the intellectual and the poetic—ironically, the relationship between the two is one of the main themes of Thomas's poetry—can be deployed to support the charge of obscurity. This last never wholly goes away, even when transformed into Spender's "opaque" and "transparent." Through the review of the books by Olson and Stanford runs the feeling that much of Thomas's work is confusing, arbitrary, and flawed.[39] Fraser—to return to his important review—tried to explain the difficulty of Thomas's poetry as resulting from "a sort of mobile stickiness, rather than because they are expressing . . . a complex of feelings bafflingly novel and alien to the ordinary reader."[40] They were also, apparently, resistant to explication: attempts by Tindall and Emery baffled more than the poems. This sense of analysis being inimical to the poetry also emerges in the review of Tindall's *A Reader's Guide to Dylan Thomas*, the widely influential line-by-line exegesis. The reviewer wondered whether this kind of "expository criticism" was merely spoon-feeding the reader. He added, confusingly, that Tindall was good on the clear poems but simply added his own confusion to the confusing ones.[41]

The charge that Thomas is deliberately obscure returns via a reader's letter from one J. H. Martin, who knew Thomas in Cornwall during the 1930s;[42] his letter may well represent only the revealed part of a lingering iceberg of denigration. His point—that Thomas was a charlatan, adopting obscurity to climb onto the modernist bandwagon and so attract public attention—drew angry rebuttals from Keidrych Rhys, former editor of the literary magazine *Wales*, with which Thomas had been associated during the late 1930s, and from Constantine FitzGibbon, then preparing his important biography. The latter made the telling point that such attacks on Thomas fly in the face of the immense care he took when writing his poems.[43]

As more became known of Thomas's life and working methods, Martin's accusation seemed wholly unjustified. Rolph's bibliography enabled that reviewer to insist, to repeat a quotation, that "Dylan Thomas was the very opposite of a careless writer."[44] The *Letters to Vernon Watkins* "finally destroy the myth that Thomas was a poet who worked quickly and easily while staggering between bar and bed."[45] G. S. Fraser regarded Thomas as a "dedicated craftsman in verse, a hard and honest worker at every job he undertook."[46] Such gratifying rehabilitation of Thomas's character was linked to a new approach to the general problem of obscurity. This last was made via attention to Thomas's prose following the publication of his broadcasts and the reprinting of much of his early fiction.

The substantial review of *Quite Early One Morning*, the volume of Thomas's pieces for radio, which appeared barely a year after his death, praised Thomas to the skies: "His place in sound radio was equivalent to Chaplin's place in the silent films. . . . The writer he most resembles, in his inexhaustible spring of language and ideas, is Dickens." Such compliments support the review's main point, that Thomas had "moved from a haunted, confused and symbol-charged shaping-place in the direction of the living voice." As in the *TLS* reviews of *Deaths and Entrances* and *Collected Poems, 1934–1952*, obscurity was seen as past history; the concern for "the living voice," evident in his broadcasts, as in *Under Milk Wood*, the "final masterpiece"[47] that emerged from them, was the way—the way of comic prose—in which Thomas was emerging into the light.

Two further reviews support this new emphasis. That of *Adventures in the Skin Trade*, though critical of the work's structure—"a thread of narrative only slightly connected to the central character"—insisted that

there is a very real sense in which his genius was best expressed in prose. What seems rhetorically obscure or merely tricky in his verse (after the first two books) is turned to outrageous verbal comedy in his heightened prose. . . . [Thomas's genius was] essentially [of] a comic character.[48]

Such a statement is the implication of the review of *A Prospect of the Sea*, which reprints much of Thomas's early fiction, including all the stories from *The Map of Love*, and four nonfictional pieces. In the former, the reviewer considered, "the volume of language oppressed [Thomas]" so that eventually he was "impelled to write about living people," as seen in the nonfictional items. None of these ranked with Thomas's best work: "Conversation about Christmas," which Thomas wrote for *Picture Post*, was a precursor of the famous "A Child's Christmas in Wales"; "How to Be a Poet" was a determinedly facetious piece from the little magazine *Circus*; "The Followers" was an inconsequential and desperate late attempt to recapture the *Portrait* manner; "A Story," mildly amusing on the page, was one of the last prose pieces Thomas wrote. Yet praise was lavished upon them because, in the reviewer's opinion, they caught "the cadence of the living voice" and because "nobody since Dickens has been able to write in this way with the incomparable invention, the accurate yet bubbling word-play, that springs from life itself."[49] Despite the flattering comparison with Dickens, this is, to say the least, a reductive view of Thomas's career.

Hardworking, conscientious, the creator of readily understandable comic pieces in prose at their most entertaining when heard: Thomas's character improved as his literary achievement declined. But that improvement was not allowed to last for long before being caught in the persisting undertow of hostility. This hostility is first detected in two early reviews of the filmscripts. One was of *The Beach of Falesá*, the adaptation of the Stevenson story, which offered a derogatory restatement of the idea of Thomas as careful craftsman: "He has bowdlerized his original in just the right way to guarantee its success at the box office."[50] The other was of *Twenty Years A-Growing*, the film version of O'Sullivan's account of life on the Blasket Islands off the coast of Ireland; this showed "how conscientious Thomas was, when he needed money, in subduing his genius to honest journeywork."[51] The untrained genius become careful craftsman is now the calculatingly commercial hack. It is a point restated in 1972 in the notice of Walford Davies's edition of *Early Prose Writings* that described Thomas as "conscientious and gifted hack-writer,"[52] and, yet again, in Stephen Knight's 1991 response to Ralph Maud's edition of *The Broadcasts*: Thomas is here described as "the jobbing broadcaster."[53] This recurring sense of "Thomas the calculating" is echoed in Neil Powell's comment, when discussing George Tremlett's *Dylan Thomas: In the Mercy of His Means*, that Tremlett's notion of a naïve genius does not square with Thomas's role as calculating scrounger, particularly since Tremlett's Thomas "sounds more than ever like a modern Harold Skimpole."[54]

Such jibes occur alongside continuing concern with Thomas's Welshness, a source of suspicion and some hostility for both Welsh-speaking and, occasionally, English-speaking Wales and the English literary world. In his indignant reply to J. H. Martin's letter Keidrych Rhys also commented that opposition to Thomas within Wales was because "Thomas, above all, has made a fool out of most of the Welsh literary Establishment who kept him out of everything until it was too late.''[55] The sourness of "The Two Literatures of Wales," an anonymous essay included in the "Special Autumn Number" of 1955, entitled "Writing Abroad," enables us to understand exactly what Rhys meant. This is one—perhaps, then, the main—voice of Welsh-speaking Wales. It noted disapprovingly that though, in English-speaking Wales, "the journalistic exploitation of moon-kissed poet and rampaging bohemian has been uncritically welcomed by patriotic and sectional pride," most Welsh-language poets and critics have been unimpressed. In any case, Welsh-language writers, to whom most of the essay is devoted, were, in the reviewer's opinion, far more important than their Anglo-Welsh counterparts, given the twentieth-century renaissance in Welsh-language writing.[56] Walford Davies's was a more considered approach in his review of *Poet in the Making*, Ralph Maud's masterly edition of the notebooks: the early writing was an attempt "to break a personal deadlock by embracing external social themes"[57] in the manner of Auden and Eliot. Thomas was thus placed wholly within the English tradition by a professor of English who was also a pillar of the Welsh-language community. The English-speaking Welsh poet Stephen Knight, in his review of *A Companion to Dylan Thomas* by John Ackerman, another and older stalwart of English-speaking literary Wales, illustrated this community's extreme responses. In Knight's opinion, Ackerman, who, since his first book on Thomas in 1964, has stressed the importance of the Welsh background, albeit in a "provincial"[58] manner, was an example of "the deification school of Dylan Thomas criticism. It seems his boy can do no wrong," so that "the *Companion* is an efficiently written fan-letter." Knight himself considered that "there has always been something ghoulish about the Dylan Thomas industry."[59] As for English reviewers,[60] two comments sum up persisting prejudice. The first, from the notice of Caitlin Thomas's *Leftover Life to Kill*, was on Caitlin's revelations of her husband's "unexpected Welsh middle-class streak."[61] The meaning is all in the noun. The second, in the review of *A Reader's Guide to Dylan Thomas*, repeated Tindall's comment that the use of sound in "The conversation of prayers" was an example of "Welsh oral trickery."[62]

The *TLS* reviews clearly demonstrate that all three communities—Welsh-speaking Wales, English-speaking Wales, the English—were uneasy about Thomas. His Welshness became even more problematic when it was linked, in a further manifestation of the charge of arrested development, to his perpetual adolescence:

Perhaps he never really in his deep heart left the Swansea bedroom where as a little boy he would write for hours, never left home, never stopped hearing, without understanding, his father reading Shakespeare. He needed to be sick; to be made a fuss of; to have a mother-figure to protect him. In the end the only bed was the grave, the only mother-figure Death.[63]

Wales and Welshness are only patronized by such sentimental-romantic touting for sympathy. It makes it easy to perceive the equally patronizing pathos—though certainly not the accuracy—of the sentence that closes the review of Maud's bibliography, *Dylan Thomas in Print*: "Perhaps the 'real' Dylan was somebody whom Wales, both then and now, understood better than London."[64]

In the mid-1960s G. S. Fraser referred to the coolness and distaste that followed Thomas's death, reinforced, he felt, by Brinnin's *Dylan Thomas in America* and Caitlin Thomas's *Leftover Life to Kill*.[65] A year later Thomas was placed with faint praise as "top of the second eleven."[66] The wonder is that Thomas's posthumous reception was described so blandly and that he was placed even that high, given, in 1962, the scorching attack on man and works, the first of five reviews that were either overtly or indirectly hostile, the last appearing in 1993.

David Holbrook's *Llareggub Revisited* was given a substantial review. The book is in two parts: a general critical survey of contemporary English poetry and a second part entitled "The Strange Case of Dylan Thomas." Holbrook, then a fellow of King's College, Cambridge, wrote in the Arnoldian/Leavisite tradition centered on the idea of poetry as criticism of life, "essentially metaphorical, concerned with the extension of physically apprehended experience over and into abstract, moral, spiritual experience."[67] With this in mind, Holbrook laid about him, attacking such Movement poets as John Wain, Kingsley Amis, and Donald Davie, as well as the overintellectual aspects of T. S. Eliot's work, for not observing his criteria. As for Thomas, he was close to being Antichrist.

The reviewer agreed. He considered that most would concur with Holbrook that Dylan Thomas was

an unintellectual poet, that his range of themes is a narrow one, that he sometimes plays about both with words and images in an irresponsible way and that a certain regressiveness, a refusal to cut himself free from a tangle of childish or adolescent fantasies, lusts, and disgusts, both gives him his peculiar flavour and helps to define his limitations. He is not either in his life or his art an example of normality.[68]

As has been seen, there is nothing new in such criticisms. What is new is the scale and viciousness of Holbrook's attack on Thomas and, in particular, the linking of man and work. Holbrook seized upon what he considered to be Thomas's moral flaws: his failure to grow up, his lack of compassion, and his neopsychopathic obsession with sexual violence and drunkenness. Further, Holbrook loathed "suburbia." In his opinion Thomas and his work were its products, reflecting in both form and content "the malaise of English suburban life itself, the formlessness, lack of shape, life, and aims . . . [its] loss of significance and purpose."[69]

Faced with such loathing, the reviewer offered an odd and loaded counter. Holbrook was criticized for not taking sufficient account of Thomas's background and, in particular, for mistakenly regarding him as a suburban poet. He was further criticized for judging Thomas against an English standard of seriousness and respectability. Later critics of Thomas are often willing to call Thomas "suburban" and do not regard the adjective as necessarily insulting. As for the remark about an "English standard," the implication that Welsh standards are lower continues the vein of patronage and prejudice detected in other reviews.

Both the Holbrook study and the review gave ammunition to Thomas's enemies. One, the famous Shakespearean scholar E. M. W. Tillyard, contributed a reader's letter on 27 April 1962 describing contemptuously Thomas's visit to Queen's College, Cambridge: drunk, pretending to be a dog, scampering around the room and under the tables, and requesting those present to pat his head.[70] Holbrook also wrote a letter to the editor, complaining that the reviewer had travestied his book. In reply, that reviewer, still anonymous, again rejected the description of Thomas as "suburban," made a strong point about literature not being necessarily moral, complained that Holbrook simply did not understand Thomas's poetry, and objected forcefully to his "personal sneers and rudeness" to a dead man whom the reviewer "knew . . . slightly and was very fond of."[71] This last is doubtless well meant but might remind the reader of Thomas as Tillyard's dog. That acquaintances took to Thomas was a point also made by the reviewer of E. W. Tedlock's collection of memoirs and critical pieces, who reminded readers that Thomas was "much loved"[72] by his friends, a fact hardly to be grasped from the disappointing recollections by G. S. Fraser and, as will be seen later in this chapter, by Goronwy Rees. Certainly, as the Holbrook review demonstrates, Thomas continued to arouse strong feelings.

In 1967 Constantine FitzGibbon's edition of Thomas's *Selected Letters*, together with critical studies by William Moynihan and Louise Murdy and, for a second time, George Firmage's *A Garland for Dylan Thomas*, were the subjects of the front-page lead review. Though unsigned, it is now known to have been written by Geoffrey Grigson, Thomas's early supporter turned castigating enemy. Grigson commented interestingly on the critical studies—his assertion that Moynihan was wrong to compare Thomas with Hopkins because the latter's "toughness, suppleness and articulation" are lacking in Thomas's work is at least arguable—and he recognized central aspects of Thomas's poetry, including the idea of "process," his care with words, and his "determination . . . to compel symbol and reality to agree, or to make reality impart its force to symbol." This is serious engagement, but it is set aside by Grigson's belief that "Thomas's poetry owes its popularity to the romantic stereotype of its movement, its sonority and its language" and by his disturbing eagerness to mount a vicious ad hominem attack on Thomas.

He conceded that in the letters there is "a track of intellectual growth and living good sense"; however, there is also "a track of curious insensitivity—literary insensitivity, to leave an insensitive egocentricity on one side." Character assassination then follows, Grigson fiercely criticizing Thomas's self-consciousness about his suburbanism and his claims to be Welsh; in fact, he was English, not Welsh, and not even Anglo-Welsh. Grigson continued:

This poet . . . whatever the merit of his poems, is of little interest—or little adult interest—in himself. . . . the personality, squalid, repellent, sentimental and sterile. . . . his opinions were marginal and sometimes nonsense arrived at *ex post facto* in justification of his practice.

He avoided all intellectually taxing company. Further, "how ham the acting, how tiresomely over-poetic the reading on all those discs, in all those broadcasts . . . that gusher of words coated in warm maple-syrup." In the later letters, his judgments "exhibit what happens, terribly (tediously as well) when a man weak and arrested in his curriculum takes to the heroin habit of being a sponge." Grigson was repelled by "sycophancy, crawling letters." Thomas, like Vernon Watkins, was the product of "that late Victorian humus in which he was potted." For good measure, as it were, Grigson concluded by attacking Fitz-Gibbon's editing as inaccurate, "slatternly and inconsistent." More than thirteen years after Thomas's death and more than thirty years after quarrelling with him, Grigson's hatred remained astonishingly virulent and disturbing in his restated criticism of Thomas's lack of education, the nature of his Welshness, and his arrested development.[73]

The other three hostile reviews are post-1974, the year in which the *TLS* ended anonymous reviewing. The first was by Goronwy Rees, who in his lifetime was the most controversial of figures both in Wales, due to a short and controversial principalship of the University College of Wales, Aberystwyth, and elsewhere, because of his close Oxford friendship with Guy Burgess, later unmasked as a Soviet spy. Rees reviewed Paul Ferris's *Dylan Thomas* and Daniel Jones's memoir *My Friend Dylan Thomas* and, unusually, much preferred the latter to the former. Rees expressed concern about the Dylan Thomas industry, believing that Thomas gained a "rock-or-pop celebrity" status, a point later developed by George Tremlett. Ferris's biography was important, but despite the new material, Rees wondered whether yet another biography was necessary, particularly since Ferris omitted "something vital and essential," which, for Rees, was the fact that despite the problems of Thomas's life, he was "always a pleasure and a stimulation to meet and to know," thus echoing the point made by the reviewer of Holbrook's diatribe. Jones's memoir, however, was much better at conveying the essential Thomas because Jones understood the creative mind.

Neither, though, adequately explored the Welsh background, the effect of "a society in a process of rapid disintegration and decay, and of equally rapid transformation." Confronted by a much more powerful English society, Thomas's father was embittered by seeming rejection; his son took it by storm but was never at home in it. Rees added, enigmatically and as a Welsh speaker, that Thomas's loss of the Welsh language complicated matters. His conclusion, that Thomas approached London like a Red Indian or an Aborigine because he was "an urgent case for treatment for acute cultural shock," here undeveloped and stated without much apparent sympathy, is an important observation that may well reflect something of Rees's own feeling of deracination.[74]

Claude Rawson's long review of *Collected Letters* (1985) is an attack in the Grigson tradition. Rawson was eager to state that he found few pleasures in the volume; in his opinion only 20 of 982 pages were worth reading. Notwithstanding this severe judgment, he was moved, almost despite himself, to praise Thomas for some felicities, such as his descriptions of the Spenders in Florence, and because he "punned with great facility and had a real bent for comic pictorialism." Such praise—plus a few other positive nods, such as that at his "genuine gift for lively observant prose"—is submerged by the contempt that dominates the review. Thomas was criticized for his suburban mentality, Rawson insisting that even Thomas's sense of himself as a rebel, often expressed through pretentious links with such as Rimbaud and Whitman, was no more than a conforming to suburban notions of the bohemian poet. He commented, "We have only to think, again, of Genet to see how superficial and cosily self-cherishing Thomas's anti-social posture is." He was severe on Thomas's avoiding of war service, on his constant—and insincere—self-disparagement, and on his deployment of self-knowledge as an evasive strategy. The letters were "a prolonged effervescence of simpering contrition," written by a calculating and manipulative man. In seeking to place Thomas as a poet, we might think of, say, Thomas Moore, though "the comparison does Dylan Thomas too much honour." Ferris was praised because he knew "when to deflate Thomas's pretensions and does it without Thomas's pretentious pleasure in self-deflation." The volume "makes available an interesting and shabby case-history."[75]

The most recent major review, by the poet Gerald Mangan, is of Jonathan Fryer's *Dylan* and Paul Ferris's *Caitlin*. Its mocking title indicates the tone: "Ecstasies of Inspiration: Dylan Thomas's Descent from Peter Pan to Dorian Gray." Mangan asked an important question: "Should our reading of 'Fern Hill' be affected by the wealth of evidence that convicts its author of intemperance, flatulence, incontinence, egotism, exhibitionism, opportunism, masochism, puerility, promiscuity, disloyalty and mendacity?" He understood that the question is not a simple one, but he tended to offer a simple answer that seems little more than the further question, "After such knowledge, what forgiveness?" Most of the review illustrates the vices listed in the question plus the old charge of deliberate obscurity: "It is hard to avoid the feeling that the obscurity of his manner served as a convenient camouflage for murky complexes he was ashamed to spell out and permanently unable to resolve." "Fern Hill" was praised: "[It] reminds us that Thomas could surpass Wordsworth, in recapturing the pure awe of childhood in its original state of flux." It was, however, a late poem, and Mangan referred to, let alone praised, no other poem. His conclusion about Thomas's writing was bleak: "His real subject was the ecstasy of inspiration itself, and the loss of inspiration had left him without a subject."

Mangan accepted Ferris's argument that Caitlin did much to destroy her husband, but saw Thomas's problem as stemming from his "important private equation between intoxication and childhood" that, in the long run, "seems to have disabled him from living." He regarded Thomas, following Goronwy Rees, as a victim of the cultural interstice: on the one hand, Thomas subscribed to the "equation between poetry and intoxication . . . easily made in Celtic countries, where it still dominates," whereas, on the other hand, his idea of " 'the sublime/ in the old sense' had been too religiously segregated, according to English Romantic principles, from the Celtic sense of comedy that might have regenerated him." This is an interesting development of Rees's cruder point about Thomas's crisis of identity. Ultimately, Mangan joined Grigson and Rawson in succumbing to the attraction of repulsion: "He was growing old before he had grown up; and the Peter Pan inside him was horrified by the wheezing, gouty, booze-bloated Dorian Gray of his body."[76]

Given such a review, it might be said that so far as the sequence of *TLS* reviews extending over almost sixty years is concerned, in its end is its beginning. But this is not quite true, for unexpectedly and slightly paradoxically, as Thomas's life and death recede from the present, they receive more and more attention and appear to rouse ever more intense and usually hostile feelings. Distance has not yet brought objectivity. As for Thomas's writings, these, particularly his poetry, are, comparatively speaking, hardly considered, as the *TLS*'s failure to review *Collected Poems, 1934–1953* (1988) makes plain. A further notable omission is any consideration of Thomas's position vis-à-vis the breakup of English literature into British (and other) literatures in English that goes beyond the luminous suggestions of Goronwy Rees and Gerald Mangan. Such a consideration may well have to investigate the hatred Thomas seems still to inspire in some English reviewers.

NOTES

1. Jeremy Treglown, "Literary History and the *'Lit. Supp.,'* " *Yearbook of English Studies*, ed. C. J. Rawson, 16 (1986): 136, 149.

2. Review of *18 Poems, TLS*, 14 March 1935: 163.

3. Review of *Twenty-five Poems, TLS*, 19 September 1936: 750.

4. Review of *The Map of Love, TLS*, 26 August 1939: 499.

5. Review of Henry Treece, *Dylan Thomas: "Dog among the Fairies," TLS* 22 July 1949: 476.

6. Review of *Portrait of the Artist as a Young Dog, TLS*, 6 April 1940: 173.

7. Review of *Death and Entrances, TLS*, 9 March 1946: 116.

8. "Over Sir John's Hill," in a supplement entitled "The Mind of 1951," *TLS*, 24 August 1951: xxi; "In the White Giant's Thigh," *TLS*, 7 December 1951: 786.

9. Review of *Collected Poems, 1934–1952, TLS*, 28 November 1952: 776.

10. Review of *Twenty-five Poems, TLS*, 19 September 1936: 750.

11. Review of *18 Poems, TLS*, 14 March 1935: 163.

12. Review of first number of the literary magazine *Wales, TLS*, 4 September 1937: 643.

13. Review of *The Map of Love, TLS*, 26 August 1939: 499.

14. Review of *Deaths and Entrances, TLS*, 9 March 1946: 116.

15. Review of *Collected Poems, 1934–1952, TLS*, 28 November 1952: 776.

16. Review of *The Map of Love, TLS*, 26 August 1939: 499.

17. Review of *Twenty-five Poems, TLS*, 19 September 1936: 750.

18. Review of *Collected Poems, 1934–1952, TLS*, 28 November 1952: 776.

19. See the discussion of London literary life in the 1930s in Chapter 1.

20. Review of *Twenty-five Poems, TLS*, 19 September 1936: 750.

21. Review of *Portrait of the Artist as a Young Dog, TLS*, 6 April 1940: 173.

22. Review of Henry Treece, *Dylan Thomas: "Dog among the Fairies," TLS*, 22 July 1949: 476.

23. Review of *Under Milk Wood, TLS*, 5 March 1954: 148.

24. Stephen Spender, "Personal Preferences," *TLS*, 6 August 1954: vi.

25. See, e.g., Matthew Arnold, *On the Study of Celtic Literature* (London, 1867).

26. Blake Morrison, *The Movement* (London and New York: Methuen, 1986), 31.

27. Review of J. Alexander Rolph, *Dylan Thomas: A Bibliography, TLS*, 27 July 1956: 451.

28. "Experiment in Verse," *TLS*, 17 August 1956: iii.

29. Elder Olson, *The Poetry of Dylan Thomas* (Chicago: University of Chicago Press, 1954), 66.

30. H. H. Kleinman, *The Religious Sonnets of Dylan Thomas: A Study in Imagery and Meaning* (Berkeley: University of California Press, 1963), 10.

31. Derek Stanford, *Dylan Thomas* (London: Neville Spearman, 1954), 150, 151.

32. *TLS*, 7 January 1955: 10. This is a review of both Olson and Stanford.

33. G. S. Fraser, "The Legend and the Puzzle," *TLS*, 5 March 1964: 186. [Review of George Firmage (ed.), *A Garland for Dylan Thomas*; Ralph Maud and Aneirin Talfan Davies, *The Colour of Saying*; H. H. Kleinman, *The Religious Sonnets of Dylan Thomas*; and Ralph Maud, *Entrances to Dylan Thomas's Poetry*.]

34. Review of *Letters to Vernon Watkins, TLS*, 15 November 1957: 691.

35. Review of Bill Read, *The Days of Dylan Thomas*, and Constantine FitzGibbon, *The Life of Dylan Thomas, TLS*, 21 October 1965: 940.

36. G. S. Fraser, "The Legend and the Puzzle," *TLS*, 5 March 1964: 186.

37. Ibid.

38. Neil Powell, Review of George Tremlett, *Dylan Thomas: In the Mercy of His Means, TLS*, 31 January 1992: 25.

39. Review of Olson and Stanford, *TLS*, 7 January 1955: 10.

40. G. S. Fraser, "The Legend and the Puzzle," *TLS*, 5 March 1964: 186.

41. Review of William York Tindall, *A Reader's Guide to Dylan Thomas, TLS*, 21 December 1962: 987.

42. J. H. Martin, letter, *TLS*, 19 March 1964: 235.

43. Keidrych Rhys, letter, *TLS*, 26 March 1964: 255; Constantine FitzGibbon, letter, *TLS*, 2 April 1964: 273.

44. Review of J. Alexander Rolph, *Dylan Thomas: A Bibliography, TLS*, 27 July 1956: 451.

45. Review of *Letters to Vernon Watkins, TLS*, 15 November 1957: 691.

46. G. S. Fraser, "The Legend and the Puzzle," *TLS*, 5 March 1964: 186.

47. Review of *Quite Early One Morning, TLS*, 19 November 1954: 731.

48. Review of *Adventures in the Skin Trade, TLS*, 30 September 1955: 569.

49. Review of *A Prospect of the Sea, TLS*, 5 August 1955: 446.

50. Review of *The Beach of Falesá, TLS*, 30 July 1964: 670.

51. Review of *Twenty Years A-Growing*, TLS, 22 October 1964: 960.

52. Review of *Early Prose Writings*, ed. Walford Davies, *TLS*, 3 March 1972: 254.

53. Stephen Knight, review of *The Broadcasts*, ed. Ralph Maud, *TLS*, 17 May 1991: 28.

54. Neil Powell, review of George Tremlett, *Dylan Thomas: In the Mercy of His Means, TLS*, 31 January 1992: 25.

55. Keidrych Rhys, letter, *TLS*, 26 March 1964: 255.

56. "The Two Literatures of Wales," *TLS*, 5 August 1955: xii.

57. Walford Davies, review of Ralph Maud, *Poet in the Making, TLS*, 2 May 1968: 460.

58. Stephen Knight, *TLS*, 22 October 1964: 960. Part of a review of John Ackerman, *Dylan Thomas: His Life and Work*.

59. Stephen Knight, review of *The Broadcasts*, ed. Ralph Maud, *TLS*, 17 May 1991: 28.

60. Given the anonymity of reviews, this is, of course, assumption, but it is based on the reviewers' use of the word "Welsh."

61. Review of Caitlin Thomas, *Leftover Life to Kill, TLS*, 31 May 1957: 336.

62. Review of William York Tindall, *A Reader's Guide to Dylan Thomas, TLS*, 21 December 1962: 987. Tindall wrote "Such oral trickery, distantly Welsh," (*A Reader's Guide to Dylan Thomas* [1962; New York: Octagon Books, 1981], 179).

63. Review of Bill Read, *The Days of Dylan Thomas*, and Constantine FitzGibbon, *The Life of Dylan Thomas, TLS*, 21 October 1965: 940.

64. Review of Ralph Maud, *Dylan Thomas in Print, TLS*, 3 March 1972: 254.

65. G. S. Fraser, "The Legend and the Puzzle," *TLS*, 5 March 1964.

66. Review of Bill Read, *The Days of Dylan Thomas*, and Constantine FitzGibbon, *The Life of Dylan Thomas, TLS*, 21 October 1965: 940.

67. David Holbrook, *Llareggub Revisited* (London: Bowes & Bowes, 1962), 72.

68. Review of David Holbrook, *Llareggub Revisited, TLS*, 13 April 1962: 250.

69. Holbrook, *Llareggub Revisited*, 239.

70. E. M. W. Tillyard, Letter, *TLS*, 27 April 1962: 281.

71. Letter from Holbrook and the reviewer's reply, *TLS*, 4 May 1962: 309.

72. Review of E. W. Tedlock (ed.), *Dylan Thomas: The Legend and the Poet, TLS*, 2 December 1960: 826.

73. Review of Constantine FitzGibbon, *Selected Letters of Dylan Thomas*, William T. Moynihan, *The Craft and Art of Dylan Thomas*, Louise Baughan Murdy, *Sound and Sense in Dylan Thomas's Poetry*, and George Firmage (ed.), *A Garland for Dylan Thomas, TLS*, 2 March 1967: 157–58.

74. Goronwy Rees, Review of Paul Ferris, *Dylan Thomas*, and Daniel Jones, *My Friend Dylan Thomas, TLS*, 29 April 1977: 505.

75. Claude Rawson, review of *Collected Letters*, ed. Paul Ferris, *TLS*, 2 May 1986: 475–6.

76. Gerald Mangan, Review of Jonathan Fryes, *Dylan: The Nine Lives of Dylan Thomas*, and Paul Ferris, *Caitlin: The Life of Caitlin Thomas, TLS*, 12 November 1993: 4–5.

16

Dylan Thomas in Wales

The *TLS*, as the voice of the British literary establishment, took three approaches to Thomas as a Welsh writer. Two amounted to prejudice against Thomas because he was Welsh, together with a tendency to regard Thomas as the stereotypically Welsh purveyor of ''verbal adventurousness'' and what Spender referred to, sensationally and mysteriously in his *TLS* essay of 1954, as ''dreams and blood.'' But it also gave space to what can only be called the Welsh-language literary establishment, and this generally sought to put Thomas in his place, implying and at times stating that such virtues as he had reflected his debt to the Welsh-language poetic tradition and particularly to its aesthetic disciplines. The Welsh element of Thomas's critical history also involves prejudice, stereotyping, and tense discussion of his relationship with Welsh and its literature.

Such issues emerged gradually. The initial reception in Wales of Thomas's work was fairly brief and uncertain. One reason for this was that in 1934, when *18 Poems* was published, Wales had no literary magazine in English. The book pages of the newspapers provided the only reviews and were inevitably influenced by the populist nature of publications (Wales had no highbrow press) that kept auspicious eyes on the conservative sensibilities of their readers. Only the two local Swansea papers reviewed *18 Poems*, and one of these notices, in the weekly *South and West Wales Guardian*, was written, pseudonymously, by Thomas's close friend A. E. Trick. Thomas's former employer, the *South Wales Evening Post*, also showed interest. The editor, J. D. Williams, informed his readers late in 1934 that, with *18 Poems* imminent, his former junior was ''now definitely placed by the critics among our 'coming men' ''; a further puff followed in January 1935.[1] But Williams, obviously baffled by and reluctant to review *18 Poems*, on Richard Hughes's advice invited a much younger man to provide a review in the *Herald of Wales*, the daily's companion weekly.

A. Spencer Vaughan-Thomas was described by the *Herald* as ''a young man of the poet's own generation.'' He was Welsh-speaking, from a well-known Swansea family, and English master at Barnet Grammar School in Greater London. His lively review combined exhilarated admiration, bafflement, and reservation:

It is like no poetry that ever came out of Swansea before. Strange, compressed, tortuous, exciting by its wild leaps of imagination, and tantalizing by its equally strange lapses into baffling obscurity, it will puzzle, irritate, and . . . grip the interest as few modern poets do. . . . He has definitely arrived.

Vaughan-Thomas noted the influence of Hopkins and Wilfred Owen, the importance of sound, at times "a certain monotony of style and rhythm," and such technical devices as alliteration and vowel changes. These last led him to a central point, that such devices produced in Thomas's work, "for all its postulated modernity, a certain archaic trait, comparable with the *gorphwsfa* [*sic*] of Welsh *cynghanedd*," the last clause referring to traditional systems of sound chiming or consonantal harmonizing in Welsh-language poetry. The danger was, Vaughan-Thomas concluded, that strict technique would counter inspiration. That accepted, "no one can read his work without feeling that here is a poet magnificently equipped to achieve great things," an ambitious poet willing to take risks.[2]

This perceptive review touches on what were to become some of the main concerns of Welsh criticism of Thomas's work: the problem of obscurity, the relationship between sound and meaning, Thomas's place in a tradition of Welsh writing in English—interpreted freely to include Hopkins and Owen—and possible links to writing in Welsh. Such matters are handled with an intelligence and fair-mindedness that do not always characterize the reactions of Thomas's compatriots.

Despite such virtues, Vaughan-Thomas did not review *Twenty-five Poems*. J. D. Williams tried his hand, only to admit that "as I cannot say much about [the poems], I may say a little about [the poet]." Most of what follows consists of reminiscences of Thomas's short career as a local reporter, plus the admission that one or two lines and two poems, "This bread I break" and "Was there a time," had impressed the reviewer. Williams, describing himself as a "child of the Victorian Day," found all else incomprehensible.[3]

Here is provinciality in action, the new judged solely in terms of the old, the main charge—one that surely haunted Thomas—being obscurity. Oddly, the next local critic, Thomas's friend and fellow poet Charles Fisher, one-time member of the "Kardomah circle," who reviewed *The Map of Love* for the *South Wales Evening Post*, pleaded guilty on the poet's behalf, quoting in evidence the opening of the volume's first poem,

Because the pleasure-bird whistles after the hot wires,
Shall the blind horse sing sweeter?

surely lines of comparative transparency. The volume was not, Fisher asserted, an advance from obscurity to a new clarity, as the publishers claimed. That said, about ten of the poems should be clear to "the dullest, least imaginative man who was ever told to open an anthology." Here was work of "indisputable genius." As for the fiction, it showed "strangeness and originality," the author being "pre-occupied with his chimeras and illusions. His world is a world of dreams, madness and frustration."[4] Fisher's subtext, that the best Thomas is the most approachable, recurs frequently in the later criticism.

Eight months later Fisher reviewed *Portrait of the Artist as a Young Dog* and was disappointed. The stories reflected

the sensitive use of deliberately flimsy material. . . . Having deserted the great expanse in which he walked superbly but almost alone, Dylan Thomas has sought no compromise but set down the commonplaces, the dull, well-intentioned talk of everyday affairs so photographically that it makes us squirm.

He concluded, "One cannot but be conscious of great powers unused."[5] To imply that clarity is not enough is understandable but hardly consistent with the earlier review; the confusion was not unique.

The *Evening Post* reviewed *Deaths and Entrances* in 1946: Dilys Rowe assessed the "Place of Dylan Thomas in Modern Poetry." She considered that "the fault in modern poetry is less that it is obscure than that it is esoteric. At its worst it is not poetry that can be shared." Of the twenty-four poems in Thomas's new volume, she concluded that though "a few of them could . . . be called obscure," they were "never ungenerous like the obscurity of his imitators." Thomas was primarily concerned "with the glory of youth . . . and the full circle of youth to age, the one shadowing the other." Perhaps significantly, two of Thomas's more approachable poems were given particular attention. These are "The conversation of prayers" and "Fern Hill," the latter having "lines so full of human longing and hiraeth that it should be remembered long after the mechanics of this age's poetry are forgotten." She then made a more general point. After asserting that Thomas was "in tune with all men and not with a clique," she continued:

It is a pity that Wales, which is everywhere in his poetry, has failed to follow him and been content to relegate him to the English.

As yet another wireless comic gathers more derision for Welshmen, little national interest is shown in the Welsh writer who is one of the dozen or so recent poets to lead poetry out of the gloom.[6]

The second paragraph refers to postwar radio productions such as the plays of E. Eynon Evans and "Welsh Rarebit," to which Evans also contributed, a comedy program produced in Wales that relied on Welsh characters and accents exaggerated for comic effect. Rowe's review as a whole, favorable though it is, does imply that it was written in the face of ambivalent attitudes to Thomas's literary worth and Welshness, particularly in the Welsh-language community. These are points to which this chapter will return.

In Thomas's lifetime the local paper offered only one further notice: John Ormond Thomas, born locally and who, as John Ormond, was to have a distinguished career both as poet and BBC producer, reviewed *Collected Poems, 1934–1952*. His aggressive tone reflects the exasperation of Thomas's supporters at attacks upon him at a time when Movement hostility was at its peak. Ormond certainly came out fighting: Thomas, he stated, "divines complexities that are too great to be simplified for the benefit of a number of one-eyed, half-eyed critics" who simply cannot deal with his originality but "call for their usual jelly." He was not "a twentieth century Welsh verbal trickster and unreasoning obscurantist" but a poet with similarities to Vaughan and Traherne who "has set himself the task of revealing the grandeur and purity of Man and how 'with much ado' he is corrupted. . . . He teaches the mortality and the immortality of Man," concerning himself, Ormond Thomas continued with grand eclecticism, with "Time, death, unkindness, lack of charity and love." He was celebratory, essentially religious, creating "work of major status and importance."[7]

This is adulation and a sweeping rejection of criticism. Yet within the rhetoric is a recognition of the main questions that recur through Welsh criticism of Thomas's work: the problems of obscurity and difficulty, Thomas's relationship to a tradition of Welsh writing in English, and the general question of Thomas's Welshness. In addition, Ormond Thomas's description of Dylan Thomas's themes suggests their distance from ordinary life in all its realist detail.

After Thomas's sensational death, which drew a number of expressions of sympathy, *Evening Post* reviews were less frequent and more perfunctory. In reviewing Daniel Jones's edition of *Under Milk Wood* (1954) and *A Prospect of the Sea* (1955), D. H. I. Powell was relieved to find both volumes approachable: "Dylan writes of the common man for the common man," he commented on the former; of the latter he considered that whereas the early stories were "eerie studies in insanity," the postwar work was "straightforward and amusing."[8] This eager seizing upon Thomas's relatively simpler prose as it appeared in posthumous editions and the comparative neglect of the poetry—a case of populist provincialism—were trends of the 1950s, further defensive gestures in the face of criticism. In 1964 J. Gwyn Griffiths, a prominent Welsh nationalist and member of the Classics Department of the University of Wales, Swansea, noticed Aneirin Talfan Davies's study, *Dylan: Druid of the Broken Body*. He was unconvinced by Davies's argument that in Thomas's work an increasing acceptance of Roman Catholicism could be discerned, asserting that Thomas invariably used Christian symbols merely as embellishments and had only fitful moments of faith. He also objected to the suggestion that turning to Catholicism was a reaction against suffocating Nonconformity, a statement that, given Griffiths's membership in the predominantly Nonconformist Welsh-speaking establishment, was as much a cultural as a critical gesture.[9]

Thus the Swansea press, though fumbling at times, wrestled valiantly with Thomas's originality and provides a microcosm of wider Welsh critical approaches. Meanwhile the *Western Mail*, the Cardiff-based "national newspaper of Wales," began its checkered relationship with Thomas with three undistinguished reviews, all by A. T. G. Edwards, of *Twenty-five Poems, The Map of Love*, and *Portrait of the Artist as a Young Dog*. Though agreeing with the publisher's blurb that *Twenty-five Poems* was " 'poetry that merits attention'— serious and thoughtful attention, let us add," Edwards also felt that readers used to more traditional poetry "will find it rather heavy going."[10] The poetry in *The Map of Love* simply confused him: "In Mr. Thomas genuine native genius is being increasingly thwarted by a mistaken devotion to the doctrines of surrealism—to a fashionable intellectual pose. I got on better with the stories."[11] *Portrait of the Artist as a Young Dog* came as blessed relief. Thomas was, Edwards considered, more likely to make his mark as a short-story writer: "As a poet he may be incoherent; in prose (when he gets clear of surrealistic dogma) he is superb."[12]

Edwards tended to hedge his bets, at least a little, possibly because elsewhere in the *Western Mail*, other opinions were being rehearsed. Some of these found expression in an article by the famous Welsh-language poet and scholar T. Gwynn Jones entitled "The Modern Trend in Welsh Poetry." This is a lament for the deplorable standard of poems in Welsh submitted for various eisteddfod competitions. The fault, Jones implied, was Dylan Thomas's (though Jones never mentioned him by name). Too many submissions had been obscure, due to the "influence of those who evidently think that 'pure poetry' need not be intelligible, at least to anyone but the author, who may even make his own vocabulary." This was because of "our national tendency to follow every new fashion from the outside, at least for a while."[13]

T. Gwynn Jones was (and remains) a towering figure in Welsh-language literary life and culture. His implied attack on Thomas the Outsider attracted much attention. There followed, during August 1939, a fierce and mainly three-sided correspondence between Keidrych Rhys, poet and, as editor of *Wales*, publisher of Thomas and other Anglo-Welsh writers, poet and short-story writer Nigel Heseltine, and Pennar Davies, then writing as "Davies Aberpennar," poet, novelist, scholar, and another important figure in Welsh-language literary life. Predictably, Pennar Davies supported T. Gwynn Jones; he also had Dylan Thomas in his sights when he stated that a Welsh writer should be one who "regards Wales not merely (or even at all) as a source of subject matter but as the place of his milieu and his audience . . . the map of England should be, except for special reasons, out of bounds." The alternative was "to seek his fortune in the midst of a cosmopolitan confusion of poetasters and minors and literary racketeers of all kinds." Heseltine tended to provide ammunition for Davies in being sceptical about the extent of contemporary Anglo-Welsh talent and concerned that no one seemed to deal with current crises and happenings. But he was more moderate than Davies regarding relations with England: though it was wrong to exploit Welsh foibles to provoke English laughter, it was also wrong to exclude English influence.[14]

Rhys was far more aggressive. In his opinion, T. Gwynn Jones knew little about younger Welsh-language poets, let alone of "young Welshmen who write in English." It was wrong that Dylan Thomas and others should "go on being relatively unknown in their native country." More notice should be taken of Anglo-Welsh writers. As it was, the Welsh-language community appeared to hate them: "People like Mr Iorweth C. Peate seem to consider the destruction of periodicals printing the work of Welshmen writing in English as important an effort as the destruction of Hitler—perhaps a bit more important." The result was that Anglo-Welsh writers were driven out of Wales.[15] Rhys's point about hatred drew a letter of general support from the Anglo-Welsh poet Huw Menai, who, however, encapsulated a further Welsh difficulty about Dylan Thomas by nailing his colors, alongside those of J. D. Williams, to the mast of poetic tradition. His heroes were poets such as Milton, Wordsworth, Browning, and Tennyson, who wrote "not in nihilistic vers libre or prose, but in disciplined and ordered metrical form."[16] At the end of August 1939 Menai was supported by a vicious attack on "Because the pleasure-bird whistles," the opening poem of *The Map of Love*. This was by one "Shinkins Abercwmboi," who insisted that no one should expect your "average Welshmen . . . to waste time on these fruitless inanities . . . the charlatanry of cloud-cuckoo stuff packed in bales of obscurity."[17] Thomas was thus savaged by the twin hatreds of some members of the Welsh-language community and traditionalist English speakers. All this occurred within days of the start of World War II.

After the war *Western Mail* reviewing of Thomas was taken over by A. G. Prys-Jones. He was then an inspector of schools in Wales and a firmly traditionalist poet wholly out of sympathy with modern literary trends who was on his way towards becoming the grand old man of Welsh letters (he died in 1987, aged ninety-eight). Prys-Jones began cautiously with *Deaths and Entrances*, the volume that made Thomas famous. He described it as "an unusual and rather terrifying portent in modern poetry," seized on the approachable poems, "which have a rare and simple beauty," and concluded, not altogether consistently, that Thomas was "undoubtedly among the major voices in modern poetry. . . . What is much less certain is whether the general reading public will take the trouble to try to understand him; and, even if they do, whether they will ever succeed."[18]

In his notice of *Collected Poems, 1934–1952* he came to much the same conclusion in much the same way. He scattered adulatory clichés, praised the simpler poems, approved of the appearance of "a greater clarity and precision," regarded some poems as "beyond any explanation," and ended magisterially by discerning "a new fire and flexibility . . . an astonishing magic."[19]

In 1954 came another reviewer who could mint clichés with the best of them: Gwyn Jones reviewed *Under Milk Wood*. Jones, then at the height of his powers, was a distinguished Welsh professor of English literature, an important Anglo-Welsh writer and editor, and champion of Thomas. The review heaped high praise on the play—"Surely the best script ever written for broadcasting"—but was mainly concerned to counter statements that the play was about Laugharne and its inhabitants. Rather, Jones insisted, it was "a quintessence of Laugharne; it is Laugharne lifted above particulars and raised to universals."[20] Though this was overstated, there was sense in it, but because it was said at a time when the play was controversial, Thomas being regarded by many as exploiting Welsh life for commercial purposes and English predilections, it can now seem merely defensive special pleading.

With few exceptions—Vaughan-Thomas's piece on *18 Poems*, possibly that by Dilys Rowe—the attention given to Thomas's work by Welsh English-language newspapers hardly reassures. When Thomas published his first book in 1934, the greatest poetic achievements of the modernist movement—Eliot's *The Waste Land* and Pound's *Hugh Selwyn Mauberley* and the early *Cantos*—were some years in the past, yet Welsh newspaper reviewers judged his work in terms of Victorian or, at best, Georgian poetics and inevitably found much of it wanting. Blinkered traditionalism rejected Thomas as obscurely strange; many in the Welsh-speaking literary world, blinkered or not, hated Thomas for many of the same reasons, as well as for becoming famous through writing in English and rejecting the age-old communal role of the Welsh poet. With notable exceptions—Keidrych Rhys, for example—implicitly or overtly hostile conservatism, passing itself off as critical engagement, shaped reviews and on occasion dominated the letter columns, sometimes as spiteful glee. Thus in a letter to the *Western Mail* shortly after Thomas's death, one D. L. Evans of Carmarthen took pains to exclude Thomas from a list of eminent Welshmen, citing in support the Anglo-Irish writer Lord Dunsany, who had stated that Thomas was "totally unable to express his real affection for rural scenes in plain English."[21] Here fear of the new unites with cultural cringe.

The rising star of Thomas's career through the 1930s was part of a burgeoning of Welsh writing in English that fuelled the development of what might be called an appropriate infrastructure. *Wales*, the literary magazine edited by Keidrych Rhys, began life in 1937, Gwyn Jones's *Welsh Review* in 1939. Thomas, the first modern Welsh writer to move steadily towards an international reputation, forced the Welsh-language literary world to give serious attention to its English-speaking compatriots. But any notion that Thomas was now working in a more congenial critical climate is, at least initially, difficult to sustain in the face of two responses.

Nigel Heseltine reviewed *Twenty-five Poems* in the second issue of *Wales*. The notice is hardly favorable. There was, considered Heseltine, more promise than achievement; overwriting was a recurring fault. He continued:

Whether Mr. Thomas' poetry is worth the trouble must remain undecided for the present. . . . [There is] a greater reliance on the echo of sound-association than the more rational association of ideas. . . . The richer products of his imagination roar away in unrestricted floodtorrents and leave only chirpings and scrapings of intelligibility.[22]

An absence of meaning, sound dominating sense, general obscurity: such writing would have been at home in the correspondence columns of the *Western Mail* or in the *TLS*'s sourer notices.

The second response came in an influential lecture by Saunders Lewis given in Cardiff during 1938 and published the following year as *Is There an Anglo-Welsh Literature?* Lewis is commonly regarded as the outstanding Welsh-language writer and intellectual of his generation. Fiercely nationalistic, he was then at the height of his fame, having been jailed during 1936 for arson in support of his political and cultural aims. His formidable intellect replaced T. Gwynn Jones's fear of the new with what, from one point of view, might be seen paradoxically as principled prejudice, but, from a Welsh-language perspective, as precise and powerful argument. Lewis offered a narrow definition of the Anglo-Welsh writer: "a Welshman who writes of Wales and of Welsh life in the English language." The literature was the product of industrial South Wales, and in his opinion, industrialization destroyed nationhood by reducing all to "a grey sub-human uniformity." He was quite prepared to accept that Thomas was a writer of high quality, but insisted that he belonged to "the main stream of the English literary tradition . . . there is nothing hyphenated about him. He belongs to the English."[23]

Heseltine and Lewis may have been an unlikely duo, but their combined influence can be detected in three pieces on Thomas in *Wales* before the journal suspended publication in 1949. The earliest, a review of *The Map of Love*, is by Davies Aberpennar, already encountered writing letters to the *Western Mail*. He noted, nodding towards Lewis, that the Welshness of Thomas's work was controversial, and, gesturing towards Heseltine, that there was a lack of clear narrative. He also, predictably, had his own reservations. The inclusion of a number of poems "about the problems of his craft" suggested that Thomas had "obviously, indeed avowedly, reached a crisis." His poetry was a minority interest, because very few could "enjoy an almost (not quite) pure aestheticism of image and word." Whole poems tended to be "elusive," despite good individual lines. The stories, in his opinion, were "far more compelling than the poems." The total effect of the volume was "a developed compound of the law-breaking imaginations of the child, the madman, the lover and the dreamer," which Aberpennar linked to surrealism. This is a fine insight, but he made little of it; certainly he did not recognize that this effect was necessarily incompatible with what he wanted from Thomas's work, which was implicit in his main criticism, that though

he has something important to say and knows, in spite of some hesitations, how to say it movingly and suggestively . . . he does not attempt to answer the question: what shall we do about it? An emphatic ethic seems as urgently necessary in these desperate days as an honest statement of experience.[24]

The reviewer, as Pennar Davies, had a distinguished career as a Nonconformist minister. It is not surprising—though all too typical of Nonconformist Wales

and hence disappointing in a man so obviously gifted intellectually—that, uneasy about the anarchic thrust in Thomas's work, he judged it against a narrowly
moral and didactic standard. Aberpennar may have been implicitly comparing
Thomas with the great twentieth-century Welsh-language poet Gwenallt Jones,
whose Marxist-Christian principles were evident in his writing, but oddly, in
English literary terms, in asking for a "message" Aberpennar was asking for a
poet more like the socially conscious, left-wing writers of the Auden group, that
is, more like the English.

The second discussion of Thomas is by W. Moelwyn Merchant, another
Welsh speaker, in a general article on Anglo-Welsh writing. He quoted approvingly from Saunders Lewis's lecture that Dylan Thomas belonged to the English,
and he agreed that Anglo-Welsh writing was dissociated from the Welsh tradition and so led inevitably to caricature.[25] The third item is a letter from John
Idris Jones in 1959, in the very last issue of *Wales*. He condemned *Under Milk
Wood* as "that regrettable pantomime" and as a "laborious hack-piece," praised
the poetry, then regretted—did he have Aberpennar and Merchant in mind?—
that *Wales* was too traditionally respectable and religious, too concerned with
the language, to be other than "slow in seeing [Thomas's] genius."[26]

As has been noted, Keidrych Rhys was a great supporter of Thomas and his
Anglo-Welsh contemporaries; Thomas contributed to *Wales* and had helped with
the editing. The carping tone of the magazine's reviews is thus surprising and
very different from that of its rival, Gwyn Jones's *Welsh Review*. In its issue of
October 1939 Glyn Jones reviewed *The Map of Love*. He considered it an advance on Thomas's earlier work, praising "the unexpectedness of his verbal
patterns" and the "experiment and development in the matters of theme, vocabulary and rhythm." He felt that too much had been made of the difficulty
of Thomas's work.[27]

In a review of Rhys's own anthology, *Modern Welsh Poetry*, W. D. Thomas,
professor of English at University College of Swansea, complained that Thomas's work would "cause . . . exasperation. . . . [It shows] the employment of
work in search of an experience."[28] This blimpish response is untypical of the
magazine's view of Thomas. Beryl Jones's review of *Deaths and Entrances* was
lavish with praise for Thomas's "ability to reveal to the reader the nature of
joy and Entrances, of sorrow and Deaths." Jones considered that Thomas "has
come clear of a period of great promise into assured production of pure poetry";
wisely, she did not attempt to define what she meant by "pure."[29] In an article
on the Welsh short story, Michael Williams praised *Portrait of the Artist as a
Young Dog*, in which "symbolism is replaced by imaginative naturalism," not
only for "the music of words" but also for good "naturalistic conversation."[30]
In the final issue of the magazine E. Glyn Lewis replied robustly to the virulent
criticism of Thomas made by Geoffrey Grigson in the little magazine *Polemic*
and in his book *Harp of Aeolus*. Lewis insisted that Thomas was "articulate,"
did say something, and did use language in an understandable and traditional

way. Rather than pine for Aberpennar's "emphatic ethic," Lewis accepted the nature of Thomas's work, his "amoral acceptance of all experience," the fact that his "early poetry is . . . an expression of the erratic sensual lure . . . without the formulation of a metaphysic to explain that attitude." There might be an "infantile fixation," often revealed in sea imagery, but Thomas's modernity was reflected in his "hypersensitive reaction to society" and in the lack of universal values that throws the poet back upon himself.[31]

Gwyn Jones supported Thomas not only in his magazine but also in his academic life. In 1953 he wrote of Thomas and others in the scholarly annual *Essays and Studies*. Though Jones's florid, self-indulgent style draws attention more to itself than to the literature it purports to discuss, there is no doubting his enthusiasm for Thomas's work and, here, his essential shrewdness about its nature. For example, while asserting, inimitably, that "it is expected that Anglo-Welsh prose should be poetic, or even 'bardic', and all aglow as a fire-crimsoned gorseroot," he pointed to Thomas's departure from that Anglo-Welsh norm in *Portrait of the Artist as a Young Dog*: "The high bardic note is gone, [leaving] the half-strangled importance of the diction."[32] Jones's obituary of Thomas was hyperbolic: "The world is a prodigy around us, and Dylan's world a singing miracle." The 1930s were described as "the gold-browed years when, sown in seasand, he grew from dragon's tooth to druid," and Thomas as one who "lived unchained by fact and indifferent to circumstances,"[33] comments hardly confirmed by the facts of his life. Jones's strained, overlyrical style at times seems almost a parody of the Anglo-Welsh stereotype; in assimilating Thomas it did the latter no favors.

In the early 1950s two other Welsh journals began life. One was the *Welsh Anvil*, published by the University of Wales Guild of Graduates and thus, then, dominated by Welsh speakers. It gave space to three writers who developed Saunders Lewis's attack on Anglo-Welsh literature. Ioan Bowen Rees was sceptical, insisting that such distinctive qualities as were possessed by Anglo-Welsh literature were derived from Welsh-language literature. In any case, Thomas's Wales was really only Swansea and district.[34] Aneirin Talfan Davies echoed Rees's point about the Anglo-Welsh: "We are allowed the luxury of the 'Anglo' because some people remain stubbornly Welsh." The impact of "After the Funeral" was derived, in part, from her grave being, in part, the grave of her language. Only if Welsh decayed could English be successfully used in a Welsh way. As it was, the Anglo-Welsh writer addressed the English middle class. Davies ended with the point to which J. Gwyn Griffiths once objected and that anticipated Davies's later study of Thomas and Catholicism: "[He] has reacted to the suffocating puritanism of nonconformity by a flight to a richly furnished imaginative world, where the priest is in the ascendant rather than the prophet."[35]

The third contributor was Bobi Jones, also a prominent nationalist. He considered Thomas to be a dire example of national decline:

His exuberant but irresponsible concoction of verbal cleverness . . . smart exhibitionism . . . undisciplined decorative flaccidity has not gone unnoticed in England. . . .

With all the advantages that we have in Wales of a living traditional community and literature . . . it is incongruous that we should spy cravingly on such a decadent pretence at literature.[36]

All three protested too much and so, doubtless to their mutual chagrin, implicitly rejected Saunders Lewis's argument by recognizing the abiding presence and increasing importance of Anglo-Welsh literature. That said, the accompanying insistence on its dependence on the Welsh language allowed Anglo-Welsh literature and Dylan Thomas to know their place. The hope, presumably, was that both the literature and its leading writer would stay in it.

Given that the *Welsh Anvil* essays typified Welsh-language attitudes not only to Thomas but to Anglo-Welsh writing in general, the appearance of a magazine sympathetic to literature in the language of the vast majority of Welsh people was an urgent requirement. Hence the importance of *Dock Leaves* (which became the *Anglo-Welsh Review* in 1959), edited by Raymond Garlick. But its first references to Thomas were hardly reassuring. In 1951 A. G. Prys-Jones— he of the *Western Mail*—discussed Thomas's work in an essay on "Anglo-Welsh Poetry." In his utterly conventional view Thomas's poems of "pure beauty" would survive; others, as examples of "linguistic chaos," would become museum pieces.[37] Eighteen months later A. R. Williams did not mince matters:

There must be many an ordinary reader of poetry who, like myself, can at times see in one of his poems only a goulash composed of the chewed fag-ends of inspired phrases, pitched helter-skelter into the spittoon of memory and discharged in a dishevelled stream—as a result of furious agitation—to form a string of mincemeat phrases, grouped like sausages denuded of their enveloping and connecting tissue of significance.[38]

He exempted a few of the more approachable poems from this subtle criticism, noted that a dictionary helped when reading Thomas, and concluded, unsurprisingly, that understanding Thomas's work required an unjustifiable amount of work on the reader's part.

Such an extreme reaction is at odds with the magazine's response to Thomas's death. This was in two parts. First was an obituary, followed by two "Obituary Statements" by Daniel Jones and Aneirin Talfan Davies, the latter including two important statements about Thomas. The first was a description of Thomas as a "skilled craftsman," a recurring point in the posthumous criticism. The second was yet another attempt to give Thomas acceptable Welsh credentials: "Although he himself was not Welsh-speaking, he had a great love for Wales, and always regretted that he had not been taught the language when he was young. He paid tribute to the language in the names of his children."[39] A competition was announced, offering a "Dylan Thomas Award" for the best poem in tribute to the dead poet.

"A Dylan Thomas Number" followed.[40] The editorial, by Raymond Garlick, sought to influence opinion: Thomas's "wide and warm personality" (1) had dominated responses to his death, and we must remember that his "greatness" (1) depended on the poems. His Welshness could not be overstressed: he sounded Welsh, he was formed by Wales, and in his work "the topography of Wales is his Map of Love" (2). *Under Milk Wood* was a "major work of art born of modern, bilingual Wales" (2); Anglo-Welsh literature spoke to English-speaking Wales, which was different from England. Thomas was part of a tradition of Welsh writing in English stemming from the seventeenth century; this tradition, plus Hopkins, had a strong influence on him.

Louis MacNeice judged the Dylan Thomas Award, which was won by Tony Conran, whose critical work is to be discussed. There followed tributes by Saunders Lewis, the ubiquitous Aneirin Talfan Davies, Henry Treece, and Glyn Jones, and a substantial critical essay by Roland Mathias. This issue is thus an important indication of how Thomas was regarded in Wales at the time of his death. The contributors tended to focus on a cluster of recurring ideas.

Garlick referred to Thomas's relationship to Wales as being "that of a lover" (2), a sentiment echoed in Conran's prizewinning poem, "For Dylan Thomas (On Hearing He Was Dead)," in that it highlighted the positive and celebratory aspects of Thomas's work, the "lovelit mazes" (7) through which the poetry moved. The poet as celebrator was also Saunders Lewis's point, particularly when seen in the context of modern writing: "He sang of the glory of the universe when it was the fashion for every prominent poet in Europe to sing despairingly and with passion and anguish of the end of civilization" (9). Prys-Jones touched on the same point in noting that Thomas, though initially struggling with "fear and darkness" (27), eventually "emerged into the radiant sunlight and the lyric splendour of his finest poems" (27).

Three of the contributors, Saunders Lewis, Glyn Jones, and Roland Mathias, considered his Welshness. Lewis, once disinclined to recognize Thomas as a Welsh writer, had shifted his position, describing him as the preeminent English-speaking Welsh poet. He continued, carefully: "The English critics see Welsh characteristics in his work. He brought honour to Wales, and in his latter years became increasingly Welsh in his sympathies, and found his themes in Welsh society" (9). Moral magnanimity is also present, Lewis urging us to accept "that great creative powers are rarely unaccompanied by a devil-may-care extravagance" (9).

Glyn Jones's piece was entitled "Dylan Thomas and Welsh" and was concerned to dispel what he regarded as myths. Jones asserted that in his opinion, Thomas knew next to no Welsh and nothing about Welsh poetry. If Welsh poetic techniques such as versions of *cynghanedd* appeared in his poetry, they did so either accidentally or through the influence of Gerard Manley Hopkins. Saunders Lewis was correct insofar as the "outward form" (25) of Thomas's poetry belonged to the English. But such poems as *"Fern Hill* and *Poem in October* and *In Memory of Ann Jones* . . . could only have been written by a poet profoundly at one with his own people and country'' (25). Prys-Jones followed Glyn Jones's common sense with a romantic view of Thomas's relationship with Welsh-language poetry: though he knew no Welsh and had no knowledge of Welsh prosody, ''these influences had always been in his environment: and substantially, perhaps, in his subconscious'' (27). This is a potentially alarming and wholly unconvincing example of osmosis and/or the collective unconscious.

Mathias, following Garlick, assimilated Thomas into an Anglo-Welsh poetic tradition centered on the seventeenth century. In describing *The Map of Love* in relation to the two earlier volumes, Mathias argued for the importance of Thomas's Welsh upbringing:

The Map of Love was not spread out in a Welsh dawn. It was the product of London, of lionisation, of exposure to new and not-so-wonderful influences. The spiritual conflict, the passion which burned sustainedly in his earlier work, faded slowly as the walls of Wales fell. (37)

Eventually, Mathias suggested, Thomas's writing problems returned him to Wales: ''Perhaps it was no more than instinct, the aborigine seeking cooling herbs for an overheated stomach, that brought him back to Laugharne'' (38). This might seem an odd view of such a sophisticated and worldly writer.

Two further important points also flicker through these commemorative articles. One is the insistence that Thomas was a careful and conscientious craftsman, a point made by Aneirin Talfan Davies in his account of Thomas as a broadcaster, and by Glyn Jones, who protested: ''The view that Dylan Thomas was a kind of irresponsible rhapsodist from whom poured effortlessly a spate of brilliant but largely unintelligible verse is no longer tenable. He was a careful and endlessly patient craftsman'' (25).

The other is the emphasis on Thomas's childlike qualities, strangely present even in Saunders Lewis's piece: ''We have lost the most splendid Englishspeaking child Wales has produced for centuries'' (9). Henry Treece considered Thomas to be

the Young Rip we all envy and wish we could be, but dare not. The enormous majority of us ''grow up'', get old and anxious and responsible. . . . But Dylan just remained himself, his honest scallywag self, and was inevitably destroyed, like all other perpetual boys.'' (19)

Prys-Jones's Dylan was ''the terrible boy with 'the lovely gift of the gab' '' (27) in whom ''there lay just beneath the surface—the clear, still waters of a child-like innocence'' (28).

Only Mathias developed such sentimental patronizing into a critical argument: Thomas moved from ''schoolboy flamboyance'' (31) to a later poetry, that of

Deaths and Entrances and after, in which a lost sense of place and familial security was countered by "a return to one sustained image—the image of childhood. . . . the only one sweet and powerful enough to father and hold in family so many others, central enough in his feeling to recapture the dynamic of his first writing" (38). Setting aside the piece by Aneirin Talfan Davies, which is a mainly factual account of Thomas as broadcaster, Mathias's essay is a refreshing contrast to the slight "appreciative" pieces that precede it. It may provoke objections: at the heart of Mathias's argument may be a narrow notion of Welshness. Nonetheless, almost uniquely, a Welsh literary figure examined texts and weighed relationships carefully in order to argue seriously that Thomas was "the last great Romantic poet" (39). In 1954 this was virtually the only essay by a Welshman to stand comparison with the weighty critical attention that had long been accorded to Thomas in the United States.

Because of the Mathias essay and because it brought together in tribute leading figures from both sides of the Welsh linguistic divide, the "Dylan Thomas Number" of *Dock Leaves* is a milestone in the Welsh section of Thomas's critical history. Sweetness and light, however, did not last long: two issues later Pennar Davies (the Davies Aberpennar of earlier criticism) attacked as overdone the adulation following Thomas's death.[41] Once again the attack was led by Welsh-speaking Wales: Thomas, "the irresponsible thumb-to-nose adolescent who was determined not to finish growing up" (15), was no more than "an interesting minor poet" (17). Criticism of Thomas in the *TLS* and in *Scrutiny* was not unfair. Thomas's merits as a poet had been greatly overstated, but, whatever his merits, there were finer poets writing in Welsh. Enter Kitchener Davies, in Pennar Davies's view a far more important poet than Thomas. Unlike Kitchener Davies, Thomas

did not address himself to the Welsh people or even seek to give a portrayal of Wales with anything like the loving care shown by many an English regional writer towards his region. He saw Wales from the outside and with the help of the distorting mirror provided by Caradoc Evans. . . . His picture of the Reverend Eli Jenkins seems to represent the sum total of his knowledge and appreciation of the vast heritage of Welsh literary culture. He made no serious attempt to acquaint himself with the language. . . . Dylan Thomas's art is certainly . . . no more Welsh than a supply of Idris Waters bought at Llareggub. (17)

His work "lacked moral substance" (16) and was never wholly free from "pretentious incoherence" (16), his "religious" gesturings were "devoid of moral affirmations" (16), his obscurity was "partly a matter of deliberate cultivation"(16).

Such charges are all too familiar, the depth of the hostility disturbing. To judge from such reviews, the Welsh-language literary world found it almost impossible to come to terms with the fact that modern English-speaking Wales had at last a writer whose high quality and international reputation validated and publicized Anglo-Welsh literature. What Welsh speakers feared was the increased self-confidence of English-speaking Wales, a fear implicit in Pennar Davies's denouncing of a Welsh politician of the day who suggested that Thomas's example made learning Welsh less important.

In 1956 John Ellis Williams reviewed a stage performance of *Under Milk Wood*. He praised Thomas's dramatic qualities and popular appeal but also used the review to attack John Malcolm Brinnin's book *Dylan Thomas in America* as "not worth the ink used in its printing."[42] The following year Raymond Garlick's editorial, part of which discussed Caitlin Thomas's memoir, *Leftover Life to Kill*, stressing the Thomases' "strange jealousy of each other" in "a sad book . . . heartrending,"[43] attacked the Movement as ludicrously overhyped. Both review and editorial are edgily defensive gestures in the face of Brinnin's presentation of Thomas as a dishonest drunk and the enormously influential Movement's rejection of Thomas as man and poet.

During the 1950s, despite the indignation of Williams and Garlick, Thomas's stock was low, in Wales no less than in England. This could seem particularly the case in Wales as Welsh writers sought to escape from his influence. Two of the most prominent Anglo-Welsh poets of the postwar period, Dannie Abse and Leslie Norris, each wrote first volumes heavily influenced by Thomas and then eliminated them from their literary histories.[44] Raymond Williams, Wales's most famous writer since Thomas, made a conscious decision that his fiction would avoid the verbal exuberance that, in his view, turned Welsh writers into garrulous eccentrics.[45] Likewise, the novelist Emyr Humphreys was concerned to "use as few words as possible" and so depart from a South Wales tradition (Humphreys is from North Wales) "where the flourishing of many words is considered to be the acme of 'the bard.' "[46] Welsh writing in English changed: it can be said that almost all after Dylan Thomas aspired to the condition of the Movement.

In 1959 *Dock Leaves* became the *Anglo-Welsh Review*. The latter continued to give space to old prejudices. Thus R. George Thomas, later to become a prominent Cardiff academic and a leading authority on Edward Thomas, reviewed E. W. Tedlock's *Dylan Thomas: The Legend and the Poet* (1960) and revived the "warbling woodnotes wild" view of Thomas as inspired innocent: "One wonders, with all respect, whether he really understood what he was doing himself."[47] The following year Terence Hawkes, also Cardiff based and with an even more substantial academic career ahead of him as a Shakespearean critic and literary theorist, reviewed Holbrook's *Llareggub Revisited*, ridiculed the Thomas industry, and echoed Pennar Davies's view (though Hawkes did not refer to it) that "Thomas is little more than a minor poet." More followed:

His pages are simpered over by the lovers of "beautiful words", the image-bibbers, the Rhiwbina romantics and Sketty scholars who know poetry is somehow connected with magic, and that the streets of South Wales ring nightly to the (beautifully sung) extempore verses of poets going home from the pit.

Of his poems, "less than a dozen are worth reading, let alone preserving."[48] The attack on sentimental Welshness and sentimental Welsh adulation of the sound of Thomas's work may have been well founded. But Hawkes's broad agreement with Holbrook and his insistence that "Dylan must be cut down to size" tend to eject baby with bathwater.

In 1961 Roland Mathias took over the editorship of the *Anglo-Welsh Review* from Raymond Garlick. He remained editor for fifteen years, during a period when books on Thomas, mainly but not exclusively from the United States, were beginning to appear. Time passing fostered objectivity; Mathias published a number of fine essays on Thomas by Welsh critics.

One such was by Anthony Conran,[49] an early contribution to a brilliant career, conducted mainly in Wales, as critic, poet, and translator. His study put its finger on the Welsh-language community's problems about Thomas's rise to fame. The rise of Anglo-Welsh writing reflected a decline in the speaking of Welsh and the end of Wales as a homogeneous community. A consequence of the latter, with the collapse of shared concerns that fostered the chaos of the time, was that "poetry degenerates into heroic self-worship" (12). Thomas, "arch-hero of the Anglo-Welsh" (12), engaged in a discourse with himself; his "early poems all ponder the life of an individual alone in a horrid world" (12). In this he reflected the condition of modern Wales, in which so many were driven in on themselves. Thomas's work illustrated

the Anglo-Welsh predicament: the poet is caught between two fires. He is neither English nor Welsh; neither a member of the anglicised middle-class, nor of the Welsh-speaking peasantry. Indeed, he may despise both. . . . What is there left for him to praise and mourn but his own self's legend, the glory of himself and the pathos of his bewilderment? (14–15)

In a country in which the preacher had replaced the priest, Thomas offered preaching, hence the appeal of his grand rhetorical flourishes. Two poems were great exceptions: "Especially when the October wind" and "After the funeral," the latter in particular. In both, in different ways, he achieved objectivity and escaped from himself.

Another essay was a further study by R. George Thomas. His theme was a recurring refrain in Thomas criticism: Thomas's first three volumes contained many poems that "are so personal—and even obscurely wilful in their private statements—that they stand as a permanent obstacle between the reader's understanding and the poet's intention in writing them." But the critic was here more patient than many of the earlier reviewers in separating the obscure from the difficult. He argued that several of the best early poems, examples being "The hand that signed the paper," "And death shall have no dominion," and "I have longed to move away," release meaning when "they are placed against that background of terror, pity and uncertainty which dominated the years before the second World War." The change in Thomas's poetry was due in part to his experiences as broadcaster and scriptwriter, through which he escaped from a wholly private self and was required to discipline his rhetoric, so that the later poetry succeeded in giving "expression to universal experiences which are readily accessible to every reader."[50]

A third essay was by Richard A. Davies, who identified a unifying theme in *Portrait*: the "gradual loss of courage and boldness, a consequent increase in fears and terrors." He gave detailed attention to that area of Thomas's work, the prose fiction, that had been comparatively neglected.[51] A fourth essay, by Peter Elfed Lewis, was on *Under Milk Wood*. This was the second of three essays by Lewis on Thomas's play for voices, building on detailed attention to the piece that began in 1959 with a seminal essay by Raymond Williams that suggested that the play's antecedents included Joyce's *Ulysses* and *King Lear*, and examined the various discourses in Thomas's radio play: narrative, dialogue, and song.[52] In his *Anglo-Welsh Review* essay Lewis argued that Thomas's work can only be properly understood if its true nature is recognized: it is more radio poem than radio play. His earlier essay argued that its nature as a play for voices had not been sufficiently taken into account. The third piece outlined antecedents and critical reception in drawing earlier work together into a statement that *Under Milk Wood* is not great literature but great radio.[53]

The *Anglo-Welsh Review* essays testify to a new spirit governing Welsh attention to Thomas's work. The writers were all graduates of the University of Wales during the postwar period who became university teachers. They examined old prejudices—particularly those concerning the Welsh language—with a new objectivity and as trained scholars and literary critics. Theirs is the approach that dominates the rest of this chapter.

Certainly it is the approach of other essays in other modern Welsh literary magazines. One of the latter was *Poetry Wales*, which published the first of Peter Lewis's three essays. In 1973 it published a further piece by R. George Thomas that examined the readership of Thomas's early works. R. George Thomas touched on the tension generated in the Welsh-language community by the rise of the Anglo-Welsh during the 1930s, and on that between Thomas and the politically conscious writing of the Auden group. Thomas was presented as a creation of the 1930s literary world, in which it was comparatively cheap to live and when, beyond reviewing, literary criticism was at a premium. There he was known only to a minority of intellectual readers. *Deaths and Entrances* made Thomas famous in a postwar world—expensive, dominated by the academy—with which he failed to come to terms. The concern with literary and historical context evident in R. George Thomas's earlier *Anglo-Welsh Review* essay was thus developed, a further indication of the increasing sophistication of Welsh critical attention.[54]

This piece by R. George Thomas and Peter Lewis's first essay on *Under Milk Wood* were both included in *Poetry Wales*'s "A Dylan Thomas Number" that in 1973 marked twenty years since Thomas's death. The number also contained detailed factual reminiscences of Thomas's work for the BBC by the radio producer Douglas Cleverdon and a short piece by Glyn Jones that in suggesting that Thomas's poetry "is the sort that benefits *least* by explanation. . . . When magic fails it cannot be made to work by explanation,"[55] in its Celtic vagueness now seems more gauche than perceptive. More in accordance with new rigor was Raymond Garlick's reexamination of the influence on Thomas of Donne and Herbert. Garlick's sense of a tradition of Welsh writing in English to which Thomas belongs was here more implied than stated, for his main concern was to explicate "Vision and Prayer" as a poem about birth and death without resurrection, in which emotion is contained by shape and poetic patterns.[56] In the same number Barbara Hardy wrote with similar detailed seriousness on the way in which deep human feeling can enter Thomas's generally abstract lyrics, offering, as one example, the close of "Over Sir John's Hill."[57] Roland Mathias's essay "A Niche for Dylan Thomas," later reprinted in *A Ride through the Wood*, is the number's outstanding study, a brilliant and provocative exploration of Wales and Welshness in Thomas's work.[58] It begins by referring to the hostility towards Thomas felt by many in Wales, particularly by Welsh speakers, stemming from their apprehension of "what was felt to be the anti-Welshness, the general disservice to Wales which Dylan's attitude had appeared to represent" (51). The relationship between Thomas and Wales was complex, considered Mathias, hence the starting point for his argument:

His own attitude to Wales was based first on deprivation and the clever hostility that sometimes comes from it, then on a gradual realization of loss and a disillusionment with the ambitions that had created that loss (in his parents and himself). (52)

Mathias regarded Thomas as an example of cultural dissociation, cut off from "real" Welsh community life that was underpinned by the Welsh-speaking nonconformist tradition. Thomas rejected the traditional Welsh idea of the poet as a member of that community who spoke to his fellows out of experience and learning. Rather, he adopted the traditional romantic English notion of the poet as the man apart and subjectively obsessed. As for learning, though he read much in his teens, he ignored academic work, did not develop intellectually, read little after his teens, and ever after lacked the resources of "an educated and thoughtful mind" (64). Without roots and adequate resources, he retreated from a world, literary and adult, in which he felt dislocated, inferior, and overwhelmed. He returned to Wales to write about "childhood and its memories, the countryside and its 'holy' or sacramental qualities, and death. There is almost nothing about the matter of living as an adult" (71). Even the finest poems of his finest period—which include "Fern Hill," "Holy Spring," and "A Winter's Tale"—"demonstrate such a narrowing and closing of poetic interest that the end is clearly foreshadowed" (74).

Later Welsh critics, including Conran and the present writer, have taken issue with Mathias's argument. This might seem to be weakened by his odd assumption that the only "real" Wales is the traditional one he described. A counter-argument is that Thomas is preeminently the poet of middle-class suburbia—an equally "real" Wales—and important because of this. That said, all considerations of Thomas and Wales must engage with Mathias's powerful criticism. He moved those considerations beyond prejudice and polemic. The "Dylan Thomas Number" of *Poetry Wales* is further evidence that Welsh criticism was increasingly inhabiting the uplands of academic precision and objectivity.

The demise of the *Anglo-Welsh Review* and the emergence of the *New Welsh Review* in 1988 did not, however, wholly further that inhabiting. Under the editorship of Robin Reeves, the latter has taken a less academic approach to Thomas. This is very evident from the populism of its "Dylan Thomas Special" in 1992.[59] A defensive editorial referred to Welsh ambivalence towards Thomas, to the "myth" that he was other than disciplined and hardworking, and to the "irritating" notions that Thomas is the only poet of merit Wales has produced and that Wales is somehow too provincial properly to appreciate him, all to some extent a refighting of battles already won on the Welsh academic front. Too much of the "Special" is a mixed bag of confused criticism, adulation, and anecdotage, plus some discussion of Thomas's work on film. After such a contradictory final paragraph as that of John Idris Jones on *Under Milk Wood*,

It fails as a whole because it lacks stylistic cohesiveness, has no intrinsic development of character and theme and has a serious structural imbalance. Its tone varies from the sublime to the ridiculous; and worse, it is at times pantomimical, trivial and smutty.... It is vivid, moving and beautiful, and therefore it succeeds as a work of art,[60]

John Ackerman's bland praise, and Aeronwy Thomas's chatty account of a return visit to Laugharne, pieces by Peter Stead and Richard Jones come as blessed intellectual relief. Stead demolished Karl Francis's film *Rebecca's Daughters*—"a disgrace ... this awful film"[61]—and Richard Jones gave George Tremlett's biography *Dylan Thomas: In the Mercy of His Means* a balanced notice.[62]

In 1994 a younger critic, Katie Gramich, reviewed new editions of Thomas's work. She made four urgent points. The first drew attention, almost for the first time, to the unreconstructed "male bias" of Thomas's attitude to women in his work. The second took issue with Daniel Jones's claim that Thomas's work broadly divides into private poetry and public prose, arguing that both, quoting Leslie Norris, "came from the same source." The third protested against the involvement, often as editors, of friends and relatives in the publication of Thomas's work and called for more scholarly input (the case for this last being made immediately following Gramich's piece: Aeron Thomas reviewed Ferris's *Caitlin* and Jonathan Fryer's *Dylan*, virtually ignoring the latter in order to attack Ferris for being too hard on her mother). The fourth was that Thomas's character and life should not affect judgment of the works. Gramich's informed modern viewpoint suggested modern issues and was impatient with old approaches.[63] What it did not succeed in doing was to change the emphasis in the *New Welsh*

Review's approach to Thomas. In its "Swansea Special" of 1995 the two short pieces on Thomas—on school-magazine contributions and on memories of Dylan Thomas at dame-school—interesting and thoughtful though they were, both eschewed serious critical engagement for biographical interest.

Though serious critical engagement has remained in short supply in Welsh literary magazines, this lack has been countered, to a great extent, elsewhere. In 1963 T. H. Jones published the first critical book on Thomas written by a Welshman, a useful survey that was concerned to separate the man from the works and that insisted that Thomas wrote several great poems, including "Fern Hill" and "A Refusal to Mourn." But as these two titles perhaps indicate, Jones's views are conventional: for example, Thomas was Welsh but not Welsh-speaking; his work was a progress to greater clarity and objectivity. An acute review of Jones's book by Brian Way suggested that Jones was good on individual poems but evaded larger issues and never established a coherent critical position. He contributed to

the impasse in Thomas criticism. There are three main positions in this area: sour, undiscriminating detraction, represented by David Holbrook; an ecstatic, undiscriminating acceptance which has produced some of the most extraordinary excesses of American myth-criticism; and an acceptance of Thomas's own vatic or bardic projection of himself.

Jones, argued Way, was too inclined to accept the third position uncritically, tending to agree that academic training would have harmed Thomas's genius, that social irresponsibility was necessary to protect his gift, and that he wisely stayed aloof from the propagandism of the 1930s to concentrate on "universals." Jones, Way continued, was one of Thomas's anti-intellectual supporters, romanticizing the life as if to criticize it would affect the quality of the work. Way's account is a useful piece of ground clearing, even though his conclusions are as conventional as Jones's and reflect Roland Mathias's influence: Thomas had extraordinary command of a child's vision but failed to handle adult experience because he evaded adult responsibility.[64]

During the 1960s three books by Welsh authors between them pointed to the two main trends in later Thomas criticism. Aneirin Talfan Davies's *Dylan: Druid of the Broken Body* (1964) considered Thomas as a religious poet, one who even in his early work "discerned the sacramental nature of the universe."[65] Thomas moved from a Welsh nonconformist upbringing, evident in the religious imagery of his early poems, more and more towards Roman Catholicism as the result of the influence of Hopkins and of an interest in liturgy fostered by the parish priest at Laugharne. Davies's Thomas is one to whom his Welsh upbringing was important, but univeral concerns even more so.

The other books are John Ackerman's *Dylan Thomas: His Life and Work* (1964) and Glyn Jones's *The Dragon Has Two Tongues* (1968). Both are seminal works. The former is a detailed scholarly discussion of Thomas's Welsh background. Ackerman claimed Thomas for Wales, stressing the influence of his father, the puritan Nonconformist conscience and chapel experience, left-wing political feelings, Welsh poetic techniques, what Ackerman believed to be the influence of Welsh working-class routine, and what he described as a ''Celtic'' familiarity with the divine. The book is all too open to the criticisms that it offers a narrow stereotype of Welshness and lacks critical edge. As one reviewer put it, Ackerman generalized too much about Wales and evaded the difficult poems and stories.[66] But he replaced previous gestures at Thomas's Welshness and its effect on his work with detailed investigation. His conclusion, echoing Mathias, that Thomas's ''needs as an artist became increasingly rooted in his love for Wales''[67] has been widely influential.

Glyn Jones's book—one of the first substantial studies of Anglo-Welsh writing—is more discursive and less scholarly, more belles lettres than literary criticism. His concept of Welshness is also narrowly conceived, and he failed to free himself from familiar prejudice. Thus Thomas the Anglo-Welsh writer was dissociated from fundamental aspects of what Jones regarded as ''proper'' Welshness, such as links with the Welsh language and a sense of the poet as part of the community. Jones was troubled by Thomas's lack of clarity and by the way he lived his life. What attracted him to Thomas was also conventional, a ''Celtic twilight'' romanticism as suspect as Ackerman's narrow Welshness: ''the best of Dylan's early poems are pure sensation, they have in fact achieved the condition of music.''[68] Whereas Talfan Davies moved Thomas outward into mainstream English religious poetry, both Ackerman and Jones sought to reclaim him for Wales.

In 1965 Constantine FitzGibbon published the authorized biography based on much newly available material. The following year he edited a selection of Thomas's letters, the first since *Letters to Vernon Watkins* (1957). FitzGibbon's biography was superseded in 1977 by Paul Ferris's fuller *Dylan Thomas*. This argued that Thomas manufactured a character, at once poet and clown, to enable him to cope with life, and thus, disorientated from his real self and unsure what was real and what was assumed, he was trapped and eventually destroyed both by his assumed persona and by a world the overwhelming nature of which had made that persona necessary. Himself a Swansea man, Ferris understood Thomas's background but seemed out of sympathy with both man and works. Nonetheless, because of its masterly research and use of much new material, his is now the standard biography. It has been followed by Ferris's edition of Thomas's *Collected Letters* (1985), which corrected FitzGibbon's often inaccurate texts and set new scholarly standards, and by *Caitlin: The Life of Caitlin Thomas* (1993), Ferris's superb study of the marriage that concluded that Thomas's downfall was hastened by his wife's behavior. This stream of biographical work has created new interest in Thomas as fact replaces legend; it has also supplied both background and basic material for the scholarly editing of Thomas's works, the Welsh contribution to which can now be noted.

This contribution began in 1971 with Walford Davies's valuable edition of *Early Prose Writings*, reprinting scarce items from *Swansea Grammar School*

Magazine and other uncollected early material, and with Daniel Jones's edition of *The Poems*. Jones's edition reprints over one hundred poems not included in *Collected Poems, 1934–1952*, but its editorial principles are suspect, as John Pikoulis pointed out in a fierce attack in the *Anglo-Welsh Review*. He demonstrated that the edition is not complete, that Daniel Jones failed to distinguish clearly between finished and unrevised poems, and that the chronology of composition is faulty because Jones sometimes placed a poem according to the date of its first draft, even when—for example, in the case of "Why east wind chills"—the draft was extensively revised years later for publication.[69]

In 1974 Walford Davies brought out the first annotated edition of Thomas's poems; a revised edition followed in 1993. These contain valuable exegeses, though the longer and most difficult poems are not included. An important introduction catches up ideas developed in Walford Davies's books on Thomas, considered later.

The high point of the sequence of editing remains *Collected Poems, 1934–1953*, edited by Walford Davies with the English-born Canadian academic Ralph Maud. This is superbly edited and is the standard edition. It is not, however, strictly a collected edition: it contains only the contents of Thomas's collected edition of 1953 plus "Paper and Sticks" and two unfinished poems. But the texts are authoritatively edited, dated, contextualized, and selectively annotated. John Ackerman has edited Thomas's filmscripts, restoring accessibility to many rare items but with insufficient production detail. Davies and Maud have brought out a new edition of *Under Milk Wood*, invaluable for its apparatus and for a substantial introduction by Walford Davies that draws together previous work on the play, but damaged by "reading edition" ambitions that, as has been noted, have led to a major unscholarly alteration to the text, the conflating, without any textual authority, of the two narrative voices.

This stream of life writing and scholarly editing is one of two major Welsh contributions to Thomas studies, one that continues to transform our understanding of relationships within Thomas's work as well as with his historical context. The second, a series of critical studies, is enabled by the first. Both have freed themselves from the parochial prejudice and hostility and sour carping—particularly that generated by tensions between English and Welsh—that mark the early stages of the Welsh critical history. The critical studies link with those few earlier exceptions—for example, essays by Conran and Mathias—to form a distinguished tradition.

Three of these studies—mainly of the poetry—are by Walford Davies, the leading Thomas scholar. His approach can only be called magisterial, in the sense that he offered no narrow special pleading but sought to place Thomas in a matrix of suggestive, rather than ambivalent, associations. This is clearly seen in his introduction to the revised edition of *Selected Poems*. Walford Davies noted Thomas's Welshness and the extent to which knowledge of the (Welsh and English) literary and historical context can illuminate the poems. He had no time for the "pure poetry" or "pure sound" school of Thomas appreciators.

Rather, though alive to the danger of thinning complex effects through paraphrasing, in his view meaning is a constant: "In Thomas's poems the realities
of birth, sex, and death are referentially and very concretely there."[70] The stress
on the "concrete" and on the "thinginess" of Thomas's poetry points to his
concern with craftsmanship, with the poet as maker.

The same approach was adopted in the same author's *Dylan Thomas* (1972;
revised, 1990), in which he charted a progress towards the triumph of "Fern
Hill." In citing Thomas's most famous poem as one of wholeness and organic
affirmation, the greater clarity of which enables the personal to become generally
available, he did not wholly avoid the conventional view that Thomas eventually
escaped from clotted obscurity to the sunlit uplands of conventional English
lyricism. But crucial here, and anything but conventional, is the reference to
"too much verbal glamour"[71] in the later poems, those after "Fern Hill." This
connects with a published lecture of 1986 in which Walford Davies wrote:

And the later poems are indeed generally more accessible. That accessibility involved
what was in many ways a withdrawal from the dense imagistic techniques of Modernism.
In the last phase of all (1946–1953) Thomas is a fairly conventional poet meditating on
the realistic landscapes of West Wales. And the poems of that period remain attractive
and often moving. But it is also possible to feel that they lack the creative textural
tensions that come from the very density of the early style. It is in that density that I
feel the trapped ambiguities and contradictions of experience to have been most effectively and affectively caught.[72]

The 1990 revision of *Dylan Thomas* made two important changes. First,
greater emphasis was placed on Thomas's poems about World War II, poetry
about noncombatants that was "the most positive of the poems produced by
that war . . . [and] closer to the real temper of the time—to the resilience and
the guts."[73] Second, there was greater stress on Thomas's Welshness and what
he may have learned of the Welsh poetic tradition from friends such as Glyn
Jones and Aneirin Talfan Davies. There was also more stress on Thomas's
osmotic Welshness (already noted): that is, on what he absorbed, as it were
despite himself, through his upbringing. In this we can hear echoes of 1930s
attitudes to Thomas. We can certainly detect the whiff of a new zeitgeist: the
concern, mainly on the part of Welsh-speaking nationalists, to conceive of Wales
as a Welsh-language-centered entity and so, as far as possible, to effect links
even with monoglot English-speaking Thomas. It must also be said that Walford
Davies's concern to effect these links was accompanied by a willingness to
recognize Thomas's place in mainstream English literature. Implicitly, Walford
Davies's is the "interstitial perspective," even though he did not use that term.

His second book (a critical study of Thomas's poetry written for the Open
University) has remained the best introduction to Thomas's poetry. It is invaluable for its close reading of a number of Thomas's poems and for its emphasis
on the poems about poetry. Despite its introductory function, the volume is an

important contribution to Thomas studies for three reasons. One is its further detailed discussion of the complexities of Thomas's Welshness. Walford Davies here was guarded about the influence on Thomas of Welsh-language poetry and instead advocated attention to the "un-English" qualities of his writing, such as the slightly odd use of particular words and grammatical structures and the extent to which Thomas can be seen as "preserving his [Welsh identity] . . . by subverting the cultural expectations normally associated with the English tradition" (106). Second, accepting that being drawn towards English literature can be cultural gain, Walford Davies was illuminating on Thomas's place within the English tradition. He examined and clarified the difference between Thomas and the surrealists and symbolists of the 1930s by stressing the strong narrative element even in the early poetry, which we now see leads to "Fern Hill." He commented valuably on the influence of modernism on "the discontinuity of disparate images" (112) in Thomas's work, and the "irreducibility" (112) of its "concreteness" (113). Further, he rejected oversimplified accounts of Thomas in relation to Audenesque social poets—let alone the idea that Thomas's work had nothing to do with the world in which he wrote it—by emphasizing the way in which "social" metaphors are embedded in Thomas's work and ways in which the poems are shaped by and comment on the historical context. Thus, of his 1930s poetry:

He shows a remarkable resistance to that decade's fashion for socially and politically committed poetry. . . . [Yet] his emphasis on a basically physical concept of human energy and potential may still be related (if only in reaction) to the 1930s' sense of political and social collapse.[74]

Thomas was a social poet of a special kind.

The sections on Dylan Thomas in Anthony Conran's *The Cost of Strangeness* (1982) reinforce this sense of the social. Conran made a brilliant and unexpected comparison of Thomas with John Betjeman to emphasize their common middle-classness and suburbanism. He studied Thomas as "the poet of suburban man standing on the threshold of power," before "the suburbs lost their soul to Education and Television." For Conran,

Eighteen Poems are not simply expressive of the suburbs of Swansea, nor yet simply of Anglo-Welsh revolt against the Chapel and the Welsh Way of Life. They also register a mood, a polarity, a revolution in sensibility, of the British middle class as a whole.

Conran's second chapter on Thomas considered "After the funeral" not only as a poem of "full social reality," but also in relation to the Welsh-language tradition of praise-poetry.[75] He thus, like Walford Davies, placed Thomas in that tense interstice between Wales and England.

John Ackerman knows much about Thomas, but his *Dylan Thomas Companion* (1991) is a missed opportunity. Its sanitized account of the life and uncritical approach to the work hardly build on earlier work and seem strangely out of place in modern Thomas studies. The general thrust of these studies, particularly the concern with the Welsh/English relationship, was continued by M. Wynn Thomas in *Internal Difference* (1992). He qualified Mathias's account of a Dylan Thomas saddened by cultural dislocation:

Instead of feeling disinherited and deracinated . . . he simply wanted to be closer to what, from his point of view, seemed to be the cultivated centre of things; and his self-consciously avant-garde adolescent poetry was his passport to sophistication. In this sense his provincialism was the very making of his genius."[76]

Wynn Thomas also argued that Dylan Thomas ignored Welsh social realities for a concern with the helplessness of the individual within eternal natural processes. Thus in the fine "After the funeral," Ann Jones was detached from social realities and turned into a pagan priestess of nature. Paradoxically, as M. Wynn Thomas also noted, this was, in a very basic sense, a peasant outlook.

In 1986 the present writer examined Thomas as Welsh, bourgeois, and suburban, seeking to build on Conran to demonstrate how that upbringing informed Thomas's work and, in particular, how its restrictive patterns of social behavior, the order and control of contemporary middle-class life, were mirrored within the poems in the relationship between tight structures and emotional force, and in the themes of a number of the stories.[77] Two later essays, also by the present writer, are among the most recent by a Welsh critic. Both are in *Welsh Writing in English: A Yearbook of Critical Essays*, the first scholarly journal devoted to the field.[78] Both, like the 1986 essay, are concerned with the relationship between Thomas's work and the sociohistorical context. The first studies Thomas's relationship with his father and its effect on Thomas's poetry to suggest a concern in the latter with social mobility and class tension. The second examines Thomas's obsession with the Great War in his juvenilia of the 1920s, the poetry and prose of the 1930s, and his broadcasts of the early 1940s. It argues that proper awareness of this obsession generates new readings of important poems, notably of "And death shall have no dominion," which can be read as a poem about the Great War. All three essays insist on the social thrust of Thomas's poetry and on his suburban middle-class sensibility.

Welsh criticism of Dylan Thomas has not yet brought to bear on its subject the full force of modern literary theory, even though its influence can be detected. The historicizing tendency of recent work is one example. The interest in reader expectations in relation to Thomas's often unpredictable syntax evident in Walford Davies's work has similar implications. Other postmodernist perspectives will doubtless be adopted. What seems certain is that as "English literature" continues to lose its monolithic quality, and the limitations of postcolonial discourse for understanding the relationships between British literatures become ever more apparent, Welsh writing in English will require more theoretical attention. As this volume's section on "Fern Hill" has sought to show, a reassessment and resiting of Dylan Thomas's work will almost certainly follow.

NOTES

1. The Listener [J. D. Williams], "Our Young Poets," *South Wales Evening Post*, 19 November 1934: 4; The Listener [J. D. Williams], "Gossip of the Day: Poems of Dylan Thomas," 1 January 1935: 4.

2. A. Spencer Vaughan-Thomas, "Significance of Dylan Thomas's '18 Poems,'" *Herald of Wales*, 12 January 1935: 6. *Cynghanedd* depends on sound relationships between the two halves of a line of poetry. *Gorphwsfa*, the correct spelling of which is *gorphwysfa*, is the pause or caesura between the two halves.

3. J. D. Williams, review of *Twenty-five Poems, Herald of Wales*, 19 September 1936: 1, 12.

4. Charles Fisher, review of *The Map of Love, Herald of Wales*, 26 August 1939: 4.

5. Charles Fisher, review of *Portrait of the Artist as a Young Dog, South Wales Evening Post*, 26 April 1940: 4.

6. Dilys Rowe, "Place of Dylan Thomas in Modern Poetry," *South Wales Evening Post*, 6 April 1946: 3.

7. John Ormond Thomas, review of *Collected Poems, 1934–1952, South Wales Evening Post*, 8 November 1952: 4.

8. D. H. I. Powell, "The Words and Music of 'Under Milk Wood': Dylan Thomas's Last Masterpiece," *South Wales Evening Post*, 6 March 1954: 4; D. H. I. Powell, "The Mystical Prose by a Master of Poetry: *A Prospect of the Sea*," *South Wales Evening Post*, 13 August 1955: 4.

9. J. Gwyn Griffiths, "Was Dylan's Vision 'Catholic?'" *South Wales Evening Post*, 11 July 1964: 4.

10. A. T. G. Edwards, review of *Twenty-five Poems, Western Mail*, 10 September 1936: 10.

11. A. T. G. Edwards, review of *The Map of Love, Western Mail*, 24 August 1939: 9.

12. A. T. G. Edwards, review of *Portrait of the Artist as a Young Dog, Western Mail*, 4 April 1940: 7.

13. T. Gwynn Jones, "The Modern Trend in Welsh Poetry," *Western Mail*, 19 July 1939: 11.

14. For the letters from Davies and Heseltine, see *Western Mail*, 8 August 1939: 9; 10 August 1939: 9; 15 August 1939: 9; 22 August 1939: 11. At this time the image of Wales in London was much influenced by plays by Jack Jones and Emlyn Williams, which stereotyped for commercial effect.

15. For the letters from Keidrych Rhys, see *Western Mail*, 3 August 1939: 9; 17 August 1939: 9; 23 August 1939: 9. Iorweth C. Peate (1901–82) was a prominent nationalist who became the first curator of the Welsh Folk Museum.

16. Huw Menai, letter, *Western Mail*, 30 August 1939: 9.

17. Shinkins Abercwmboi, letter, *Western Mail*, 31 August 1939: 9.

18. A. G. Prys-Jones, review of *Death and Entrances, Western Mail*, 15 May 1946: 2.

19. A. G. Prys-Jones, review of *Collected Poems, 1934–1952, Western Mail*, 10 November 1952: 2.

20. Gwyn Jones, review of *Under Milk Wood, Western Mail*, 17 March 1954: 6.

21. D. L. Evans, letter, *Western Mail*, 23 January 1954: 6.

22. Nigel Heseltine, review of *Twenty-five Poems, Wales* 2 (August 1937): 74–75.

23. Saunders Lewis, *Is there an Anglo-Welsh Literature?* (Caerdydd: Guild of Graduates of the University of Wales, 1939), 9, 5.

24. Davies Aberpennar, review of *The Map of Love, Wales* 11 (Winter 1939–40): 306–8.

25. W. Moelwyn Merchant, "The Relevance of the Anglo-Welsh," *Wales*, 2nd ser. 1 (July 1943): 17–19.

26. John Idris Jones, letter to the editor, *Wales*, n.s. 8 (April 1959): 74.

27. Glyn Jones, review of *The Map of Love, Welsh Review* 2, no. 3 (1939): 179–80.

28. W. D. Thomas, review of *Modern Welsh Poetry*, ed. Keidrych Rhys, *Welsh Review* 3, no. 3 (September 1944): 220.

29. Beryl Jones, review of *Deaths and Entrances, Welsh Review* 5, no. 2 (June 1946): 145–50.

30. Michael Williams, "Welsh Voices in the Short Story," *Welsh Review* 4, no. 4 (Winter 1947): 295, 296.

31. E. Glyn Lewis, "Dylan Thomas," *Welsh Review* 7, no. 4 (Winter 1948): 270, 272–3, 273, 276, 279.

32. Gwyn Jones, *Essays and Studies* 6 (1953): 108, 110.

33. Gwyn Jones, "Welsh Dylan," *Adelphi*, 1954: 108, 115, 116.

34. Ioan Bowen Rees, "Wales and the Anglo-Welsh," *Welsh Anvil* 4 (1952): 23.

35. Aneirin Talfan Davies, "A Question of Language," *Welsh Anvil* 5 (1953): 19, 28.

36. Bobi Jones, "Imitations in Death," *Welsh Anvil* 7 (1955): 85, 86. Jones was concurring with *Scrutiny* attacks on Thomas. See chapter 17.

37. A. G. Prys-Jones, "Anglo-Welsh Poetry," *Dock Leaves* 2, no. 5 (May 1951): 8.

38. A. R. Williams, "A Dictionary for Dylan Thomas," *Dock Leaves* 3, no. 9 (Winter 1952): 31.

39. Aneirin Talfan Davies, "Obituary Statement," *Dock Leaves* 4, no. 12 (Winter 1953): 6–7.

40. *Dock Leaves* 5, no. 13 (Spring 1954): 1–41. "Editorial," 1–5; Louis MacNeice, "A Dylan Thomas Award," [includes Anthony Conran, "For Dylan Thomas" (poem)], 6–7; Saunders Lewis, "Dylan Thomas," 8–9; Aneirin Talfan Davies, "The Golden Echo," 10–17; Henry Treece, "Chalk Sketch for a Genius," 18–23; Glyn Jones, "Dylan Thomas and Welsh," 24–25; A. G. Prys-Jones, "Death Shall Have No Dominion," 26–29; Roland Mathias, "A Merry Manshape (or Dylan Thomas at a distance)," 30–39; R. N. G., review of *Under Milk Wood* and Henry Treece, *Dylan Thomas: "Dog Among the Fairies,"* 40–41.

41. Pennar Davies, "Sober Reflections on Dylan Thomas," *Dock Leaves* 5, no. 15 (Winter 1954): 13–17.

42. John Ellis Williams, review of a stage performance of *Under Milk Wood, Dock Leaves* 7, no. 20 (Winter 1956): 51.

43. Raymond Garlick, editorial, *Dock Leaves* 8, no. 21 (Summer 1957): 6–8.

44. See Dannie Abse, *After Every Green Thing* (1948), and Leslie Norris, *Tongue of Beauty* (1941) and *Poems* (1944). Abse's volume is never included in his own bibliographies; Norris's *Collected Poems* (1996) reprints only one poem from his first two volumes, and this because it was reprinted as part of a later sequence. The poem, interestingly, is "At the Grave of Dylan Thomas."

45. Raymond Williams, *Politics and Letters: Interviews with New Left Review* (London: Verso, 1979), 279.

46. Quoted in Emyr Humphreys, *Toy Epic*, ed. M. Wynn Thomas (Bridgend: Seren Books, 1989), 12.

47. R. George Thomas, review of E. W. Tedlock (ed.), *Dylan Thomas: The Legend and the Poet, Anglo-Welsh Review* 11, no. 27 (1961): 55.

48. Terence Hawkes, review of David Holbrook, *Llaryeggub Revisited* 12, no. 30 (1962): 68, 69, 70.

49. Anthony Conran, "The English Poet in Wales," *Anglo-Welsh Review* 10, no. 26 (1960): 11–21.

50. R. George Thomas, "Bard on a Raised Hearth: Dylan Thomas and His Craft," *Anglo-Welsh Review* 12, no. 30 (1962): 11, 14, 16.

51. Richard A. Davies, "Dylan Thomas's Image of the 'Young Dog' in the *Portrait*," *Anglo-Welsh Review* 26 (1977): 68–72.

52. Raymond Wilson, "Dylan Thomas's Play for Voices," *Critical Quarterly* 1 (1959): 18–26.

53. Respectively, Peter Elfed Lewis, "*Under Milk Wood* as Radio Poem," *Anglo-Welsh Review* 64 (1979): 74–90; "Return Journey to *Under Milk Wood*," *Poetry Wales* 9 (1973): 27–38; "The Radio Road to Llareggub," in *British Radio Drama*, ed. John Drakakis (Cambridge: Cambridge University Press, 1981), 72–110.

54. R. George Thomas, "Dylan Thomas and Some Early Readers," *Poetry Wales* 9 (1973): 3–19.

55. Glyn Jones, "*18 Poems* Again," *Poetry Wales* 9 (1973): 23.

56. Raymond Garlick, "The Shapes of Thought," *Poetry Wales* 9 (1973): 40–48.

57. Barbara Hardy, "The Personal and the Impersonal in Some of Dylan Thomas's Lyrics," *Poetry Wales* 9 (1973): 75–83.

58. Roland Mathias, "A Niche for Dylan Thomas," *Poetry Wales* 9 (1973): 51–74.

59. "Dylan Thomas Special," *New Welsh Review* 16 (Spring 1992): 1–29.

60. John Idris Jones, "*Under Milk Wood*" *New Welsh Review* 16 (Spring 1992): 9.

61. Peter Stead, "Rebecca's Seed Falls on Stony Ground," *New Welsh Review* 16 (Spring 1992): 12.

62. Richard Jones, "Delinquent Free Spirit or Astute Operator?" *New Welsh Review* 16 (Spring 1992): 24–27.

63. Katie Gramich, "Dylan Thomas: Forty Years On," *New Welsh Review* 24 (Spring 1994): 30–32.

64. Brian Way, review of T. H. Jones, *Dylan Thomas, Anglo-Welsh Review* 14, no. 33 (1964): 119–20.

65. Aneirin Talfan Davies, *Dylan: Druid of the Broken Body* (London: Dent, 1964), 20.

66. Kent Thompson, review of John Ackerman, *Dylan Thomas: His Life and Work, Anglo-Welsh Review* 14, no. 34 (Winter 1964–65): 113–14.

67. John Ackerman, *Dylan Thomas: His Life and Work* (1964; Basingstoke: Macmillan, 1991), 183.

68. Glyn Jones, *The Dragon Has Two Tongues* (London: Dent, 1968), 184.

69. John Pikoulis, "On Editing Dylan Thomas," *Anglo-Welsh Review* 21, no. 48 (1972): 115–28.

70. Walford Davies, introduction, *Selected Poems*, by Dylan Thomas (1974; rev. Everyman ed., London: Dent, 1993), xxxi.

71. Walford Davies, *Dylan Thomas*, Writers of Wales (1972; rev. ed., Cardiff: University of Wales Press, 1990), 62.

72. Walford Davies, *Dylan Thomas: The Poet in His Chains* (Swansea: University College of Swansea, 1986), 26.

73. Walford Davies, *Dylan Thomas*, Writers of Wales, 42.

74. Walford Davies, *Dylan Thomas*, Open University Guide, 106, 112–13, 45–46.

75. Anthony Conran, *The Cost of Strangeness* (Llandysul: Gomer Press, 1982), 178, 179, 177, 187.

76. M. Wynn Thomas, *Internal Difference* (Cardiff: University of Wales Press, 1992), 31.

77. James A. Davies, "A Picnic in the Orchard: Dylan Thomas's Wales," in *Wales, the Imagined Nation*, ed. Tony Curtis (Bridgend: Poetry Wales Press, 1986), 45–65.

78. James A. Davies, " 'Hamlet on his father's coral': Dylan Thomas and Paternal Influence," *Welsh Writing in English: A Yearbook of Critical Essays* 1 (1995): 52–61; " 'A Mental Militarist': Dylan Thomas and the Great War," *Welsh Writing in English* 2 (1996): 62–81.

17

Dylan Thomas in England

In 1993 an article on Dylan Thomas by Philip A. Lahey described its aim as follows:

This article, in seeking to answer the argument from biography, and the corresponding animosity towards the poetry based on a moral objection to the man, will examine the texts as the primary documents in an attempt to assess the poetry.[1]

That such a statement should still be made forty years after Thomas's death is a reminder that, as has been seen in the *TLS* reviews by Grigson and Rawson, English literary criticism of Thomas has been dominated by fierce attacks, extreme reactions, that too often link man and works. Fortunately for Thomas, his work has been championed by some of the century's leading critics, among them William Empson and John Bayley, though even their writings have struggled against the hostile tide.

"Our eunuch dreams," published in *New Verse* in April 1934, drew the first important critical response. It was resoundingly negative: Edith Sitwell described the poem as "An appalling affair! . . . The idea is really of no importance" and condemned "the thick squelching, cloying, muddy substance" of the diction.[2] The charge of having little to say is a recurring one, as has been seen. So, too, are the objection to language—a gesture at Thomas's obscurity—and the angry tone, as if responding to a personal affront.

This attack came only a few months before the publication of *18 Poems*. In general Thomas's first book was still well received, though reviewers worried about obscurity. Desmond Hawkins was Thomas's first metropolitan reviewer, finding him to be an original voice, the first since the Auden group: Thomas used "an unborrowed language, without excluding anything that has preceded him. . . . Thomas's poetry is personal or universal, but not social. He is therefore purer than the fashionable."[3] Personal poetry, pure poetry, become distracting legacies.

After the publication of *18 Poems* Edith Sitwell changed her mind about

Thomas's poetry. An article in *Life and Letters Today*, written jointly with Robert Herring, cited his "remarkable promise" but warned about narrowness, meaning here his recurring bodily metaphors. The same issue contained the first seven sonnets of the "Altarwise" sequence; the notes on contributors refer to the "favourable impression" created by Thomas's first volume.[4] In 1936 Sitwell went further: *18 Poems* "contained many beauties," but a more recent poem, "A grief ago," "shows an enormous advance." It was

so beautiful and moving for all its obscurities. Here, I said to myself, is a young man who has every likelihood of becoming a great poet, if only he will work hard enough at subduing his obscurity. I know of no young poet of our time whose poetic gifts are on such great lines.[5]

Her review of *Twenty-five Poems* began:

A year ago, the present reviewer became convinced that a new poet had arisen who shows every promise of greatness. The work of this young man . . . is on a huge scale, both in theme and structurally—his themes are the mystery and holiness of all forms and aspects of life.

She made much of Thomas's religious sense, praised the "superb" form of many of the poems, and, though she worried about their "difficulty, which is largely the result of the intense concentration of each phrase, packed with meaning," responded to the "poignant and moving beauty" even of the most difficult image. Particular praise was given to the "Altarwise" sonnet sequence, in which "the theme treats of the dark soul in the midst of the death-like state of the modern world," a tentative gesture towards context. Sitwell concluded, echoing her earlier review, "I could not name one poet of this, the youngest generation, who shows so great a promise, and even so great an achievement."[6]

Privately, Thomas was uneasy about Sitwell's propensity to interpret his poems as reactions to contemporary life, but he was quick to recognize that she found his work attractive because she considered it to be, as he told her, like her own, "right outside the nasty schools and the clever things one (me) doesn't want to understand, like surrealism and Cambridge quarterlies and Communism and the Pope of Rome."[7] Thomas was a kindred spirit. On his part he recognized the importance to him of the connection. As Ferris noted, the *Sunday Times* review made him well known in literary circles and caused the first printing of *Twenty-five Poems* to sell out.[8]

This success occurred despite murmurs from elsewhere. For example, Michael Roberts, also writing in the *London Mercury*, found *Twenty-five Poems* at times "a mere riot of noise" because of uncontrolled "purely verbal associations."[9] In the American magazine *Poetry*, Geoffrey Grigson flexed his muscles in "A Letter from England." Grigson, the early supporter become implacable enemy and, of course, the editor of the influential and prestigious *New Verse*, let rip:

"My opinion of Mr. Dylan Thomas's new *Twenty-five Poems* . . . must be honest—that twenty-four twenty-fifths of them are psychopathological nonsense but done with a remarkable ineptitude of technique."[10]

Until 1939 and *The Map of Love*, apart from general murmurings about obscurity, often linked to Thomas's surrealistic tendencies, the only English response of note, apart from that of the *TLS*, was that of Irish-born Louis NacNeice in 1938. His complaint about obscurity and incoherence was tempered slightly by an insistence that Thomas's writing had more humanity than surrealism proper. But his general conclusion had a Grigsonite edge more ad hominem than literary-critical: "He is like a drunk man speaking wildly but rhythmically, pouring out a series of nonsense images . . . [the] message being adolescence."[11] Until *The Map of Love* Edith Sitwell was Thomas's only English champion with literary substance.

Despite publication being overshadowed by the start of World War II, *The Map of Love* received a number of reviews. Two are typical. One was in the *Listener*, which contrasted Thomas's work with the emphasis on the intellect in such contemporary poetry as that by Eliot and Auden: Thomas

is a bard, he has no university education, he does not think intellectually, he expresses elemental passions and extreme conditions of human existence, birth, death, despair, violence, in an enlarged and primitive Welsh landscape. His obscurity cannot be puzzled out; it is the darkness of drunken rhetoric. He is an unique poet, and at the age of 24 he has succeeded in creating a rhetorical language of great power, which is impassioned, austere, and serious.

"After the funeral" was praised: "Where the occasion is simple and clear . . . the result is magnificent."[12] The other was by Hugh Gordon Porteous. It is an odd affair: Porteous played with the book's title—"A map is a representation of surface features. To snatch and fix the living surface is a Welsh gift"—mocked the Augustus John portrait that served as frontispiece, and presented a Thomas who had gained a public by mastering "a few tricks of verbal and metaphorical violence" before, illogically, recommending the book.[13] Both reviews offer early examples of the anti-Welsh prejudice and stereotyping that were later to intensify.

More considerable voices joined the debate. Edwin Muir was uncertain about Thomas and distracted by "the 'natural magic' which Arnold attributed to the Celtic genius." Despite the obscurity, he found "lines of extraordinary beauty and imaginative force."[14] Herbert Read was more confident, believing that "immaturities have now entirely disappeared." Though "the verse-form seems sometimes to cramp the syntax, and the punctuation of the verse is often so arbitrary that it would be clearer with none," yet this third volume demonstrated "poetic genius." Further:

It is mainly a poetry of the elemental physical experience: birth, copulation, death. But not entirely: there are poems, such as No. 7, "The spire cranes", which are quite abstract, or arabesque, in their beauty. The birth and death poems are not less absolute in their beauty, but they have reverberations in sentiment which add another dimension. I know of no poem since Hopkins which has the pathetic intensity of the elegy "In Memory of Ann Jones". . . . These poems cannot be reviewed; they can only be acclaimed.[15]

As will be seen, the first hostile stirrings of *Scrutiny* reviewers began at about this time. Those apart, the first substantial work to be published in England was, alas, two essays in "New Apocalypse" publications. Even though Thomas always kept his distance from this group of wildly romantic minor writers reacting against Auden's "classicism," the two essays, despite some shrewdness about Thomas's work, effected a damaging association. One was by Henry Treece, who argued for a distinction between Thomas's work and surrealism in that the former had a degree of intellectual control.[16] The other was by G. S. Fraser, who suggested that Thomas, as a neoromantic concerned with social disintegration, had links with the "New Apocalypse" group.[17]

Horizon, which under Cyril Connolly's editorship became the decade's leading literary magazine, began life in 1940. Its first notice of Thomas was a review of *The Map of Love* by archenemy Geoffrey Grigson. Relatively speaking, this was a balanced assessment: Thomas's poems, he considered, were still very much about himself, but there was now some talk of love other than self-love. In support, he quoted two lines from "After the funeral." He continued through slightly gritted teeth: the volume "still contains ripe nonsense which pretends to be sensual wisdom; but the poems are better written, and sound less monotonous. Whether a better and saner poetry will emerge from these poems . . . I do not know."[18] In May 1940 *Horizon* printed "There was a saviour" with the editorial comment that it was "governed by a kind of wild bleak inspiration" and that Thomas "resembles a kind of mad hit-or-miss experimental scientist who may at any moment either split the atom or produce from his laboratory a few test-tubes fizzing with coloured water."[19] The line of vituperative metaphor begins to lengthen.

In a swing to the opposite extreme, in November 1940 *Horizon* published "The Poetry of Dylan Thomas" by Francis Scarfe, poet, critic, and academic, at that time the most substantial essay on Dylan Thomas to be published in England.[20] It took Thomas seriously, finding the poetry difficult but suggesting ways of proceeding, engaging in detail with some of Thomas's most problematic poems, such as the "Altarwise" sonnets. Scarfe argued that the poetry could be understood in relation to James Joyce, the Bible, and Freud, meaning that Thomas used many of Joyce's tricks with language, much biblical mythology, and Freud's psychopathology. Scarfe found meaning and thus had little time for "pure poetry": for example, he considered Thomas to be much concerned with "the reconciling of the creative and destructive elements of sex." Scarfe also found poetic form and narrative line. He was on Thomas's side, but not uncritically, having reservations about what he called the "overlaying of images" in some of the poems. He also questioned Thomas's originality: "his personal rhythms,'' for example, ''are not unusual when compared with those of Hop-kins.'' With an eye on Grigson, who favored the Auden group, Scarfe suggested that Thomas must be assessed for what he was, a plea that many critics of Thomas hardly heed:

Dylan Thomas is fundamentally a poet of the feelings, and is not a visual poet. He does not see clearly, and consequently is a cuckoo in the nest of the *New Verse* observation poets. His main object is to feel clearly, which he has not yet achieved. . . . His future depends on an enlarging of his simple vision of the sexual basis of life, and it is to be hoped that he will not abandon his essential subject.

We need not agree with all Scarfe's judgments to recognize the injection of much-needed objectivity, free of anti-Welsh prejudice, ad hominem transposi-tions, and class positioning, into the increasingly polemical beginnings of this section of the critical history. Here at last, ''now and in England,'' was consid-ered work of a kind that was appearing in the United States.

Horizon was to publish eleven of Thomas's poems, six during 1945, for which he received the ''Horizon Prize.''[21] It had moved a long way from Grigson and ''test-tubes fizzing,'' as is also evident from a Stephen Spender essay during 1946. Spender became a strong admirer of Thomas's poetry, and a generous one in that Thomas did not much like him and had slated Spender's *Vienna* in a review in *New Verse*.[22] Spender's admiration was important to Thomas; though the support of such figures as Edith Sitwell and Herbert Read was invaluable, both were of an older generation, and the former was notably eccentric. Spen-der—later, like Thomas, a target of the Movement—was, as a member of the Auden group and a founder of *Horizon*, at the center of London literary life. His essay described Thomas's early work as that of ''another 'opaque' poet who writes poetry for poetry's sake,'' the obscurity stemming from the lack of ''any strong principle of selection.'' Such poems were ''often just collections of won-derful poetic insights, sustained by no unifying thought or experience behind them.'' But, Spender continued, Thomas gained much from his war work and had developed new rhythms, often close to speech rhythms, ''slightly empha-sizing and conventionalizing them.''[23] In *Poetry since 1939*, his survey for the British Council, he went further in regarding Thomas as ''a poet of whom, at times, we can use the word 'genius.' '' He placed Thomas as part of

a reaction . . . away from a conscious and intellectual style of writing towards the invol-untary, the mysterious, the word-intoxicated, the romantic and the Celtic. . . . Dylan Tho-mas . . . is a ''bardic'' poet . . . an elemental writer dealing with ideas and images which seem on the verge of disintegrating into a formless chaos; they are saved by a simple and grandiose structure and by Thomas's commanding and picturesque poetic person-ality.

. . . In 1943 he began publishing poems again . . . These poems are undoubtedly his greatest achievement. The verboseness of his early work has disappeared. . . . He uses language with a power he has never displayed before. And he has invented new forms of stanza which are likely to have a lasting influence on the future of English poetry.

Thomas is a poet who commands the admiration of all contemporary English poets.[24]

This is high praise and a welcome shift from "poetry for poetry's sake" to "ideas," even though Thomas (and we) may well have had reservations about the lack of conscious control implicit in "involuntary" and the anti-Welsh prejudice in the Arnoldian stereotyping of the Celtic imagination.

Two anonymous notices in the *Listener* during the 1940s each illustrate continuing extremes. The first, of *Deaths and Entrances*, considered that

it is probable that not one of his contemporaries has been responsible for so much loose and fatuous writing—by others. Reviewers have tended to hedge over the poems in *Deaths and Entrances*, acclaiming their authentic genius but finding themselves unable to analyse them with any real confidence or to relate them to any school or influence. Mr. Thomas must simply be regarded as a phenomenon; he exists, he writes, and the result is a poetry that has all the marks of greatness.

The reviewer begged to differ, accepting that Thomas was "a remarkable, if wayward, poet," but, nonetheless, able to be precise about content: the theme of the volume was "innocence regained," and the poems embodied "the thread between reason and imagination."[25]

The second reviewed Treece's *Dylan Thomas: "Dog among the Fairies,"* the first book-length study. The reviewer noted the romantic impulse behind Thomas's poetry and that obscurity was his "most obvious quality." He noted also that Treece wrote mainly on the early poetry, and considered that this was because

Deaths and Entrances (1946) is an uneven volume in which the earlier facility gives place too often to mere exercise, coupled with a less acceptable obscurity. But the exceptions are among Thomas's very best poetry; and these, besides exploring new techniques, contain a new element of objectivity.[26]

Here is yet another extreme reaction, what amounts to the dismissing of almost all Thomas's work except a few of the later more approachable poems, such as "Poem in October" and "Fern Hill."

Though Treece's book was first published in 1949, Treece had prepared much of it during the late 1930s, which explains his concentration on the earlier work. It remains useful for suggestive comments on Thomas and surrealism and Thomas and his Welsh background, and, of course, as an example of a late 1930s reaction. Treece sought to establish Thomas as the most gifted and original of modern poets. His approach, however, was patronizing and irritating: Thomas was "the least intellectual poet we have had this century" and was linked— doubtless to Thomas's anger—to Treece's "New Apocalypse" group. The cause was not helped by Treece's membership in that school of obfuscatory literary criticism that insisted that Thomas's obscurity was either deliberate or the result of semiautomatic writing, and that the simplest, most readily approachable poems were the best. The book has a subtext that hints at Grigsonian prejudice against engaging with Thomas on his own terms. Thomas was doubtless comforted that the book received a very mixed reception. Spender, for example, reviewed Treece as a partisan writer whose book nevertheless evaded the difficult work and failed to add to general understanding.[27]

During the late 1940s Grigson's main attack came in 1947 in the "little magazine" *Polemic*. This is the much-reprinted "How Much Me Now Your Acrobatics Amaze," hatred masquerading as literary criticism. He began by castigating George Barker, Spender, and Edith Sitwell for purveying "romance without reason," formless writing greeted by "a hallelujah of reviews." This brought him to Dylan Thomas, before whose work "even the conventional critics have begun abasing themselves." He continued: "The self in Mr. Thomas's poems seems inhuman and glandular. Or rather like water and mud and fumes mixed in a volcanic mud-hole, in a young land . . . [a] meaningless hot sprawl of mud." Thomas did not *say* anything; even *Deaths and Entrances*

shows, not a theme, not meditation, but simply obsession;—obsession with birth, death, and love, and obsession mainly in a muddle of images with only the frailest ineptitude of structure. Rhyme schemes begin and break. Rhythms start off and falter into incoherent prose. Image repeats image in a tautology of meaning.

As always in these attacks, Grigson judged Thomas with a closed mind, a strangely personal sense of poetic decorum, stranger still when he turned to Thomas's lines. Thus he quoted the opening of the moving "Lie still, sleep becalmed" as an example of "ineptitude" because Thomas used "afloat" and "sheet" as rhymes. Grigson remained oblivious to the poem's emotional power, intensified by being almost unbearably close to breaking through the last vestiges of control suggested by these imperfect sound links. Grigson was too concerned to twist the knife, as when, knowing Thomas's anger at being so accused, he described, oddly given its comparative transparency, the opening of "A Refusal to Mourn" as "nearly automatic, his words come bubbling in an automatic muddle." In general, Thomas's was "the poetry of a child, volcanic, and unreasoning," part of the current slide into "idiot romance." Here, as elsewhere, what appalls is the violence of the language.[28]

Kenneth Allott offered more reasoned criticism in one of the most influential anthologies of the postwar period. It includes four of Thomas's poems: "A grief ago," "In Memory of Ann Jones," "The hunchback in the park," and "Poem in October." Allott's introduction quoted Grigson's comment in "How Much Me Now" that contemporary "romance" was "self-indulgent and liquescent" as part of a general statement that in the 1940s there had been much "loose, obscure, slapdash verse-making." As for Thomas,

[He] has in the 'forties come a long way from the riddling darkness of some of his earlier poems in the direction of greater discipline over his very considerable gifts, and in the direction of a continuous, rather than a spasmodic, attempt at narrative meaning.

This owes much to Grigson, as is clear from the editorial notes on Thomas's poems. In these, Allott summed up the extremes of critical opinion regarding Thomas's work and, though he shrewdly recognized that Grigson's attacks on Thomas were, in part, in defence of Auden, again nodded approvingly at the archenemy's objections to Thomas "for his neglect of a continuous line of meaning and for being, at times, fantastic and slovenly." "A grief ago" was offered by Allott as salutary example, "full of towering phrases and with a real structure, but arbitrarily obscure for lack of a central theme or any clear impulse on the poet's part beyond that of wishing to produce a poem." Allott concluded that Thomas had "moved in his later work towards the decorum of a more continuous 'narrative' of meaning," the use of "decorum" indicating judgment in terms of what might be called a traditional norm and a gesture towards increasingly dominant Movement respectability.[29]

By far the most valuable critical support during the 1940s and after was provided by William Empson, now, of course, generally recognized as one of this century's seminal critical minds. His reviews and short pieces on Thomas are fine examples of profound common sense. The earliest was a review of *Selected Writings*, the first postwar American edition of Thomas's poetry and short fiction, in February 1947. It began negatively: Empson objected to the selection—he would have liked more early poems—and to John Sweeney's "well-informed introduction" for praising Thomas's shift "from the womb and the grave to the world of light." Empson commented on the latter:

I am not sure that the change need be described so rosily. Anyone who starts bang off with a highly original and within its limits perfect technique is bound to have trouble in getting out of the limits; Dylan Thomas has been courageous in refusing to repeat his successes, and I expect this will repay in the end as it deserves to. But so far I like the earlier poems better. They have such concentration that they seem to be constructed of exploding bombs.

Then followed close and revealing analysis of the final lines of the "Altarwise by owl-light" sequence, an example of "poetry you can live with, because it opens on you gradually." It also contained "a good deal of horror," which Empson also found in the later work, an example being "Vision and Prayer." The change might not be as great as Sweeney had suggested, though Empson also considered that Thomas moved beyond "the mighty-line technique" of the earlier work, in which "the thought is so packed that the mighty lines are very detachable," to such a poem as "direct and enchanting" "Fern Hill," the kind of thing that he had hitherto done only in prose; and the technical invention of an elaborate but unrhymed stanza form is just what it needed. But I am not sure about "turning towards the world of light"; it is a lament for lost youth. . . . The change is one of technique rather than of mood.

In fact, the attractions of that "world of light" were not beneficial: "A Winter's Tale" failed because Thomas deserted realism for the ecstatic, "turning to the world of light to be sure, as much as you could wish." In the course of a short review Empson demonstrated the value of working at even the most difficult of Thomas's poems, rejected simplifications about development, and pointed tactfully to the problems of willed optimism in the later work.[30]

Empson followed the review with a short study of "A Refusal to Mourn."[31] It opened, "The critics agree with hardly a dissenting voice that Dylan Thomas is a splendid poet, but it is unusual for anyone to undertake to say what he means, as I am doing here." Empson offered candid general statements about Thomas's work: his suggestiveness was traditional, though Thomas might pile up more suggestions than most; such writing was resistant to paraphrasing; he had a small number of "fundamental ideas"; "what stick in our minds are single rich phrases rather than a connected argument," though *Deaths and Entrances* "has a higher proportion of poems which you would remember as units, though it is still using the same concentrated technique." He then brilliantly explicated "A Refusal to Mourn," particularly concerned, as might be expected, to tease out ambiguities, to stress beauties, and to indicate the "pervading pantheism" of Thomas's ideas. What impresses is the sheer sanity of Empson's literary criticism, its freedom from class, national, or aesthetic prejudice. One of the strongest arguments for Thomas's importance is that his work demonstrably fascinated and rewarded a great mind.

Viewed from the 1990s, Empson's attention is one guarantee of Thomas's status. In the late 1940s, however, though it seems a weighty riposte to, say, Grigsonian irritations, it could do little to counter the main source of hostility to Thomas in the years surrounding his death. This was the Movement. Its effect on Thomas can be gauged from the "Prologue" to *Collected Poems, 1934–1952*, the defensive self-consciousness, stereotypical "bardic" quality, and parodic bravado of which, as reactions to Movement hostility, have already been discussed in detail. As he wrote the poem, Thomas knew that the enemies were massing at the Boat House gate.

As early as 1949 *Oxford Poetry*, of which Kingsley Amis was a joint editor, rigorously excluded poems written under the "harmful influence"[32] of Dylan Thomas. During the summer of 1953 John Wain organized a series of radio programs featuring poetry written on what we now recognize as Movement principles. In that same year G. S. Fraser and Ian Fletcher brought out *Springtime*, an anthology that demonstrated, at least to Donald Davie, that others shared his own "indignant distaste for the Dylan Thomas or George Barker sort of poetry which had been *de rigueur* in London for a decade."[33]

Thomas's *Collected Poems, 1934–1952* was published in 1952 to considerable acclaim. Philip Toynbee, in the *Observer*, described Thomas as "the greatest living poet";[34] Cyril Connolly in the *Sunday Times* and Stephen Spender in the *Spectator* were equally adulatory. This was high and typical praise from the nonacademic world; the publication of *Collected Poems* was one of the last occasions when a serious and difficult poet was championed by representatives of the general reader. Apart from Empson and one or two other lesser exceptions, so far as *Collected Poems* was concerned, the opinion of what might be called "higher academia" was invariably unfavorable but not, at that time, generally influential. The main example is that of the Cambridge journal, *Scrutiny*.

From *Portrait of the Artist as a Young Dog* onward, *Scrutiny* had castigated Thomas, in a manner now all too familiar, for being, as W. H. Mellors put it, "the overgrown schoolboy," and for "the immaturity of adolescence." Mellors also attacked Thomas's assumption of "the mantle of distraught romantic genius" and added, grimly: "His Welsh nonconformist background effectively sets off this posture in that it encourages the bardic gesture, the Dionysiac vision, the rapture of hell-fire." Wolf Mankowitz accused Thomas of "playing at games" and "clever-boy pranks." For R. G. Cox, "Thomas's romantic subjectivism looks for the most part like an excuse to avoid the trouble of precise communication." Robin Mayhead went even further in referring to Thomas's "self-indulgent religiosity . . . pseudo-liturgical verbal juggling" and "a downright disgusting self-righteousness." Mayhead considered that in Thomas's work "without any disrespectful feelings towards the country of the poet's origin— the idea of the bard counts for not a little." That idea, he was quick to assure his readers, had little to do with intelligence.[35]

Scrutiny exerted a powerful influence on Movement thinking, not only because Donald Davie, Thom Gunn, and D. J. Enright had been at Cambridge, but also because all three acknowledged the powerful effect upon them, as teacher and critic, of *Scrutiny*'s chief editor, F. R. Leavis, Fellow of Downing College, Cambridge, who, at that time, bestrode the academic literary-critical world like a colossus. *Scrutiny*'s aesthetic objections to Thomas—his lack of seriousness and intellectual grip, the absence of clarity, and his all-pervading self-indulgent emotionalism—form the intrusive subtext of much Movement response to Thomas's work. This can be seen in the review of *Collected Poems, 1934–1952* by John Wain, then a young lecturer at Reading University.

Wain praised Thomas—"he is a fine, bold, original, and strong poet"—then damned him with strong criticism of his "disastrously limited subject matter" (childhood, the viscera, religion) and his tendency to "quasi-automatic" writing that suggested that he did not really care about meaning. We may be glad to be told that Thomas was not a divinely inspired simpleton; rather, he had a great deal of "ordinary common-or-garden cleverness and capability of the bread-winning, examination-passing type."[36] In these reluctant statements we catch echoes of *Scrutiny*'s references to Thomas's obscurity and "clever-boy pranks."

Similar points—some now famous or notorious—were made by Wain's

Movement colleagues. Thus Donald Davie, in *Articulate Energy*, attacked Thomas for exploiting what Davie called "a pseudo-syntax. Formally correct, his syntax cannot mime, as it offers to do, a movement of the mind."[37] In any case, Davie continued, Thomas obscured his poems with images. This last point was also implied by Kingsley Amis, who concluded: "For long stretches very little can be extricated beyond a general air of bustling wildness allied to a vague sexiness or religiosity of subject-matter."[38] D. J. Enright was even more scorching: Thomas's poetry lacked thought because he forgot that "poetry is like the human body in needing bones as well as flesh and blood."[39] In Robert Conquest's introduction to *New Lines*, with its stress on the need for poetry to have "the necessary intellectual component" and to refuse "to abandon a rational structure and comprehensible language,"[40] Dylan Thomas was obviously crushed between the lines.

To quote Blake Morrison, the Movement prized "rationalism, realism, empiricism."[41] John Lehmann described it as well as anyone as having "a dry anti-romantic flavour, and using the contrast or conflict of a conversational tone and an exacting technical pattern."[42] In the eyes of some members of the Movement, Thomas's late and extreme romantic manner made him a necessary evil.

To say, carefully, "some members" is to emphasize that the Movement's response to Thomas was not homogeneous. Indeed, John Wain's review catches something of the general ambivalence: in mixing praise and criticism Wain at times threw himself firmly onto the fence. The others knew which side of the fence they were on but were not all on the same side all the time. Thus Davie, despite his strictures, could still refer to Dylan Thomas as "the greatest talent of the generation before ours."[43]

Philip Larkin is another case in point. His relationship with Thomas, never more than slight, began at a reading in Oxford at which Thomas read hilarious parodies of contemporary poets and then two of his own poems, "which seem very good," Larkin commented to J. B. Sutton. A year later Larkin was subjecting a visitor "to a daily battery of jazz & Dylan Thomas—he likes the latter." Only in letters to Amis did Larkin's attitude change, and then not completely: "I think there is no man in England at now who can 'stick words into us like pins' . . . like he can," he wrote, rather ungrammatically, in 1947, and then complained about Thomas's obscurity and "shocking influence." Many years later he wrote to Amis about Thomas's letters, which he "read with almost supernatural boredom," and praised Amis's parodies of Thomas in *The Old Devils*, which recalled "that wonderful stuff from *That Uncertain Feeling*."

Here, of course, is the letter writer as chameleon, for elsewhere, in two responses to Thomas's death, the emotional charge seems more intense, more sincere. As Larkin wrote to Patsy Stone, in a reaction already quoted in part: "I can't believe D. T. is truly dead. It seems absurd. Three people [the others were T. S. Eliot and W. H. Auden] who've altered the face of poetry, & the *youngest* has to die." Three years later he told Vernon Watkins "how shocked [he] had been (like everyone else) by Dylan Thomas's death."[44]

The Movement's ambivalence towards Thomas's work may well have stemmed in part from the uneasy feeling—one that Grigson would have done well to take on board—that poetry of consequence cannot be judged simply in terms of reactionary principles, and that adherence to those principles could not counter Thomas's ability to "stick words into us like pins." It might also have owed something to the sense Davie and others certainly had, that Thomas had been a victim: the literary/social world had destroyed the great talent; the innocent provincial had been corrupted by the great city. Thomas was, in Enright's marvellous analogy, a "Bubbles who fell among literary touts."[45] He fell, of course, with some eagerness.

The view of Thomas as the victim of big bad literary London raises questions of origin. Here we might be reminded of *Scrutiny*'s hostility to the Welsh sources of Thomas's faults and its stereotyping of Thomas as the Welsh Nonconformist preacher-bard. D. J. Enright echoed this in his seminal anthology, *Poets of the 1950s*, in which he commended the richness of Thomas's imagination, then cited its "deficiency in intellectual conviction" and poetry's "own kind of logic" before asserting that "*Welsh* rhetoric seems a deadly enemy to all varieties of logic, even the poetic."[46]

The Movement had strong Welsh connections. Donald Davie, for instance, described his wife's Plymouth family as having been "profoundly matriarchal." But her father was a Welsh shipwright, and her home was "seen less as the domain of her mother than of her father."[47] Though we tend traditionally to think of Wales as a matriarchal society, Davie took the opposite view. "Barnsley, 1966" is a poem about his own father, and he commented that if Yorkshire had been Wales his father would have dominated as a "Word-spinner, teller of tales." Davie was glad this had not been the case and that his father was not to be remembered as a Dylanesque stereotype:

> I should not have liked him rich,
> Post-prandial, confident, bawdy.

In "Monmouthshire," strangely included in that very English volume *The Shires*, Davie described his marriage as "Anglo-Welsh" and ends: "Our sons are a quarter Welsh if they care to think so."[48] The edge apparent in this final line—in a poem that uses the term "Anglo-Welsh" in a nonliterary way as meaning half-English, half-Welsh, as distinct from Welsh writing in English— is at best sardonic, at worst close to contempt. This attitude may well stem in part from what appears to have been an uneasy relationship with his father-in-law; in turn, it may well have influenced Davie's view of "that Welsh miracle, half-prodigy half-charlatan, the doomed and disgusting, self-diagnosing and at last self-denouncing Dylan Thomas." There may also have been jealousy of the way Thomas—and Brendan Behan later—commanded the literary headlines while Davie's own work was little noticed. Further, there was, as Davie later realized, a fatal tendency to stereotype:

What I did not sufficiently allow for is the pressure exerted by the dominant British culture, English, so as to distort exponents of the other British cultures—Welsh and Irish and Scottish—into becoming just what Thomas and Behan became: licensed buffoons and zanies, stage-Welshmen and stage-Irishmen, rewarded by the English for exposing all over again the picturesque incapacity of the Brython or the Gael when released from England's apron-strings.[49]

The "apron-strings" reference has echoes of John Wain and *Scrutiny*'s charges of immaturity and, here again, does not wholly escape the patronizing. But the key lines, penetrating to the heart of Davie's and the Movement's attitude to Dylan Thomas and reminding us that whatever sympathy existed for what happened to Thomas's life was more than outweighed by the hostility to what he represented as poet and by being Welsh, are in the *Shires* poem on "Herefordshire." In wartime—the year is 1944—Davie walks with a friend down country roads near Hay, on the English-Welsh border and, conscious of the looming Welsh hills, moves from thoughts of German barbarism to a more localised threat. He comments feelingly: "with atavistic Englishness I saw / the black Black Mountains menacing our acres."[50]

Larkin's Welsh connections were very different; they involved influence and friendship. Together with the influence of Dylan Thomas—and Larkin would not be unique among writers in resenting that which, he may have felt, delayed the finding of his own voice—a second influence (part of a long friendship) was that of Vernon Watkins. He so impressed the young Larkin that "his likes became my likes, his methods my methods, or attempted methods. At the same time I could never quite expel from my mind a certain dubiety, a faint sense of being in the wrong galley."[51] The galley was the one marked "ecstatic" and "bardic." Despite Larkin's aesthetic unease, an affectionate friendship persisted and on occasion brought Larkin to Swansea.

It is surely significant that Larkin's closest encounters with Welsh poetry were via links with two—so-to-say—rhapsodic bards, one of whom (Watkins) hero-worshipped the other (Thomas). One effect of such encounters is the generous selection from Thomas, and from Watkins at his most bardic, in the *Oxford Book of Twentieth-Century English Verse*, which Larkin edited in 1973. But the background to these links appears to be overt prejudice of a kind that now, following the publication of *Selected Letters*, we recognize to be typical of the man and is here evident in two enigmatic quotations. The first is from Larkin's first description of Watkins, in a letter to J. B. Sutton: "He is nearly 40 & has just published a book of poems which I don't like an awful lot, but I like him enormously. . . . He is also an intimate friend of Dylan Thomas. I hope someday you can meet him. He's Welsh. [. . .]" The second is a remark about R. S. Thomas, "Arse Thomas" in Larkin's letters: "Our friend Arsewipe Thomas suddenly was led into my room one afternoon last week, and stood without moving or speaking: he seems pretty hard going. Not noticeably Welsh, which is one comfort.[. . .]"[52] The tone of both statements, we might think, makes

Welshness something of a problem for Larkin. But "enigmatic" must be stressed because of the editor's deletion marks, which probably indicate further derogatory comments. There seems no other point to them.

One reason why we should not be surprised at Larkin's anti-Welsh feeling is his friendship with Kingsley Amis, which also took Larkin to Wales. Amis lectured at the University College of Swansea from 1949 to 1961 and retained strong links with the area until his death. His dislike of Thomas's work was long-standing and of two kinds. First, there were the aesthetic objections proffered by all good Movement men. These are summed up in Amis's poem "Against Romanticism," which argues vehemently against garishly anarchic and oversensual language tricked out with abstractions—Amis's notion of Thomas's poetry—and for plain imagery.[53] Even more vehement are objections to the man: Thomas as charlatan inspired two of Amis's best-known fictional characters. The pretentiously bardic Gareth Probert in *That Uncertain Feeling* gave Amis the opportunity for viciously amusing parody both of the poetry and of the Captain Cat sequences in *Under Milk Wood*. *The Old Devils* also savaged Thomas and the Dylan industry through reactions to Bryden, the dead Welsh poet who is now an all-things-to-all-men tourist attraction. All this emerges more directly in Amis's essay "Thomas the Rhymer," where bardic Thomas is dismissed as worthy of attention only from those who, Amis commented with heavy irony, "hanker after something sublimer than thinking."

But Amis went further. The poem sequence "Evans Country," based on Swansea, is a harsh and patronizing attack on what he regarded as the philistine Welsh. Amis suggested nastily that Swansea's city center, cited by some architects as the worst in the country, in its ugliness reflected its inhabitants' "Permanent tendencies of heart and mind."[54]

The Movement's view of Thomas resulted from a combination of aesthetic disgust based on a misunderstanding of Thomas's work and of extreme anti-Welsh prejudice. The first was, of course, fuelled by the second, and the second was fuelled by the fact that Thomas was the only Welsh writer to mount a serious challenge to an English/metropolitan hegemony. Animus strengthens the willingness to stereotype: to be a Welsh poet is to be like Dylan Thomas, and this means being rural-lyrical, ecstatic, inspired, bardic, undisciplined, immature. Years later John Wain was still purveying similar ideas:

Thomas wrote in the way he did because he was a Welshman. . . . [Thomas and Yeats] are Celtic in their basic attitudes to poetry. That is, they have no dealings with English understatement or English casualness; they love form, they love to sing; they love striking imagery; they respond ecstatically to natural sights and sounds. . . . [Thomas] was a poet of the hill and the estuary.[55]

To complete the picture, all we need is "bardic," and that, of course, is heavily implied.

In England, certainly, and possibly in Wales, Thomas's reputation has been slow to recover from the Movement's onslaught. The persisting hostile reviews in the *TLS* are evidence of this. Thomas's cause was further undermined by Robert Graves's influential Clark Lectures of 1954–55, part of which were published in *Essays in Criticism* and later as *The Crowning Privilege*. Graves did not hesitate to provide his Cambridge audience with anti-Welsh prejudice, making what would have been regarded, at that time, as demeaning comparisons of a member of a Welsh choir with an Egyptian fellah and a Majorcan shepherd. All work instinctively, stated Graves; the Welshman sings, but "seldom really cares what the tune is." Similarly, "Dylan Thomas was drunk with melody, and what the words were he cared not. He was eloquent, and what cause he was pleading, he cared not. . . . Dylan's golden voice could persuade his listeners that he was divulging ineffable secrets," even though what he wrote was nonsense.[56]

In 1961 David Holbrook, the Leavisite Cambridge don, began what, after that of the Movement, has been the most influential attack. The first salvo was in his essay on Thomas in *The Pelican Guide to English Literature*, the series that did much to form the literary opinions of generations of British undergraduates. He wrote to put the record straight, fearing the pernicious effect of those who took Thomas seriously as an artist. For Holbrook in 1961, Thomas suffered from "a disabling amorality, leading towards the trivial and ultimately the inarticulate. In metaphor he is impotent." His work reflected "his own failure to grow up and accept adult reality." He lacked sympathy, empathy, and compassion; his "repulsive disdain of humanity" led to the nasty and salacious laughter of *Under Milk Wood*, "watered-down Joyce" that offered no more than "a spiteful childish moral anarchy."[57]

During the following year Holbrook published *Llareggub Revisited*, which even more vehemently reiterated objections and added to the list. The main charge was one that has persisted from the very first reactions to Thomas's published poems, blindly ignoring numerous refutations through exegesis and put bluntly and inaccurately by Holbrook: "42 of the 90 poems in . . . *Collected Poems* [are] meaningless, or [yield] no meaning worth possessing even with the most considerable effort." Much stress was laid on Thomas's infantilism: "His poetry is as much baby-talk." All moved towards the Leavisite statement: "The lack of true criticism of life in his writing—of a true search for the vital reality— makes him unable to offer a true vitality of language." His work illustrated a "failure to develop mature powers—to come to terms with adult sex, with death, time and circumstances."[58] Lahey may well have been right in complaining that Holbrook regarded Thomas as a "psychopath."[59] What is apparent is that a line of moral seriousness links Leavis, the Movement, and Holbrook. What is certain is that Holbrook's criticism blurs the line between literary criticism and ad hominem viciousness. Further, in his use of the Welsh word *hwyl*, used to describe both Thomas's brand of too-often-persuasive emotionalism—Elder Olson was offered as an example of a critic "hypnotized by Thomas's *hwyl*"—and the irrational "indulgence in the emotional satisfactions" of Thomas's poetry by the same critic, as well as an attack on "Welsh scholar-apologists," E. Glyn Lewis being cited, Holbrook sustained English prejudice against the Welsh that the Movement did so much to foster.[60]

The effect of constant and influential criticism is apparent in the apologetic manner even of reviews by those drawn to Thomas's work. One example is reviews in the *Listener*, beginning with Raymond Preston's mixed review of *Collected Poems, 1934–1952*. Preston opined that "Mr. Thomas has left a mass of incorrigible rubbish in his stuffed drawers, but remains the most alive, and growing, of English poets of my generation." "Poem in October" and "Over Sir John's Hill" were praised for being "the very opposite of the mechanical formalism which Mr. Thomas has too often displayed." Preston concluded: "Tempted to vaporous mumbo-jumbo, he nevertheless obeys the command of the psalmist, to sing to the Lord a new song."[61] Implicit in this was yet more stereotyping of Welshness in terms of chapel going and a tendency to be wordily windy. This is close to the prejudice implicit—in the abusive fashion of the period—in the *Listener*'s anonymous review of *Under Milk Wood*. This notice, after stating that Thomas's "most essential genius was for lightness and comedy and a deceptively wandering fantasy. Tragic feelings he could rarely sustain," observed that the change from "Llareggub" to "Llaregyb" was "a piece of nasty genteelism. . . . It is literary welshing, with a vengeance."[62] Today this last sentence may well be actionable.

The *Listener* reviews are, from Thomas's point of view, at best equivocal. Thus Bernard Bergonzi, reviewing William Tindall's *Reader's Guide to Dylan Thomas*, wondered about Tindall's exegetical approach, "as though Professor Tindall had accepted a bet to prove that some sort of paraphrasable meaning could be extracted from every poem," and commended Holbrook for at least attempting to provide what Thomas's poetry needed so badly: "some attempt at real assessment and responsible judgement."[63] The ubiquitous and persistent Geoffrey Grigson was never lacking in prejudice. In a *New Statesman* notice of books by John Ackerman and Aneirin Talfan Davies, he commented that the writers of "Anglo-Wales" had a sense of inadequacy that led them to "promote the poems in the glow of the legend." That inadequacy was because "not entirely Anglo, they are not entirely Wales. They fear contempt from either side. They require, in a milieu notably provincial and mediocre, a genius dependent neither on local nor English recognition." He considered that Ackerman was out to claim for Wales, at all costs, "a poet who farted so contemptuously in the face of that kind of Welshness" (that is, "nonconformist, narrow, moralistic and enraged by Caradoc Evans"). Grigson dismissed Ackerman's claims for the importance of the Welsh background, and Davies's attempts to present Thomas as religious. He patronizes Welshness: Thomas was "a provincial of poetry, smoozing, if with the best hopes and intentions, a masticated old manner with a pop modernism."[64] Grigson made his last flourish—inserted the knife for the last time—in the *Listener* during 1976 in a review of *The Death of the King's Canary*, easy meat for the hostile critic:

In this little knockabout, I found the two authors technically biting their own backsides; and I reflect that publishing it . . . is about as low as English publishing . . . can descend. Or is there still something to be fished, cynically or pertinaciously, out of the supplementary bottom of the barrel of Dylan Thomas?[65]

Only Kingsley Amis—who, irony of ironies, because of his friendship with the senior executor of Thomas's estate, the Swansea solicitor Stuart Thomas, himself became an executor—could compete with such venom. His *Memoirs* (1991) sustained the hostility of his Movement days:

[Dylan Thomas] is a pernicious figure, one who has helped to get Wales and Welsh poetry a bad name and generally done lasting harm to both. The general picture he draws of the place and the people, in *Under Milk Wood* and elsewhere, is false, sentimentalising, melodramatising, sensationalising, ingratiating.[66]

Grigson, the Movement, Holbrook, Graves, Amis once more, and Rawson in the *TLS* were all close to apoplexy with anger and disgust, their language sweepingly uncontrolled. They communicated a fierce resentment of Thomas's work and of Thomas himself. English reserve and critical decorum were set aside as attitudes became more extreme.

If such abuse had been the only reaction, Thomas's work would have sunk without a trace. Fortunately, a parallel sequence, involving weighty academic names, has kept Thomas's work critically alive and available for restorative reassessment. Initially, its effect was undermined to some extent by too great a stress on what can be called the anecdotally biographical. One example is the memorial number of *Adam International Review*, which published some of Thomas's juvenilia and other information on his earlier life—defensively insisting on Thomas's normality—but did little with the work. Only W. S. Merwin's essay, to be considered in the next chapter, engaged seriously with Thomas's poetry.[67] The same can be said of *Encounter*, which devoted a special section to ''Dylan Thomas: Memories and Appreciations.'' It lives up to its title: items include information from Daniel Jones on the early juvenile collaborations and a piece by Louis MacNeice defending Thomas's obscurity (''never the obscurity of carelessness''), stressing the care he took with his work, and praising his human qualities. The whole does little for Thomas the writer.[68]

The same can be said of tributes by Thomas's two staunchest supporters: the *Times* obituary by Vernon Watkins and Edith Sitwell's eulogy in the American magazine the *Atlantic Monthly*. The former—a Welshman's reaction, of course, but, through its placing, a part of the English perception of Thomas—was sharp in places, in others blind to Thomas's faults. To say of Thomas, as Watkins did, that ''none has ever worn more brilliantly the mask of anarchy to conceal the true face of tradition'' is arguable but brilliantly suggestive. To state, also, that Thomas was ''a poet who was able to live Christianity in a public way'' is to move hero-worship beyond belief.[69] The latter's style is high adulation: the young Thomas was like the young Blake, with the "look of archangelic power." Ironically in the light of later revelations, Thomas was praised as a man and as a husband ("There was never anyone but her"). Sitwell quoted copiously from the poetry:

It was not until I began this tribute of love to the ever-young, un-dying Dylan in his grave, that I began to realize that I shall never hear that golden speaking voice, that voice of the lion, the eagle, the dove, the sun, again.[70]

After such writing, what forgiveness? With such friends, who needs enemies?

Thomas's critical standing depends not on such outpourings but on serious literary advocacy that begins, after Thomas's death, with reviews by William Empson, all redolent of "higher commonsense" and fine insights.[71] He always took the poetry seriously. He accepted that much of it is obscure, but did so with a rare humility, willing to state that he still did not understand everything. Ambiguity and multiple meanings also had to be accepted; the suggestiveness of many of Thomas's lines could be a source of pleasure. Empson's flair for teasing out meanings is always evident. To him the meaning always mattered; he was fiercely against all attempts to argue the contrary in the manner of, say, Daniel Jones, who described the "Altarwise by owl-light" sequence as "absolute poetry."[72] In general, he prefered the earlier poems because of their suggestive difficulty, though a number, despite superb individual lines, did not work well as units. For good measure he added an attack on Holbrook, suggesting that the latter misunderstood Thomas because of his (Holbrook's) narrow sensibility. As clinchers, Empson threw in comparisons between Holbrook and Malvolio and Holbrook and Chadband.[73]

G. S. Fraser was temperamentally probably less sympathetic to Thomas than was Empson, but succeeded in furthering Thomas's reputation by finding him not just a "good rhetorician"[74] but also a writer of fire and passion, offering genuine praise of the Divine. He tried to explain Thomas's appeal and, in a slightly later essay, found it in the "baffling simplicity" at the heart of his work, that is, a rejection of modern doubts and divisions. Like Empson, Fraser accepted some obscurity but insisted on the presence of meaning.[75]

Derek Stanford's *Dylan Thomas* was one of the first attempts to counter the burgeoning biographical myth by stressing what A. G. Prys-Jones described as a "child-like innocence" that lay beneath the turbulent surface. The strength of the book is its detailed exegesis of individual poems, even though Stanford had reservations about Thomas's obscurity. Despite the "major" status of such a poem as "Fern Hill" and the high quality of other later poems, Stanford believed that, in general, the lack of moral excitement in Thomas's work placed him as a minor poet. In a later edition he considered Thomas's status in the light of the attacks by the Movement and Robert Graves, and of John Malcolm Brinnin's account of Thomas drinking himself to death because his creative powers were waning. While recognizing that Thomas's reputation had suffered by the replacement of the "muse-poet" by the "scholar-poet"—the terms are those of Robert Graves—he pointed to his continuing popularity with the common reader and insisted that despite changing critical fashions, he would remain important as a "poet of religious temperament nourished in a literary culture of doubt."[76]

In a solid and balanced essay first published during 1954, David Daiches complained that "there are still some people who talk of Thomas as though he were a writer of an inspired mad rhetoric, of glorious, tumbling, swirling language which fell from his pen in magnificent disorder." Rather, he was a conscientious craftsman creating "a ritual of celebration" who moved from congested early poetry to a "more limpid, open-worked poetry." He was not a moralist but a relisher of humanity.[77] This was the first of two essays by distinguished academic critics. The second was a substantial section of John Bayley's *The Romantic Survival* (1957), which remains one of the finest and most suggestive explorations of the poetry. Essentially, like all the best criticism of Thomas, this is a study of his language. Indeed, Bayley placed Thomas in relation to his contemporaries in terms of language: against Yeats's and Auden's norm of "fluency, conversation" was set Thomas's norm of "incantation." Within Thomas's work Bayley pointed to changes in linguistic usage: the "metaphysical 'sense' [followed by] . . . associational 'sound.' " Bayley rejected as inadequate such generalizations as "rhetorical" or "Biblical," examined the language itself, and found diversity. He placed Thomas within the English tradition, finding the *hwyl*-like quality of Thomas's work a reminder of the tradition of Milton and Spenser, but also recognized "an un-English fullness of articulation," a "dual function" of combining self with an almost physical presence. Thomas's importance was in part that he achieved "a balance" between "the meaningless exuberance of surrealism" and "the self-conscious precision of poets influenced by positivistic theory" (160). Both served Thomas's "obsessional theme, the telescoping of existence," the linking, for example, of growth and decay, as in "Time held me green and dying."[78] Bayley's distinguished essay offers intriguing possibilities for modern literary interests, such as those in Bakhtinian language theories and in British literatures.

Two close readings point to the textual possibilities of Thomas's poetry. One, relatively brief, is in Christine Brooke-Rose, *A Grammar of Metaphor* (1958). She considered Thomas's "shattered sacramental view of life" and Thomas's frequent demonstrations of "a fusion of grammatical metaphor and symbolism."[79] The other is Winifred Nowottny's detailed investigation of "There was a saviour" in *The Language Poets Use* (1962). To date, this is probably the most detailed analysis of any single poem by Thomas. She began with bafflement, then countered it with detailed exegesis of syntax and word usage, teasing out turns in the argument and demonstrating the symbolic use of language. Nowottny traced Thomas's links with and allusions to earlier poets, including Keats, Blake, and Swinburne, and so, perhaps too readily, placed Thomas squarely within the English tradition. She concluded:

The scope, depth and multiplicity of reference in *There Was a Saviour* is necessitated by the ambitiousness of its purport; the poet in time of war examines the religious and cultural symbols that have themselves in great measure shaped the intelligence and feeling that turn to question the meaning of their world.[80]

Here is a powerful plea for the large-scale importance of Thomas's work and, which is perhaps the same point, for the way it expands the English language. Once again a powerful mind demonstrates what can be found through detailed, "objective" attention.

The final stage thus far in this English critical history could be said to begin in 1966 with a collection of critical essays edited by C. B. Cox. The editorial introduction is glibly inconclusive: "His poetry remains confusing, disturbing, never completely explicable. . . . The explanations are inadequate; so it may well be that when we, his twentieth century critics, are forgotten, Thomas's poetry will continue to stimulate controversy, and to give pleasure 'for as long as forever is.' "[81] The collection strives for a balanced view and so reprints John Wain's loaded notice of *Collected Poems* and Holbrook's furious attack on *Under Milk Wood*. But there is little doubt that despite editorial indecision, the weight of criticism is in favor of Thomas: as well as supportive pieces by American and Welsh critics, Cox reprinted the essays by Daiches and Bayley, part of Nowottny's essay on "There was a saviour," and Empson's *New Statesman* review in 1954 of *Collected Poems and Under Milk Wood*.

In 1972 a volume of essays edited by Walford Davies brought together new work by a group of English academic heavyweights. Though John Wain and F. W. Bateson—"the Welsh imagination becomes diffuse, Swinburnian, when expressed in English poetic diction"—proceeded on stereotyping autopilot to offer versions of Arnoldian Celticism, the collection in general is a substantial counter to the tradition of hostility. Examples are a thoughtful and balanced essay by Claude Rawson, who, despite reservations, seized brilliantly—if in a slightly patronizing manner—on the bourgeois qualities that made Thomas "a suburban Larkinized Pope, or Horace of the fish-and-chip shop." John Bayley once more stressed Thomas's important originality as

the first great and evident talent of the modern movement in poetry to have no truck with literature or belief or the contemporary apparatus of science and ideology, but to concentrate on what it felt like to be himself, to make his poetry the feeling of his being.

Bayley bravely listed what for him were Thomas's best poems, taken from all stages of his career, with "Twenty-four years" as the masterpiece. Martin Dodsworth argued that Thomas extended modernist practice through his resistance to Audenesque rational discourse. The ubiquitous David Holbrook argued for his new view of Thomas that he developed in *Dylan Thomas: The Code of Night*, also published in 1972: he was now seen as a schizoid person whose work was "a strategy of survival" that made art out of personal chaos, achieving "integration and coherence" in his later work.[82]

Dylan Thomas: New Critical Essays illustrates two movements in Thomas criticism. The first is detailed analysis of individual poems, or, to put this another way, a general willingness to pay attention to what is there, rather than condemning poems simply because they are different or because of Thomas's personal faults. The results, invariably, are illuminating. Second, there is a distinct preference for the earlier poems. Even though Alistair Fowler analyzed "Fern Hill" and demonstrated its place in the English tradition, and Laurence Lerner placed *Under Milk Wood* as an example of pastoral, most preferred poems more difficult to assimilate into English literary history. That is, this volume implicitly added to the groundwork for the later preoccupation with British literatures.

A lively collection of essays edited by Alan Bold and published during 1990 introduced a number of new voices. More directly than the Walford Davies collection, it suggested and at times demonstrated fresh, fruitful lines of approach. One such is a more detailed and refined account of Thomas in his time; Stewart Crehan's essay on Thomas and the 1930s is an example of what can be achieved by moving beyond generalizations. Others pointed to the possibilities of psychological and linguistic approaches and, urgently, of feminist readings.[83]

In slightly impatient fashion, John Powell Ward and Neil Corcoran—the latter an Oxford-educated Irishman whose academic career has been wholly in British universities—invoked a sense of déjà vu, tending to fight old battles long won. Ward worried about Thomas's concern with self and womb fixation, his "obsession with pre-infancy," and suggested that "much of the time Thomas is . . . probably meaningless," then offered fine insights into his romanticized suburbanism and the way his work "stands in mixed relation to any 'English line,' " a further pointer to the need to place Thomas in relation to mainstream English literature.[84] Corcoran's treatment of Thomas was altogether more conventional. For him, "A Refusal to Mourn," "In my craft or sullen art," "Fern Hill," "Do not go gentle," and, unexpectedly, "Into her lying down head" were

the poems on which Thomas's reputation will ultimately rest. . . . Poems such as these turn the mesmerised and self-obsessed narcissism of the earlier work outwards to a recognizable external world of action, event, suffering, and relationship.[85]

This is well-trodden ground. What intrigues here, as throughout his treatment of Thomas, is that the tone always threatens to become insulting. Even in 1993, to adapt Larkin, the idea of Thomas stuck like a pin into some critical sensibilities. It is no accident that in the very same year Lahey complained about a critical tradition redolent with misplaced animosity.

NOTES

1. Philip A. Lahey, "Dylan Thomas: A Reappraisal," *Critical Survey* 5 (1993): 53.

2. Edith Sitwell, *Aspects of Modern Poetry* (London: Duckworth, 1934), 149–50.

3. Desmond Hawkins, review of *18 Poems, Time and Tide*, 9 February 1935: 204, 206.

4. Edith Sitwell and Robert Herring, "A Correspondence on the Young English Poets," *Life and Letters Today*, December 1935: 16–24. See also "Notes on contributors," 232; these were presumably written by the editor, who was Robert Herring.

5. Edith Sitwell, "Four New Poets," *London Mercury*, February 1936: 386–88.

6. Edith Sitwell, review of *Twenty-five Poems, Sunday Times*, 15 November 1936: 9.

7. *CL*, 210. Letter to Edith Sitwell, dated 17 January 1936.

8. Paul Ferris, *Dylan Thomas* (1977; Harmondsworth: Penguin Books, 1978), 147–48.

9. Michael Roberts, "The Brassy Orator," *London Mercury*, October 1936: 555.

10. Geoffrey Grigson, "A Letter from England," *Poetry* November 1936: 101–3.

11. Louis MacNeice, *Modern Poetry: A Personal Essay* (London: Oxford University Press, 1938), 160.

12. Review of *The Map of Love, Listener* 9 October 1939: 780, 782.

13. Hugh Gordon Porteous, "Map of Llareggub," *New English Weekly*, 7 September 1939: 269–70.

14. Edwin Muir, *The Present Age from 1914* (London: Cresset Press, 1939), 220–21.

15. Herbert Read, *Seven* 6 (Autumn 1939): 19–20.

16. Henry Treece, "An Apocalyptic Writer and the Surrealists," in *The New Apocalypse*, ed. J. F. Hendry (London: Fortune Press, 1940), 49–58.

17. G. S. Fraser, "Apocalypse in Poetry," in *The White Horseman*, ed. J. F. Hendry and Henry Treece (London: Routledge, 1941), 3–31.

18. Geoffrey Grigson, review of *The Map of Love, Horizon* January 1940: 58.

19. Dylan Thomas, "There was a saviour," *Horizon*, May 1940: 318–19; [Cyril Connolly] "Comment," *Horizon*, June 1940: 390, 391.

20. Francis Scarfe, "The Poetry of Dylan Thomas," *Horizon*, November 1940: 237, 238, 239. The essay has been reprinted in Francis Scarfe, *Auden and After* (London: Routledge & Sons, 1942), 101–17; and in E. W. Tedlock (ed.), *Dylan Thomas: The Legend and the Poet* (London: William Heinemann, 1960), 96–112.

21. Announcement of "Horizon Prize," *Horizon*, January 1946: 7. The poems were "Vision and Prayer," "Holy Spring," "Poem in October," "Fern Hill," "A Refusal to Mourn," and "A Winter's Tale."

22. Dylan Thomas, review of Stephen Spender, *Vienna, New Verse* 12 (December 1934): 19–20.

23. This is a discussion of *Deaths and Entrances* within a longer piece by Spender entitled "Poetry for Poetry's Sake and Poetry beyond Poetry," *Horizon*, April 1946: 233–34.

24. Stephen Spender, *Poetry since 1939* (1946; London: Longmans, Green, for the British Council, 1950), 44–50. The international distribution of British Council publications made this praise of Thomas's work important for his reputation.

25. Review of *Deaths and Entrances, Listener*, 9 May 1946: 622.

26. Review of Henry Treece, *Dylan Thomas: "Dog among the Fairies,"* *Listener*, 19 May 1949: 861. For the quotations from Treece: Henry Treece, *Dylan Thomas: "Dog among the Fairies"* (London: Lindsay Drummond, 1949), 104.

27. Stephen Spender, "Dylan Thomas," *New Statesman*, 18 June 1949: 650–52.

28. Geoffrey Grigson, "On a Present Kind of Poem," *Polemic* 7 (March 1947): 52–64. Grigson combined this article with an earlier piece with the well-known title in *Polemic* 3 (May 1946): 8–13, reprinting both as a single essay, "How Much Me Now Your Acrobatics Amaze," in *The Harp of Aeolus and Other Essays* (London: Routledge, 1948), 151–60.

29. Kenneth Allott (ed.), *The Penguin Book of Contemporary Verse* (Harmondsworth: Penguin Books, 1950), 25–26, 225.

30. William Empson, "Death and Transfiguration," *Nation*, 22 February 1947: 214–16.

31. William Empson, "To Understand a Modern Poem: 'A Refusal to Mourn the Death, by Fire, of a Child in London,' by Dylan Thomas," *Strand*, March 1947: 60–64.

32. Kingsley Amis, quoted in Blake Morrison, *The Movement* (1980; London and New York: Methuen, 1986), 25.

33. Donald Davie, quoted in Morrison, *Movement*, 47.

34. Philip Toynbee, review of *Collected Poems, 1934–1952, Observer*, 9 November 1952: 7.

35. W. H. Mellors, "The Bard and the Prep School," *Scrutiny* 9 (1940): 77; Wolf Mankowitz, review of *Deaths and Entrances, Scrutiny* 14 (1946): 65, 67; R. G. Cox, review of Henry Treece, *Dylan Thomas: "Dog among the Fairies," Scrutiny* 16 (1949): 249; Robin Mayhead, review of *Collected Poems 1934–1952, Scrutiny* 19 (1952–53): 146, 143.

36. John Wain, *Mandrake* (Summer–Autumn 1953): 261–63. This review is conveniently found in C. B. Cox (ed.), *Dylan Thomas: A Collection of Critical Essays*, Twentieth Century Views (Englewood Cliffs, NJ: Prentice-Hall, 1966), 9–13.

37. Donald Davie, *Articulate Energy* (1955; London, Henley, and Boston: Routledge & Kegan Paul, 1976), 126.

38. Kingsley Amis, "Thomas the Rhymer," *What Became of Jane Austen?* (1970; London: Panther, 1972), 5.

39. D. J. Enright (ed.), *Poets of the 1950s* (Tokyo: Kenkyusha, 1955), 8.

40. Robert Conquest (ed.), *New Lines* (London: Macmillan, 1962), xv–xvi.

41. Morrison, *Movement*, 9.

42. John Lehmann, quoted in Morrison, *Movement*, 43.

43. Donald Davie, quoted in Morrison, *Movement*, 146.

44. Philip Larkin, *Selected Letters, 1940–1985*, ed. Anthony Thwaite paperback edu. (London and Boston: Faber and Faber, 1993), 28, 46, 133, 758, 218, 264.

45. D. J. Enright, quoted in Morrison, *Movement*, 146.

46. Enright, *Poets of the 1950s*, 8–9; my emphasis.

47. Donald Davie, *These the Companions* (Cambridge: Cambridge University Press, 1982), 69.

48. Donald Davie, *Collected Poems* (Manchester: Carcanet, 1990), 150, 261.

49. Davie, *These the Companions*, 91.

50. Davie, *Collected Poems*, 256.

51. Philip Larkin, *Required Writing* (London and Boston: Faber & Faber, 1983), 41.

52. Larkin, *Selected Letters*, 55, 341.

53. Kingsley Amis, "Against Romanticism," in *New Lines*, ed. Robert Conquest (London: Macmillan, 1962), 45.

54. Kingsley Amis, *A Look Round the Estate* (London: Jonathan Cape, 1967), 53, 45.

55. John Wain, "Druid of Her Broken Body," in *Dylan Thomas: New Critical Essays*, ed. Walford Davies (London: Dent, 1972), 7–8.

56. Robert Graves, "These Be Your Gods, O Israel!" *Essays in Criticism* 5 (1955): 147–50. Graves quoted the first five lines of "If my head hurts a hair's foot" as an example of "nonsense." During his lecture he offered a pound to anyone who could make sense of the lines. M. J. C. Hodgart, then a fellow of Pembroke College, Cambridge, did so, only for Graves to bluster and refuse to pay. The Clark Lectures are included in Graves's *The Crowning Privilege* (London: Cassell, 1955; Garden City, NY: Doubleday, 1956; reprint, Harmondsworth; Penguin Books, 1959). Part is reprinted in John Malcolm Brinnin (ed.), *A Casebook on Dylan Thomas* (New York: Crowell, 1960) 160–66, together with Graves's account of the "Hodgart affair."

57. David Holbrook, "Metaphor and Maturity: T. F. Powys and Dylan Thomas," in *The Pelican Guide to English Literature: The Modern Age*, ed. Boris Ford (Harmondsworth: Penguin Books, 1961), 415–28.

58. David Holbrook, *Llareggub Revisited: Dylan Thomas and the State of Modern Poetry* (London: Bowes & Bowes, 1962), 127, 129, 238. The American edition was published in 1964.

59. Lahey, "Dylan Thomas: A Reappraisal," 54.

60. Holbrook, *Llareggub Revisited*, 108, 87, 112.

61. Raymond Preston, review of *Collected Poems, 1934–1952, Listener*, 4 December 1952: 947.

62. Review of *Under Milk Wood, Listener*, 27 May 1954: 937.

63. Bernard Bergonzi, review of William York Tindall, *A Reader's Guide to Dylan Thomas, Listener*, 3 January 1963: 37–38.

64. Geoffrey Grigson, "Dylan and the Dragon," *New Statesman*, 18 December 1964: 968–69. Grigson reviewed John Ackerman, *Dylan Thomas: His Life and Work*, and Aneirin Talfan Davies, *Dylan: Druid of the Broken Body*.

65. Geoffrey Grigson, "Sub-satirical," *Listener*, 30 September 1976: 409.

66. Kingsley Amis, *Memoirs* (London: Hutchinson, 1991), 132–33.

67. *Adam International Review* 238 (1953), ed. Miron Grindea.

68. "Dylan Thomas: Memories and Appreciations," *Encounter*, January 1954: 9–17.

69. Vernon Watkins, "Mr. Dylan Thomas: Innovation and Tradition," *Times*, 10 November 1953: 11.

70. Edith Sitwell, "Dylan Thomas," *Atlantic Monthly*, February 1954: 42–45.

71. From 1953 onwards, William Empson's reviews are as follows: "A Poem by Dylan Thomas" (source unknown, 1953); "The Collected Dylan Thomas," *New Statesman and Nation*, 15 May 1954: 391–95; "Dylan Thomas," *Essays in Criticism* 13 (1963): 396–403; "Dylan Thomas in Maturity," *New Statesman*, 29 October 1965: 647–48; and "Some More Dylan Thomas," *Listener*, 28 October 1971: 408–12. All are conveniently reprinted in William Empson, *Argufying*, ed. John Haffenden (London: Hogarth Press, 1988).

72. Empson, "Dylan Thomas in Maturity," 648.

73. Empson, "Dylan Thomas," *Essays in Criticism*, 403.

74. G. S. Fraser, *The Modern Writer and His World* (1953; Harmondsworth: Pelican Books, 1964), 334.

75. See Fraser's reprinted reviews in *Essays on Twentieth-Century Poets* (Leicester: Leicester University Press, 1978), 182–203.

76. Derek Stanford, *Dylan Thomas* (1954; revised and extended ed., New York: Citadel Press, 1964), 29, 110, 203.

77. David Daiches, "The Poetry of Dylan Thomas," *Literary Essays* (London: Oliver & Boyd, 1956), 52, 58.

78. John Bayley, *The Romantic Survival* (London: Constable and Oxford University Press, 1957), 190, 195, 215, 216, 220.

79. Christine Brooke-Rose, *A Grammar of Metaphor* (London: Secker & Warburg, 1958), 320–23.

80. Winifred Nowottny, *The Language Poets Use* (1962; London: Athlone Press, 1972), 215.

81. C. B. Cox (ed.), *Dylan Thomas: A Collection of Critical Essays* (Englewood Cliffs, NJ: Prentice-Hall, 1966), 8.

82. Walford Davies (ed.), *Dylan Thomas: New Critical Essays* (London: Dent, 1972), 226, 103, 57–58, 168–69, 198.

83. Alan Bold (ed.), *Dylan Thomas: Craft or Sullen Art* (London: Vision Press, 1990).

84. John Powell Ward, *The English Line* (London: Macmillan, 1991), 168–74.

85. Neil Corcoran, *English Poetry since 1940* (London and New York: Longman, 1993), 45.

18

Dylan Thomas in North America

The first works by Dylan Thomas to be published in North America were his short story "The Visitor" in 1935[1] and, two years later, his poem "We lying by seasand," the latter in an "English Number" of *Poetry* edited by W. H. Auden and Michael Roberts. In 1938 *Poetry* published four more poems and awarded Thomas its Oscar Blumenthal Prize. This was a triumph of quality over prejudice: as has been noted, in 1936 Geoffrey Grigson had vilified *Twenty-five Poems* in "A Letter from England" in the same magazine.[2] Yet in America Grigson had little effect, and other magazines published further poems before *The World I Breathe*, the first American edition of Thomas's work, appeared in 1939. During the same year the *Kenyon Review* paid the first substantial critical attention to Thomas, published "If my head hurt a hair's foot," and described Thomas as "a young Welshman whose daring verse is now heavily under discussion on both sides of the Atlantic."[3]

From 1939 through 1961 the *Kenyon Review* published a series of reviews and articles that together comprise a microcosm of the American critical history of Thomas's work. That series began with Philip Blair Rice's review of *New Directions 1938*, which included two of Thomas's stories and three of his poems. Rice focussed on "I make this in a warring absence," then known as "Poem for Caitlin" and one of Thomas's most difficult poems. He acknowledged the difficulties but also suggested the rewards of grappling with them:

Any term of the two principal systems of imagery may itself suggest a new metaphor of an unrelated type, and often this appears subjective and impenetrable. . . . The closely packed lines that result are exciting and perturbing. . . . [I]ndividual images . . . are strange, violent, frequently beautiful; the rhythms keep one lurching; and the verbal texture is exquisite. But the total effect is extremely rococo: the poem is lost in the detail; imagination and intelligence are drowned in fancy and sensibility.[4]

In issues following the one that included "If my head hurt a hair's foot" were two pieces by English critics. First came praise by Herbert Read, one of Thomas's most fervent supporters: "Here, as nowhere else in modern poetry, beauty and terror reach a rare union," he wrote, with *The Map of Love* in mind.[5] Second, early in 1940, was a mixed response from Julian Symons, who stated, Grigson-like, that "frequently [Thomas's] poems are jokes, rhetorical intellectual fakes of the highest class," and

what is said in Mr. Thomas's poems is that the seasons change; that we decrease in vigour as we grow older; that life has no obvious meaning; that love dies. His poems mean no more than that. They mean too little.

Yet he concluded, mollifyingly and puzzlingly, that his piece was "not in any way an 'attack' on Mr. Thomas's poetry; if he were not a good poet, there would be less reason to write critically about his work."[6]

A few months later John Berryman noticed *The World I Breathe*, using the review in part to refute Symons's charges. He agreed that Thomas's themes "are simple, but not I think so unimportant as Julian Symons calls them in a very bad article." The reference to Thomas's lack of important meaning he considered to be part of "Mr. Symons's nonsense": Symons seemed not to realize "that a poem means more than the abstract, banal statement of its theme. . . . What Mr. Symons misses is the value of presentation, the dramatic truth of metaphor." Berryman analyzed Thomas's diction, noted that "the principal sources of imagery are the sea and sex," and discussed Thomas's technique and, in his opinion, the much-exaggerated difficulty of the writing. Though he had reservations about Thomas's future development, the best of his "brilliant" work "has extended the language and to a lesser degree the methods of lyric poetry."[7]

Four years after Berryman's rebuttal of Symons and following the publication of *New Poems* (1943), Thomas's second American volume, Arthur Mizener complained that Thomas, like too many other modern poets, was more interested in expression than content and so tended to heap up elaborate details.[8] This time it was Robert Horan's turn to oppose criticism, which he did in a substantial essay that opened with a rejection of Mizener's argument. In Horan's view "the complexity of Thomas's ornamentation [is] an expression of the necessities of his subject matter, rather than . . . indulgent verbalizing." This was because of his modernity, his concern

to free memory from the strictures of paternity, from religion and from death; to establish the unique individual, not merely as the victim, but as the agent of choice; not alone *created by history*, but *creative in history*. . . . [and] his effort to bring the diverse and almost uncontrollable poles of his observation and sympathy into the same poem, or into the same system of consciousness and value . . . with finer precision of feeling and more developed insight. . . . [so that] his grasp of reality is more shocking, and correspondingly more sensitized than those around him.[9]

This is high praise. More came from Howard Moss in a review of *Selected Writings* (1946). He linked Thomas with Robert Lowell and William Carlos Williams: "they are genuine creators: They do not describe nor interpret reality as much as construct it." For Moss, Thomas was "the most original poet to have appeared in English since Hopkins." In what could be seen as a further rejection of Julian Symons's criticism, he continued: Thomas's "subject matter is simple: it is chiefly concerned with an individual awareness of the duality of birth and death. What he does with this primary idea is astonishing." Moss was excited by the range of Thomas's symbolism and by the rich complexity of his language. Though some of the early poems were obscure, the later ones "have moved towards statement without losing richness of speech, or technical fluidity. . . . Thomas has all the earmarks of a major poet."[10]

John Crowe Ransom, in a survey of twentieth-century poetry, placed Thomas with Houseman, Wallace Stevens, and Auden in the major or minor ("I cannot tell") category.[11] Howard Nemerov, however, knew exactly where he stood. His review of *Collected Poems, 1934–1952* was candid: "Not a great deal of Thomas's poetry does succeed, to my mind; and when he is bad I believe he is very bad indeed. But there are a few poems, and few poets have more, which strike me as perfected results, and very beautiful." These included "After the funeral," "Over Sir John's Hill," and, surprisingly, "Hold hard, these ancient minutes in the cuckoo's month." This last work was analyzed in some detail as a poem "about *process*," more specifically, about "the *fall* . . . from nature into history, from the timeless to the organic." Nemerov believed that the characteristic violence of Thomas's style on occasion became "rather mechanical than muscular," that his technical skill was not always what it appeared to be, and that in the later poetry, energy was not always subject to formal control. His rhetoric could seem empty. "But," Nemerov concluded, "[Thomas] has written a few beautiful poems."[12]

In 1955, the British critic Geoffrey Moore contributed an essay setting Thomas in his Welsh context—suggesting some similarities between Thomas's style, particularly in "The conversation of prayers," and *cynghanedd*—and in the history of twentieth-century poetry. Moore concluded that Thomas was the heir to the romantic tradition, a counter to contemporary low-key poetry, and a reminder of a celebratory and affirmative Hopkins.[13]

However, Moore's article, though it helped sustain Thomas's work as a literary presence, was not part of the *Kenyon Review*'s American sequence. This was continued in 1957 by Richard Ellmann, and in a most significant manner. Ellmann's essay was on Wallace Stevens and used Thomas as a point of comparison—as, for example, "in Thomas . . . the main revelation is that death pervades life, while in Stevens it is that life pervades death"[14]—thus demonstrating Thomas's centrality in contemporary American literary thought. However, in 1961 George Steiner sounded a jarring note, describing Thomas as a "showman" of whose work it had to be said that "barring certain eloquent exceptions, there is in his poems less than meets the dazzled eye."[15]

The attacks by Symons and Steiner were by Europeans. The *Kenyon Review*'s home team offered generally favorable accounts. In so doing they demonstrated the fundamental and admirable characteristics of American critical approaches to Thomas. One is, from the first, sustained intellectual argument, often in substantial essays and reviews, proceeding from a basic but far-from-uncritical acceptance of Thomas's great literary worth. A second is close textual analysis, even of Thomas's most difficult work, that reflects the influence of "New Criticism" and is a reminder that John Crowe Ransom founded and edited the *Kenyon Review*. Indeed, the "New Critics" were drawn to Thomas's work: in 1950 Cleanth Brooks and Robert Penn Warren included "The force that through the green fuse" in *Understanding Poetry*, their widely influential "New Critical" bible. A third is an openness to new experiences and ideas that can lead to interpretive excesses but is invariably exhilarating and always free from the prejudices of class or nationality. Another is the sense of serious critical debate: Berryman replied to Symons, Horan to Mizener; Brewster Ghiselin, in the *Western Review*, countered one of Nemerov's criticisms by pointing to formal measures in Thomas's later poetry.[16]

An early example of such qualities at work is Marshall W. Stearns's essay in the *Sewanee Review* during 1944. He offered a clear and measured summary of critical views on Thomas. Stearns was anxious to reject Symons's view that Thomas's poems contained very thin thematic material: he stressed "the fallacy in Symons' line of criticism, which paraphrases a poem and then criticises the paraphrase." He was, in particular, sceptical about the influence of Freud: Thomas's idea of writing as catharsis "springs apparently from a strong personal need rather than any thorough understanding of Freud." At the center of Stearns's essay was the view that "the major theme of man in Thomas's poetry is variously accompanied by the minor themes of religion and sex, which are sometimes fused at a high temperature." Supporting analyses of a number of Thomas's poems then followed, including, in great and illuminating detail, one of sonnet 8 of the "Altarwise" sequence—read as a poem about Mary's view of the Crucifixion—and of "Light breaks where no sun shines," a poem about "the process of living" that illustrated Thomas's "dialectical method in practice." That dialectic might be a functional device to express Thomas's "inner confusion," but in general, Stearns accepted the obscurity that "seems to arise in part from his fluid syntax," but worried about the dangers of multiple meanings. He also worried about "the problem of the poet in our time," needing "a highly individual idiom" in order to attract attention. Stearns doubted whether Thomas would solve the problem, become "more easily-classified," and attain greater lucidity. "His historical importance is assured," but his difficulty might well limit his readership.[17]

John L. Sweeney's introduction to *Selected Writings* (1946) is another considered statement. For him, Thomas's "poetry springs directly from primitive and traditional sources, but it is peculiarly the poetry of his own time. It is the record of a struggle toward spiritual rebirth." Sweeney found a strong Freudian influence, "especially evident in the sexual emphasis of Thomas' early poetry, in its preoccupation with birth and the informative period of childhood . . . [and] in its synthesis of unconscious experience." He quoted from Marshall Stearns's essay Thomas's description of breeding images in which the reference to applying "intellectual and critical forces" distanced Thomas from surrealism. Sweeney was perceptive about the Welshness of Thomas's writing, citing cadence, rhythm, and rhymes.

Since the air-raid poems of 1940, Sweeney considered that in his latest work Thomas "has turned from the womb and the grave to the world of light; from contemplation of the flesh and its declension to a metaphysical vision of resurrection." This led to analyses of "Holy Spring" and "Vision and Prayer." Sweeney discussed Thomas's short story "The Burning Baby" and the life of William Price that inspired it. Dr. Price, Sweeney concluded, was "a symbol of those who fearlessly seek their selfhood and speak its truths," as did Thomas.[18]

The essays by Stearns and Sweeney are impressively researched; both contain much perceptive close reading. David Aivaz's study has similar virtues.[19] He too referred back to Julian Symons, agreeing with the objections of Berryman and Stearns, and to Grigson, who, ignoring the element of thought in Thomas's work, found only automatic writing. Certainly Thomas had faults: Aivaz was well aware of initial confusion, occasional cleverness, strained syntax, and a tendency to complicate. He also believed that close reading cleared up much seeming difficulty, proving his case by means of perceptive analyses of poems on all levels of difficulty. Aivaz wrote after the publication of Treece's book-length study, which printed in full Thomas's description of the "dialectical method" that resulted from "breeding images."[20] Such a method, involving, as it did, images conflicting and contradicting, was a source of Thomas's obscurity. Another source of difficulty was what Aivaz called "residual imagery," one example of which occurred when what an image meant in one poem obscured what that same image might mean in another. A further complication was ambiguity: "Too many connotations weaken the image."

In a version of Sweeney's description of Thomas's work as a progress "to the world of light," Aivaz considered that the early imagery of denial was transformed by process into "later imagery of affirmation." He applied the idea of the dialectic to that of "process," the latter being "the basic theme of all Thomas's poems. . . . Process is unity in nature; its direction is the cyclical return; the force that drives it is the generative energy in natural things," which was, in Thomas's own words quoted by Aivaz, dialectically "destructive and constructive at the same time." What we find in Thomas, argued Aivaz, is that "Man is Thomas's metaphor. . . . The consciousness of man shapes the natural world by its awareness of it; man is the metaphor through which the qualities of things find expression." Further and finally, Aivaz insisted, he sought to answer critics like Grigson and "those of [Thomas's] admirers who damn him with diffuse praise'' by demonstrating that ''he deserves to be read as much for his sense as for his sound and fury.''

In 1951 Babette Deutsch published ''The Orient Wheat.'' The title points to the essay's thematic heart. It comes from Thomas Traherne's meditation on childhood: ''The corn was orient and immortal wheat, which never should be reaped, nor was ever sown,''[21] suggesting a view of Thomas's work as strangely radiant, long-lasting, with great potential, and much concerned with childhood. However, Deutsch opened by placing Thomas as a fervent religious poet and as a difficult writer because he ''combines with equally private references both Freudian and Christian symbols and allusions to Welsh mythology.'' She considered his work in relation to ''the elaborate consonantal harmonies'' of traditional Welsh-language poetry. Her close reading of ''Poem in October'' then demonstrated such patterns of sound. She examined his treatment of children and childhood. Once again an American critic referred to and quoted from Thomas's description of breeding images and dialectical method. She noted the value of ''the inevitable conflict of images,'' though she suggested that the conflict in Thomas's poetry

is not between images, but between the ideas and attitudes they represent. The Freudian recognizes the generous beauty of sexuality. The Christian, shadowed by the sense of sin of his chapel-going forbears, would destroy the body to liberate the spirit.

Further, ''Nearly every poem moves tempestuously among contradictory themes.'' Ultimately, ''the beclouded pantheism of his early work gives place to a more orthodox religiosity.''

His poetry, she believed, ''ignores social issues''; even in the war poems ''the political significance of the bombings is scarcely glanced at.'' Accepting that ''many of Thomas's lyrics are undecipherable,'' Deutsch moved into explication of three of the more approachable: ''The hunchback in the park,'' ''After the funeral,'' and ''Among Those Killed in the Dawn Raid.'' She concluded that the poetry was essentially a search for ''the wisdom and power of God exhibited in a world subjected to the fires of a man-made inferno'' and that ''it is . . . in his poems praising earthly things and the waters that hold the earth, and the lovers who for a little while rejoice in it, rejoicing in each other, that Dylan Thomas speaks most tellingly.'' In what is the first important essay on Thomas by an American woman, he is presented to us as the archromantic.[22]

Deutsch's conclusion can be compared to John L. Sweeney's in his review of *In Country Sleep* (1952). Sweeney asserted what is surely the eclectic absolute, that the poems all deal with ''life, death, love, country matters and Wales.'' He insisted again on the importance of the Welsh background, here particularly evident in ''Over Sir John's Hill,'' and touched interestingly on differences (a Celtic emphasis on ''sound'' being one) between the Welsh literary tradition to which Thomas belonged and the English tradition of, say, Wordsworth's *Prelude*, before his peroration:

Thomas still stands alone among the poets near him in age. . . . Thomas is not a philosophical poet . . . but there is a deep and rich vein of poetic thought in his reverberating affirmations of life and intimations of mortality.[23]

In the studies by Deutsch and Sweeney such moments—fortunately preceded in both cases by insightful scholarship—remind us of Aivaz's witty reference to "admirers who damn [Thomas] with diffuse praise."

Cid Corman certainly did not. Her review of *Collected Poems, 1934–1952* was mixed and uncertain. It began combatively: "That Thomas is a very limited poet . . . is almost a constant self-testimony. . . . There is a note of self-pity." That said, Corman, having studied the drafts of a Thomas poem, knew "that his seeming spontaneity is a studied grace. . . . [The drafts] testify to a keen critical self-scrutiny and an ear that will not work without the mind." In so saying, Corman became another American critic to stress Thomas's intellectual force. She, like Sweeney and others, also stressed the importance of place: most of his poems reflected, she noted mysteriously, "the Welsh locale . . . a haunt where music and reverence are companionable and ripe." This translated into "his powerful rhetoric, his Biblical breath, and his Anglo-Saxon vocabulary." Mainly through an analysis of "Over Sir John's Hill" Corman found that Thomas's poetry "grieves . . . for a world pledged to war, for the weak, the innocent, the many. . . . He reveres the individual soaked in sense." Compassion was at the center of work that was often ritualistic. Like Stearns, nine years before her, Corman considered Thomas a victim of a success "that has prodded him to repeat his past performances excessively," so that poetic effects could be overstated because he "is pinched in by self-definition." He had also suffered from having imitators to draw attention to his weaknesses. Yet

his verve, his crying spirit, his naughtiness, his rhetorical romancing, are wide attractions. It is worth more of our careful consideration as to how deep and insighted are his poems and how superficial and rhetorically blinding, as well as captivating.[24]

Such careful rapture—also found in Sweeney's description of the same volume as "impressive and delightful. Achievement and promise striding along together" and, via a change of metaphor, in his further comment that "the sense of loss runs like a mine through most of Thomas's poetry but it is almost always at some point shafted for light"[25]—is an acknowledgment of Thomas's mesmeric powers. But though never unilluminating, it is too close to Sitwellish praise for complete critical comfort. Fortunately, a harder-edged critical force made its first appearance in print in October 1954, within a year of Thomas's death.

This was that of English-born Ralph Maud, whose professional academic career was spent wholly in North America. His study, published in *Essays in Criticism*, the English academic journal, sought to describe the basic character of Thomas's poetry. An analysis of "I see the boys of summer" demonstrated

Thomas's craftsmanship; it also demonstrated that though Thomas's syntax could be difficult, invariably it created "soluble difficulties and not enigmas." The poetry, Maud contended, was based on "the short rhetorically coherent phrase," which tended to lengthen through Thomas's career, at times at the expense of "the remarkable concentration of power" found in the earlier poems. Thomas's poetry was rewarding because "almost every phrase of a poem will exhibit the interplay between the descriptive, metaphoric and conceptual levels of meaning." The later poems were less obscure "because they are usually unified on a narrative level."[26] As will be seen, Maud's scholarship and the scholarly clarity of his writing make him a central force in Thomas studies.

The most important considered American response to Thomas's death was the November 1954 number of the *Yale Literary Magazine*, the whole of which was devoted to Thomas.[27] Whereas, as has been seen, British equivalents tended to be mainly anecdotal-biographical, here were, for the most part, serious arguments that at times addressed ideas with relevance beyond Thomas's death. Possibly because of this wider range, some essays can at times be coolly abstract, one example being Winfield Townley Scott's piece, which asked, "Why do people *like* to have a poet die?" (*Y*, 13), and cited jealousy, fear of a poet's dangerous truth, the controlling of the once-wild, and a desire not to witness literary decline. Richard Eberhart's praise of the poems for their "struggle . . . dynamic energy . . . [and] sly, cool, subtle, controlled intellectual craftsmanship" (*Y*, 5) and his conviction that "a drive to destruction was inextricably bound up with his genius" (*Y*, 6) were countered by equally sly suggestions that he could tell the full (and presumably scandalous) truth about Thomas's life.

But generally, and even at times in the tributes by Scott and Eberhart, this number demonstrated respect for and warmth towards the dead man and his achievements. Such feelings were evident, for example, in William Jay Smith's moving recollections of lunching with Dylan and Caitlin as guests of the historian A. L. Rowse at august All Souls College, Oxford. Smith's delicate symbolism lifted the piece above the conventional memoir as he recalled Thomas as a fine craftsman and brilliant talker on both life and, occasionally, literature. The whole occasion, let alone the venue, boosted Thomas's literary status. The other contributions include poems by Babette Deutsch and Kenneth Rexroth, a meditation on the death of a poet, and essays on *Under Milk Wood* and on Thomas's romantic heritage. This last essay was a reprint of Horace Gregory's scholarly essay in *Poetry*[28] that related Thomas, in the customary American way, to aspects of modern romanticism, both English and Welsh, commented on his Welshness, and considered his place in the modern contemporary pantheon: "Among his elders only Yeats and Edith Sitwell and Walter de la Mare are poets of greater and more accomplishment than he" (*Y*, 33). Gregory, whose essay was written in 1947, praised *Deaths and Entrances* for achieving "a greater integration of [Thomas's] imaginative life." Gregory added a postscript lamenting Thomas's death. It is a reminder of the extent to which the volume

is haunted by Thomas's dreadful demise and what it might mean. As Wallace
Fowlie put it, "The real lover of death is the real lover of life and beauty" (*Y*,
29). That death tended, with hindsight, to affect recollections of the readings: a
number of the poems revealed how deeply listeners were touched by them, an
example being Marguerite Harris's "Cherry Lane," which described Thomas's
"public-ravaged face" and "the seething stresses lancinating there" (*Y*, 10). As
in earlier essays, here is Thomas as victim, a view perhaps intensified by the
second point, that Thomas may have been in decline as a poet. As Scott put it,
Thomas's early death "may mean he was spared a long Swinburnian death-in-
life" (*Y*, 14). A sympathetic piece by Kimon Friar on *Under Milk Wood* implied
much the same in surmising that a potentially great dramatist was lost, who
could have moved on from "the more expanded dramatic objectivity of his later
prose and poetry" (*Y*, 17), a dramatic phoenix rising from the ashes of a poetic
career.

The final memorializing word was that of William Carlos Williams. He celebrated unequivocally the Welshness that led to "song," and Thomas's packed
lyricism:

Thomas was a lyric poet and, I think a great one. Such memorable poems as "Over Sir
John's Hill" and, even more to be emphasized, "On His Birthday", are far and away
beyond the reach of any contemporary English or American poet. . . . You may not like
such poems but prefer a more reasoned mode but this is impassioned poetry, you might
call it drunken poetry, it smacks of the divine—as Dylan Thomas does also. . . . He had
passion and a heart which carried him where he wanted to go, but it cannot be said that
he did not choose what he wanted. (*Y*, 21–22)

Though here the intellectual element is downplayed, possibly indicating the poet
rather than the (American) critic, Thomas as tragic chooser is more dignified
than Thomas as victim. It may not be true, but we wish to believe it was so.

As has been seen, Thomas's preoccupation with religion has been discussed
by a number of American critics. W. S. Merwin devoted a whole essay to the
subject, considering him to be a great religious poet. In most of the early work,
Merwin argued, "the 'I' is 'man' trying to find a means of imagining and
thereby redeeming his condition; much of the seemingly baroque and motiveless
'agony' of the earlier poems stems from the desperateness of this need," an
idea that, in terms of style, has been developed by Eleanor McNees. In the later
poems Merwin argued that Thomas progressed to the belief that love is more
powerful than death.[29]

Merwin's essay provides a focus for those early religious concerns and thus
a useful prelude to the first book-length study of Thomas by an American. This,
published in 1954, was by Elder Olson.[30] As befitted a distinguished member
of the Chicago school of criticism, Olson offered an approach through structure
that emerged from an examination of texts as close as that of any New Critic.
In the history of Thomas criticism Olson is the North American equivalent of

England's William Empson: a major critic who wrote brilliantly on the early work and general poetic techniques. That early work created a universe dominated by the "enormous range and power" of a poetic imagination that defamiliarized the world: "We should see flowers on a grave; he sees the dead 'who periscope through flowers to the sky.' " Olson understood Thomas's career in terms of religious faith. In the early poems we are shown that "to a serious and sensitive individual, life in the absence of a sustaining faith is a nightmare." The turning point in Thomas's progress is the "Altarwise by owl-light" sonnet sequence, Olson's detailed analysis of which has become the volume's most controversial section. He argued for the unity and coherence of the sequence, detecting six different levels of recurring symbolism. The most debated of these have been those of Greek myth, astronomical symbolism, and Christianity, or, as Olson wrote:

(4) a level based on ancient myth, principally Greek, representing the fortunes of the sun in terms of the adventures of the sun-hero Hercules;

(5) a level based on relations of the *constellation* Hercules to other constellations and astronomical phenomena; and

(6) a level derived from the Christian interpretation of levels 4 and 5.

The sequence was seen as one version of Thomas's "struggle from darkness to light" that here insisted on the redeeming powers of God's mercy. The objections—and there have been many—are predictable and are directed against Olson's assumptions regarding the kind of arcane, scholarly knowledge that the lightly educated Thomas could have possessed. Brian Way's reference, already quoted, to "the most extraordinary excesses of American myth-criticism"[31] has doubtless spoken for many. We feel instinctively that Olson's structure does not reflect Thomas's poetic procedures and probably not his knowledge. But we also feel that Olson's interpretations are not wholly imposed upon the poem; rather, the difficulty in accepting them results from the extrapolation of a complete scheme from individual instances of, say, astronomical imagery. Olson cannot be dismissed. At the very least he exhibited the structural complexity and coherence of Thomas's work; he pointed to a way of reading the poems as wholes or interconnected wholes and to the necessity of close reading. He also wrote with a chastening humility that is a pleasing contrast to the prejudiced utterances of some British critics. He regarded Thomas as the author of great poems, including, particularly, the sonnet sequence, "A Refusal to Mourn," "Vision and Prayer," and "Ballad of the Long-legged Bait." But he kept in mind that

those of a poet's own age do not have the last word about its value; they do, however, have the first word, and . . . this much we who have the first word may say: that he seemed to us one of the great artists of our time, and that, in his struggle from darkness to light, he uncovered darknesses in him that we should otherwise not have known, and brought us to a light we should not otherwise have seen.

In 1955 John Malcolm Brinnin published *Dylan Thomas in America*, the best-selling account of the last three years of Thomas's life.[32] Brinnin described Thomas's American reading tours in great and sensational detail: the drunkenness and dreadful behavior, and the vicious public quarrels between husband and wife when Caitlin accompanied him. Thomas was the driven, self-destroying writer who knew that he was over the hill and sought to escape that fact. Whereas in Britain Thomas's faults of character influence too many critical ventures, in America, where the impact of Brinnin's book was greatest, the serious critical debate continued, not, of course, unaffected by the revelations, but still objective.

For 1955 saw two responses to Olson's book. Ralph Maud criticized its strained and unconvincing interpretations; Brewster Ghiselin, however, more open-mindedly praised it for "reasoned explications . . . fresh information and rich insights . . . or alternative readings which, compelling or not, must stimulate reconsideration and sometimes enlarge understanding."[33] In November 1955 *Poetry* published its own memorial tribute to Thomas that, in part, pointed to one future development in Thomas studies.[34] It reprinted four transcriptions of notebook poems from the manuscript notebooks in Buffalo and facsimiles of worksheets for "Poem on his Birthday" held in the Houghton Library at Harvard: initial gestures at necessary textual studies. Of the other contributions, which included poems and reviews, the most important was Karl Shapiro's essay.

Shapiro tried to analyze the effect on readers of Thomas's work, of the kind of poetry "that touched the raw nerve of the world and that keeps us singing with pain." Though he found nothing original in either meter or language and regarded Thomas as often "a quite derivative, unoriginal, unintellectual poet . . . [who] sometimes attempted to keep people from understanding his poems," yet, Shapiro continued, he would wish to keep more than thirty of Thomas's poems that "stand with the best poems of our time." The simplest poems were the best, despite the fact that—and here he may have had in mind Brinnin's revelations—"through the obscurity of the poetry everyone could feel the scream of desperation." This was one reason why Thomas found such a large audience that also seemed an "impossible one: a general audience for a barely understandable poet." Shapiro concluded:

It is easy to dismiss him, but he will not be dismissed. . . . What he said was that man is a child thrust into the power of self; an animal becoming an angel. But becoming an angel he becomes more a beast. There is no peace, no rest, and death itself is only another kind of disgusting sex. Yet man must not believe so little. He must invent a belief in love, even if it doesn't exist.

Despite his intellectual reservations, Shapiro found himself responding to Thomas's emotional power.[35]

The 1960s, in which American critical engagement with Thomas reached its apogee, began with salutary warnings from Monroe C. Beardsley and Sam Hynes. They used Thomas's "Altarwise" sequence in order to highlight unsound critical approaches, from the rejection of explication to the imposing of critical systems in the Olson manner.[36] We are again forcibly made aware of the critical struggle waged over Thomas's texts.

That struggle continued during the same year in M. L. Rosenthal's *The Modern Poets*. Seven years after Thomas's death he offered honest doubt. Thomas's achievement was "romantic, incantatory, 'bardic', though not really . . . nonintellectual." Despite the latter, the reader gained sufficient "sensuous gratification" (the phrase is D. H. Lawrence's) to make understanding unnecessary. Ultimately,

Thomas's poetry is a reaction away from the topical, the "social," and the ratiocinative to a realm of introspective personalism which is at the same time inclusively human. It was that reaction, as well as the native genius he revealed, which so surprised and overwhelmed Thomas's first audience and persuaded their affection.[37]

Ralph Maud was in no doubt. *Entrances to Dylan Thomas' Poetry* (1963) is a general study that remains one of the best introductions.[38] With an unrivalled knowledge of Thomas's working methods, gained from studying the manuscripts, Maud argued for close attention to Thomas's uniqueness, rather than the approach through literary tradition that has been a staple of American engagement. He began by dismissing the "Welshness" question as irrelevant: "Thomas was not a 'Welsh bard'; he was an English poet." Knowing what he read did not help much; for example, "The similarity between Hopkins and Thomas is only superficial." Through detailed exegesis, including an exemplary section on "I see the boys of summer," and wide-ranging reference, Maud joined the long line of American critics who use Thomas's letter to Henry Treece to demonstrate his "dialectical method," the constant presence in his poems of polar opposites. Maud argued for the importance of the unit, such as the individual image. He also insisted that "the full significance of a poem will be in the literal narrative plus the central concept inherent in the symbolic power of the wording." For Maud, Thomas was a writer of poems in which the processes of the body provide metaphors for external natural processes. The result was a poetry that gave "a sense of the interplay of forces beneath the ordinary events of life." In support, he offered the most detailed account of "process" vocabulary and themes in the poems. Maud faced the question of difficulty, arguing that the slow gaining of understanding is a way of distancing intimately sexual and religious material, and the question posed by the later clarity, using worksheets to demonstrate Thomas's search for language that was at once descriptive and symbolic. The appended "Chronology of Composition" reprints material from an earlier article to show that the order in which Thomas's poems were published is very different from the order in which they were written.[39] Such basic and meticulous scholarship, together with his edition of Thomas's notebooks[40] and his later collaboration with Walford Davies to edit *Collected Poems, 1934–1953*, represents a major and indispensable contribution to Thomas studies.

A further account, H. H. Kleinman's study of the religious sonnets, was also published in 1963.[41] Kleinman drew on a deep knowledge of biblical scholarship and seventeenth-century poetry and has been wrongly accused of turning Thomas into an expert theologian with a special interest in the Caroline divines. Unlike, say, Olson, who uncovered deliberate astronomical patterns in the "Altarwise" sequence, Kleinman was mainly concerned with similarities between Thomas's work and other kinds of religious writing. He argued that the sonnets explored "a fearful struggle of the poet with his God" that began with mockery and ended with faith. That general progress was not in itself startlingly original, but Kleinman also offered much brilliantly illuminating close reading. Though Kleinman's scholarship sometimes risks overwhelming the sonnets, here is yet another example of the rewards of close engagement with Thomas's most difficult work, and of the deep suggestiveness of Thomas's text.

Four other important studies appeared during the mid-1960s. That by Jacob Korg is a Twayne English Authors volume, thus recognizing continuing wide interest in the poet.[42] The series format required a biographical account, which Korg duly provided, despite his view that "Dylan Thomas' life and times have only a limited relevance to his poetry." The earlier poetry, having little to do with external reality, exhibited a mystic and mythic consciousness, concerned with "a number of convictions about time, immortality, personal identity, the unity of existence, and similar matters which are the familiar principles of intuitive religion." Such metaphysical concerns were a source of Thomas's obscurity. In the later poems, however, "ultimate realities are approached through nature and daily life instead of visionary imagery," which might seem to cast doubt on Korg's opening assertion about the irrelevance of life and times. But, in general, he offered a coherent explanation of Thomas's increasing approachability from within the work rather than in terms of the external influences of, for example, radio and film scriptwriting. Korg is a member of the large group of American critics who regard Thomas as primarily a religious poet. His central contention about Thomas's language—that its innovative strangeness jolts the reader out of his or her everyday understanding of words into a "rhetoric of mysticism"—is another idea that, as will be seen, has been developed by Eleanor McNees.

In 1966 William T. Moynihan published what is still an essential study of Thomas.[43] Like Korg—and thus part of a reaction against the scandalous legend—he insisted on a firm distinction between the life and the works. At times this is just as well, given some overstatement regarding Thomas's life: Moynihan believed that Thomas belonged to the "upper-middle-class" and had, on his mother's side, a "long clerical heritage." More convincingly, he argued that obscurity can result from investing the ordinary with cosmic meaning, and that syntactical complexity can be a serious defect. Nonetheless, Thomas had important things to say. His "early work is principally concerned with themes of revolt, the middle work with themes of reflection and debate, the late work with themes of praise and consent." Overall, that work shows "a mythic perception of the human condition . . . from origin to regeneration." We see from this that like so many of his American predecessors, Moynihan was much concerned with the religious elements in Thomas's poetry, concluding that the poems use Christian imagery in a non-Christian way to celebrate the creative powers of love and nature. Thomas was not "a howling iconoclast raging in his animality" but "the celebrant of a secular . . . [and] unified state of existence between man and nature where there is no death." Once again, there is much close reading, with illuminating material on recurring imagery. A section on sound patterns in Thomas suggests the influence of traditional Welsh-language poetry and asserts that as Thomas's career developed, there was a consistently supportive relationship between sound and meaning. (Louise Murdy's more comprehensive analysis of Thomas's use of sound reached much the same conclusion.[44]) In Moynihan's opinion, Thomas was "one of a half dozen major poets writing in English in the first half of our century."

The most important volume of the decade was that by J. Hillis Miller, now famous for his association with deconstruction and for having been "the leading polemicist for the Yale School."[45] In the 1960s, however, he practiced the "criticism of consciousness" of Georges Poulet, concerned to reveal the consciousness of the author in his work.[46] Apart from Thomas, Miller's "poets of reality" include Conrad, Yeats, T. S. Eliot, and Wallace Stevens, modernist writers who stated, "If there is to be a God in the new world it must be a presence within things and not beyond them." Miller thus sought to reveal Thomas's religious consciousness. In so doing he accepted, with Thomas, the literal meaning of the poetry: "The difficulty of so many of his poems derives from this assertion as literally true of what would usually be thought of as metaphorical relations." In insisting, further, that Thomas's work reflected the "passionate apprehension of things through the senses" and the "coincidence of self and world," and, in conclusion, that "self, world, and deity dwell together in the ark of the poem," Miller exhibited the unified nature of Thomas's vision.

As has been noted, from the first the influential American critical studies of Thomas have invariably included illuminating close analysis, reflecting New Critical dominance. Also from the first, such studies have been written against a background of what can be described as concentrated exegesis, the main example of which is the series of detailed elucidations of poems, or parts of poems, in the *Explicator*.[47] Massive consolidation plus further original analysis had come in 1962 in two detailed, line-by-line—at times word-by-word—explications of the poetry, neither of which has been wholly superseded.

The first was by William York Tindall.[48] His introduction was an important general survey that noted the several ways in which Thomas—as man and as poet—has been regarded, that

Thomas had no interest in politics and society; that he was a religious poet, a surrealist, a disciple of Freud, a composer of nonsense verse, and a student of Welsh "cynghan-nedd" [sic]—that he was deeply learned or incredibly ignorant. Though each of these notions has something to commend it, none fits Thomas exactly.

The explication that follows employs the scattergun approach, hurling sugges-tions at Thomas's text. The target is sometimes hit with brilliantly stimulating results; sometimes it seems to be missed altogether. Even though Beardsley and Hynes may well have had Tindall in mind when they wrote of interpretation without any real context, the effect of his approach can still be exhilarating. Tindall was more concerned with local effects than with the poem as a unit, but his approach, though at times uncontrollably associative, again and again dem-onstrated Thomas's poetic intelligence at work, offering meaning, making con-nections, and deploying a surprisingly wide range of reference. Tindall was also not afraid to doubt received opinion: he questioned Thomas's description of "breeding images" and wondered whether "the process is systematically 'di-alectical.' " He wondered whether Thomas was a religious poet in the conven-tional way: "God and Christ are always around in Thomas's poetry—not in their proper capacities, however, but as metaphors for nature, poet, and their creative powers." In Tindall's view, hinting at Shapiro's "scream of despera-tion," the poetry conveyed "the sadness of a man aware of time and death." That said, Tindall then asserted, in the face of so much of his exegesis, that "though important, these themes are less important than his genius and his craft with words." In this we hear, unexpectedly, an echo of early critical fatuities about sound rather than sense and Thomas's "pure poetry."

The second work, by Clark Emery, also explicates more or less line by line.[49] His book, however, transforms our sense of Thomas by organizing his poetry in terms of theme: "poems revealing the poet as a human being; as a student of human relationships; as a practicing poet; as a war poet; as a seeker of God; as an amateur philosopher." Emery thus disposed of any notion of Thomas as a writer endlessly preoccupied with "process" and little concerned with external reality. Emery's approach is more discursively reflective than Tindall's and, perhaps because of this, lacks the latter's clarity. His interpretations can be as difficult as the poems themselves. Yet he presented a coherent, if conventional, overview of Thomas's work: his poetry, as a "a movement from darkness to light", was, like the work of so many poets, "seeking God: a lost Christian God, the true Christian God, or a substitute in Nature or Art or History or Man." It was a modern search: Thomas seeks a Christianity that "assimilates Frazer, Freud, Darwin."

Since 1970 there have been a number of important American studies of Tho-mas's work building on the earlier firm foundations. The earliest was Annis

Pratt's study of the prose, part of which was included during 1966 in C. B. Cox's edition of essays.[50] Pratt reversed received opinion to make a case for the early prose, regarding the later, from *Portrait of the Artist as a Young Dog* onwards, as "a minor genre within his writing."[51] Her stress was on the mythical, religious, occult, and surreal elements of that early writing. She investigated possible sources of these elements and suggested the influence of T. F. Powys, the stories of the Welsh writers Arthur Machen and Caradoc Evans, Thomas's knowledge of Welsh and Egyptian mythology, and surrealist writing of the 1930s and the work of Carl Jung, the last two available to Thomas through the magazine *transition*, which he is known to have read and to which he contributed a poem and a story in 1936. The result was a fictional world in which Thomas's heroes searched "for an eternally creative Word at the center of the universe," and in which Thomas used surrealistic effects in an intellectually controlled way to dramatize extreme states of mind. Though there may be doubts about the range of reading Pratt claimed for the young Thomas, her importance is in pointing to the rich suggestiveness of the prose. She applied to it the kind of scholarship and close reading her predecessors applied mainly to the poetry.

In 1973 Rushworth Kidder's study of Thomas as a religious poet sought to clear ground in the interests of greater precision. He considered terms frequently applied to Thomas, such as "mystic," "pantheistic," and "sacramental," finding each to be inadequate both in terms of definition and application. The fundamental impulse for Thomas's poetry was religion; Kidder demonstrated through superb close analysis the extent to which biblical imagery penetrates Thomas's work. His conclusion was that Thomas's work exhibits a fascinating inconsistency in moving to a greater spiritual commitment.[52]

The most important general American study of Thomas since 1970 is R. B. Kershner's magisterial survey of Thomas's biographical and critical history up to 1975.[53] Kershner examined every aspect of Thomas's literary career, from the legend of the life to serious biography to Thomas as religious poet and, importantly, to the general and particular contexts out of which he came, plus the poetics that he developed. His survey sought to counter all previous critical and biographical excesses and to conclude that though cast by many as a romantic victim-hero, a victim both of society and his own romantic ego, Thomas's tendency to humorous self-deprecation meant that he never quite played such roles.

One of Kershner's important themes was that there had been a lack of precision in Thomas studies: for example, not until Kidder's book had there been a systematic attempt to place Thomas precisely as a religious writer. The same could be said about Thomas in relation to twentieth-century literary movements from modernism to the Movement; there was a need to recognize the implications of stating that "belonging to no group or movement, Thomas has affinities with many." As for the question of Thomas's Welshness, in arguing that he fitted into Welsh literature "as uneasily as he does in the British," Kershner anticipated the urgent modern necessity of clarifying distinctions between British literatures in English, given, as has been stated, the increased questioning of monolithic "English Literature" His main conclusion was the present writer's recurring theme:

> Thomas's poems will continue to attract imaginative minds and acute sensibilities. They demand reading in their own terms; if we must find new methods for unravelling them and a new vocabulary to hint at their workings, then that is one measure of their success.

One aspect of Kershner's concern with the Welsh literary context was Thomas's relationship with Welsh-language poetic traditions. He stressed that Welsh speakers either reject or have strong reservations about English-speaking Thomas's knowledge and use of traditional Welsh poetic techniques. His call for "something more than impressionistic criticism" was answered by Katherine T. Loesch, who quoted the phrase and certainly responded to it. Her papers made a strong case for Thomas having had some access to knowledge of Welsh poetic forms.[54] Her study of "I dreamed my genesis" not only argued against suggestions that Hopkins was the source of Thomas's knowledge of the Welsh *englyn* but also showed that the poem observes traditional rules. Given the already-mentioned scepticism on the part of Welsh speakers and the fact that Thomas's sources for that knowledge remain a matter for speculation, the jury is probably still out, but it is thinking hard and is grateful for Loesch's new precision.

Echoes of early prejudice are still occasionally heard, ignoring later developments. Hugh Kenner, for example, believed that Thomas "took no account at all of the public world and what had been happening to it." Early promise came to nothing.[55] Two distinguished modern writers were, however, more considered. Louis Simpson furthered the exploration of Thomas's literary context by linking him to Allen Ginsberg, Robert Lowell, and Sylvia Plath in a tradition of poetry as "passionate speech."[56] Seamus Heaney, whose Bennington College lecture on Thomas might be considered as part of the American literary scene, argued powerfully that "Thomas's achievement rests upon a number of strong, uniquely estranging, technically original and resonant poems, including one of the best villanelles in the language." He praised early poems such as "Before I knocked," "The force that through the green fuse drives the flower," and "A process in the weather of the heart," in which "affections and impulses have been stabilized not into dogma but in the form." But the later, famous poems "avert the eyes from the prospect of necessity," all except "Do not go gentle," where "craft has not lost touch with a suffered world."[57]

A final example of greater precision entering the ongoing critical debate is Eleanor J. McNees's *Eucharistic Poetry*.[58] She described Thomas's work as "today discredited or ignored by many critics." She then examined in detail ways in which Donne, Hopkins, Thomas, and Geoffrey Hill "force their words to mime the fraction and communion of the eucharistic ceremony." In her section on Thomas she moved beyond generalities about the religious poet to investigate textual effects. She noted that previous writers on Thomas and religion, such as Olson, Kidder, and Aneirin Talfan Davies, charted "a steady progression toward a Christian sacramental vision." Others—Stanford, Merwin, and Stuart Holroyd in *Emergence From Chaos* (London: Gollancz, 1957)—argued for an "innate 'animal faith.' " McNees demonstrated that in his earlier work Thomas disrupted and distorted language—syntax, diction, rhythms, the relationship between sound and sense—to suggest tension with God and "to *manifest* the experience instead of to *tell* it." We encounter a "realization of a simultaneous secular and sacred presence" and "a deepening sense of the inevitability of sacrifice." In Thomas's later work, "as he relinquishes his rivalry with God and Adam [his] syntax grows less contradictory," and rhythm and sound become increasingly supportive of meaning. McNees's central thesis, that Thomas's poems constantly reenact a sacrificial/redemptive sequence, is a theologically more precise restatement of Thomas's "individual struggle from darkness towards some measure of light."[59] Her close encounter with Thomas's writing—focussing on the religious element that has preoccupied so many American and other critics—is a demonstration of the persisting richness of Thomas's writing that may well begin a new critical phase.

NOTES

1. Dylan Thomas, "The Visitor," in *Best British Short Stories of 1935*, ed. Edward O'Brien (Boston: Houghton Mifflin, 1935), 193–200.

2. Geoffrey Grigson, "A Letter from England," *Poetry*, November 1936: 101–3.

3. *Kenyon Review*, Summer 1939: 351.

4. Philip Blair Rice, "Twenty-five Directions," *Kenyon Review*, Winter 1939: 109–10.

5. Herbert Read, "The Present State of Poetry: I. In England," *Kenyon Review*, Autumn 1939: 367.

6. Julian Symons, "Obscurity and Dylan Thomas," *Kenyon Review*, Winter 1940: 71.

7. John Berryman, review of *The World I Breathe, Kenyon Review*, Autumn 1940: 482–485.

8. Arthur Mizener, *Kenyon Review*, Winter 1944: 123–26.

9. Robert Horan, "In Defense of Dylan Thomas," *Kenyon Review*, Spring 1945: 304, 305, 310; emphasis in the original.

10. Howard Moss, "Ten Poets," *Kenyon Review*, Spring 1947: 290, 291, 292.

11. John Crowe Ransom, "The Poetry of 1900–1950," *Kenyon Review*, Summer 1951: 452.

12. Howard Nemerov, "The Generation of Violence," *Kenyon Review*, Summer 1953: 478, 479, 481, 483.

13. Geoffrey Moore, "Dylan Thomas," *Kenyon Review*, Spring 1955: 258–77.

14. Richard Ellmann, "Wallace Stevens' Ice Cream," *Kenyon Review*, Winter 1957: 101. See also 97.

15. George Steiner, "The Retreat from Word," *Kenyon Review*, Spring 1961: 207.

16. Brewster Ghiselin, "The Extravagant Energy of Genius," *Western Review*, Spring 1954: 245–49. This is a review of *Collected Poems, 1934–1952*.

17. Marshall W. Stearns, "Unsex the Skeleton: Notes on the Poetry of Dylan Thomas," in E. W. Tedlock (ed.), *Dylan Thomas: The Legend and the Poet* (London: Heinemann, 1960), 116, 120, 119, 126, 129, 130, 131. Stearns's essay was first published in *Sewanee Review* 52 (1944): 424–40.

18. John L. Sweeney, Introduction to *Selected Writings*, by Dylan Thomas (New York: New Directions, 1946), x, xv, xx, xxiii.

19. David Aivaz, "The Poetry of Dylan Thomas," *Hudson Review* 3 (Autumn 1950): 386, 385, 394, 390, 400, 404.

20. Thomas's full description of his approach to composition is in *CL*, 281–82. Letter to Henry Treece, 23 March 1938.

21. Thomas Traherne, "The Third Century—3," in *Poems, Centuries, and Three Thanksgivings*, ed. Anne Ridler (London: Oxford University Press, 1966), 264.

22. Babette Deutsch, "The Orient Wheat," *Virginia Quarterly Review* 27 (Spring 1951): 226, 222, 229, 228, 235, 234, 231, 234, 236.

23. John L. Sweeney, "Intimations of Mortality," *New Republic*, 17 March 1952: 18, 22–23.

24. Cid Corman, "Dylan Thomas: Rhetorician in Mid-Career," *Accent* 13 (Winter 1953): 56–59. Quotations from E. W. Tedlock (ed.), *Dylan Thomas: The Legend and the Poet* (London: Heinemann, 1960), 223, 225, 223.

25. John L. Sweeney, "The Round Sunday Sounds," *New Republic*, 6 April 1953: 24–25.

26. Ralph Maud, "Dylan Thomas's Poetry," *Essays in Criticism* 4 (1954): 411–12, 415, 417, 418.

27. *Yale Literary Magazine*, November 1954. Its contents are as follows: Richard Eberhart, "Some Memories of Dylan Thomas," 5–6; William Jay Smith, "Life, Literature, and Dylan," 7; Babette Deutsch, "For Dylan Thomas on the Day of His Death" (poem), 8; José Garcia Villa, "Death and Dylan Thomas" (poem), 9; Marguerite Harris, "Four Poems," 10–12; Winfield Townley Scott, "The Death, and Some Dominions of It," 13–14; Kimon Friar, "Dylan Thomas and the Poetic Drama," 15–19; Alastair Reed, "A First Word," 20; William Carlos Williams, "Dylan Thomas," 21–22; Isabella Gardner, "When a Warlock Dies" (poem), 22; Joseph Tusiani, "For Dylan Thomas on the Day of His Death" (poem), 23–25; Kenneth Rexroth, "Lament for Dylan Thomas" (poem), 26–27; Wallace Fowlie, "On the Death of Dylan Thomas," 28–29; Horace Gregory, "The Romantic Heritage of Dylan Thomas," 30–34. References to this issue, abbreviated as *Y*, are included in the text.

28. Horace Gregory, "The Romantic Heritage of Dylan Thomas," *Poetry*, March 1947: 326–36.

29. W. S. Merwin, "The Religious Poet," *Adam International Review* 238 (1953): 73–78.

30. Elder Olson, *The Poetry of Dylan Thomas* (Chicago: University of Chicago Press, 1954), 12, 18, 64, 19, 88–89.

31. Brian Way, review of T. H. Jones, *Dylan Thomas, Anglo-Welsh Review* 14, no. 33 (1964): 119–20.

32. John Malcolm Brinnin, *Dylan Thomas in America* (Boston: Atlantic–Little, Brown, 1955).

33. Ralph Maud, "Dylan Thomas Astro-Navigated," *Essays in Criticism* 5 (1955):

164–68; Brewster Ghiselin, "Critical Work in Progress," *Poetry*, November 1955: 118–19.

34. *Poetry* (special issue), November 1955: 63–129.

35. Karl Shapiro, "Comment: Dylan Thomas," *Poetry*, November 1955: 100, 103, 104, 107, 109.

36. Monroe C. Beardsley and Sam Hynes, "Misunderstanding Poetry: Notes on Some Readings of Dylan Thomas," *College English* 21 (1960): 315–22.

37. M. L. Rosenthal, *The Modern Poets: A Critical Introduction* (New York: Oxford University Press, 1960), 203, 207, 219.

38. Ralph Maud, *Entrances to Dylan Thomas' Poetry* (Pittsburgh: University of Pittsburgh Press, 1963), 2, 4, 49, 80.

39. See Ralph N. Maud, "Dylan Thomas' *Collected Poems*: Chronology of Composition," *PMLA* 76 (1961): 292–97.

40. Ralph Maud (ed.), *The Notebooks of Dylan Thomas* (New York: New Directions, 1967).

41. H. H. Kleinman, *The Religious Sonnets of Dylan Thomas: A Study in Imagery and Meaning* (Berkeley: University of California Press, 1963), 11.

42. Jacob Korg, *Dylan Thomas*, Twayne's English Authors Series (New York: Twayne, 1965), 13, 27, 29, Chapter 2, passim.

43. William T. Moynihan, *The Craft and Art of Dylan Thomas* (1966; Ithaca, NY: Cornell University Press, 1968), 16, 18, 159, 217, 292, 295.

44. Louise Baughan Murdy, *Sound and Sense in Dylan Thomas's Poetry* (The Hague: Mouton, 1966).

45. Imre Salusinszky, *Criticism in Society* (New York and London: Methuen, 1987), 210.

46. See J. Hillis Miller, *Poets of Reality: Six Twentieth-Century Writers* (Cambridge, MA: Harvard University Press, 1966), 10, 194, 196, 215, 216.

47. A list of articles on Thomas's works in *The Explicator* during the period 1945–1967 is in Ralph Maud, *Dylan Thomas in Print* (London: Dent, 1970), 185–86.

48. William York Tindall, *A Reader's Guide to Dylan Thomas* (1962; New York: Octagon Books, 1981), 7, 18, 8, 16.

49. Clark Emery, *The World of Dylan Thomas* (Coral Gables, FL: University of Miami Press, 1962), 28, 7, 15.

50. Annis Pratt, "Dylan Thomas's Prose," *Dylan Thomas: A Collection of Critical Essays*, ed. C. B. Cox, Twentieth Century Views (Englewood Cliffs, NJ: Prentice-Hall, 1966), 117–29.

51. Annis Pratt, *Dylan Thomas' Early Prose: A Study in Creative Mythology* (Pittsburgh: University of Pittsburgh Press, 1970), xii, 84.

52. Rushworth M. Kidder, *Dylan Thomas: The Country of the Spirit* (Princeton: Princeton University Press, 1973).

53. R. B. Kershner, Jr., *Dylan Thomas: The Poet and His Critics* (Chicago: American Library Association, 1976), 150, 230.

54. Katherine T. Loesch, "Welsh Poetic Syntax and the Poetry of Dylan Thomas," *Transactions of the Honourable Society of Cymmrodorion*, 1979: 159–202; "Welsh Poetic Stanza Form and Dylan Thomas's 'I dreamed my genesis,' " *Transactions of the Honourable Society of Cymmrodorion*, 1982: 1–24. Neither article is included in Georg Gaston's *Dylan Thomas: A Reference Guide* (Boston: G. K. Hall, 1987).

55. Hugh Kenner, *A Sinking Island: The Modern English Writers* (1988; Baltimore: Johns Hopkins University Press, 1989), 232.

56. Louis Simpson, *A Revolution in Taste: Studies of Dylan Thomas, Allen Ginsberg, Sylvia Plath, and Robert Lowell* (New York: Macmillan, 1978), 3–42.

57. Seamus Heaney, *Dylan the Durable? On Dylan Thomas* (Bennington: Bennington College, 1992), 15, 18, 31–32, 25.

58. Eleanor J. McNees, *Eucharistic Poetry* (London and Toronto: Associated University Presses, 1992), 9, 114, 115.

59. Dylan Thomas, ''Answers to an Enquiry,'' *New Verse*, October 1934: 8.

Selected Bibliography

WORKS BY DYLAN THOMAS

18 Poems. London: *Sunday Referee* and the Parton Bookshop, 1934.

Twenty-five Poems. London: Dent, 1936.

The Map of Love. London: Dent, 1939.

The World I Breathe. Norfolk, CT: New Directions, 1939.

Portrait of the Artist as a Young Dog. London: Dent, 1940.

New Poems. Norfolk, CT: New Directions, 1943.

Deaths and Entrances. London: Dent, 1946.

Selected Writings. Intro. John L. Sweeney. New York: New Directions, 1946.

Collected Poems, 1934–1952. London: Dent, 1952.

In Country Sleep and Other Poems. New York: New Directions, 1952.

The Collected Poems of Dylan Thomas. New York: New Directions, 1953.

Quite Early One Morning. London: Dent, 1954.

Under Milk Wood. Preface by Daniel Jones. 1954. London: Dent/Everyman, 1992.

A Prospect of the Sea. Ed. Daniel Jones. London: Dent, 1955.

Adventures in the Skin Trade. Aldine paperback ed., 1955. London: Dent, 1965.

Letters to Vernon Watkins. Ed. Vernon Watkins. London: Dent and Faber & Faber, 1957.

The Beach of Falesá. 1964. New York: Stein and Day, 1983.

Twenty Years A-Growing. London: Dent, 1964.

Me and My Bike. London: Triton, 1965.

Rebecca's Daughters. 1965. London: Grafton, 1992.

The Doctor and the Devils, and Other Scripts. New York: New Directions, 1966.

Poet in the Making: The Notebooks of Dylan Thomas. Ed. Ralph Maud. London: Dent, 1968.

Early Prose Writings. Ed. Walford Davies. London: Dent, 1971.

The Poems. Ed. Daniel Jones. Revised ed. 1974. London: Dent, 1982.

Selected Poems. Ed. Walford Davies. 1974. Revised Everyman ed. London: Dent, 1993.

The Death of the King's Canary (with John Davenport). 1976. Harmondsworth: Penguin, 1978.

Collected Stories. Ed. Walford Davies. 1983. London: Dent/Everyman, 1995.

The Collected Letters. Ed. Paul Ferris. London: Dent, 1985.

Collected Poems, 1934–1953. Ed. Walford Davies and Ralph Maud. London: Dent, 1988.
The Notebook Poems, 1930–34. Ed. Ralph Maud. London: Dent, 1989.
The Broadcasts. Ed. Ralph Maud. London: Dent, 1991.
Letter to Loren. Ed. Jeff Towns. Swansea: Salubrious Press, 1993.
The Filmscripts. Ed. John Ackerman. London: Dent, 1995.
Under Milk Wood. Ed. Walford Davies and Ralph Maud. ''The Definitive Edition.''
      London: Dent, 1995.

MANUSCRIPTS

The main collections are in the following repositories:

Austin, TX: Harry Ransom Humanities Research Center, University of Texas.
Buffalo, NY: Lockwood Memorial Library, State University of New York.
Cambridge, MA: Houghton Library, Harvard University.

Smaller collections are in the following:

Aberystwyth, Wales: National Library of Wales.
Bloomington, IN: Lilly Library, Indiana University.
London: British Library.
Newark, DE: University of Delaware Library.
New York: Berg Collection, New York Public Library.

BIBLIOGRAPHIES

Davies, James A. ''Dylan Thomas.'' *Annotated Bibliography of English Studies*. Abing-
      don: Swets & Zeitlinger, 1997. CD-ROM.
Gaston, Georg M. A. *Dylan Thomas: A Reference Guide*. Boston: G. K. Hall, 1987.
Harris, John. *A Bibliographical Guide to Twenty-four Modern Anglo-Welsh Writers*. Car-
      diff: University of Wales Press, 1994.
Maud, Ralph. *Dylan Thomas in Print: A Bibliographical History (with Appendix)*. Lon-
      don: Dent, 1970.
Rolph, J. Alexander. *Dylan Thomas: A Bibliography*. London: Dent, 1956.

WORKS ON DYLAN THOMAS: A SELECT LIST

This section does not include all the items discussed in Part 3: Critical
History.

Ackerman, John. *Dylan Thomas: His Life and Work*. 1964. Basingstoke: Macmillan,
      1991.
———. *Welsh Dylan*. 1979. London: Granada, 1980.
———. *A Dylan Thomas Companion*. Basingstoke: Macmillan, 1991.
Bates, H. E. *The Modern Short Story*. London: Thomas Nelson, 1941.
Bayley, John. *The Romantic Survival*. London: Constable, 1957.

Bigliazzi, Sylvia. "Fable versus Fact: Hamlet's Ghost in Dylan Thomas's Early Poetry," *Textus* (Genoa) 5 (1992): 51–64.

Bold, Alan (ed.). *Dylan Thomas: Craft or Sullen Art*. London and New York: Vision Press and St. Martin's Press, 1990.

Brinnin, John Malcolm. *Dylan Thomas in America*. London: Dent, 1956.

———. (ed.). *A Casebook on Dylan Thomas*. New York: Crowell, 1960.

Brooke-Rose, Christine. *A Grammar of Metaphor*. London: Secker & Warburg, 1958.

Burns, Richard. *Ceri Richards and Dylan Thomas: Keys to Transformation*. London: Enitharmon Press, 1981.

Cleverdon, Douglas. *The Growth of "Milk Wood."* London: Dent, 1969.

Conran, Anthony. *The Cost of Strangeness*. Llandysul: Gomer Press, 1982.

Cox, C. B. (ed.). *Dylan Thomas: A Collection of Critical Essays*. Twentieth Century Views. Englewood Cliffs, NJ: Prentice-Hall, 1966.

———. "Welsh Bards in Hard Times: Dylan Thomas and R. S. Thomas," In *The New Pelican Guide to English Literature*. Vol. 8, *The Present*, ed. Boris Ford. Harmondsworth: Penguin, 1983. 209–23.

Daiches, David. *Literary Essays*. Edinburgh: Oliver & Boyd, 1956.

———. *The Present Age in British Literature*. Bloomington: Indiana University Press, 1958.

Davie, Donald. *Articulate Energy*. London: Routledge & Kegan Paul, 1955.

Davies, Aneirin Talfan. *Dylan: Druid of the Broken Body*. London: Dent, 1964.

Davies, James A. "Dylan Thomas' 'One Warm Saturday' and Tennyson's *Maud*." *Studies in Short Fiction* 14 (1977): 284–86.

———. " 'Crying in My Wordy Wilderness.' " *Anglo-Welsh Review* 83 (1986): 96–105.

———. "A Picnic in the Orchard: Dylan Thomas's Wales," In *Wales: The Imagined Nation*, ed. Tony Curtis. Bridgend: Poetry Wales Press, 1986. 45–65.

———. *Dylan Thomas's Places: A Biographical and Literary Guide*. Swansea: Christopher Davies, 1987.

———. " 'Hamlet on his father's coral': Dylan Thomas and Paternal Influence," *Welsh Writing in English: A Yearbook of Critical Essays* 1 (1995): 52–61.

———. " 'A Mental Militarist': Dylan Thomas and the Great War," *Welsh Writing in English: A Yearbook of Critical Essays* 2 (1996): 62–81.

———. "Questions of Identity: Dylan Thomas, the Movement, and After." In *Appropriations and Impositions: National, Regional and Sexual Identity in Literature*, ed. Igor Navrátil and Robert B. Pynsent. Bratislava: Národné literárne centrum, 1997. 118–29.

———. "Dylan Thomas in Oxford: An Unpublished Poem." *Notes and Queries* n.s. 44 (1997): 360–61.

Davies, Richard A. "Dylan Thomas's Image of the 'Young Dog' in the *Portrait*." *Anglo-Welsh Review* 26 (1977): 68–72.

Davies, Walford. "Imitation and Invention: The Use of Borrowed Material in Dylan Thomas's Prose." *Essays in Criticism* 18 (1968): 275–95.

———. *Dylan Thomas*. Writers of Wales. 1972. Revised ed. Cardiff: University of Wales Press, 1990.

———. (ed.). *Dylan Thomas: New Critical Essays*. London: Dent, 1972.

———. *Dylan Thomas*. Milton Keynes: Open University Press, 1986.

———. "Bright Fields, Loud Hills, and the Glimpsed Good Place: R. S. Thomas and

Dylan Thomas.'' In *The Page's Drift*, ed. M. Wynn Thomas. Bridgend: Seren, 1993. 171–210.

Deutsch, Babette. *Poetry in Our Time*. New York: Holt, 1952.

Emery, Clark. *The World of Dylan Thomas*. Coral Gables, FL: University of Miami Press, 1962.

Empson, William. *Argufying*. Ed. John Haffenden. London: Hogarth Press, 1988.

Farringdon, Jillian M., and Farringdon, Michael G. *A Concordance and Word-Lists to the Poems of Dylan Thomas*. Oxford: Oxford Microform Publications, 1980.

Ferris, Paul. *Dylan Thomas*. 1977. Harmondsworth: Penguin Books, 1978.

———. *Caitlin: The Life of Caitlin Thomas*. London: Hutchinson, 1993.

FitzGibbon, Constantine. *The Life of Dylan Thomas*. London: Dent, 1965.

Fraser, G. S. *Essays on Twentieth-Century Poets*. Leicester: Leicester University Press, 1978.

Gaston, Georg M. A. (ed.). *Critical Essays on Dylan Thomas*. Boston: G. K. Hall, 1989.

Grindea, Miron (ed.). *Adam International Review* 238 (1953). Dylan Thomas Memorial Number.

Hardy, Barbara. *The Advantage of Lyric: Essays on Feeling in Poetry*. London: Athlone Press, 1977.

———. *Dylan Thomas's Poetic Language: The Stream That Is Flowing Both Ways*. Cardiff: University College, Cardiff, 1987.

———. "Region and Nation: R. S. Thomas and Dylan Thomas." In *The Literature of Region and Nation*, ed. R. P. Draper. Basingstoke: Macmillan, 1989.

Heaney, Seamus. *Dylan the Durable? On Dylan Thomas*. Bennington, VT: Bennington College, 1992. Reprint. Seamus Heaney. *The Redress of Poetry*. London: Faber, 1995. 124–45.

Holbrook, David. "Two Welsh Writers: T. F. Powys and Dylan Thomas." *Pelican Guide to English Literature: The Modern Age*, ed. Boris Ford. Harmondsworth: Penguin Books, 1961. 415–28.

———. *Llareggub Revisited: Dylan Thomas and the State of Modern Poetry*. London: Bowes & Bowes, 1962.

———. *Dylan Thomas: The Code of Night*. London: Athlone Press, 1972.

Johnson, Pamela Hansford. *Important to Me: Personalia*. London: Macmillan, 1974.

Jones, Daniel. *My Friend Dylan Thomas*. London: Dent, 1977.

Jones, Glyn. *The Dragon Has Two Tongues*. London: Dent, 1968.

Jones, T. H. *Dylan Thomas*. Edinburgh: Oliver & Boyd, 1963.

Kershner, R. B., Jr. *Dylan Thomas: The Poet and His Critics*. Chicago: American Library Association, 1976.

Kidder, Rushworth Moulton. *Dylan Thomas: The Country of the Spirit*. Princeton, NJ: Princeton University Press, 1973.

Kleinman, H. H. *The Religious Sonnets of Dylan Thomas*. Berkeley: University of California Press, 1963.

Korg, Jacob. *Dylan Thomas*. New York: Twayne, 1965.

Lahey, Philip A. "Dylan Thomas: A Reappraisal." *Critical Survey* 5 (1993): 53–65.

Lewis, Peter Elfed. "Return Journey to Milk Wood." *Poetry Wales* 9 (1973): 27–38.

———. "*Under Milk Wood* as Radio Poem." *Anglo-Welsh Review* 64 (1979): 74–90.

———. "The Radio Road to Llareggub." In *British Radio Drama*, ed. John Drakakis. Cambridge: Cambridge University Press, 1981. 72–110.

Loesche, Katherine T. "Welsh Poetic Syntax and the Poetry of Dylan Thomas." *Transactions of the Honourable Society of Cymmrodorion*, 1979: 159–202.

———. "Welsh Poetic Stanza Form and Dylan Thomas's 'I Dreamed my genesis.' " *Transactions of the Honourable Society of Cymmrodorion*, 1982: 29–52.

———. "An Early Work on Irish Folklore and Dylan Thomas's 'A grief ago.' " In *Celtic Language, Celtic Culture*, ed. A. T. E. Matonis and Daniel F. Melia. Van Nuys, CA: Ford & Bailie, 1990. 308–21.

Mathias, Roland. *A Ride through the Wood*. Bridgend: Poetry Wales Press, 1985.

Maud, Ralph. *Entrances to Dylan Thomas' Poetry*. Pittsburgh: University of Pittsburgh Press, 1963.

———. (ed.). *Wales in His Arms: Dylan Thomas's Choice of Welsh Poetry*. Cardiff: University of Wales Press, 1994.

Maud, Ralph, and Davies, Aneirin Talfan (eds.). *The Colour of Saying: An Anthology of Verse Spoken by Dylan Thomas*. London: Dent, 1963.

McKay, Don. "Dot, Line, and Circle: A Structural Approach to Dylan Thomas's Imagery." *Anglo-Welsh Review* 18 (1969): 69–80.

———. "Crafty Dylan and the 'Altarwise' Sonnets." *University of Toronto Quarterly* 55 (1986): 375–94.

McNees, Eleanor J. *Eucharistic Poetry*. London and Toronto: Associated University Presses, 1992.

Miller, J. Hillis. *Poets of Reality: Six Twentieth-Century Writers*. Cambridge, MA: Harvard University Press, 1966.

Morrison, Blake. *The Movement: English Poetry and Fiction of the 1950s*. 1980. London and New York: Methuen, 1986.

Moynihan, William T. *The Craft and Art of Dylan Thomas*. 1966. Ithaca, NY: Cornell University Press, 1968.

Murdy, Louise B. *Sound and Sense in Dylan Thomas's Poetry*. The Hague: Mouton, 1966.

Nowottny, Winifred. 1962. *The Language Poets Use*. London: Athlone Press, 1972.

Olson, Elder. *The Poetry of Dylan Thomas*. Chicago: University of Chicago Press, 1954.

Peach, Linden. *The Prose Writing of Dylan Thomas*. Basingstoke: Macmillan, 1988.

Pratt, Annis. *Dylan Thomas' Early Prose: A Study in Creative Mythology*. Pittsburgh: University of Pittsburgh Press, 1970.

Pratt, Terrence M. "Adventures in the Poetry Trade: Dylan Thomas and Arthur Rimbaud." *English Language Notes* 24, no. 4 (1987): 65–73.

Rawson, Claude. "Dylan Thomas." In *Talks to Teachers of English 2*. Newcastle upon Tyne: Department of Education, King's College, Newcastle, 1962. 30–56.

Ray, Paul C. *The Surrealist Movement in England*. Ithaca, NY: Cornell University Press, 1971.

Read, Bill. *The Days of Dylan Thomas*. London: Weidenfeld & Nicolson, 1964.

Rosenthal, M. L. *The Modern Poets: A Critical Introduction*. New York: Oxford University Press, 1960.

Rosenthal, M. L., and Gall, Sally M. *The Modern Poetic Sequence*. New York: Oxford University Press, 1983.

Scarfe, Francis. *Auden and After*. London: Routledge & Sons, 1942.

Seib, Kenneth. "*Portrait of the Artist as a Young Dog*: Dylan's *Dubliners*." *Modern Fiction Studies* 24 (1978): 239–46.

Simpson, Louis. *A Revolution in Taste*. New York: Macmillan, 1978.

Sisson, C. H. *English Poetry, 1900–1950: An Assessment*. New York: St. Martin's Press, 1971.

Smith, A. J. "Ambiguity as Poetic Shift." *Critical Quarterly* 4 (1962): 68–74.

Spender, Stephen. *Poetry since 1939*. 1946. London: Longmans, 1950.

———. *The Making of a Poem*. London: Hamish Hamilton, 1955.

Stanford, Derek. *Dylan Thomas*. 1954. Revised and extended ed., New York: Citadel Press, 1964.

Tedlock, E. W. (ed.). *Dylan Thomas: The Legend and the Poet*. London: William Heinemann, 1960.

Thomas, Caitlin. *Leftover Life to Kill*. London: Putnam, 1957.

———. *Not Quite Posthumous Letter to My Daughter*. London: Putnam, 1963.

Thomas, Caitlin, with Tremlett, George. *Caitlin: A Warring Absence*. London: Secker & Warburg, 1986.

Thomas, R. George. "Dylan Thomas and Some Early Readers." *Poetry Wales* 9 (1973): 3–19.

Tindall, William York. *A Reader's Guide to Dylan Thomas*. 1962. New York: Octagon Books, 1981.

Treece, Henry. *Dylan Thomas: "Dog among the Fairies."* London: Lindsay Drummond, 1949.

Tremlett, George. *Dylan Thomas: In the Mercy of His Means*. London: Constable, 1991.

Trick, Bert. "The Young Dylan Thomas." *Texas Quarterly* 9 (Summer 1966): 36–49.

Volsik, Paul. "Neo-Romanticism and the Poetry of Dylan Thomas." *Études Anglaises* 42 (1989): 39–54.

Watkins, Gwen. *Portrait of a Friend*. Llandysul: Gomer Press, 1983.

Williams, Raymond. "Dylan Thomas's Play for Voices." *Critical Quarterly* 1 (1959): 18–26.

Williams, Robert Coleman (ed.). *A Concordance to the Collected Poems of Dylan Thomas*. Lincoln: University of Nebraska Press, 1967.

Young, Alan. "Image as Structure: Dylan Thomas and Poetic Meaning." *Critical Quarterly* 17 (1975): 333–45.

Index

About the Author

JAMES A. DAVIES is Senior Lecturer in English at the University of Wales, Swansea. He has been visiting professor at Baylor University, Texas, and Andrew W. Mellon Foundation Fellow at the Harry Ransom Humanities Research Center at the University of Texas at Austin. He is secretary of the Region and Nation Literature Association, and treasurer of the Association for Welsh Writing in English. In addition to many articles and reviews he has published *John Forster: A Literary Life* (1983), *Dylan Thomas's Places* (1987), *The Textual Life of Dickens's Characters* (1989), and *Leslie Norris* (1991). He has also edited Dannie Abse, *The View from Row G: Three Plays* (1990), and two anthologies: *The Heart of Wales* (1994), and *A Swansea Anthology* (1996)

ISBN 0-313-28774-0

9 780313 287749

90000>

HARDCOVER BAR CODE

EAN